HOLY WAR

IAN CAMPBELL

Holy War

The Untold Story of Catholic Italy's Crusade Against the Ethiopian Orthodox Church

HURST & COMPANY, LONDON

First published in the United Kingdom in 2021 by
C. Hurst & Co. (Publishers) Ltd.,
83 Torbay Road, London, NW6 7DT
This paperback edition published in 2023 by
C. Hurst & Co. (Publishers) Ltd.,
New Wing, Somerset House, Strand, London WC2R 1LA

Copyright © Ian Campbell, 2023

All rights reserved.

Printed in the United Kingdom by Bell & Bain Ltd, Glasgow

The right of Ian Campbell to be identified as the author of this publication is asserted by him in accordance with the Copyright, Designs and Patents Act, 1988.

Distributed in the United States, Canada and Latin America by Oxford University Press, 198 Madison Avenue, New York, NY 10016, United States of America.

A Cataloguing-in-Publication data record for this book is available from the British Library.

ISBN: 9781805260240

www.hurstpublishers.com

By the same author

The Plot to Kill Graziani:
The Attempted Assassination of Mussolini's Viceroy

* * *

The Massacre of Debre Libanos—Ethiopia, 1937:
The Story of One of Fascism's Most Shocking Atrocities

* * *

The Addis Ababa Massacre:
Italy's National Shame

This book is dedicated to the memory of
Richard Keir Pethick Pankhurst

CONTENTS

List of Maps	xiii
List of Tables	xv
List of Illustrations	xvii
List of Abbreviations	xxi
Notes on Transliteration	xxiii
Glossary and Explanatory Notes	xxv
Preface	1
Prologue	11

PART ONE
PRELUDE

1.	A Most Ancient Church	15
2.	Bad Neighbours	33
3.	An Unholy Alliance	43

PART TWO
A HOLY WAR

4.	Missionaries of the Cross	67
5.	A Happy Triumph	103
6.	Civilising Actions	125

CONTENTS

7.	Terror in the Capital	139
8.	A Bungled Mission	157
9.	A Beautiful Conquest	163

PART THREE
A STRIKE AT THE HEART

10.	Preparing the Killing Fields	173
11.	Encirclement and Captivity	181
12.	Death in the Afternoon	189
13.	Massacre at Borale River	201
14.	Telling the Story	209

PART FOUR
ONWARD, CHRISTIAN SOLDIERS

15.	Persecution of the House of Tekle Haymanot	221
16.	An Italian Jihad	233
17.	The Holy War Turns Full Circle	241

PART FIVE
AN IGNOMINIOUS END

18.	A Wind of Change	249
19.	More Clergy to the Sword	257
20.	Kissing the Cross	269
Epilogue		275
Reflections		293

Appendix I: The Final Toll	311
Appendix II: Spoils of War	319
Appendix III: Major Quercia's Report of 14 March 1937 (page 1)	331

CONTENTS

Appendix IV: Telegram No. 35049, Pietro Maletti to Rodolfo Graziani, 22 May 1937	333
Appendix V: Telegram No. 9325, Rodolfo Graziani to Pietro Maletti, 24 May 1937	335
Appendix VI: Telegram, Graziani to the *Residente* at Fiché, 27 October 1937	337
Appendix VII: The Italian Inventory of Items Removed from Debre Libanos	339
Acknowledgements	341
Notes	349
Bibliography	391
Index	419

LIST OF MAPS

1. Ethiopia: dioceses of the Ethiopian Orthodox Church 9
(based on *The Ethiopian Orthodox Church* (1970), map,
p. 179)
2. The invasion of Ethiopia: principal invasion routes 69
(© Ian Campbell)
3. Wag and Wello (based on *Encyclopaedia Aethiopica*, 89
vol. 4, map 'Wag')
4. Eastern Ethiopia: Dire Dawa, Harar and Jijiga 98
(based on *Guida dell'Africa Orientale Italiana*, map, p. 448)
5. Southern Ethiopia: Yirga Alem and Hagere Maryam 114
(© Ian Campbell)
6. Lake Zway, Mount Ziqwala and Midr Kebd (based on 129
Ethiopia: Around Ziquala, map)
7. Western Ethiopia: Gore, Addis Alem (© Ian Campbell) 133
8. Plan of the monastery of Debre Libanos 158
(© Ian Campbell)
9. Northern Ethiopia: Begémdir and Western Tigray 165
(© Ian Campbell)
10. Gojjam and the Blue Nile (© Ian Campbell) 168
11. The massacre of Debre Libanos: The execution site at 177
Laga Weldé (© Ian Campbell)

LIST OF MAPS

12. The massacre of Debre Libanos: The execution site at Borale, Ingécha (© Ian Campbell)   179
13. Central Ethiopia: Northern Shewa (© Ian Campbell)   222
14. Addis Ababa, Dire Dawa and Harar (© Ian Campbell)   225
15. Northern Shewa: The *jihad* of June 1937 (© Ian Campbell)   236
16. Ankober district: church burning of October–November 1937 (© Ian Campbell)   259

Note: As far as possible, these maps reflect diocesan boundaries of the Ethiopian Orthodox Church, rather than the administrative areas adopted by the Italians from 1936 to 1941. However, there may be slight variations between maps, particularly in the demarcation of Shewa and its zones, several of which, such as Merhabété and Menz, had either indeterminate or frequently changing boundaries.

LIST OF TABLES

14.1. Number of victims killed in the massacre of Debre Libanos   212

A.1. Ethiopian death toll submitted at the Paris Peace Conference   311

LIST OF ILLUSTRATIONS

1. Pope Paul III with St Ignatius of Loyola and Tesfa Siyon (© Zeno Colantoni)
2. The centre panel of a 15th-century Ethiopian icon (© Ian Campbell)
3. The church of Santa Maria degli Angeli, Rome (© Azurevanilla Ash, https://creativecommons.org/licenses/by-sa/4.0/deed.en)
4. Our Lady and the Seven Archangels at the church of St Tekle Haymanot at Azezo (© Ian Campbell)
5. Church of St Tekle Haymanot at Debre Libanos before the Italian invasion (public domain, en.wikipedia.org)
6. The Catholic Cathedral in Addis Ababa (© A. Savin, WikiCommons)
7. Pope Pius XI (public domain, Alberto Felice, WikiCommons)
8. Jesus Christ guiding the Italian troops (postcard, C.G.M.)
9. Madonna of the Manganello (public domain, https://it.wikipedia.org/wiki/File:Madonna_manganello.jpg)
10. Father Reginaldo Giuliani (public domain, https://it.wikipedia.org/wiki/File:Reginaldo_Giuliani.jpg)
11. Emperor Haile Selassie prays for peace (Ian Campbell archive; origin unknown)

LIST OF ILLUSTRATIONS

12. *Li'ul-Ras* Kassa Haylu (courtesy, *Weyzero* Herane Birhane Mesqel Kassa)
13. Italians with severed heads (courtesy, Richard Pankhurst archive)
14. Ildefonso Cardinal Schuster (public domain, https://commons.wikimedia.org/wiki/File:Schustercardinal.jpg)
15. Missionaries of the Gospel (Fitur Abriham, 1947 E.C.)
16. The Day of Faith (Ian Campbell archive; origin unknown)
17. Archbishop Ascalesi at Naples (postcard, Edizione Avino Pasquale, Pompei Santuario)
18. Public hangings (courtesy, Richard Pankhurst archive)
19. Blessing Machine-Guns (Ian Campbell archive; origin unknown)
20. Victory Celebration in Udine (Ian Campbell archive; origin unknown)
21. Marshal Graziani 1936 (public domain)
22. Victory at the Crucifix (postcard, A.V.E, Rome)
23. A Picture for Mother (Ian Campbell archive, origin unknown)
24. Bishop Petros (https://creativecommons.org/licenses/by-sa/3.0/deed.en)
25. Archbishop Castellani with *Federale* Guido Cortese (© Archivio Luce)
26. The Church of Gebre Menfes Qiddus at Midr Kebd (© Ian Campbell)
27. Bishop Mikaél (courtesy, Mahbere Kidusan)
28. Children thrown into the flames, Martyrs Monument (© Ian Campbell)
29. Menelik Square before the Italian invasion (courtesy, Richard Pankhurst archive)
30. Bodies at the Church of St Peter and St Paul, Addis Ababa (courtesy, Richard Pankhurst archive)
31. The Menelik Mausoleum (Ian Campbell archive, © Burton Holmes Archive)

LIST OF ILLUSTRATIONS

32. Meggabi Welde-Tinsa'e (*If Only I were that Warrior*, © Awen Films)
33. Public hangings on prefabricated gallows (courtesy, Richard Pankhurst archive)
34. General Pietro Maletti (courtesy, Luigi Panella archive)
35. Borale, Ingécha, 1997 (© Ian Campbell)
36. The 45th Colonial Battalion (postcard, V.E. Boleri, Rome)
37. Clergy at Debre Libanos awaiting execution (courtesy, Luigi Panella archive)
38. Debtera Zelleqe at the Fincha Wenz, 1994 (© Ian Campbell)
39. Debtera Zelleqe seated, with Meggabi Fiqre-Iyesus, 1994 (© Ian Campbell)
40. Possible massacre scene at Laga Weldé (YEQEDAMAWI HAYLE SILLASSÉ TOR TIMHIRT BÉT, 1950 EC)
41. Feqyibelu Yirgu and family with Professor Pankhurst, 1997 (© Ian Campbell)
42. Negash Yirgu with Professor Shiferaw and Ian Campbell, 2015 (© Ian Campbell)
43. Mulatwa Yirgu, 1997 (© Ian Campbell)
44. Sketch of executions at Borale, Ingécha (LEIJONHUFVUD, E.S.A., 1948)
45. Italian soldiers at a mass grave (YEQEDAMAWI HAYLE SILLASSÉ TOR TIMHIRT BÉT, 1950 EC)
46. Bodies in trench (DEPARTEMENT DE LA PRESSE ET DE L'INFORMATION DU GOUVERNEMENT IMPERIAL D'ETHIOPIE, n.d.)
47. Pope Pius XII, formerly Eugenio Cardinal Pacelli (public domain)
48. A section of the Mohammed Sultan Group (courtesy, Luigi Panella archive)
49. The severed head of *Dejazmach* Haylu Kebbede (PANKHURST, S., 1946, courtesy, Richard Pankhurst archive)
50. The Holy Synod of the Ethiopian Church: canonisation of Bishop Mikaél (courtesy, Mahbere Kidusan)

LIST OF ILLUSTRATIONS

51. The Graziani Room (*Gli Annali dell'Africa Italiana*, II, 2, 2 July 1939, © Mondadori Portfolio)
52. Italian partisan leaders with Ethiopian crowns (*Storia Illustrata*, June 1971, © Mondadori Portfolio)

LIST OF ABBREVIATIONS

ACS	Archivio Centrale dello Stato, Rome
AESI	Segreteria di Stato, Affari ecclesiastici straordinari, Italia
AISS	Ambasciata d'Italia presso la Santa Sede
ASDMAE	Archivio storico diplomatico del Ministero degli Affari Esteri
ASMAE	Archivio storico, Ministero degli Affari Esteri, Rom
ASV	Archivio Segreto Vaticano, Vatican City
BCMS	Bible Churchmen's Missionary Society
CR	Segreteria particolare del duce, Carteggio riservato
DAGR	Direzione generale pubblica sicurezza, Divisione affari generali e riservati
DDI	Documenti Diplomatici Italiani
EOC	Ethiopian Orthodox Church
IES	Institute of Ethiopian Studies, Addis Ababa University
MAI	Ministero dell'Africa Italiana
UN	United Nations
USSME	Ufficio storico dello stato maggiore dell'esercito
USNA	United States National Archives, Maryland

NOTES ON TRANSLITERATION

The following system has been used for the transliteration of Amharic words into English.

Vowels:

The seven orders are represented as follows:
1st: be   ('e' as in 'open'). First order 'h-' is represented by 'ha'; the open vowel form is represented by 'a'.
2nd: bu   ('u' as in 'rude')
3rd: bi   ('i' as in 'piano')
4th: ba   ('a' as in 'fast')
5th: bé   ('é' as in the French 'détente')
6th: bi   ('i' shortened; similar to 'eu' in the French 'peu'). Where the sixth order vowel is silent, no vowel is shown.
7th: bo   ('o' as in 'core')

Explosives:

To minimise the need for diacritical markings, no distinction has been drawn between the explosives and non-explosives, with the exception of the most common: 'q' for explosive 'k', and 'ts' for explosive 's'.

NOTES ON TRANSLITERATION

'zh' is pronounced as 's' in 'pleasure'.
'ñ' is pronounced as in 'señor'.

The use of double consonants normally employed in English to indicate pronunciation (such as the double 's') is retained. Double consonants are also used to indicate gemination in Amharic names, as in 'Iyyasu'.

Proper names have also been transliterated according to the above system, with the exception of:

(i) the following names, which are written as conventionally spelt: 'Menelik' rather than 'Minilik', 'Haile Selassie' rather than 'Hayle-Sillassé', and 'Lorenzo' rather than 'Lorénso';

(ii) the following common place names, which are written as conventionally spelt: 'Addis Ababa' rather than 'Addis Abeba', 'Dessie' rather than Dessé', 'Dire Dawa' rather than 'Diré Dawa', 'Gore' rather than 'Goré', and 'Harar' rather than 'Harer'.

It should be noted that when the name of an Ethiopian author of a European language publication cited in this book appears in that publication using a different system of transliteration (such as Tamasgen Gabre), this spelling has been retained in the Bibliography and in the citations, and thus will be different from the spelling of the name in the text (i.e., Temesgen Gebré).

Foreign words are italicised where they are not already naturalised in the English language, apart from dates in the Ethiopian calendar, e.g., Ginbot 10, Yekatit 20. However, the date of the attempt on Graziani is italicised (*Yekatit 12*) when it refers to the event rather than the date.

GLOSSARY AND EXPLANATORY NOTES

(All terms and titles are Ethiopian unless otherwise stated)

Abba	title: Father, used particularly for monks
abun	leader of the Ethiopian Orthodox Church
Abune	title: leader of the Ethiopian Orthodox Church; also used as a courtesy title for senior clerics such as a bishop (lit. 'Our Father')
Afa Negus	title: Chief Justice (lit. 'Mouth of the King')
Agafari	title: Superintendent of Banquets
Aleqa	title: Head of a church
amba	steep-sided natural fortress
angach, pl. angachoch	retainer, usually assistants to Patriot fighter
arbeñña; pl. arbeññoch	partisan, Patriot; *ye wist arbeñña*: urban, 'underground' Patriot
askari	(Swahili) native soldier, guard
Ato	title, equivalent to Mr
awraja	district
Azajh	title: Commander; Chief of the Imperial Court
balabbat	hereditary landowner; roughly equivalent to country squire

xxv

GLOSSARY AND EXPLANATORY NOTES

Balambaras	military title: lit. 'Head of an *Amba*'; Head of a fort
banda	(Ital.) group (esp. of soldiers); term also used by Ethiopians to refer to an individual Ethiopian collaborating with, or fighting for, the Italians
bande irregolari	local troops (typically Ethiopian) fighting for the Italians
bande militari	trained and uniformed colonial soldiers (typically Eritrean, Libyan, Somalian or Ethiopian) fighting for the Italians
Basha	military title, derived from the Turkish *pasha*
Bejirond	title: Royal Treasurer; Guardian of Royal Property
bét	house
Blatta	title, awarded to government officials at director-general level; lit. youth, signifying learning
Blattén Géta	title, awarded to officials at ministerial level; lit. Master of the *Blatta*
carta bianca	(Ital.) carte blanche
debtera	unordained ecclesiastic of the Ethiopian Orthodox Church, situated between clergy and laymen; scholar; specialist in theology, music and esoteric knowledge.
Dejazmach	military title: lit. 'Commander of the Gate' or 'Commander of the Threshold'; rank just below *Ras*
Dyakon	title: Deacon; a position normally held by young men, following which they may become a monk or a priest
eqa-bét	church treasury or store for sacred artefacts
Fitawrari	military title: lit. 'Commander of the Vanguard'

GLOSSARY AND EXPLANATORY NOTES

gebez	sacristan; an important ecclesiastic who manages church property; usually next to *aleqa*
gibbi	palace or nobleman's residence or compound
Gi'iz	ancient language of the Ethiopian Orthodox Church
Grazmach	military title: lit. 'Commander of the Left Wing'
Ichegé	title: traditionally the highest ecclesiastic in the Ethiopian Orthodox Church
Immahoy	title, particularly for a nun
Itegé	title: Empress
kabba	decorative ceremonial Ethiopian gown, for men and women
Kentiba	title, roughly equivalent to Mayor
liq	scholar; also chief (e.g., *Liqe Papas*, Archbishop)
Li'ilt	title: Princess
Lij	title: sometimes used as equivalent to Prince (lit. child)
Liqe Mekwas	title given to official serving as the double of the sovereign
Liqetebebt	an honorific title of the Ethiopian Orthodox Church
Li'ul	title: Prince
Li'ul-Ras	title: Royal Duke (lit. 'Prince-Duke')
malkaña	local representative of the Italian *residente*
Meggabi	In the case of Debre Libanos, the *meggabi* is in command of the entire monastery, below the *tsebaté*. The position of *meggabi* is not to be confused with seven specialised subsidiary positions unique to Debre Libanos, such as *Meggabi-Hadis* (expert on the New

GLOSSARY AND EXPLANATORY NOTES

	Testament) and *Meggabi-Beloy* (expert on the Old Testament).
memhir	teacher, particularly in a monastery; sometimes used as a title, meaning head of a monastery or Abbot
Memiré	title: senior ecclesiastic in a monastery
mengist	government
meqdes	the inner sanctum of an Ethiopian church, where the *tabot* is kept
mesqel	the Christian cross
Neggadras	title: Head of Merchants; Head of Customs
Negus	title, equivalent to King
papas	bishop
Qeññazmach	military title: lit. 'Commander of the Right Wing'
Qés	(Amharic) title: Priest
Qéssis	(Gi'iz) title: Priest
qiddist	the inner of two concentric aisles in a circular Ethiopian church, accessible to the priests
qiné mahlét	the outer of two concentric aisles in a circular Ethiopian church, accessible to the laity
Ras	title, roughly equivalent to Duke or Lord
Regia Aeronautica	(Ital.) Royal Air Force
residente	(Ital.) resident district officer under the Fascist administration
sefer	district authority, settlement
Shaleqa	military title, equivalent to major (also, *Shaqa*)
Shambel	military title, below *Shaleqa*
shamma	Ethiopian toga-like shawl worn by men and women
shimagilé	respected elderly man, particularly as interlocutor

GLOSSARY AND EXPLANATORY NOTES

Shum-Bashi	title: the highest rank given by the Italian military to a colonial officer
sistrum; pl. sistra	traditional jingling instrument or rattle used by *debteras*
tabot; pl. tabotat	holy altar slab unique to the Ethiopian Orthodox Church, symbolising the Ark of the Covenant
tsalihun	ecclesiastical artefact
Tsebaté	title: Head of the Monastery of Debre Libanos
Tsehafe Ti'ezaz	title: Head Scribe; Minister of the Pen
tsuwa	traditional drink; chalice
tukul	traditional Ethiopian cottage or hut (term commonly used by non-Ethiopian writers; language unknown)
wereda	administrative district
Weyzerit	title roughly equivalent to Miss
Weyzero	title roughly equivalent to Mrs

The term 'Coptic' was often used by the Italians to denote Ethiopian Christians. Although the Ethiopian Church had an arrangement with the Egyptian Church for the provision of an archbishop, the Ethiopians were not Copts, for the term 'Copt' means Egyptian, and these days is normally applied only to Egyptian Christians. Nonetheless, the misused term appears in some quoted Italian sources.

The Ethiopian Calendar

The Ethiopian calendar is approximately seven years and eight months behind the international, or Gregorian, calendar. It begins and ends in September. Unless otherwise stated, all years in *Holy War* refer to the international calendar. Where the year refers to the Ethiopian calendar, it is written, for example, 1929 EC, which spans 12 September 1936 to 11 September 1937. An event occurring in 1929 EC would then be recorded as having occurred in 1936–7.

GLOSSARY AND EXPLANATORY NOTES

Italian Military Units

During the invasion and occupation of Ethiopia, the Italian military arrangements were complicated, due to the deployment of Blackshirts, colonial soldiers and irregulars alongside the regular army, and a certain flexibility in organisation. The present author makes no pretence to be a military specialist, but since terms such as 'division', 'battalion' and 'platoon' appear from time to time in the text, the following notes on Italian military units in diminishing order of size, together with some of the key ranks, will assist readers unfamiliar with military terms. However, these notes are by no means exhaustive or precise, and the translation of the Italian terms into English does not imply exact equivalence.

- A field army can consist of hundreds of thousands of soldiers, and is typically commanded by a general. Mussolini also created the higher rank of marshal of Italy, a special rank for outstanding generals.
- The army that invaded Ethiopia consisted of a number of divisions, each of which consisted of several thousand soldiers (sometimes more than ten thousand) organised into brigades or regiments or both. A division was usually commanded by a general or major general.
- The size of brigades and regiments varied. They each generally consisted of less than ten thousand soldiers, but a brigade was often larger than a regiment. Both brigades and regiments, each of which would usually be commanded by a colonel, usually consisted of a number of battalions.
- The most frequently mentioned military unit in this book is the battalion, which usually contained at least five hundred men, and sometimes more than a thousand. A battalion was typically commanded by a lieutenant colonel.
- Within a battalion there would be a number of companies, each headed by a captain commanding generally one or two hundred men, and sometimes more.
- Within a company there would be a number of platoons, each of which could consist of less than around fifty men, commanded by a lieutenant.

GLOSSARY AND EXPLANATORY NOTES

- Within a company there would be sections or squads, sometimes containing just a few men, and commanded by the equivalent of a staff sergeant or sergeant.
- Below a sergeant there could be a (non-commissioned) corporal.
- There were many other ranks, not mentioned here, including variations of marshal (not to be confused with marshal of Italy) for non-commissioned officers.
- Among the ranks of colonial soldiers, a *muntaz*, which appears occasionally in this book, was more or less equivalent to a corporal, and refers to a non-commissioned commander of *askaris*, the lowest rank of Italian colonial soldier.

PREFACE

Thirty-one years ago I was in the Ethiopian highlands conducting a socio-cultural study of the communities in a large valley in the rugged district of Northern Shewa. The principal centre of population in the gorge was a monastery named Debre Libanos. Dating from the 13th century, it constituted one of the greatest and most revered institutions of the Ethiopian Orthodox Church, to which the majority of Ethiopians belonged. But to my surprise, I was informed by the priests that in 1937 the entire monastic community had been brutally massacred by Italians.

Massacred? By Italians? I knew that in October 1935 Ethiopia became the world's first sovereign state to fall victim to Fascist invasion. I also knew that it was not the last, for Mussolini's attempted annexation of Ethiopia inspired Adolf Hitler and the Nazis, disempowered the League of Nations, and triggered a chain of military invasions that culminated in the Second World War. However, I was under the impression that, unlike the Nazis and the Japanese, Italian soldiers of the 1930s were bumbling, harmless and friendly young men fighting reluctantly in a war in which they had been drafted against their will; atrocities were not something I associated with Italians.

It turned out that whatever was known about the incident was based on a couple of Italian military telegrams, and that no historians had conducted any in-depth research into the tragedy. I was intrigued by the lack of information about an atrocity of such magnitude, and over the coming months my co-researcher, Degife Gebre-Tsadiq of Addis Ababa University, and I dedicated ourselves to solving the mystery: Was the story true? What exactly happened, and why?

Sadly, Degife would pass away before our research into the massacre of Debre Libanos was complete, but historian and Ethiopianist Richard Pankhurst of Addis Ababa University, whose anti-Fascist mother Sylvia had led an international lobby against the Italian invasion, and who had himself conducted pioneering archival research into the occupation, joined forces with me to support the project, which would span another two decades.

As it turned out, the story of what happened at the monastery was far more complex than we had imagined. It took extensive fieldwork—site visits, false starts and dead ends, interviews of eyewitnesses and trawling through dusty archives—before the pieces of the puzzle started coming together. In the process I also explored the links between the massacre at the monastery and the slaughter that had taken place in Addis Ababa after an abortive attack on the Italian High Command. The massacre of Addis Ababa was common knowledge in Ethiopia, but I had presumed that it was a 'hiccup' in an essentially peaceful occupation—a momentary aberration. I could not have been more wrong, for gradually, over the years, a very different picture emerged. Italy's invasion of Ethiopia introduced to the world a new form of warfare that would be known as 'total war', in which large-scale war was deliberately waged against civilians as well as the military—a precursor of what occupied Europe would suffer in the years that followed.

The massacre of Debre Libanos turned out to have involved slaughter on a far larger scale than was reported in the fragmentary Italian sources, but even worse was to come: it was actually the tip of the iceberg. As I dug deeper, I discovered that the Italians had conducted a massive and deadly campaign against the Ethiopian Orthodox Church (hereafter, the Ethiopian Church)—a pogrom against one of the world's oldest national Churches. While the massacre of Debre Libanos was specifically ordered in writing by the Italian High Command, it transpired that hundreds of other churches and monasteries had also been systematically attacked and the clergy

PREFACE

slaughtered, but without a mention either in Italian archives or in the history books. To my horror, it gradually emerged that in town after town, village after village, rampaging soldiers had turned the churches into funeral pyres.

What possessed the Italians to behave in this manner? I found this question very difficult to answer, but I came to realise that there had been some sort of conditioning. From time to time while in the countryside I had heard it said that 'the pope in Rome had blessed the invading armies', but I had not taken the story seriously, until I discovered that the Italian Catholic episcopate had actually promoted and sanctified the invasion, granting it the status of a crusade—a holy war against what they referred to as the 'heretics' and 'schismatics' of the ancient Ethiopian Orthodox Church. The flood of volunteer militiamen and recruits that the war-mongering bishops managed to rally to the cause manned a campaign that took the lives of thousands of Ethiopian Christian clergy, while numerous monasteries and churches suffered bombings, burning, and pillage of their cultural patrimony. It is the promotion, conduct and outcome of that campaign that are the subject of this book.

In a commentary on the enduring influence of the medieval crusaders, Professor Jonathan Riley-Smith ventured that the 'wash' of the First Crusade of 1096–1102 'could still be felt almost within living memory'. There is more truth to that statement than perhaps even he realised, for the preaching of the crusade from 1935 to 1937 by cardinals, archbishops and bishops, which was widespread throughout Italy, was almost indistinguishable from the rhetoric and exhortations of their medieval forebears.

* * *

Why did this pogrom never feature in historical memory? Although news of the brutality of the invasion appeared on the front pages of European newspapers at the time, the suffering of the Ethiopian clergy and the destruction of that nation's age-old Christian institutions passed almost unnoticed by the outside world, for many of the churches and monasteries targeted were in remote areas, and the clergy and monks present were typically executed, leaving few witnesses to tell the tale.

HOLY WAR

I also discovered that almost all non-Ethiopian historians of the period were, and still are, under the illusion that hostilities in Ethiopia ended on 9 May 1936, because that was when Mussolini announced that the war had ended. The world's attention then turned to the Spanish Civil War and the deteriorating situation in Europe. However, in reality, war correspondents in Ethiopia were prohibited by the Italians from reporting that both armies actually continued to be engaged in battle long after that date. The fact is that with the international spotlight now off Ethiopia, more Ethiopians died at the hands of the Italian military after, than before, 9 May 1936.

Pioneering historians such as Professor Angelo Del Boca and Anthony Mockler, who studied the Italian invasion in depth, soon discovered that the war did not end in 1936. However, the study of war crimes in Ethiopia, being largely undocumented, was much more difficult, which meant that many atrocities remained entirely unknown to international scholarship.

Finally, international politics blocked any reckoning with the past. Upon Ethiopia's liberation in 1941, Emperor Haile Selassie had to operate under the auspices of the British Occupied Enemy Territory Administration, which obstructed Ethiopian attempts to document Italian war crimes. Following Italy's surrender to the Allies in 1943, the Italian Catholic Church rapidly disengaged itself from Fascism, and the episcopate's sacralisation of the invasion of Ethiopia was quickly and conveniently forgotten, and even denied. Furthermore, when the Second World War ended in 1945, the British government acted rapidly to protect its new-found ally from the ignominy of war crimes trials.

For these reasons hardly anything had ever been published on Italy's war on Ethiopian Christendom.

* * *

I have attempted to remedy this lacuna to the extent possible. Fortunately, during the 1990s I was able to meet survivors and eyewitnesses in Ethiopia to determine what happened when their oases of peace were invaded by the marauding soldiers. Multiple interviews and discussions over several years have thus enabled

PREFACE

me to tell some of the stories in detail—not through the memoirs of European travellers, but through the voices of Ethiopians who lived through that tragic episode. It should be noted that these were not people struggling to recall events that had occurred in places they had left behind decades before; they were for the most part witnesses who had never left the hamlets where they were born and where the atrocities took place. They knew every household and every nook and cranny of the places concerned, and retained crystal-clear memories of the incidents they were describing, often providing blow-by-blow accounts of what occurred in the context of the immediate environment—the lie of the land, the cottages, the mule tracks, the trees, the rocks and the streams.

A major breakthrough in my research was the discovery of important written testimonies of the 1940s. After the expulsion of the Italians and re-establishment of the Ethiopian government in 1941, some of the surviving residents of the rural settlements ravaged by the invading forces were able to submit reports to their local diocesan offices regarding the attacks on their parish churches, their clergy and parishioners during the occupation. I was given access to transcripts of some of these records, many of which recount the events in considerable detail.

Finally, rich testimonies have been provided by Addis Ababa University scholars who conducted field research principally in the 1970s and 1980s, interviewing witnesses and participants in the conflagrations of the invasion and occupation.

I am thus fortunate to have been able to compile and analyse a considerable amount of original material on the fate of the Ethiopian Church during both the invasion and occupation.

Few of the approximately ten thousand Ethiopian churches and monasteries existing in 1935 survived unscathed. Yet only a selection of the violent incidents that affected Ethiopian Christendom can be described in a single volume such as this. Nonetheless, the data collection and analysis conducted have made possible at least a partial reconstruction of Italy's war on the Ethiopian Church, told here for the first time.

* * *

HOLY WAR

It is difficult to put across to a non-Ethiopian readership the gravity of the Italian onslaught, particularly, for example, across the central and northern Ethiopian highlands, at the cathedral of St George in Addis Ababa, and at the monastery of Debre Libanos. For Italians it would be equivalent to an alien force invading Italy, destroying hundreds of churches and slaughtering their clergy, despoiling, looting and burning St Peter's Basilica in Rome, desecrating the holy sites, rounding up and executing by firing squad all the clergy of St Peter's, and dispatching to concentration camps their surviving relatives, friends and associates. However, like so many of the crimes against humanity carried out by the Italians during their military occupation of Ethiopia, these atrocities were subsequently largely covered up by the British and American governments. The resultant failure of the UN Italian War Crimes trials thus facilitated the propagation and dissemination of the myth of benign Fascism that still prevails today in some quarters.

Nonetheless, as the veil of silence and collective amnesia in Italy regarding the truth of that nation's invasion of Ethiopia is drawn aside, there is a growing awareness—encouraged by the current climate of openness of the Holy See under His Holiness Pope Francis—of the excesses of the occupying forces during the campaign. In that regard, I am grateful to the Italian Catholic Church television channel, tv2000, for producing a docu-film inspired by my book *The Massacre of Debre Libanos* (Addis Ababa University Press, 2014). This book uncovered for the first time the story of one of the most chilling massacres of the occupation, the principal findings of which have been updated and incorporated into the present volume.

Entitled *Debre Libanos*, and billed as *Il più grande massacro di cristiani in Africa* (the greatest ever massacre of Christians in Africa), the tv2000 docu-film, by Antonello Carvigiani, has been screened several times on Italian television and in theatres across Italy since May 2016, to favourable reviews in leading Italian newspapers and journals.[1]

On 1 December 2016 a private showing of *Debre Libanos* was arranged at the Vatican for an invited audience. I was honoured to be a guest and to speak at that memorable event, which marked the first occasion for the subject of the Italian atrocities against the Ethiopian

PREFACE

Church to be tabled and openly discussed in Rome by senior officials of the Holy See, together with Catholic and Orthodox Ethiopians.

In March 2017 the noted historian Andrea Riccardi, founder of the global peace community Sant'Egidio and former Minister of International Cooperation and Integration, made an appeal in the columns of *Corriere della Sera* for 'concrete gestures' by national authorities to recognise and apologise for the Italian massacres of Ethiopian clergy. Pointing out the 'collusion in the mobilisation of the Catholic Church' in the military invasion of Ethiopia, he called attention to the recent visit of Pope Francis to the basilica of St Bartholomew in Rome, where the Holy Father prayed before the Icon of the New Martyrs in which the victims of the massacre of Debre Libanos are depicted.[2]

Riccardi's appeal was followed by an interview in May 2017, published in *Avvenire*, in which he expressed dismay that 'no Italian personality had felt the need even to bring a wreath to Debre Libanos'.[3] The historian's voice did not go unheard, for on 22 May the Italian Ministry of Defence confirmed the facts of the massacre, which it described as 'cruel and methodical', and announced that 'to keep alive the memory of those facts and reaffirm the universal values of human civilisation, the Ministry of Defence would constitute a working group composed of scholars, military and other experts, aimed at a historical deepening of the story'.

Shortly afterwards, I was invited by the Community of Sant'Egidio to attend their annual Paths of Peace meeting in Münster in September 2017, to present stories of Ethiopian Christian martyrdom during the occupation to a distinguished gathering under the chairmanship of Catholic Archbishop Nikola Eterović, apostolic nuncio to Germany.

In May 2019, more than eighty years after the sacralisation of the invasion of Ethiopia, an international forum was convened at the United Nations Economic Commission for Africa in Addis Ababa, to examine the prospects for a process of truth and reconciliation between the two Churches.

These welcome developments have come too late for the survivors I met over the last three decades, all of whom lost family members, friends and colleagues in the massacres, and most of whom have now died. But thanks to them, at least part of the story of what happened when Italy invaded that sovereign state in its homicidal quest for power and prestige through foreign conquest can now be told for posterity and the education of future generations, in the hope that such abominations will never occur again.

Ian Campbell
Addis Ababa
June 2021

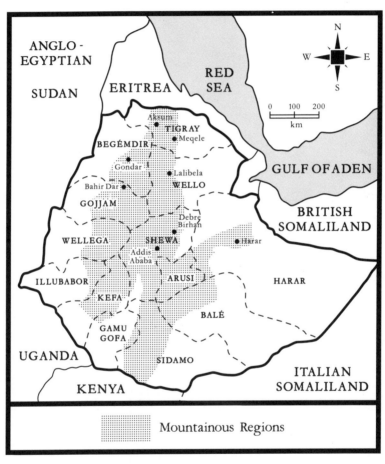

Map 1: Ethiopia: dioceses of the Ethiopian Orthodox Church

PROLOGUE

NAPLES, 26 FEBRUARY 1936

His Eminence Cardinal Archbishop Alessio Ascalesi was not unaccustomed to appearing in public with high dignitaries when giving his benedictions on ceremonial occasions, but this time he excelled himself. An imposing figure in his ecclesiastical regalia—his mitre gleaming in the afternoon sun, and his crosier in his left hand—flanked by a large retinue of bishops donning black birettas, he strode slowly but purposefully through the city's ancient streets. Behind him, borne aloft below a canopy surmounted by a high Latin cross, progressed majestically the gilt-framed holy icon, Our Lady of the Rosary of Pompei, which he had blessed before a massive crowd of clergy and military at the Pontifical Shrine of the Blessed Virgin in Pompei. The great flower-bedecked platform was, in turn, followed by countless thousands of devotees, the moving throng now swelling the crowds that had been gathering since early morning on the streets, in the piazzas, at the windows and on the balconies, to welcome the procession.

It seemed that the entire populations of both cities had come to witness the benediction by Monsignor Ascalesi, head of one of the most important archdioceses of the Roman Church, for the Mother of Christ was to embark at the port of Naples on a long voyage to the Horn of Africa. Now honoured with the title 'Patron of the Italian Army Invading Eastern Africa', the Holy Virgin and Her Beloved

Son would attract more volunteers for Mussolini's Blackshirts, demonstrate divine support for their military adventure, and empower the conquering heroes to strike down the 'heretics and schismatics' against whom the cardinals and archbishops of Italy had risen in their righteous fury.

This was a crusade par excellence. As the Regia Aeronautica (the Royal Italian Air Force), overhead dropped flowers, and flyers extolling the inseparability of the new Trinity—Fascism, the Mother of Christ and the invasion of Ethiopia—nothing like this had been seen since 1209, when the great crusading Catholic armies set out down the Rhone valley to wreak havoc among the heretical Cathars in the Languedoc.

A roar of approval arose from the crowd as the archbishop invoked the name of Jesus Christ and the Holy Blessed Mother to again bless the icon that was to assure victory in Ethiopia. The citizens of that ancient Christian polity had not only dared to challenge the invading armies; they had even had the temerity to fight back—sometimes bare-handed—against the bombs of the Regia Aeronautica, the tanks and the asphyxiating gases. So now the forces of invasion that the senior Italian clergy had been enthusiastically promoting and cheerleading, and who had nonetheless been struggling to reach Addis Ababa for almost five long months, would be boosted by the presence of the Mother of Christ. Now her black-shirted Missionaries of the Cross, as they were designated by the cardinals, would surely open the gates of Ethiopia to 'Roman culture', and eliminate once and for all the 'obstacle' of the Ethiopian clergy.

If there had ever been any doubt that the brutal invasion of Ethiopia was a holy war, and that it had the support of the highest levels of Italy's Catholic Church, advocating untrammelled violence in the name of Christ, those doubts were dispelled by the glory and the majesty of that procession. As countless clergy and their flock bid the Madonna of Pompei a thunderous farewell at the quayside, she boarded ship on her providential quest for victory, accompanied for good measure by several thousand well-armed militiamen.

PART ONE

PRELUDE

1

A MOST ANCIENT CHURCH

'We who profess Christianity ought to be ashamed of ourselves, since the Ethiopians seem to surpass us in regard to the cult and observance of the religion.'

Adamus Carolus to Domião de Góis of the Imperial Portuguese court, 1540

In 2016 the American Pew Research Center found that Ethiopians, consisting overwhelmingly of Christians and Muslims, are the most religious people in the world.[1] This is not altogether surprising, given that it is generally agreed by scholars that by the year 340 the emperor of Ethiopia had declared Christianity the state religion, making Ethiopia the second country in the world to do so, after Armenia.[2] It would be almost another half-century before the Roman Empire followed suit.[3] Moreover, Ethiopia was the first country in the world to mint coins bearing the Christian cross, and with an unbroken record of continuity to the present day, the Ethiopian Church remains one of the world's most ancient and venerable national Churches.[4] Ethiopia also traces its encounters with Islam back to the earliest times; the Prophet Muhammad advised his followers to escape persecution at Mecca by going to Ethiopia, where there was 'a king under whom none are persecuted. It is a land of righteousness where God will give you relief from what you are suffering.'[5]

The practices and doctrines of the Ethiopian Church incorporate unchanging traditions dating back to the earliest Christian Church, one of the most fundamental being the institution of monasticism rooted in the traditions of Pachomius, as practised by the Desert Fathers of Egypt. Ethiopia is today one of the few countries in the world in which Christian monasticism, which is widespread and strongly associated with the national spirit, is still to be found in its original, highly ascetic form.

When Christianity was declared the state religion, the state capital was the city of Aksum in today's northern province of Tigray. Soon churches and monasteries had been constructed, or carved into the mountains and high pinnacles of that province, while several Ethiopian monks ventured as pilgrims to the Holy Land.

By the 6th century the monastery of Debre Damo, built on a steep-sided, flat-topped mountain known as an *amba*, had been founded, and soon became one of Ethiopia's principal centres of theological learning.

When the Prophet advised his followers to take refuge in Ethiopia, they did so. In the year 615 or thereabouts the first group of twelve arrived in the holy city of Aksum, including the Prophet's daughter and her husband. They were hospitably received and lived happily in Aksum. Many more followed in due course, including Umm Habibah, who in due course was betrothed to Muhammad, and left a vivid description of the 4th-century church of Aksum St Mary of Zion and its interior adorned with pictures of the saints.[6]

From the inception of monasticism, the establishment of a monastery in Ethiopia required a royal charter, and a combination of the monasteries and the royal court provided Ethiopia's principal socio-cultural and socio-economic infrastructure, as would in due course be the case in medieval Europe. The monastic settlements, which were permanent while the royal court was often on the move, also contributed to the expansion of the Ethiopian polity and the incorporation in it of different ethnic groups.[7]

The Jewel in the Crown

By the time of the Italian invasion of 1935 there were hundreds of monasteries in Ethiopia, but the greatest Christian centre was the monastery of Debre Libanos. Christianity had been the state religion for more than eight hundred years when the monastery was founded, at the northern boundary of the plateau of Shewa, some 460 km due south of Aksum (see Map 1), by an Ethiopian monk named Tekle Haymanot (pronounced 'Teck-leh High-ma-nought'), meaning 'Plant of Faith'. Born in 1214, Tekle Haymanot was descended from a community that had migrated down from the north of Ethiopia centuries before. As a young man he travelled widely and studied in some of the great and ancient monasteries of Ethiopia, including Debre Damo. He also became a disciple of one of 13th-century Ethiopia's most revered holy fathers, Iyasus Mo'a ('Jesus Has Conquered'), abbot of the monastery of Istifanos in the Lake Hayq area.

By this time the capital of Ethiopia had been re-established at the site known today as Lalibela (Map 1), where, during Tekle Haymanot's lifetime, a complex of rock-hewn churches—now a Unesco World Heritage site—was being completed under the Zagwé dynasty of kings.

Eventually Tekle Haymanot returned as a learned ascetic to the Shewan plateau and set about establishing a community of monks and nuns in a cave set in the wall of a great canyon of the Siga Wedem River, a tributary of the Blue Nile.

Tekle Haymanot and his followers were pioneers, in that, instead of withdrawing from the world as ascetics, their objective was apostolic—to reach out and evangelise in frontier districts where the Church was weak. The areas in which they would work were dangerous, but fortunately the site for their retreat was well chosen. Tucked away inside the wall of the gorge, the cave, which overlooked a terrace, not only provided ready access to the plateau above, but also preserved the secrecy and seclusion necessary for protection of the community from marauding bands serving local chiefs and warlords intent on maintaining their control over the plateau and its inhabitants.[8]

The indomitable Tekle Haymanot named his monastery Debre Asbo ('Mount of the Rock'), and partitioned off part of the cave as a church, which he dedicated to the Virgin Mary, known in Ethiopia as Maryam.

The founder of Debre Asbo is said to have retired in his old age to a solitary existence as a lone anchorite in a cave near his church, engaged in prayer and self-denial until his death in 1313. After several years in a shrine, his remains were moved in 1370 to a site in the cliff face above Debre Asbo, eventually being ceremoniously relocated to the terrace below.[9]

Debre Asbo came to particular prominence under the renowned Emperor Amda Siyon (r. 1314–44), when the monks, preferring to maintain their ascetic life, refused royal jurisdiction and denounced royal excesses.[10] By the early 15th century, under Téwodros (Theodore), the fourth abbot, the monks had moved their monastery onto the terrace below the cave of Debre Asbo and had made their peace with the imperial court. Under Yohannis Kama, the highly revered seventh abbot, the monks built a new church and had it well endowed by Emperor Yeshaq (r. 1412–27).

Debre Asbo achieved its apogee under Emperor Zer'a Ya'iqob ('The Seed of Jacob', r. 1434–68), who bestowed great wealth and prestige on the monastery, elevating it to the most influential position in both Church and state. In 1450 he renamed it Debre Libanos, thereby symbolising the rebirth of a renowned 5th–6th-century monastery of the same name that had wielded considerable influence when the capital was at Aksum.[11] For the Ethiopian Church, in which the monastic tradition plays such a central role, Debre Libanos became the jewel in the crown. This was the monastery's golden age. Sacred books were written praising the earthly struggle of St Tekle Haymanot, and the first church of St Tekle Haymanot was built over a crypt containing the saint's mortal remains. The abbot of Debre Libanos was made an *ex officio* high-ranking member of the imperial court and was raised to the illustrious level of *ichegé*, the head monk of Ethiopia and the second-highest official of the Ethiopian Church below the archbishop, who, by agreement with the Alexandrian Patriarchate, was a Copt (i.e. an Egyptian Christian).[12] In practice, the abbot being obliged to spend much of his time at the imperial court, Debre Libanos was, and still is, actually run not by the abbot, but by an official known as the *tsebaté*, with the assistance of his deputy, the *meggabi*, who presides over a council of twelve monks.[13]

The rules of the monastery of Debre Libanos can be traced back to those of the 3rd-century St Anthony, who is generally considered to be the founder of monasticism, and is venerated in Ethiopian Christianity. At various times several 'daughter' monasteries following the same order were established in Ethiopia, creating a 'House' of St Tekle Haymanot.

Ethiopians Abroad

Ethiopian monks often travelled to religious centres such as Alexandria, Jerusalem and Rome. Egyptian monasticism being highly revered by the Ethiopians, Ethiopian Christian pilgrims en route to the Holy Land frequently visited Egypt. By the end of the 12th century there was an Ethiopian community at Scetis, where the Ethiopian monastery of St Elija was located. By the beginning of the 15th century the Ethiopians had also established a church of St George near Cairo, following which they developed more monasteries in Egypt.[14]

Letters written by notables such as the 4th-century St Jerome mention Ethiopian Christian pilgrims in Jerusalem, and later manuscripts record contacts between the Ethiopian emperors and the basilica of the Holy Sepulchre. By the 14th–15th centuries the Ethiopian community in Jerusalem was flourishing; it possessed four chapels within the church of the Holy Sepulchre, and a monastery on Mount Zion.[15]

Some scholars suggest that as early as 1310 there were Ethiopian pilgrims at the complex of St Stephen Protomartyr in Rome. It is certain that an embassy of the Ethiopian emperor Widim Re'ad (r. 1299–1314)[16] was in Rome to visit the tombs of the Apostles. In 1402 Ambassador Antonio Bartoli was in Venice on a diplomatic mission for Emperor David II (r. c.1379/80–1413), who is credited with bringing to Ethiopia a piece of the True Cross, in addition to icons of the Virgin Mary reputedly painted by St Luke.[17] This visit was followed up in 1404, when a delegation of Ethiopians arrived in Rome to find out whether the pontiff had received gifts sent earlier by the Ethiopian sovereign.[18]

In all, between 1403 and the Council of Florence in 1441, the Vatican archives registered twelve pilgrimages of Ethiopians to

Rome. They were given hospitality by four popes, namely Boniface IX (r. 1389–1404), Gregory XI (r. 1406–15), Martin V (r. 1417–31) and Eugene IV (r. 1431–47).[19]

In 1439 the Ethiopian Church sent a delegation to the Council of Florence convoked by Pope Eugene IV,[20] and in the mid-15th century Emperor Zer'a Ya'iqob dispatched an embassy that met with Pope Nicholas V (r. 1447–55). The historic meeting was reciprocated in 1451, when the pontiff sent his representative to Ethiopia.

In November 1481 a more formal and momentous meeting between the Roman Church and the Ethiopian Church occurred, when an imposing Ethiopian delegation arrived in Rome. Pope Sixtus IV (r. 1471–84) then decided to assign the church of St Stephen Protomartyr in Rome to the Ethiopian monastic community, and renamed it St Stephen of the Abyssinians.[21] Four of the Ethiopian delegates are believed to have been subsequently immortalised by Botticelli and Tucci in frescoes on the walls of the newly built Sistine Chapel, where they can be seen today.[22] By the early 1500s St Stephen's monastery hosted the largest Ethiopian community in Europe.[23]

Under a succession of notable abbots, the monastery of Debre Libanos maintained a prominent position and a high profile in the affairs of the Ethiopian empire. When a Portuguese delegation arrived at Debre Libanos to meet Emperor Libne Dingil (r. 1508–40) in October 1520, the Catholic mission chaplain, Father Francisco Alvares, found he could discuss matters of faith with the Ethiopian clergy in an atmosphere of mutual respect and admiration.[24] He also remarked upon their level of scholarship and the asceticism of the monks. He found the abbot to be 'a man of holy life conversant with Latin and also with Portuguese and an accomplished scribe ... he wrote in his own handwriting the Gloria of the Mass, and the Creed and Paternoster, and Ave Maria, and the Apostles' Creed and the Salve Regina, and he knew it in Latin as well as I did. He also wrote out the gospel of St John and all very well ornamented.'[25]

A Devastating Jihad

However, the golden years at Debre Libanos came to an end when disaster struck the monastery. Deploying soldiers armed with matchlock guns—both provided by the expanding Ottoman Empire—*Imam* Ahmed bin Ibrahim (now popularly known as Ahmed Grañ) from the Muslim city of Harar in what was then known as the state of Adal, to the east of Ethiopia, overcame the emperor's less well-armed forces. Then in 1529 the *imam* went on to launch a devastating *jihad* throughout the Christian highlands, burning and pillaging the churches and putting the clergy to the sword. In July 1531 soldiers of Ahmed Grañ's cavalry arrived at the edge of the plateau above the monastery of Debre Libanos. Looking down on the magnificently endowed church of St Tekle Haymanot, they 'watched it from the edge of the precipice and were amazed at its golden dome and golden cross'.[26]

Grañ's army descended on the monastery, massacred 450 priests and monks, looted the premises of its gold and silver, and razed the church to the ground. The *imam's* Muslim chronicler, who was embedded with the army and witnessed the onslaught, was moved to write that so terrible was the grief of the monks at the sight of the destruction of the church, they 'plunged into the fire, as moths dive into the wick of a lamp; all but a few of them'.[27]

Ahmed Grañ's *jihad* burned and pillaged numerous churches and massacred their clergy, including the royal church of Mekane Sillassé ('Place of the Trinity'), a church affiliated to Debre Libanos and situated about 125 km to the north-east (see Map 11). Father Alvares and his delegation had earlier visited the emperor at this same church, describing in his memoirs a welcoming throng of twenty thousand, and a very large three-aisled basilica with walls of white stone, curtains of rich brocade, the principal door decorated with metal plates inlaid with stones, and above it icons of the Blessed Virgin and angels.[28] In 1531 Ahmed Grañ accompanied his soldiers in their onslaught on the church, his chronicler recording the event at the time in Arabic:

> His close friends entered with him. When he saw it, he was about to be blinded by its dazzling brilliance. The church was embellished with gold and silver plates, encrusted with pearls ... The church was one hundred cubits long ... They were stupefied by the workmanship ... So they set to work with a thousand axes, ripping out the gold and the precious stones ... Each took as much gold

as he could carry ... The Imam asked all the Arabs who were with him, 'Is there the like of this church, with its images and its gold, in Byzantium, or in India, or in any other place?' They replied, 'We never saw or heard its like in Byzantium or India or anywhere in the world.'[29]

In 1540, Emperor Libne Dingil died, a somewhat forlorn figure, at the monastery of Debre Damo, having sought military assistance from the Portuguese but not having lived to see the result. He was succeeded by his son Gelawdéwos (r. 1540–59; named after the Roman–Antiochan martyr Claudius), who attacked the problems of the Christian kingdom with renewed vigour. The following year a Portuguese military unit led by the intrepid Christóvão da Gama (a son of the explorer Vasco da Gama) finally arrived in Ethiopia to support the Christian army. Following several battles, Ahmed Grañ was defeated and killed in 1543. But the devastating *jihad* had lasted fourteen years, during which much of the rich material and spiritual culture of Ethiopian Christendom was destroyed.[30]

Debre Libanos in the Eternal City

During the Grañ *jihad* some of the younger Christian monks fled the onslaught to join their fellow countrymen overseas. There was thus an expansion of the Ethiopian monastic community in Rome, which led to a further strengthening of the cultural and religious ties between the Ethiopian and Roman Churches. Ethiopian monks had long travelled to distant monasteries, engaging with other Christian Churches, and achieving distinction as theologians, writers and scholars. Being the leading Ethiopian monastery, and with its abbot as *ichegé*, Debre Libanos was usually well represented in these overseas communities. In 1536 or thereabouts, three young monks from Debre Libanos arrived in Rome from Jerusalem, of which one, Father Tesfa Siyon, achieved particular distinction.[31] This was during the reign of Pope Paul III (r. 1534–49), who as a cardinal had been protector of the Monastery of St Stephen of the Abyssinians, and under this pontiff the monastery rose to greater splendour.[32]

Born around 1508, and with the monastic name of Pétros (Peter) or Pedro, Tesfa Siyon was a scholarly theologian, fluent in Italian,

Latin and Arabic, as well as Amharic and the ancient language of Gi'iz (also known as Ethiopic, the Ethiopian equivalent of Latin) used by the Ethiopian Church. When Grañ's army burned the monastery of Debre Libanos in 1531, Tesfa Siyon, who never forgot the horrors of that onslaught, was in his early twenties. One of the few monks who, as mentioned by Ahmed Grañ's chronicler, did not perish in the fire, he left Ethiopia for Jerusalem shortly afterwards, spending a number of years there before arriving in Rome.

The three new arrivals, who brought with them a number of codices they had managed to salvage during the *jihad*, joined the Ethiopian monks at Santo Stefano (St Stephen's monastery). The community was already renowned for its scholarship; by 1513 it had published the first Ethiopic Book of the Psalms of David, a psalter produced jointly by the Ethiopian Brother Thomas Welde-Samuél and a German member of the Roman Curia, Father Johannes Pottam. Thomas became prior of the monastery, and Father Tesfa Siyon became senior scholar, working with ecclesiastics and scholars such as Canon (later, Bishop) Mariano Vittori of the Roman Curia, and Cardinal Cervini, who would ascend briefly to the papal throne as Marcellus II (r. April–May 1555).[33]

Although there were doctrinal differences between the Ethiopian and Catholic Churches regarding the nature of Christ, an esoteric theme which many theologians—both Ethiopian and Roman—loved to discuss and debate, Tesfa Siyon considered such differences to be quite insignificant, compared to the similarities between the two Churches. Furthermore, of the various Christological beliefs within Ethiopia, those of Debre Libanos were the closest to those of Rome, and for that reason the theologians of Debre Libanos were sometimes referred to by their fellow Ethiopians as Catholics.[34]

Increasingly anxious about Ottoman expansion, the attitude of the Roman Church towards the representatives of a Church they regarded as long-lost was quite ecumenical and pragmatic. In turn, the approach of the Ethiopians towards the Roman Church was exemplified by that of Emperor Libne Dingil: 'a nuanced policy of rapprochement', presenting his faith 'as legitimate and his country as a rightful member of the assembly of Christian nations, side by side with Europe's'.[35]

Father Tesfa Siyon was responsible for several pioneering works of ecclesiastical and literary importance, including the first translation into Ethiopic of the New Testament, published in two volumes in 1548–9—a project sponsored jointly by Pope Paul III and the Ethiopian emperor Claudius. Tesfa Siyon also published Ethiopian religious books in Latin, as well as the first Ethiopic grammar. He knew Ignatius of Loyola, the founder of the Jesuits, and became a familiar of Pope Paul III and Filippo Archinto, the vicar general of Rome, with whom he is depicted in a painting in the Jesuit mother-church of Il Gesù in Rome (Fig. 1). Clearly two of the pope's most trusted associates, they are standing immediately behind him.

Much disturbed by the *jihad* against Ethiopian Christendom that he had experienced as a young man at Debre Libanos, Father Tesfa Siyon foresaw that only good could come of a stronger partnership between the Ethiopian Church and the Jesuits, and it was certainly at least partly due to his efforts that Ignatius of Loyola eventually sent a Jesuit delegation to Ethiopia.[36]

In due course Tesfa Siyon of Debre Libanos was appointed abbot of Santo Stefano, and subsequently met in Rome a Sicilian friar, Father Antonio Lo Duca—a meeting that would lead to yet another chapter in the story of collaboration between the Churches of Rome and Ethiopia.[37]

The Host of Seven

Several years before, in a small church in Sicily, Lo Duca had seen an ancient painting of the archangels Michael, Gabriel, Raphael, Uriel, Raguel, Ramiel and Sariel. Despite veneration of the Seven Archangels not being traditional in the Roman Church, the friar was inspired to become a devotee, and resolved to have a church built in their honour. However, recognition of what was known as the 'Host of Seven' was not only unrecognised in Rome, but was prevalent in ancient Judaic traditions. Jews at that time being regarded by the Roman Church as enemies of Christ, it is not entirely surprising that Lo Duca's attempts to persuade the pope that his project should go ahead were unsuccessful, and the friar had left Rome in despair.[38]

In 1539, after being further inspired by visions, Father Lo Duca returned to Rome, where he met Tesfa Siyon. The situation now changed, for in Tesfa Siyon the Sicilian found an energetic champion for his cause. The Ethiopian was very supportive of Lo Duca's proposals, the Seven Archangels being venerated only in the Ethiopian Church (see fig. 2), and being recognised in the ancient Book of Enoch, which was accepted as canonical only in Ethiopia.[39]

Being well connected with the powerful Farnese family, of which Pope Paul III was a member, Tesfa Siyon was in a position to lobby for the project, repeatedly taking up the matter with the pontiff. Although Paul III was not keen on the idea of the new church, he was nonetheless well disposed towards the Ethiopians and the Ethiopian Church. At the request of the Ethiopian monks in Jerusalem, he intervened in favour of the Ethiopian monastery of the Saviour of the World in Nicosia on the island of Cyprus, which is believed to have hosted an Ethiopian community since the 1189 conquest of Palestine by Saladin.[40] And in 1540 Tesfa Siyon succeeded in obtaining from Paul III what was, in essence, a charter for the monastery of St Stephen of the Abyssinians and the guest house attached to it for Ethiopian pilgrims. Finally, on 14 September 1548, through an Apostolic Letter, the pontiff made the concession of the monastery definitive.[41]

After the death of Pope Paul III the following year, his successor, Julius III (r. 1550–5), was more amenable to the proposals for the new church, and in due course the project's proponents, numbering twelve, banded together in a confraternity known as the Brotherhood of the Seven Angels, an exclusive group of high ecclesiastics and dignitaries committed to turning the friar's dream into reality, under the patronage of the Holy Roman Emperor.

The new pontiff moved rapidly on the project. Despite much controversy and debate, in 1550 he instructed Filippo Archinto, who was still vicar general of Rome, to sign the decree for consecration of the church, the site of which was controversial, being the overgrown remains of the public baths of the ancient Roman emperor Diocletian. Tesfa Siyon was undoubtedly pleased that the project for which he had lobbied for eleven years was finally going ahead but, sadly, he died shortly afterwards.[42]

The Chapel of the Saviour

Work finally began on the site in 1563 under Pope Pius IV (r. 1559–65), and the massive edifice, which was the last architectural project designed by Michelangelo, took several years to build. In fact, by the time it was completed, both Michelangelo and the originator, Antonio Lo Duca, had also died. Nonetheless, the contribution of Lo Duca, Tesfa Siyon and their collaborators was not forgotten, for in the 1570s a painting depicting them was hung in the first of several chapels that would be constructed within the basilica: the Chapel of the Saviour, where it can still be seen. It shows the twelve members of the Brotherhood of the Seven Angels responsible for the founding of the edifice, the group being led in prayer by Pope Pius IV followed by Antonio Lo Duca; Cardinal Fabrizio Serbelloni (a papal legate related to Pius IV); Filippo Archinto, vicar general of Rome; Father Tesfa Siyon of Debre Libanos; Matteo Catalani, the owner of the Chapel of the Saviour; and the Holy Roman Emperor, Charles V.[43]

A painting of the Virgin Mary enthroned and surrounded by the Seven Archangels, commissioned by Father Antonio Lo Duca in Venice in 1543, can also be seen in the apse of the basilica. The adoption by the pope of such a non-canonical theme for the cavernous new church—a theme recognised only by the Ethiopian Church—is a reminder of the esteem in which Tesfa Siyon of Debre Libanos was held, and of the mutual respect that had developed over the centuries between the two Churches.

The great basilica of Santa Maria degli Angeli, as it is usually known, would eventually become the state church of the newly created Kingdom of Italy (see Fig. 3). It is then a terrible irony that under the flag of that kingdom, Debre Libanos, the sacred home of one of the basilica's founders, would be desecrated and its congregation brutally massacred.

A Striking Counterpoint

By 1558, Ethiopian Christendom was in the process of recovering from the *jihad* of Ahmed Grañ, and under Emperor Gelawdéwos and Yohannis (John) I, the fourteenth abbot of Debre Libanos (1552–

9), the church of St Tekle Haymanot was reconstructed. 'Seeing that its rule were splendid', the emperor adorned it 'with precious vestments and spread carpet on the floor of its hall ... Love and honour for Debre Libanos showed all the kings during their reign, but he surpassed his predecessors.'[44]

In 1586 a great migration of the Oromo, an ethnic group hailing from south of the Shewan plateau, swept across the Siga Wedem gorge, leaving a trail of devastation from which Debre Libanos was not spared. As a result the sixteenth abbot, Zatra Wengel (r. 1560s–91), and the majority of the clergy, trekked northwards with Emperor Sartsa Dengel (r. 1563–91) to the relative safety of the Lake Tana district, where they settled. For the first time since the days of its founder, the monastery of Debre Libanos had had to abandon the Siga Wedem gorge.

In the Lake Tana area another notable and historic interaction occurred between the Roman and Ethiopian Churches when a Spanish Jesuit priest, Father Pedro Páez, arrived in Ethiopia to minister to the Luso-Ethiopian community descended from members of an earlier Catholic delegation. Originally chosen to go to Ethiopia in 1589, he finally arrived in 1603. Popular and talented, Páez was eager to study the doctrine, history and practices of the Ethiopian Church. In a striking counterpoint to the work of Tesfa Siyon in Rome, Páez was involved in the foundation of magnificent churches in Ethiopia, published a history of the nation, and translated the hagiographical work of *The Contendings of St Tekle Haymanot* into Portuguese.

The most obvious difference between the practices of the Ethiopian Christians and the Jesuits was actually not doctrinal; it was principally concerned with cultural expression—something that Páez, like Tesfa Siyon, did not consider a critical issue. He happily adopted the Ethiopian rite, and enjoyed extraordinary success in working with his Ethiopian Orthodox counterparts, including the conversion of Libne Dingil's son, Emperor Susinyos (r. 1607–32), to Catholicism.

However, by that time the attitude of the Portuguese Catholics towards the Ethiopian Church had begun to assume a character rather different from that of the papacy that Tesfa Siyon had experienced. As Matteo Salvadore explains, in the wake of the

Counter-Reformation that was under way, 'the paradigm of religious sameness and ecumenism was being replaced by a new discourse of difference and proselytism'.

Inevitably, the new aggressive approach led to confrontation between the two Churches.[45] After Páez's death this shift was exemplified by the arrival in Ethiopia in 1622 of his successor, Archbishop Alfonso Mendez, a prelate of a different sort. This pompous and arrogant appointee attempted to capitalise on the success that his predecessor had enjoyed at the imperial Ethiopian court, but his attempts to impose the Latin rite by force undid the good work that Páez had done. Mendez lacked respect even for Debre Libanos, where he had the body of one of the revered former abbots, who had been buried in the church, rudely disinterred and cast out. Despite the Ethiopian belief that the mentally disturbed are under the protection of God, he also declared an unfortunate woman a witch and had her thrown into prison.

During the time of Battra Giyorgis, the nineteenth abbot of Debre Libanos (r. 1623–32), such outrages led to serious conflicts between supporters of the emperor (who had been captivated by Páez) and the Orthodox clergy. Mendez destroyed the mutual trust that Páez had built, escalated minor cultural differences, and politicised them to the point of civil war. The resultant widespread bloodshed and devastation culminated in a decision by Emperor Susinyos to abdicate, and permit his son, Fasiledes (r. 1632–67), to take over and restore Orthodoxy as the state religion.

Following his coronation in 1632, Emperor Fasiledes concluded that in order to bring peace to Ethiopia, it was necessary to expel all foreign Catholics from the country, and did so. The legacy of the blundering Mendez was to haunt relations between the Ethiopian and Roman Churches for more than two hundred years.[46]

Debre Libanos in a Jesuit Estate

Under Emperor Fasiledes the monastery of Debre Libanos was re-established at Azezo, the newly vacant Jesuit centre combined with a royal complex originally built for Emperor Susinyos south of the present-day city of Gondar and near the northern shore of the lake.

The idyllic 17th-century development, which had been constructed by Portuguese Jesuits who had arrived from Goa with their Indian masons, consisted of a Catholic church with residential quarters for the clergy, together with a seminary, and an imperial palace with private access for the sovereign to a replica Mughal water-garden complete with pavilion. Had they lived to see it, both Tesfa Siyon and Pedro Páez would doubtless have been surprised to know that this miniature estate, which had been planted with 'lemons, apples, figs of India and Portugal, sugar cane and spinach, as well as plants already known in Ethiopia such as false banana and coffee', would eventually become the site of the monastery of Debre Libanos, and remain so for more than two hundred and fifty years, until the end of the 19th century.[47]

In due course, when the ageing former emperor Susinyos died, despite his personal adherence to Catholicism, he was buried with great respect and ceremony at the church at Azezo. Today the church complex of St Tekle Haymanot at Azezo remains a striking synthesis of Orthodox and Catholic cultural and architectural influences. Not only does the present church incorporate masonry from the original Jesuit-built complex, but the murals inside include an Ethiopian depiction of the Seven Archangels, echoing Tesfa Siyon's legacy in the iconography of the basilica of Santa Maria degli Angeli in Rome.

Scholarship at St Stephen's

While the monks of Debre Libanos were settling into the former Jesuit centre at Azezo, in Rome the monastery of St Stephen of the Abyssinians was becoming the focal point of Ethiopian studies in Europe. It was through St Stephen's that the German scholar Hiob Ludolf (1624–1704) obtained most of the information on Ethiopia for his magisterial treatise *Historia Aethiopica*, which he would publish in 1681. His principal informant was Father Gorgoryos (Gregory), a monk from the Ethiopian church of Mekane Sillassé, the church affiliated to Debre Libanos that had so impressed Ahmed Grañ when his matchlock-bearing men from the Ottoman Empire arrived to destroy and plunder it in 1531 (see Map 10).[48] The joint work of Hiob Ludolf and this scholarly monk, much of which was carried out in Germany under the patronage of the Duke of Gotha, would lay the foundation of Ethiopian studies in international scholarship.

Another Golden Age

Emperor Yohannis IV (r. 1872–89) partially restored the monastery of Debre Libanos in the Siga Wedem gorge,[49] but it was not until Emperor Menelik II (r. 1889–1913) succeeded him that the House of Tekle Haymanot was fully reinstated on the community's original site.

The reign of Emperor Menelik would be another golden age for Debre Libanos. The sovereign established his imperial court in Shewa, eventually settling in a well-watered valley where he built his capital, named Addis Ababa ('New Flower'). The Siga Wedem gorge being readily accessible from the capital city, Menelik embraced Debre Libanos as the empire's premier monastery, and the House of Tekle Haymanot as its leading monastic order.

Within a few years the emperor had built an impressive new octagonal stone church over the tomb of the saint. Opposite the front of the church, across the churchyard, stood a tall bell-tower, pierced on all sides by double windows, where the tolling of a great bell called the faithful to prayer. The new church of St Tekle Haymanot was a magnificent edifice in a majestic setting.

The sovereign had Tekle Haymanot's original *tabot*, or altar slab, and the cross that he is believed to have owned, installed in another building constructed next to the abbot's residence. Known as the House of the Cross, or Mesqel Bét, the plan took the form of a Greek cross, with a tower at the centre, the upper room of which housed the saint's sacred artefacts.

Endowing it generously, Menelik breathed new life into the monastery, which was able to continue its traditional role in the affairs of Church and State. Life at Debre Libanos was thus able to continue much as it had always done.

Over the centuries several churches were founded in the Siga Wedem gorge by disciples of Tekle Haymanot who left the monastery to establish their own communities. This trend was particularly pronounced during the 15th century, when the wealth and status bestowed on Debre Libanos led some of the more ascetic clergy, wishing to hold true to the principles of their founder, to leave the monastery to dwell in poverty in caves, and establish rock-cut churches and hermitages in remote parts of the gorge. Thus by the 20th century the gorge had become a vast sanctified cultural landscape, a Holy Land revered throughout Ethiopia, a retreat for those seeking the ascetic life and wishing to follow in the footsteps of the holy fathers, or simply to renounce the world.

Debre Libanos has always been primarily a seat of learning, where students and scholars study theology and Christian literature and poetry. The monks do not live communally, but maintain an ascetic existence in simple individual huts and cottages, in accordance with the order of St Anthony.

As a place of Christian pilgrimage, Debre Libanos was, and still is, unequalled throughout Ethiopia, many of the faithful coming to take the holy waters of the saint, of which the drops falling from the roof of his original cave of Debre Asbo are the most highly prized.

2

BAD NEIGHBOURS

> 'To make a people great it is necessary to send them to battle even if you have to kick them in the pants. That is what I shall do.'
>
> Benito Mussolini

As we have seen, prior to the religious crisis precipitated by Alfonso Mendez, the Ethiopian empire had excellent relations not only with Portugal, but also with the kingdoms of the Italian peninsula. Diplomacy, religious cooperation, cultural exchange and trade flourished between Ethiopia and both Venice and Naples, and an Ethiopian monastery and church had long been established in Rome. Furthermore, marriages were proposed between the royal families of the Ethiopian emperor Zer'a Ya'iqob and Alfonso V, king of Aragon, Naples and Sicily.[1]

Following the harsher distinction being drawn in Rome by the end of the 16th century between Orthodoxy and Catholicism, which contributed to the Mendez debacle, this period of cooperation was followed by a long interval during which Catholics were personae non gratae in Ethiopia. However, by the second half of the 19th century, Catholic missions were once again being received, and two events presented opportunities for a new phase in the relationship between Ethiopia and her erstwhile friends: the creation of the nation-state of Italy in 1861, and the opening of the Suez Canal eight years later, which created a direct maritime route from the Mediterranean to the Red Sea. The purchase of the Red Sea port of Assab by an Italian missionary on behalf of the Rubattino Shipping Company gave the Italians a tiny foothold on the coastal strip traditionally tributary to the Ethiopian emperors, and with the opening of the canal, the acquisition took on a strategic importance.

Conquest and Expansion

Had the Italians continued the good relations with Ethiopia that they had maintained in centuries past, Italy's acquisition of Assab could have been of mutual benefit. However, it was not to be, for under the new government of Italy, the desire for collaboration, trade and joint scholarship was replaced by a drive for conquest and expansion. With a view to extending their presence on the southern shores of the Red Sea, the Italians occupied the port of Massawa, thereby coming into conflict with the Ethiopian emperor Yohannis IV. While battling with Yohannis, they entered into a treaty of friendship with his rival, Menelik, then king of Shewa (r. 1865–89). Upon Yohannis's death in 1889, Menelik succeeded him as emperor, and in that capacity signed an agreement with the Italians now known as the Treaty of Wichalé. Under the treaty the Italian government recognised Menelik's sovereignty, and, in return, he granted Italy hegemony over a substantial tract of land consisting of the southwestern coastal strip of the Red Sea. The Italians were delighted. They now had not only a nation-state of their own; they had also acquired their first colony, which they named Eritrea.

Many Ethiopians, however, were unimpressed, including the sceptical and shrewd Empress Taytu. Having no trust in the Italians, she feared a foreign power achieving a stranglehold on Ethiopia. She thought Menelik foolhardy and naive to give up part of the empire, including Ethiopia's access to the sea, notwithstanding the right granted to him to import arms through Massawa as well as a loan to finance their purchase. Furthermore, the land handed over to Italy included Adulis, the ancient port of the empire when its capital was at Aksum, as well as a slice of the Christian Ethiopian highlands that encompassed the 5th–6th-century monastic centre of Debre Libanos of Ham and the most illustrious monastery of northern Ethiopia, the 14th-century Debre Bizen.

The Humiliation of Adwa

One of the clauses of the Treaty of Wichalé provided Ethiopia with the right to communicate with other foreign powers through the Italian government. However, apparently unknown to Menelik, the Italian-language version of the treaty made it mandatory for Ethiopia to do so, thereby purporting to make Ethiopia an Italian protectorate. Claiming he had been deceived, Menelik declared the treaty invalid.

But it was too late. From the start the Italians proved to be bad neighbours, for they wasted no time in crossing the newly created border into Ethiopia. Menelik repeatedly warned them against further advances, and gave them every opportunity to turn back, but received only scorn and derision in return. Empress Taytu had been proved right, but the damage was done. The Italians penetrated further into Ethiopia, reaching Meqele, the capital of the Ethiopian province of Tigray. Despite the crushing defeat of their advance unit of two thousand soldiers on the mountain-top of Amba Alagi, the Italians unwisely entrenched themselves in a hurriedly built fort. Surrounded by Menelik's forces, with limited food rations and no water supply, the Italians would have starved to death were it not for Menelik's chivalry in allowing them to evacuate the fort and return to their lines unmolested.

Finally, on 1 March 1896, still intent on invading Ethiopia, the Italians regrouped, reached further into Ethiopia, and engaged Menelik's massed armies at Adwa, a small settlement in Tigray. The attack was a costly mistake, for the invaders were routed; over four thousand Italian soldiers died. The magnanimous Menelik sent the Italian prisoners of war, numbering around two thousand, back home unharmed, and allowed the invaders to retain the colony of Eritrea. But the Italians earned the scorn of Europe, and their defeat at Adwa was to haunt them for decades to come.

The Rise of the Duce

Italy fared little better as a result of her involvement in the First World War (1914–18). It left her economy in ruins, and despite having been on the winning side, the Italians never received what they considered their fair dues at the Treaty of Versailles. The country was thus ripe for revolution, and ready for a hero who would restore national pride. A radical young journalist, political activist and former socialist named Benito Mussolini had emerged as the leading light in the militant and pro-war Fascist Party, named after the *fasces*—an axe wrapped in a bundle of rods—the symbol of the magistrates of ancient Rome. Backed by armed thugs, Mussolini garnered sufficient support to transform the party into a political force. In 1922 King Umberto I, overestimating Mussolini's popularity, asked him to form a government. The die was cast; Mussolini was now in control.

By the early 1930s the *Duce* ('Leader'), as he was known by his followers, needed a military conquest to galvanise support for himself and his Fascist 'revolution', to give substance to his claim that the 'soft, mandolin-playing' Italians had now become hardened warriors able to emulate their Ancient Roman forebears, and—most important of all—to launch a programme of international expansion through conquest. The lands to the south of the Mediterranean Sea were controlled largely by two of what were then known as the 'great powers', Great Britain and France, with which Mussolini did not yet want a confrontation. But beyond British-controlled Egypt and the Sudan lay Ethiopia, with relatively easy access for the *Duce*'s forces through the Italian colonies of Eritrea and Italian Somaliland.

Ethiopia would be the first of several nation-states to be invaded by Italy, and Mussolini intended that the annexation of Ethiopia would play a key role in his expansion programme. Eventually, he planned, Italy would extend her hegemony around the Mediterranean, westwards to consume French-controlled North Africa, and eastwards to reach the Balkans.

The plan for Ethiopia was two-fold. First, in order to gain sufficient prestige and credibility to launch his expansion programme, the *Duce* needed what he could present to his domestic audience as a glittering victory.[2] Offered the prospect of negotiating a protectorate arrangement with Ethiopia, he is said to have refused, declaring that he did not want Ethiopia 'on a plate'; he needed a war. The next step was to annex the Ethiopian state and dismantle it. The land of Ethiopia would become a military-industrial complex for Italy. A million Ethiopians would be drafted into what Mussolini called a 'black army', to fight the wars of conquest that would follow, in his quest to establish what he referred to as Fascism International. The Italians would establish country-wide infrastructure including 'fifty or so airfields' to facilitate military and administrative control, and would manufacture armaments using the mineral deposits thought by the Italians to exist in Ethiopia.[3] The invasion, which was to be supported by the deployment of chemical weapons by the Royal Air Force, was scheduled to commence in October 1935.[4] These geopolitical aims were disguised by claims that the objective of the invasion was to 'civilise' the 'barbaric' Ethiopians, in support of which, as we shall see, the Italian Catholic Church would play a critical role. A war that began with a purely secular purpose would soon acquire a powerful religious dimension.

Selling the Invasion

Emperor Menelik, the founder of modern Ethiopia, and more tolerant towards the Catholic Church than his predecessor, permitted the resumption of Catholic missions. As a young prince, the future emperor Haile Selassie was tutored by the well-known French Catholic bishop André Jarosseau, who had arrived in Ethiopia in 1882. Jarosseau was consecrated bishop in 1900, and by 1904 had established a leprosy centre in the Ethiopian town of Harar known as St Anthony's, as well as a seminary.[5] The Catholic Church soon had 232 clergy in Ethiopia, to minister to some sixteen thousand Ethiopian Catholics.[6]

In 1924, as *Ras* Teferi, the future emperor embarked on a European tour that included a state visit to Italy, where he was well received by both Mussolini and Pope Pius XI. Although Orthodox, the *Ras* was well disposed towards the Catholic Church, and encouraged Catholic missions to Ethiopia. Indeed, the Ethiopian government permitted the Catholic Church to establish three jurisdictions in the country, and Bishop Jarosseau would remain an influential personal advisor to the emperor until the prelate's death in 1941.[7]

However, despite the apparently good relationship between the governments of Ethiopia and Italy, by the spring of 1934 Italy's preparations to attack Ethiopia were well under way, with Mussolini spinning several different stories to justify the invasion, depending on the audience. There was a story for everybody. One rationale was a claim that Italy was overpopulated, and that acquiring the land of Ethiopia would provide Italians with more 'living space'—a theme that would inspire Hitler in his justification of Nazi Germany's invasion of Poland. Italians who might have baulked at the idea of an illegal armed invasion of a far-away nation were meant to be reassured by the argument that an Italian conquest of Ethiopia would constitute a 'civilising mission', and, to support this claim, a new narrative was rapidly developed, for which denigrating picture postcards supposedly depicting Ethiopians were produced and circulated in their thousands. In the process, Emperor Haile Selassie—the dapper young prince who had charmed the Italians in the 1920s—was transformed into a grotesque monster. At the same time, ironically, photographs of actual Ethiopian women were distributed to entice volunteers to join the Blackshirts, in order to man the invasion.

For the Italian military and the ultra-nationalists, a great victory would avenge the defeat at Adwa, and restore Italy's long-sought-after 'prestige' following the humiliation at Versailles. But for the peasant farmers of rural Italy, the tale was that the invasion of Ethiopia was 'colonisation', a label also intended to give the invasion a fig leaf of legitimacy. However, Ethiopia was manifestly not *terra nullius*—an unclaimed land without a recognised polity—and thus was not a candidate for colonisation. Ethiopia, like Italy, was a sovereign state, with an imperial pedigree as old as the ancient Roman Empire. In fact, both Ethiopia and Italy had achieved modern nation-state status in the second half of the 19th century. Ethiopia was also a member of the League of Nations and the Universal Postal Union, with diplomatic representation in many countries, including an ambassador in Rome at the court of King Victor Emmanuel III.[8] There had also long been several embassies in Addis Ababa including

British, French, American, German, Russian and Italian. Moreover, Italy had the largest number of diplomats of any nation with an envoy accredited to the court of Emperor Haile Selassie; there were Italian diplomats not only in Addis Ababa, but also in consulates in several of Ethiopia's secondary towns. Having thus recognised Ethiopia's status as one of the world's nation-states, Mussolini was well aware that to invade that country would be not a colonial adventure, but a criminal act in international law, and indeed it was declared to be so by the League of Nations. However, Ethiopia was now a tempting and relatively soft target, not having undergone an industrial revolution since the Battle of Adwa, and thus having no modern armaments industry or air force. For the *Duce*, it remained only to find an excuse to trigger an invasion.

After Emperor Haile Selassie's coronation in 1930, the Italians had begun a series of incursions into Ethiopia from Italian Somaliland, and in November 1934 there was an incident at a desert oasis named Welwel, about a hundred kilometres inside Ethiopian territory, where the Italians had unilaterally established a military post. Following the arrival of an Anglo-Ethiopian border survey commission, shooting broke out, in which more than 100 Ethiopians and 30 Italian colonial troops died. It has never been entirely clear whether Mussolini's government deliberately provoked the battle at Welwel as an excuse for war, or whether it simply took advantage of an unexpected but fortuitous incident. In his detailed written account of what occurred, Colonel A.T. Curle, a British member of the border commission, expressed the opinion that the Welwel incident was deliberately engineered by the Italian authorities in order to provoke the Ethiopian government.[9] This belief is supported by the fact that a few weeks after the Welwel incident, Mussolini signalled his intentions clearly in a letter to General De Bono: 'In case the *negus* [Emperor Haile Selassie] has no intention of attacking us, we ourselves must take the initiative.'[10]

Claiming that Welwel lay within their colony of Italian Somaliland, the Italian government demanded apologies and damages. Outraged, the emperor took the case to the League of Nations, in which he put great faith. However, the League procrastinated for eleven months, thus allowing Italy to complete a massive build-up in military capacity. Choosing appeasement in the expectation that that would avoid Mussolini joining forces with Adolf Hitler's Nazi movement—a movement inspired by the *Duce*'s success in launching Fascism—the French and British made Ethiopia their sacrificial lamb by declaring themselves neutral.

Italian society was supported and controlled by three pillars: the state, represented by the king; the government, represented by Mussolini; and the Catholic Church, represented at the highest level by Pope Pius XI (r. 1922–39), the former Achille Cardinal Ratti, who as pontiff was also primate of Italy and bishop of Rome. The state had been weakened by Mussolini's rise, and despite his personal dislike and disdain for the *Duce*, the king generally preferred to take a back seat and let him have his way. That left the Church. Before the Italian invasion most Ethiopians never equated the Catholic Church with Italian nationalism; they respected the pope as the head of the universal Catholic Church.

There was, in fact, no reason for the Ethiopians to think otherwise, because previously the popes had not sided with Italy. The Holy See had opposed Italy's policy of penetration into Ethiopia that had culminated in the Battle of Adwa in 1896, and had actually censured Italian Catholic clergy who offered soothing patriotic remarks at memorial services for the dead of Italy's earlier defeat at the Ethiopian battle site of Amba Alagi. And after Adwa, the bishop of Nardo, in Puglia, sought guidance from Pope Leo XIII (r. 1878–1903), fearing that honouring the fallen would glorify the 'usurper', i.e., the Italian state, in its pursuit of its expansion programme in Ethiopia, which did not have the approval of the Holy See.[11] Furthermore, the pontiff offered to mediate between the Italian government and Emperor Menelik to negotiate the return of the Italian prisoners of war, and sent a mission to Addis Ababa for that purpose. Similarly, during the First World War, Pope Benedict XV (r. 1914–22) had not been allied to a particular nation. On the contrary, within a week of his appointment to the papal throne, he had vociferously condemned the war, and did all he could to promote peace. In 1917 he went so far as to draw up peace proposals, which, although they failed, were treated by the warring powers as a serious basis for negotiation.[12] However, when Emperor Haile Selassie appealed to Benedict's successor, Pope Pius XI, to mediate during the run-up to the Italian invasion, the Ethiopian sovereign and his government seemed to be unaware that since the Lateran Treaty of 1929, the Holy See was now beholden to Italy and, furthermore, had become, in effect, a centre of Italian nationalism. Most of the cardinals in the Curia were Italian, and some of them could be described as ultra-nationalists.

Nonetheless, the question remained: What would be the stand of the Catholic Church towards the invasion of Ethiopia? Would the Holy See under Pius XI denounce the horrors of a war of conquest, or would it acquiesce in evil in order to support the *Duce*? And if the Italians managed to annex Ethiopia, what then would be the attitude of the Holy See? The answers were not long in coming.

3

AN UNHOLY ALLIANCE

'The devil hath power to assume a pleasing shape.'
William Shakespeare, *Hamlet*

Pope Pius XI was inconstant in his attitude towards the Italian attack on Ethiopia. As we shall see, at one point he expressed concerns, but then became restrained in his comments—a restraint which eventually gravitated to silence. The Lateran Treaty of 1929, which reached a settlement of long-standing problems between the Italian government and the Holy See, and created the Vatican City state, had put Mussolini's government and the Catholic Church into a situation of mutual dependence. The legacy of the First World War was a turbulent and divided society, with Fascists and Communists fighting on the streets. Italians being overwhelmingly Catholic, to rally the population behind the invasion and ensure a glittering victory, the *Duce* needed the unity of purpose that only the Catholic Church could provide. In turn, the Church needed to be in Mussolini's good books if it was to be permitted to maintain its traditional position in Italian society and hold onto the Vatican.

Being primarily concerned with the survival of the Roman Church, the pontiff decided to choose the path of caution as far as the forthcoming invasion was concerned; he would not denounce it. The Holy See was afraid that failure to support Mussolini's government might lead to the fall of Fascism and the rise, in its place, of Communism and Protestantism, which the pontiff considered the principal enemies of the Catholic Church and, thus, greater evils.

These developments were not altogether surprising, since Pius XI's position of head of state of the Vatican City and head of the Holy See often appeared to take precedence over his role as a moral compass. Much influenced by the Jesuits, his primary agenda was basically theirs: the survival and welfare of the universal Catholic Church as an institution, which was regarded in Catholicism as the Body of Christ on earth and the only channel through which souls could achieve salvation. He is on record as saying, 'I would make a concordat with the devil if it benefited the Church.'[1]

Despite the fact that Italian Catholics accounted for only thirteen per cent of Catholics worldwide, the pope also sometimes seemed to forget that he was head of the Church for all Catholics, regardless of nationality. During the 1930s he increasingly gave the impression that he was first and foremost an Italian nationalist, sometimes referring to non-Italian Catholics as 'foreigners', and belittling their views and opinions.

Ethiopia and the Roman Church

Pius XI was, of course, well aware of the long-standing relationship between the Holy See and the Ethiopians, and indeed had himself become part of that relationship. Not only had there been an Ethiopian community in the Vatican under the auspices of the Holy See for more than four hundred years, but his predecessor had decided in 1919 to establish an Ethiopian college in the monastery of St Stephen of the Abyssinians. And in 1924, at the Vatican, Pius XI had hosted Emperor Haile Selassie in his earlier role of Crown Prince *Ras* Teferi, the reception being 'almost equal to that reserved for crowned emperors'.[2] On that occasion the pontiff expressed his pleasure 'at the fact that religious freedom was now permitted in Ethiopia', and that 'the Catholic missions were now residing in Ethiopia in peace and security'. Finally, Pius XI prayed, 'May God bless the land of Ethiopia, its kings and its people.'[3]

Having been taken aback by the rather modest Catholic church he had seen in Jerusalem, *Ras* Teferi took the opportunity to tell the pope that he would buy him a site for a new one. He was as good as his word. Acquiring a piece of land next to the Holy Sepulchre, the *Ras* made over the deeds to the Holy See, a handsome gift that the pope accepted.[4]

Pius XI went on to arrange a reciprocal visit by a papal delegation to Empress Zewditu and *Ras* Teferi in Addis Ababa in November 1929. Led by the secretary of the Congregation for the Propagation of the Faith, Monsignor Marchetti-Selvaggiani, the objective was to obtain the permission of the *Ras* for Catholic missionaries to continue to work in Ethiopia, which was granted.[5]

Furthermore, in the same year, the pontiff raised even higher the esteem in which the Ethiopians were apparently held by the papacy, by building a new Pontifical Ethiopian College in the centre of the Vatican Gardens, to replace the earlier college—'a clear expression of great paternal love for and attention to the Ethiopians in his midst'.[6] The pope personally chose the site, and the Lateran Treaty of 1929 put the Pontifical Ethiopian College in an even more privileged position, for it was the only college allowed to remain in the newly designated Vatican City. All other religious institutions, including the Roman College, were transferred to Rome, outside the Vatican. Ethiopia was thus the only country in the world to claim a Pontifical College within the Vatican.

On 12 February 1930 Pius XI gave canonical status to the Ethiopian college in an apostolic constitution entitled *Curis ac laboribus*, which spoke of the college as a 'tribute to the precious heritage of the solicitude of various popes towards Ethiopian Christianity'.[7]

In fact, Pius XI had good reason to be concerned about the potential impact of the forthcoming invasion on the position of the Catholic Church in Ethiopia, for since Emperor Haile Selassie's coronation in 1930 it had been going from strength to strength. In 1931, when the Catholic bishop in Ethiopia, Monsignor Jarosseau, had requested permission to build a modest Catholic church in Addis Ababa, the emperor had not only agreed, but had insisted that it be a cathedral. He had also provided a team of Ethiopian Catholic dignitaries to facilitate the project, and made arrangements for the best architects and all that was necessary for the construction.

In an astonishingly short time the project was complete; by 8 October 1933 Jarosseau was consecrating the cathedral of the Nativity of the Blessed Virgin Mary. The emperor provided a great cross for the ceremonial procession, incorporating a medallion of commemoration in honour of Pope Pius XI. Finally, Secretary of State Cardinal Eugenio Pacelli wrote to Bishop Jarosseau, informing him of the satisfaction of the Holy Father on the occasion of the blessing of the new cathedral.[8]

Yet no more than two years later, the senior Italian Catholic clergy—and, increasingly, the Holy See itself—behaved as if they were completely unaware of the favourable climate for the Catholic Church in Ethiopia. As we shall see, the pope stood by in silence as the Italian clergy not only misrepresented the situation in Ethiopia, but demeaned the emperor, his government and the Ethiopian Orthodox Church without restraint. By so demonising the Ethiopians and denigrating the Ethiopian Church, they bestowed upon the invasion a bogus moral purpose. And in so doing, the Italian clergy managed largely to unite the overwhelmingly Catholic population of Italy behind Mussolini's forthcoming war of aggression.[9]

Riding a Tiger

It should be noted that not all Catholics supported the invasion; on the contrary, support was limited principally to those of Italian nationality. Catholics outside Italy were generally shocked by the Holy See's support for Mussolini's government; they had expected a clear denunciation of the aggressive war. The Vatican was flooded with letters from Catholics around the world begging the pontiff to step in and speak against it. As Church historian Mikre-Sillassie Gebre-Ammanuel observed, 'Not only non-Catholics but also Catholics throughout the world looked in vain for some pronouncement from the Pope on this evil act of Fascism against [the] innocent people of Ethiopia.'[10] However, although Pope Pius XI and the *Duce* as individuals often did not see eye to eye, the pontiff ignored the petitions. He refrained from a clear public denunciation of the invasion, and took no steps to distance himself, the Holy See or the Vatican from even the most bellicose pronouncements of the Italian episcopate.

Lucia Ceci points out that the link between Roman Catholicism and Fascism 'was not merely tactical, the result of mutual exploitation, but deeper and more substantial: a shared respect for order, obedience, authority; a shared mistrust of common enemies such as freemasons, liberalism and communism'.[11] These shared sentiments and the euphoria surrounding the signing of the Lateran accord triggered one of the pope's more notable—and later much-regretted—indiscretions, when he announced in July 1929 that the Fascist state 'in its ideas, doctrine, and actions, does not allow anything that is not in accordance with Catholic practice and doctrine'.[12]

This was, of course, an extraordinary statement for the pontiff to make, for Fascist 'morality' did not follow Christian precepts; indeed, most of its doctrines were incompatible with the teachings of the Bible. Violence and war were, in fact, central pillars of Fascist doctrine—hardly in accordance with Christianity: 'I have clearly laid down my views from the doctrinal and philosophical standpoint', said the *Duce*. 'I do not believe in perpetual peace. Nay, more, I hold it to be harmful and destructive of the fundamental virtues of man, which only manifest themselves to the full in bloody energy.'[13]

If by 1929 Pius XI had not discovered that Fascism was unchristian, he had certainly done so by 1931, for a report to the Vatican informed him,

> The government wishes to create young people who are war-like and with no inhibitions and scruples, nurtured on hatred, ready to commit violence and vendetta, proud to serve Fascism even by beating and killing. Love, gentleness and forgiveness are regarded as vices of weak souls who are incapable of understanding the spirit of Fascism, which is not only a party, but a doctrine, an ethic and a new religion.[14]

Nonetheless, despite the centrality of war in Fascist doctrine, Pius XI maintained solid support for Mussolini's government, and the close link between Fascism and Catholicism inevitably led to overwhelming backing by the Italian episcopate for the invasion of Ethiopia, which began to be seen in Italy as a sort of spiritual renewal. In fact, for many—perhaps the majority of—Italians, loyalty to the Catholic Church and to Mussolini's government were becoming one and the same. Furthermore, the Holy See not only encouraged this tendency; on a number of occasions, despite the papacy's precious heritage of solicitude towards Ethiopian Christianity as declared in *Curis ac laboribus*, the Vatican secretary of state's office gave the impression that opponents of the invasion of Ethiopia were regarded by the Holy See as enemies of the Catholic Church.

The inevitability of the Italian episcopate's support for the invasion did not, however, derive solely from the desire of the Holy See to remain in the good books of the *Duce*. Support for government policies in general was more or less assured by the terms of the Lateran Treaty. Article 19 of the Concordat, which constituted a section of the treaty, limited the appointment of archbishops and bishops to those whose nomination raised no objection of a political nature from the Italian government. Furthermore, article 20 required each bishop of the Italian Church to take an oath of loyalty to the state, specifically swearing that he shall 'enter into no agreement, nor attend any council, which may be prejudicial to the interests of the Italian State or to public order', and that he 'shall lay a similar prohibition' on his clergy. Finally, article 21 entitled the government to object to ecclesiastical appointees and, in effect, to block their continuance in office. For these reasons, although they were required to stay out of politics, the episcopate—at least those appointed after 1929—were most likely to support government policies.

Because Pius XI made few public statements in 1934 and the first half of 1935 about the impending invasion of Ethiopia, it is sometimes thought that the Catholic Church was in the dark regarding the military planning and preparations. Yet this is not at all the case. Correspondence of the French ambassador to the Holy See, François Charles-Roux, provides clear evidence of the close involvement of high-ranking clergy in Italian national affairs, consisting of what Annie Lacroiz-Riz terms 'a remarkable division of labour'. On the one hand, Secretary of State Pacelli continually reiterated that peace would prevail, and that military movements in preparation for the invasion were not what they seemed.[15] On the other hand, a conversation with Giuseppe Dalla Torre, head of the daily newspaper of the Vatican, *L'Osservatore Romano*, on 8 February 1935 convinced Charles-Roux that the Holy See was well aware of ongoing mobilisation for the war.[16]

The impression gained from recent studies of the Vatican Secret Archives for the period concerned is that by 1935 the pope was, so to speak, riding a tiger. Even if he was beginning to take exception to some of Mussolini's actions and policies, his great concern was for the future of the Catholic Church under a Communist government, should Fascism fall from power; he saw Fascism as the lesser evil. Furthermore, his right-hand man, Cardinal Eugenio Pacelli, was quite sympathetic to Fascism and conciliatory towards Mussolini,[17] and, finally, the overwhelming majority of the episcopate, as noted earlier, were Fascist supporters. These circumstances certainly helped to dissuade the pontiff from public denunciations, or even criticisms, of Mussolini's forthcoming war of conquest.

A Crusade in the Making

The acceptance—or even encouragement—by the Holy See of an attack on Ethiopia was itself a very serious matter, but by early 1935 there was also talk of an even more sinister development: a Catholic crusade against that nation. The French ambassador found that Catholic prelates 'were engaging in the spring of 1935 in a crusade in favour of Italian expansion', benedictions being given to the military by 'certain cardinals' which raised the eyebrows of non-Italian ecclesiastics.[18]

By April 1935 declarations of loyalty to Mussolini were being made at the opening and closing of meetings attended by members of the senior Italian clergy, such as conferences, Eucharistic congresses, Catholic assemblies and student meetings.[19] At these assemblies the senior Italian clergy, gathering in force, found common cause in orchestrating support for the proclamation of a crusade. And at the same time a parallel campaign was launched in the Catholic print media. In June *L'Avvenire d'Italia* of Bologna, described by David Kertzer as Italy's most influential Catholic newspaper, announced with the vocabulary of medieval crusaders that Ethiopians were pagan barbarians, and that war would bring them Christianity and civilisation.[20] As Philip Jenkins observes in his reflections on the period of the First World War, when religious leaders were identified with a state, they tended to abandon words of peace and reconciliation, advocating instead strident doctrines of holy war and crusade, even directed against fellow Christians.[21] So where did this notion of a crusade come from?

Christian crusades, the first of which was launched at the end of the 11th century, had originally been proclaimed as defensive wars by Catholic Christendom in order to win back Jerusalem from the Muslims. Over the centuries the concept of, and justification for, crusades had widened, some crusades combining imperial with religious aims. But in Rome the basic spirit, ideas, myths and passions associated with crusading had apparently never died out, and could at any time be awakened.

Nonetheless it was difficult to understand why Ethiopia would be a likely target for a Catholic crusade, since apart from the Ethiopian Church's legitimate properties in Jerusalem, Ethiopians were not in possession of any part of the Holy Land. Furthermore, even the medieval popes had not proclaimed crusades to invade nations just because they were regarded as pagan (although how the world's second-oldest Christian nation with at least ten thousand churches and monasteries, which proclaimed Christianity long before the Western European nations, could be regarded as pagan was not at all clear).[22] However, worse was to follow.

Opposition and Persuasion

By the summer of 1935, Italians were generally not in favour of the forthcoming war. As Alberto Sbacchi explains, they had more important, if mundane, problems to worry about, for unemployment was high, and food was scarce and often unaffordable. They also feared, quite correctly, that the war would trigger a European conflict.[23] Furthermore, some were reluctant to fight in Ethiopia as they doubted that Italy could defeat the Ethiopians—a fear based on Mussolini's claim that Ethiopia was becoming heavily armed

AN UNHOLY ALLIANCE

and posed an existential military threat to Italy. Ironically, the *Duce* had made this entirely bogus claim to convince the Italian public that Italy should attack Ethiopia with a pre-emptive strike—not to dissuade them from joining the army.

In fact, Ethiopia had very few weapons of war, and no air force. It had not industrialised since the Battle of Adwa of 1896, so the military was only lightly armed and, at times of war, relied largely on the call-up of subsistence farmers who, if they were fortunate enough, could be supplied with a rifle and a limited amount of ammunition, but nothing more. They had no experience in modern warfare, let alone familiarity with modern weaponry, and many had never seen an aeroplane. Since becoming emperor in 1930, far from spending the national budget on the military, Haile Selassie's principal focus had been on a modernisation programme, key pillars of which were a reduction in the power of the land-owning aristocracy, the dispatch of school-leavers from ordinary families for university education overseas, and expansion of the domestic education and health sectors.

The emperor also attempted to complete the abolition of the slave trade, which in the Horn of Africa stretched back at least to the 10th century. Whereas on the west coast of the African continent the Atlantic trade had met the needs of American cotton plantation owners, in the Horn it had been driven mainly by the demands of Middle Eastern potentates and the Ottoman Empire, for which slave traders had traditionally used Ethiopia as a conduit to slave markets across the Red Sea, in Egypt and in Sudan.[24]

Despite having declined dramatically since its heyday, the trade was not yet entirely eradicated. During Empress Zewditu's reign, Haile Selassie, in his former role as heir apparent *Ras* Teferi, had acted energetically against it, and what was left of the trade was mainly in the hands of wealthy Muslim businessmen. As there was often no alternative form of employment for the remaining slaves, the process of eradication was gradual and was partly dependent on cultural mores and the state of the local economy—as it was, for example, in the British colony of Kenya, where the trade still persisted in the coastal region.[25] Nonetheless, in June 1925 the Anti-Slavery Society of Italy had made Empress Zewditu and *Ras*

Teferi honorary members in recognition of their efforts, which had culminated in the Ethiopian Anti-Slavery Edict of 31 March 1924.

In March 1927, the Italian Monsignor Gaudenzio Barlassina, head of the Consolata Mission, whom *Ras* Teferi had assisted in the establishment of several villages in Ethiopia for liberated slaves, also recognised the *Ras*'s efforts, publishing the following announcement in the Italian anti-slavery journal *Antischiavismo*:

> It is especially on the hereditary Prince *Ras* Tafari [sic], who is good hearted, open-minded and energetic without violence, that the hopes of the opponents of slavery rest ... The edict [abolishing slavery] has not been shelved—it is far from being a dead document. Already many of the more notorious slave-dealers have been found guilty and hanged publicly in Addis Ababa.[26]

In October 1928 the Italian prince Francesco Massimo had sent *Ras* Teferi a long telegram of congratulation for his work in putting down slavery, and in 1932 Emperor Haile Selassie had set up the Office for the Abolition of Slavery in Addis Ababa.[27]

In fact, Ethiopia itself had never organised slavery in the sense that the term was generally used internationally, until, ironically, the Italians introduced plantation slavery in Ethiopia in 1936 on lines similar to the Italian forced-labour projects in Libya, Italian Somaliland and Eritrea. There was, however, a long-standing Ethiopian tradition of using prisoners of war (both men and women) as indentured domestic labour at the household level. In fact, by the 1930s most slaves in Ethiopia were kept as domestic workers of ordinary rural families or at the courts of the nobility.[28] This practice was adopted by the Ethiopian government after the Battle of Adwa, when thousands of Italian prisoners of war were attached to Ethiopian households in Addis Ababa before being returned to Italy. None of these prisoners were executed; indeed, few, if any, suffered as a result of this arrangement, in which the householders were obliged to accommodate and feed them. In fact, some of them chose to settle in Ethiopia and marry Ethiopian women.

By the standards of today, the employment of prisoners of war as domestic servants would, of course, be an unacceptable practice, but it was certainly more humane than the policy of killing them, as practised by the Italians during their invasion of Ethiopia. Comparing domestic slavery in Ethiopia with the brutality of slavery in some of the European colonies and in the United States, European travellers generally described it as relatively moderate. By the 1930s, many remaining slaves in Ethiopia were well fed and cared for, many were treated as members of the extended family, and some even received education.[29]

Nonetheless, the Italians broadcast the misleading notion that slavery in the American sense of the word was endemic in Ethiopia, misrepresenting the situation to the extent that the eradication of the trade in Ethiopia was even presented to Italians by the Catholic clergy as one of the purported reasons for the invasion.

Finally, as already mentioned, in another attempt to legitimise an aggressive war against another sovereign state, Mussolini also claimed that the invasion was 'colonialism'. The massive war machine, the hundreds of military aeroplanes and the thousands of bombs filled with yperite, arsine or phosgene stockpiled just outside Ethiopia's northern and eastern borders for use by the Regia Aeronautica, were thus presented as a benign expeditionary force setting out into the unknown with Bibles and beads to bring the Word of God to their unfortunate heathen brethren.[30] Nonetheless, many unemployed Italians and peasant farmers of the south in desperate need of land came to believe the tale.

We have noted that, despite these attempts to pass off an attack on another nation-state as something other than aggression and territorial ambition for geopolitical purposes, few Italians initially supported the invasion. Based on a study of the reports of informants of the Organizzazione per la Vigilanza e la Repressione dell'Antifascismo (OVRA, Mussolini's secret police in charge of the repression of anti-Fascists), private diaries and published research, Alberto Sbacchi found that many Italians were concerned about the economic strain the country would suffer in the event of war, and felt—correctly, as it turned out—that 'the war expenditure would be far greater than its returns, making Italy poorer than ever'.[31]

Nor were most Italians smouldering with hatred for Ethiopians. While many unemployed men volunteered to join the Blackshirts, the majority of the conscripts—the regulars—did not want to go to war. They were reluctant to leave their families to face an unknown future and possibly death, for they saw no worthy cause to support that would justify such sacrifice. In fact, in several incidents they demonstrated opposition to the invasion. For example, two companies of the elite Alpini refused to leave for Ethiopia. Some Alpini in Turin even lynched their officers, some garrisons mutinied, several railway stations where troops were leaving for the war were the scene of anti-war demonstrations, and there were desertions in several locations.[32] Despite all the government anti-Ethiopian propaganda, the masses in Italy were still not convinced that they had a duty to wage aggressive war against a far-away nation that posed no threat to them. The great threat to Italy as presented by the Fascists was Communism, and the Ethiopians were not Communists. The Italians were thus not taking the bait; there was no unity of purpose in the nation for the invasion of Ethiopia, until the Catholic Church came to the rescue.

The Trigger

Would Pius XI nip the crusade in the bud, or would he allow it to flourish? From the outset, despite being the primate of Italy and bishop of Rome, and despite the long-standing acceptance and engagement of Ethiopians at the heart of the papacy, he did not condemn the crusading spirit that was emerging among the Italian episcopate; he stood by in silence. Even *The Tablet*, Britain's Catholic newspaper, was surprised at the stridency of the bishops:

> The Catholic Press in Italy, with the exception of the 'Osservatore Romano', which is extra-territorial, seems strongly in favour of the conquest of Abyssinia ... The Italian bishops and clergy seem to have committed themselves wholeheartedly to the war. The attitude taken by Father Gemelli, Rector of the Catholic University of Milan, that of viewing the war as a crusade against a corrupt pseudo-Empire, seems typical ... The Church is at present extremely popular in Italy, and something like a religious revival is taking place.[33]

Apologists for the pope's failure to speak out at this point often claim that his position was necessarily one of neutrality. However, for a pontiff who normally reined in senior clergy of the national Catholic Churches when they stepped out of line, his willingness to permit Italy's archbishops and bishops to openly campaign for the invasion from their pulpits signalled that his position was actually far from neutral. On issues he felt strongly about, Pius XI would speak out courageously. But whenever the issue of the invasion of Ethiopia arose, he exhibited an uncharacteristic air of silent resignation. The most charitable explanation that might be suggested for the silence of the normally outspoken pontiff at this critical stage in the preparations for the invasion is that given the enthusiasm for the war exhibited by the senior Italian clerics, he decided that rather than risk opening a fault line within the Church (the Curia being overwhelmingly Italian), he would 'go with the flow'.

It would be misleading to suggest that during the 1930s the Holy See was a monolithic institution, for between the pope and the secretary of state, and within the Curia, there were often different opinions on key issues. But the papal silence that followed the June 1935 outburst by *L'Avvenire d'Italia* against Ethiopia's 'pagan barbarians' suggests that by then there was a growing consensus in the Holy See and in the Vatican generally of support for the forthcoming war. This would be consistent with a report by the Italian chargé d'affaires, Giuseppe Talamo Atenolfi, who, having received a confidential assurance that the Holy See 'would not treat with schismatics' in the event that the Ethiopians sought its intervention, reported that the *Avvenire* article did, in fact, reflect the attitude of the Holy See towards the Ethiopian situation.[34] And he would go on to send reports to that effect to the Italian foreign and propaganda ministries throughout July.[35]

Who in the Vatican told Atenolfi that the Holy See regarded Orthodox Christians as schismatics? Could such a belligerent term have been uttered by the peace-loving pope? The statement suggested that the ideas that drove the crusades might still be alive and well in the Holy See. Nonetheless, Rome had never launched crusades against Orthodox Christians; the Fourth Crusade of 1204, which sacked Byzantium, had been diverted from its intended course. In fact, as noted earlier, in the 16th century Catholic crusaders had

HOLY WAR

actually come to the rescue of Ethiopian Christendom, which had fallen victim to an Ottoman-backed Muslim *jihad*. Furthermore, Leo XIII had been only too pleased to mediate between the Ethiopian and Italian governments on the return of the Italian prisoners of war after Adwa.

So what was going on? Why was Pius XI taking an equivocal position? There is no doubt that at least part of the reason for the papal silence was the alliance between the Holy See and the Italian state sealed by the Lateran Treaty regarding the Vatican City. Far from being neutral, Pius XI, unlike Leo XIII who had placed Italy's earlier attempted land grab in Ethiopia on a par with its seizure of the Papal States, was hand in glove with Mussolini. Yet he felt obliged to assume a posture of neutrality. The upshot was that Pius XI adopted what can best be described as a policy of vacillation towards the invasion. Committed to his alliance with Mussolini and Fascism, yet at the same time trying to reassure the international Catholic community (which was overwhelmingly opposed to the war), and perhaps trying to appease his own conscience, he increasingly made conflicting statements and took conflicting positions. On some occasions, as we shall see, he even made speeches that propagated both causes at the same time, for and against the invasion, resulting in convoluted, 'one-size-fits-all' declarations. The result was that the Italian cardinals, archbishops and bishops carried on, unchecked.

One of the pope's notable acts that seemingly demonstrated support for Italian nationalism, the Fascist government and the invasion was reported on 13 July 1935 in the Paris newspaper *Le National*. Readers were informed that the Palatine Guards of the Vatican, for whom the Concordat provided exemption from joining the Italian military, had been included in military conscription following Pius XI's order 'that the Palatine Guards must fulfill, at the present moment, all their military obligations'. The next day *Le Temps* confirmed this report, adding, 'The Pope is pleased with the Italian action in Africa, for the success of the Italian army would assure to the Catholic Missions in Ethiopia supremacy over the Coptic [*sic*] Clergy.'[36]

It was looking as though the Holy See had decided to join hands with the Fascists over the Ethiopian war, when the pontiff

AN UNHOLY ALLIANCE

himself strengthened that impression by adding a new dimension to the emerging narrative. On 28 July, not long after the *Avvenire* denunciation of Ethiopians as pagans, he announced the forthcoming beatification of Giustino de Jacobis, a pious Catholic bishop who had served in Ethiopia in the mid-19th century. In doing so, Pius XI appeared to view the forthcoming war as an instrument for the expansion of the Catholic Church in Ethiopia.[37] Then, in a statement that was clearly not designed to foster the eternal peace about which he so frequently spoke, he referred to Ethiopians at the time of de Jacobis as 'recently converted Catholics, heretics, Muslims and pagans'.[38]

It was one thing for a 20th-century Italian pope to refer to Orthodox Christians as schismatics in a private conversation with an Italian diplomat, but to publicly designate them as heretics was something else. Heretics were regarded by the Holy See as the most dangerous enemies of the Catholic Church, and thus had been traditionally dealt with by the Supreme Sacred Congregation of the Roman and Universal Inquisition, which in 1908 had been renamed the Supreme Sacred Congregation of the Holy Office. In the 16th century, when the Inquisition was burning heretics at the stake, a Catholic army had been dispatched from Europe to rescue Ethiopian Christendom from the forces of Ahmed Grañ, many of the soldiers forfeiting their lives in the process. Yet in the 20th century, here was a supposedly enlightened pope declaring Ethiopian Christians to be heretics. Whatever the reason for his indiscreet words, the fact is that, sounding like a medieval inquisitor, Pius XI in his speech gave the green light to the Italian episcopate to step up their campaign, thereby sowing the seeds of what would soon be proclaimed a holy war.

The pope had spoken, and now, at last, the rank and file of Italy's military had a clear cause for which to go to war: the bringing of 'true Christianity' to heretics. Thus as Alberto Sbacchi noted, the Italians' state of anxiety and opposition to the invasion now began to give way to spontaneous acts of patriotic support.[39] The placing of a sacred mantle by the Italian Catholic Church over Mussolini's aspirations for conquest and expansion proved to be a masterstroke, for the joint clerico-Fascist propaganda resulted in a powerful amalgam of nationalist, spiritual and political dogma that almost overnight would transform the majority of the hesitating population of Italy into holy warriors.

A Crisis of Conscience?

Having declared Ethiopian Christians heretics, Pius XI gave the impression that he was suffering a crisis of conscience, or was at least having doubts about the wisdom of issuing that statement, for once again he was wavering. On 27 August, after addressing an audience of French nurses for over an hour, he offered his concluding benediction but then, instead of leaving, on an apparent impulse he started talking about the forthcoming invasion. In a rather muddled speech he said that if it were to be a war of conquest rather than a war of defence, it would be an unjust war—'monstrously sad and horrible'. Knowing very well that the *Duce* was planning just such a war of conquest, the pontiff seemed to be wanting to register his personal disapproval of the invasion while, confusingly, leaving Mussolini room to go ahead with it by suggesting that it might be justified as a war of defence—although it clearly wasn't.

In the event, the indications were that, despite the obvious ambiguity of the message, Mussolini would be annoyed, for shortly afterwards Pius, presumably not wanting to put his alliance with the *Duce* at risk, approved for publication a much watered-down version that had been prepared by the office of his secretary of state. The resultant text as published was even more ambiguous and confusing than the one he had delivered, being open to interpretation as a strong statement of support for the invasion just as much as a denunciation.[40]

It might be said that Pius XI was walking a tightrope, but if he was, it must also be said that he kept falling off onto one side or the other, before scrambling back on again to his self-proclaimed but unconvincing position of 'neutrality'. After the confusion of July–August, apparently torn between his conscience and the need, as he saw it, to preserve the Holy See's good relationship with Mussolini and the Fascists (probably reinforced by his own nationality as an Italian citizen), the pontiff more or less dropped the subject of the forthcoming invasion. But his silence thereafter seems to have satisfied Mussolini; as Nicolas Virtue writes, 'From the Italian perspective, silence from the Holy See was as good as support.'[41] The damage had been done; the die was cast.

The Crusade Gathers Momentum

On 5 September 1935, while the League of Nations in Geneva was discussing the forthcoming invasion, Pius XI was still vacillating. But in Italy, the train, so to speak, had left the station; the crusading spirit was now almost universal. In the city of Teramo in central Italy, not far from the Adriatic coast, a papal legate, nineteen archbishops and fifty-seven bishops were attending a national Eucharistic congress. The bishop of Teramo had already made declarations of support for the war, and at the congress the clerics prepared an encouraging message for Mussolini, assuring him that 'Catholic Italy' prayed for 'the ever-increasing greatness of the beloved mother-country, rendered more compact and stronger by your government'.[42]

It was at such meetings that the Italian clergy continued to promulgate, and strengthened, their narrative of a crusade. A week later, on 13 September, Pacelli informed the *Duce* in writing that the pope would not stand in the way of the invasion.[43]

As the Italian episcopate conveyed to the general population the message that the invasion was a crusade, that is what it became, for it had all the ingredients of a medieval crusade: a heady mixture of idealism, arrogance, courage, cruelty and greed.

And to reinforce the message that the soldiers were doing God's work, yet another media campaign was launched, in which picture postcards were produced in their thousands, showing Christ or the Virgin Mary hovering over the troops to guide them into Ethiopia, which was now being projected as some sort of Promised Land.

There had been mixed messages coming from the clerico-Fascist alliance, for while the clerics claimed that Ethiopia was full of heretics, pagans and Muslims, the government was also selling the invasion as colonialism, an undertaking that would provide vast expanses of hitherto uncultivated land for Italian peasant families, thus (as we have seen) giving the erroneous impression that Ethiopia was an empty wilderness without a polity. But the 'Promised Land' scenario was a clever combination of both projections, evoking, ironically, the iconic exodus of the Jews—traditional enemies of the Catholics—from Egypt to the Promised Land of Canaan.

As in the case of the Israelites, the Catholics would find that their Promised Land was already populated; and so, as in the crusades of old, the Catholics would replace the love of Christianity with a war of annihilation, for the Ethiopians were clearly obstructing a divine plan, and thus must be enemies of God.

Not only were the Catholics following in the footsteps of the Jews; in another irony, they were also emulating their other traditional enemy, the Protestants. The invasion of Ethiopia paralleled yet another 'Promised Land' scenario: the arrival on the coast of the New World by the Pilgrim Fathers in the *Mayflower*. Calling their Promised Land the 'English Canaan', the 17th-century Puritans, so called because of their concern for moral and religious purity, soon found that they had to grapple with the problem of the local inhabitants. Clearly these incumbents were standing in the way of the divine plan, so the invasion of the New World became a holy war, in which the inhabitants were massacred wholesale.[44]

The only essential difference between these two earlier situations and the Italian invasion of Ethiopia was the weaponry. Instead of lances and bows and arrows to decimate their victims, the invaders now had tanks, machine guns, flame-throwers and, in case the Ethiopians should continue to resist, one of Europe's largest air forces loaded with toxic gases.

The Madonna of the Manganello

In parallel with the campaign by the obliging senior clergy, the Fascists were appropriating much of the Catholic Church's iconography and even its prayers. Included in the paraphernalia were picture postcards with images remarkably similar to those depicting Christ and the Holy Virgin. The images showed the party's militia being guided into Ethiopia by iconic figures such as Mother Italy, portrayed as Magna Mater, a pagan deity believed to protect cities, wearing a turreted crown symbolising Rome. Borne aloft above the advancing Blackshirts, these deities guided them to their providential destiny. Other images showed escorting figures such as Minerva, the ancient Roman goddess of war, who was exalted in Italian Fascism.

Describing how the Fascist Party 'shamelessly plagiarised the whole repertoire of Catholic rituals and language', John Pollard may well be correct when he argues that Mussolini's attempts to sacralise the party's dogma was actually a sign of weakness.[45] But the fusion of Catholicism and Fascism was nonetheless very effective; the people of Italy soon became more united over the invasion of Ethiopia than they had been on any other issue for a long time.

Of all the images and iconographic formulae developed to win support for the crusade against Ethiopia, it would be difficult to find a more powerful portrayal of the unholy alliance between Catholicism and Fascism than that of La Madonna del Manganello (the Madonna of the Fascist Club). The *manganello* was a heavy wooden bludgeon commonly carried by the Blackshirts—the *squadristi*—during the rise to power of Mussolini's party. It was used for cracking the skulls of socialists and other anti-Fascists on the streets and in meeting halls. A prayer written at the time, to be attached to the image, ended with the words 'Manganello, Manganello, which lights up every brain, You will always be the only one the Fascists will adore'.

The statue of the Mother of Christ wielding a Fascist club in her right hand was originally created by the sculptor Giuseppe Malecore for a church at Monteleone (now Vibo Valentia), in Calabria, near Italy's southern tip. Another one was also installed in a church at nearby Nicastro, in the Sanctuary of the Madonna del Soccorso. The ultimate embodiment of the fusion of Christianity and Fascism as conceived in the minds of the philo-Fascist clergy, the image of the Madonna of the Manganello was reproduced in photographs and postcards, and by the time the invasion of Ethiopia was being launched, the cult was well established. Furthermore, statues of the Madonna of the Manganello also appeared in other Italian churches. The Mother of Christ was now clearly in the service of Fascism.[46]

A Living Icon

It was one thing for the clergy to exhort the troops to become crusading zealots; it was another to ensure that they performed as required, particularly since the commanders in the field would normally be driven principally by military strategies and tactics, and none of the cheerleading cardinals and archbishops would be on the ground in Ethiopia. Furthermore, most of the European Catholics already in Ethiopia were missionaries or teachers, and many of them were there for altruistic reasons. They had frequently developed good working relationships with the Ethiopians, and did not necessarily support the invasion. Moreover, the non-Italian Catholics were typically opposed to it. So how could the desired fusion between Fascism and Catholicism be inculcated and maintained in Ethiopia at the level of the individual Italian soldier?

Controlling and inspiring crusaders at a distance had always been a thorny problem for the Catholic Church. Traditionally the popes would appoint priestly legates and sub-legates for the task, but priests were forbidden by canon law to fight.[47] In the case of the forthcoming war, at least part of the answer was provided by the example of one man—an extraordinary and iconic figure personifying the seamless alliance between Fascism and the Catholic faith. He probably personified the theme of the Madonna of the Manganello—Catholicism in the service of Fascism—more than any other single individual on the battlefield, taking the alliance beyond declarations and imagery to action, and thereby becoming a role model for a generation of young Italians.

Father Reginaldo Giuliani was an ultra-nationalist Dominican friar who had served as a military chaplain during the First World War, in which he was a member of the Arditi, on which the German stormtroopers were modelled. He earned medals for bravery and military valour, and after the war was one of the many ex-servicemen who felt cheated by the Treaty of Versailles, which awarded Italy less than she expected for her military efforts as one of Britain's allies—a disgruntled group that included Mussolini himself.

The young Adolf Hitler—a great admirer of the *Duce*—was also driven by the legacy of Versailles, whose imposition had virtually bankrupted Germany.

Father Giuliani was an inspiring national figure who embodied the ideology, bravery, single-mindedness, arrogance and contempt for death that characterised the most battle-hardened medieval crusaders. He took part in the notorious seizure of Fiume that helped launch Fascism, and participated in the much-vaunted March on Rome in 1922, which catapulted Mussolini to power.

Giuliani was also a brilliant orator, albeit very high-flown and verbose. During the 1920s and early 1930s he travelled widely as a theology teacher and preacher, his sermons and pronouncements often speaking dramatically of the primacy of Italian civilisation and mission, self-sacrifice, and martyrdom. As the invasion of Ethiopia approached, he also became known for his contempt for Ethiopian Christians, referring to them as heretics. He was publicly vociferous in his support of the invasion, for which the Italians were making intensive preparations in Eritrea.[48]

One of the first notable Catholic clergymen to preach the crusade of 1935, and seeing what he called a 'mystic alliance' between the Catholic Church and the Fascist war machine, Father Giuliani made it clear in his personal diary that he intended to participate personally in military attacks on the Ethiopian Church.[49]

In April, at the age of 48, convinced that dying in the war would bring about his salvation, and expressing a wish 'to die with my Blackshirts',[50] Giuliani rejoined the military, choosing to serve in Eritrea as a centurion-chaplain of the '28th October' 2nd Blackshirt Division, named in commemoration of the March on Rome. Garrisoned at the small Eritrean settlement of Adi Keyih about a hundred kilometres south of Asmara, he would remain there until his unit was ordered across the Ethiopian border at the beginning of October.[51]

Lighting the Flames

Well aware of the relatively favourable situation for the Catholic Church in Ethiopia, and realising that the invasion would imperil the ongoing work of the Catholic clergy there, the pope made a belated attempt to dissuade Mussolini, pointing out that the invasion might go badly for him and for Italy. However, the message was somewhat half-hearted and only verbal, and had no noticeable impact on the *Duce*. Having already declared that the Fascist state 'in its ideas, doctrine and actions does not allow anything that is not in accordance with Catholic practice and doctrine', the pontiff had in any case left himself no room to manoeuvre, and was clearly most unlikely to withdraw those unfortunate words. It would be a few more years before he would come around to expressing regret for some of the decisions and statements he made during the early and mid-1930s, but by then it would be too late.

So it was that on 2 October 1935, with cardinals, archbishops and bishops as the cheerleaders, supported by a wealth of government and Italian Catholic propaganda, and to the clanging of church bells across the nation, the Italians announced their invasion of Ethiopia.

While the Italians were working themselves up into a frenzy of belligerence, the citizens of Ethiopia were praying for peace. Devout in his religious observances, Emperor Haile Selassie was attending prayers at the cathedral of St George in Addis Ababa.

There was widespread sympathy for the Ethiopians internationally, including among Catholics, who were astounded at the silence of the pope; Irish Catholic author Sir William Teeling wrote that 'practically without exception the whole world condemned Mussolini, all except the Pope',[52] and newspapers in Catholic France and Spain asked if Pontius Pilate was now reigning in the Vatican.[53]

Ethiopia would be the first nation-state to fall victim to Fascist invasion, but it would not be the last. The partners of the unholy alliance had lit the flames that would eventually engulf Europe.

PART TWO

A HOLY WAR

4

MISSIONARIES OF THE CROSS

> *'The soldier has got religion; I am not sure that he has got Christianity.'*
> The Reverend Neville Talbot (1879–1943)

Despite the pious speeches delivered at the League of Nations by countries such as Britain, when the hour struck, Ethiopia stood alone. Sanctions were imposed on both Italy and Ethiopia, but in restricting the importation of weapons they hurt only Ethiopia, since Italy was already heavily armed. No sanctions were placed to restrict Italian oil imports, and Britain left the Suez Canal open, so Italy was free to go ahead with the invasion.

With an army consisting initially of some two hundred thousand well-armed soldiers equipped with tanks and flame-throwers, and with the support of hundreds of aircraft equipped with machine guns and loaded with bombs and chemical weapons, the Italians launched an offensive against the Ethiopians, who despite Haile Selassie's recent attempts at modernisation were still relatively poorly armed.[1]

Under the command of the ageing Emilio De Bono, the army crossed the border from Eritrea into Ethiopia on 3 October 1935. They also penetrated from the Ogaden in the south-east, where the Italians had already established military bases resourced from Italian Somaliland, thus creating northern and southern war fronts.[2] *Li'ul-*

Ras Kassa Haylu, a highly respected dignitary of the imperial court who was a devout Christian and *gebez* (sacristan) of the monastery of Debre Libanos, took charge of Ethiopia's northern defence forces.

A word must be said here about the Italian army, which did not consist only of Italian nationals. Many of its soldiers were *askaris* from the Italian colonies of Eritrea, Italian Somaliland and Libya. Of these, the most effective were generally considered to be the Eritreans, who were relatively well trained and armed, and believed to be utterly loyal. However, the majority were members of the same Orthodox faith as their Ethiopian cousins, and thus could hardly be expected to engage in a Catholic crusade against their co-religionists. Neither, as we shall see, could they be relied upon to join in pogroms against Ethiopian Christian civilians, and indeed some of the units would in due course mutiny. These issues would lead the Italians to increasingly deploy Muslim brigades for their campaigns against the Ethiopian Church.

Penetrating from Eritrea, De Bono was a cautious commander. Worried about overstretched supply lines, he proceeded with such caution that by mid-November Mussolini had replaced him with Pietro Badoglio. De Bono, who had not penetrated beyond Tigray, did, however, attempt to address the slavery issue, announcing that any slaves in Tigray were now free. Nonetheless, De Bono soon discovered the realities with which Haile Selassie had been contending, writing in his memoir that his proclamation 'did not have much effect on the owners of the slaves and perhaps even less on the liberated slaves themselves ... Many of the latter, the moment they were set free, presented themselves to the Italian authorities, asking, "And now who gives me food?"' Most of the liberated slaves sought—and obtained—long-term employment with their former masters.[3]

Despite their grossly inferior weapons, the Ethiopians put up an extraordinary level of resistance and displayed considerable resilience, often making significant headway when fighting the Italian infantry on an equal playing field. However, in such cases the battle was usually settled by the intervention at the critical moment of the Italian Air Force, discharging poison gas onto the Ethiopians.[4] It was a war of annihilation; the Italian episcopate

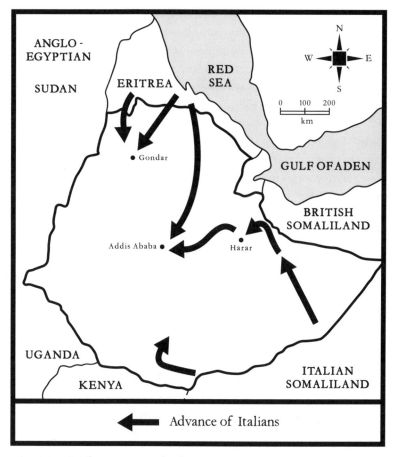

Map 2: The invasion of Ethiopia: principal invasion routes
(© Ian Campbell)

had, knowingly or unknowingly, incited the invaders to acts of terrible carnage.

Although the Italians took a few prisoners in the first few weeks of the war, the Ethiopians were faced thereafter with a ruthless 'take no prisoners' policy. Mussolini's military directive had specified not just the conquest of Ethiopia, but 'nothing less than the *complete destruction* of the Abyssinian army' (emphasis added), so that was the objective of the Italian commanders. This meant paying no heed to the Geneva Conventions—not only in the killing of prisoners and the liberal use of internationally banned weapons, but also in the adoption of inhumane methods of killing, including torturing prisoners to death and beheading. A prime example was set by none other than Achille Starace, a leading architect of Fascism, who, according to Mussolini's son-in-law Count Ciano, demonstrated to his troops how to shoot Ethiopian prisoners in the testicles first to increase their suffering before execution, which involved using them as target practice.[5]

In due course, in their implementation of Mussolini's new concept of 'total war', the Italians also tested techniques of counter-insurgency which, together with the Nazis, they would employ in Europe and the Balkans in the years to come. These techniques, designed to terrorise the civilian population into submission, and today known as 'exemplary repression', included the rounding up and killing of civilians, deportation to concentration camps, and the burning of families alive inside their houses.

Divine Backing

The barbarity of the invading forces shocked the Ethiopians, particularly those who were aware that Italy claimed to be a Christian country. However, Italian consciences were clear, for just as the weeks preceding the invasion had witnessed the propaganda campaign of religious and quasi-religious imagery backed by speeches by clerico-Fascist orators such as Father Giuliani, so October saw an extraordinary upsurge of crusading zeal on the part of the senior Italian clergy. The recruitment campaign, which might have been expected to end when the invasion was launched, instead gathered strength. There was what can only be described as a hysterical outpouring from many of the country's most distinguished and influential cardinals, archbishops and bishops—few, if any, of them ever having even met an Ethiopian—as they used their cathedrals and public forums to denigrate Ethiopians and the Ethiopian Church with almost inexplicable venom, and to convince the Italian public that the military onslaught was the will of God.

Although Mussolini had originally denied that Italy had any interest in Ethiopia apart from the security of the borders of its colony of Eritrea and protectorate of Italian Somaliland, he increasingly encouraged the Church to claim a 'civilising mission'. Thus Giovanni Cazzani, the bishop of Cremona, was moved to proclaim, 'The blessing of God be upon these soldiers who, on African soil, will conquer new and fertile lands for the Italian genius, thereby bringing to them Roman and Christian culture!'[6] And to reinforce the spoken word, each soldier en route to Ethiopia was provided with a prayer book produced especially for the occasion, with an introduction by Monsignor Agostino Gemelli, a strongly pro-Fascist prelate who was close to Pius XI and was rector of the Catholic University of Milan. Gemelli's text assured the troops that the invasion was endorsed by the Catholic Church and indeed had divine backing: 'Soldier of Italy, your sacrifice, united with the sacrifice of Our Lord Jesus Christ, God among men, will achieve the salvation and greatness of the Fatherland.'[7]

In several cases senior clerics went beyond verbal support to donate money collected from their congregations as well as gold artefacts from their churches specifically to help finance the invasion. They sent the soldiers on their way to Ethiopia with Godspeed, and blessed the machine guns and aircraft to be used to shoot down, bomb and gas the Ethiopians. 'Santa, Santa, Santa' ('Holy, Holy, Holy'), a Catholic priest intoned, captured by a Film Luce cameraman as he blessed the bombs being loaded onto a Caproni bomber of the Regia Aeronautica.

It is, of course, necessary to distinguish between the task of military chaplains ministering to soldiers embarking on dangerous missions, on the one hand, and senior clergy promoting an illegal war of conquest against another nation-state, on the other. The Italian bishops, as Gaetano Salvemini pointed out at the time, 'did not confine themselves to imparting blessings'. They delivered public addresses and circulated letters campaigning for, and directly supporting, a war of conquest which none other than the Holy Father himself had at one point denounced as 'truly an unjust war ... something beyond imagination ... something monstrously sad and horrible'.[8] And as the days of the invasion turned into weeks, the campaigning and the rhetoric intensified.

Would the Italian bishops have opposed with such impunity the policy of their own primate? As the pope had publicly denigrated

Ethiopian Christians as heretics and schismatics, and had never reprimanded the war-mongering of his episcopate, his silence since the invasion began was widely interpreted according to the principle *Qui tacet consentit* ('He who is silent consents').

Whenever energetic and spirited resistance managed to force the invading armies to a standstill, the Italians discharged air-borne poisonous gases onto the Ethiopians, who referred to them as a rain of death. Details of the resultant carnage were broadcast by the world's newspapers, and so the senior Italian clergy in Rome were certainly aware of the illegal methods that the invading forces adopted. Indeed, on 18 October a group of French Catholic intellectuals signed a manifesto solemnly protesting against the unprovoked aggression, and denouncing the Fascist argument of the 'natural inequality of races' as a repudiation of Christian teaching.[9]

A Heretical Church

Despite international protests, the Italian clergy did not regret their stance; on the contrary, several high-ranking prelates actually reiterated and even reinforced their position following revelation of the atrocities, reassuring the Italian public that the invasion was a Catholic crusade. On 19 October, the day after the French expressed their horror at the brutality of the invasion, *La Civiltà Cattolica* hit back at the critics. This was the Jesuit journal whose contents were approved by the Vatican secretary of state, and which was read by Catholics as the expression of the pope's views on the issues of the day.[10] In a remarkable article that introduced new vocabulary labelling Ethiopian clergy 'ignorant and corrupt', the message was merciless, justifying the carnage on the grounds that Ethiopia constituted a typical example of the moral and intellectual decay of a people 'detached from Rome through schism and heresy'.[11]

In labelling the Ethiopian Church heretical, *La Civiltà Cattolica* was echoing the pope's statement of July. Ethiopian Christians were now designated enemies of the faith, indicating that what had begun as a crusade had now become a holy war. In medieval Catholicism, pagans were deemed ignorant and in need of pity and conversion. However, heretics were people who professed Christianity but deviated from the doctrines of the Catholic Church, and were therefore dangerous enemies who, if they persisted in their heresies, should be dealt with decisively, which ultimately meant being burned alive.

The term 'schismatics' was an allusion to the Council of Chalcedon of the year 451, which had been divided over the definition of the nature of Christ. That Council assigned equal importance to the Church of Constantinople and the Church of Rome, a position rejected by the pope, and the disagreement eventually led to the Great Schism between the Eastern (Orthodox) and Western (Catholic) Churches in the year 1054. The Jesuits clearly had long memories, and doubtless they had also not forgotten their ignominious departure from Ethiopia in the 17th century when their mission was expelled by the Ethiopian government as a national security risk, following the civil war in which they had embroiled the country.

Since the world's first countries to declare Christianity as the state religion (Armenia and Ethiopia) were both Orthodox, it might be thought more logical to label the Catholics as the breakaway or 'schismatic' faction. However, this denigrating vocabulary had become part of Catholic tradition, and so as far as the Catholic Church was concerned, Ethiopian Christians were schismatics.

Normally, as already noted, heretics were dealt with by the Inquisition, but in the past the popes had occasionally acted against entire Christian communities regarded as heretical. The best-known case was what came to be known as the Albigensian Crusade, which was waged against the Cathars during a period of twenty years in the early 13th century. Another was waged against the Hussites in Bohemia in the 15th century. But these were instances in which the pope, as a powerful European monarch, or his allies felt threatened by the heretical communities.

What, then, was the need for a crusade against the Ethiopian Church? Although the Ethiopians had not developed the same dogma or liturgical expressions as the Roman clergy, they posed no threat to Rome. Ethiopia had not declared a holy war on Catholicism; on the contrary, by the 20th century, the Ethiopians, who could themselves have denounced the Roman Church as heretical, instead accommodated thousands of Catholics, and their government had encouraged and facilitated the building of a new Catholic cathedral on a prime site in Ethiopia's capital city.

Clearly the Ethiopians were no danger to the Catholic Church; the Italian clergy had stepped out of line on a serious religious matter, which according to the Catholic Code of Canon Law meant that they should have been reined in by Pius XI. As bishop of Rome and primate of Italy, the pontiff should also have brought into line the Jesuits, whose public declarations of heresy usurped the authority of the Holy See. Yet he maintained a stony silence.

So did papal silence mean that the Holy See approved of the October article in *La Civiltà Cattolica*? Was Pius XI, knowing very well that the Italian episcopate was likely to follow the principle of *Qui tacet consentit*, actually in favour of what had been written? The matter inevitably casts a spotlight on the Jesuits, who had considerable influence on Pius XI, and who were led by Superior General Włodzimierz Ledóchowski, a Polish aristocrat who was a hawkish supporter of the Fascist regime and strongly anti-Semitic, even by the standards of the 1930s. Ledóchowski certainly backed the invasion of Ethiopia, telling the Italian ambassador to the Holy See, Count Bonifacio Pignatti, that criticisms of the war were simply 'a pretext from which international Judaism is profiting in order to advance its attack on western civilization'.[12]

Given Ledóchowski's well-known prejudices, it was to be expected that he would see a Jewish conspiracy behind every action to which he was opposed. But why was he so strongly in favour of the invasion? Was he getting revenge for the expulsion of the Jesuits by the Ethiopian government in 1633? Or was there more to it than historical resentment? Being very ancient, and having undergone little change since the time of the early Christians, the Ethiopian Church still contained Judaic elements reflecting Ethiopia's Old Testament religious traditions. These included, and still include, for example, the presumed presence of the Ark of the Covenant in Ethiopia and its representation in every church in the form of a *tabot*; the order of the *debtera*, which has been compared to the position of the Levites in the Temple; the division of animals into clean and unclean, as in the law of the Old Testament; and the keeping of the Sabbath.[13]

Retaining these Judaic elements, and incorporating none of the changes in the liturgy introduced over the years by the Catholic Church in what Orthodox theologians regarded as 'Romish errors', the Ethiopian Church could have been a particular target for anti-Semites such as Ledóchowski, who through the pages of *La Civiltà Cattolica* continued to be one of Italy's most influential proponents of the invasion.

Semi-feral People

A few days later, doubtless inspired and emboldened by the impunity of *La Civiltà Cattolica* and the papal silence that followed, 67-year-old Bishop Nicola Cola of the diocese of Nocera Umbra–Gualdo Tadino, wrote an extraordinary pastoral letter that would have done justice to the most dedicated medieval inquisitor. Praising the carnage in Ethiopia as 'a just and holy matter', he stated that Italy had 'a great civilising mission to fulfil for the semi-feral and mentally and religiously backward people'.[14] He wrote:

> The Ethiopian war is just and holy, and it is necessary for the defence of as vital a part of the Fatherland as the colonies; for the pressing expansion of our enemies; [and] for the assertion of our right as a civilising nation. Ethiopia is but a mixture of uncivilised tribes. Its people have no true notion of the duties of man, of his rights, of its freedom.
>
> It is a people which, having become detached from Rome, cannot get the full benefit of the Christian ideas; which has not been able, therefore, to produce those beneficial conditions to which the West of Europe owes its greatness. Roman Catholic Italy has the duty of bringing to populations deprived of them, its principles of equity, charity and fraternity.[15]

Given that Ethiopia's proclamation of Christianity as the state religion predated that of the Roman Empire, the claim that the Ethiopian Church had 'become detached from Rome' was open to debate. What was certain, however, was that the Ethiopians had already discovered that whatever the invaders were bringing to Ethiopia, it did not include equity, charity or fraternity.

Moreover, Bishop Cola's vocabulary introduced a new, racial epithet in the vilification of the Ethiopians. Arousing no objections from the pope who apparently had such a high regard for Ethiopian Christianity and who hosted in the Vatican the largest Ethiopian community in Europe, these defamations were echoed by one high-ranking prelate after another. The Italian episcopate was clearly deliberately developing a narrative to convince the general Italian public that Ethiopians were subhuman, thereby promoting ultra-nationalism and strengthening support for hard-line Fascist policies and the increasingly vigorous prosecution of the war in Ethiopia.

It is remarkable how rapidly the senior clerics joined the chorus against the Ethiopians, making support of the invasion a Catholic obligation. Even Mussolini was surprised, and apparently quite amused, at how easy it was proving to get them to raise their voices. Speaking later to the German foreign minister, the *Duce*'s explanation was that by granting the clerics small favours such as railway tickets and tax concessions, he had won them over, 'so that they even declared the war in Abyssinia [Ethiopia] a Holy War'.[16] Perhaps Mussolini was recalling Hitler's remark when the two dictators had met in Venice the previous year: 'Thank goodness that you succeeded injecting more than a little paganism [into the Catholic Church], making its centre in Rome and using it for your own ends.'[17]

Hitler was not far off the mark, for Fascism using the Catholic Church for its own ends and, in turn, the Church using Fascism for its own ends had increasingly characterised the relationship welded in 1929, and the invasion of Ethiopia was demonstrating just how poisonous the product of that relationship could be. Now Fascism's most important festival—the one commemorating the March on Rome which brought the *Duce* to power—was approaching, and that would be the opportunity for the clerico-Fascist chorus to reach a climax.

An Assignment from God

During the First World War, Pius XI's predecessor, Benedict XV (r. 1914–22), had repeatedly sought peace and denounced militarism and war-mongering. Yet now, senior Catholic clerics—both young and old—were confidently using their pulpits to make the most bellicose speeches, and all with remarkably similar vocabulary. But none had quite the gravitas and power of Ildefonso Cardinal Schuster, the highly influential archbishop of Milan, who preached the crusade at High Mass in Milan cathedral on 28 October, celebrating the thirteenth anniversary of the Fascist March on Rome. On that occasion, in a carefully prepared speech, His Eminence, archbishop of Italy's largest and wealthiest archdiocese, and a powerful supporter of Fascism, went one step further than his clerical colleagues. In a homily entitled *Dei sumus adiutores* ('We are God's helpers') he announced that the invasion of Ethiopia was a task to which the Italian nation had been assigned by God.[18]

From that moment on there were no lingering doubts. As far as most Italians were concerned, the Catholic Church had spoken; the sanctification of Fascist expansionism was now complete. The 'crusade' was not a metaphor; the invasion was now officially a holy war. Until then there had been talk by the clergy of a 'just war', a concept that had been introduced into Catholic thinking centuries after the medieval notion of a holy war had run its course. In his August speech Pius XI had himself toyed with the possibility of a just war against Ethiopia, but then he had appeared to reject it, on the grounds that an armed invasion was not a war of defence, and thus could not be a just war. During the course of 1935 there had been calls for a holy war by several of the clergy, including Father Reginaldo Giuliani, but none of the highest-ranking prelates had gone that far.

Moreover, instead of moderating or qualifying his announcement, Schuster went on to reinforce his message by stating that the roads being built in Ethiopia by the Italians to transport the military were carrying 'missionaries of the Gospel', bearing 'the cross of Christ', and he prayed for the 'protection of the gallant army that, in fearless obedience to the commanders of the fatherland, is opening the gates of Ethiopia to the Catholic faith and Roman civilization'.[19]

In the absence of any objection from the Vatican, Schuster's declaration unquestionably put a divine seal of approval on the war. From 28 October 1935, the invasion of Ethiopia was a holy war.

The Great Mobilisation

For the Italians, supporting the invasion was one thing; volunteering for a military adventure from which they might never come back was quite another. So who would inspire and convince them to volunteer? This task was traditionally accomplished by what was known as 'preaching the Cross', which was usually carried out by the bishops. The crusade against the 'heretics and schismatics' of Ethiopia was no different. There were many messages to be put across, but the critical one was that a holy war meant that any of God's warriors who fell in battle would be guaranteed a place in heaven. Thus, not surprisingly, the clamour of clerical support following Cardinal Schuster's declaration was countrywide. From north to south, from east to west, the Italian clergy rallied the faithful to back the holy war, in a campaign that Mimmo Franzinelli calls the Great Mobilisation.[20] Cardinal Schuster proved to be the best recruiting officer that the Fascist military could have had, for the ports of Genoa and Naples were soon flooded with volunteers eager to join the Blackshirts in the ongoing onslaught against the heretics. Their participation being declared by Cardinal Gemelli a sacrifice to God, thousands of the militia were consecrated by the clerics to the Sacred Heart of Jesus and the Madonna of Divine Love—powerful forms of religious devotion invoking images of sacrifice and martyrdom.[21]

Within a few days of Cardinal Schuster's announcement, Archbishop Mario Taccabelli of Siena, on Italy's west coast north of Rome, who was an enthusiastic supporter of the war, endorsed the invasion both in the local Catholic paper and in Siena cathedral.[22] In fact, based on a perusal of only two or three Italian daily newspapers at the time, Gaetano Salvemini identified no less than 103 senior Italian Catholic clerics, consisting of 7 cardinal archbishops, 28 archbishops and 68 bishops, making public proclamations supporting the war—a list which, he commented, was 'doubtless far from complete'.[23] Given that there were only 274 dioceses in the entire country, such a large number of outspoken supporters of the invasion being identified from so few sources in such a short time, indicates significant support by the senior clergy. In fact, Italy's episcopate was not only supportive of the invasion; barring a few notable dissenting voices, the clerics were positively enthusiastic. The Fascist policy of national expansion through foreign conquest was now the will of God.

Gaetano Salvemini's sample of 35 publicly supportive archbishops accounted for approximately three-quarters of all archdioceses, and so most of Italy was represented by these prelates. Thus even this limited sample shows that the Italian episcopate was overwhelmingly influencing Italians across the nation to support the war. This was not a case of a few rogue priests speaking out of turn; it was clearly an orchestrated campaign. The pope remained silent, but it is hardly credible that such a campaign could have taken place without the support of the bishop of Rome.

Although the phenomenon of Italian clergy falling in line with Fascist Party policies was not new, the speed with which they took up Schuster's cry *ex cathedra* was astonishing, and indicates that Milan was the nerve centre of the campaign for the holy war—particularly as the three most notable clerics to deliver opening broadsides (i.e., Cazzani, Gemelli and Schuster) were all based in the province of Lombardy, whose capital was Milan, the birthplace of Fascism.

The majority of the nine bishops of the archdiocese of Lombardy had been appointed after the Concordat of 1929. These included Cardinal Schuster, who had actually been the first in the country to be appointed according to the requirements of the articles guaranteeing that no bishops would oppose government policies. However, the bishops of Lombardy went far beyond not opposing the government; they were active protagonists of the war. As the invasion was launched, Alessandro Macchi, bishop of Como in the same ecclesiastical province, announced that the invasion was a just war, and instructed his flock to assume 'a spirit of discipline, of deference and docility towards the supreme authority', 'without any debate or discussion'. Back in July, while blessing Blackshirts departing for Ethiopia, his colleague Domenico Menna, bishop of Mantua, had identified historical, political and religious reasons why the invasion was justified, adding that God would support the 'civilising work' involved. Bishop Cazzani again added his voice, exhorting the people of Italy to cooperate with and obey the king and Mussolini, and accept the sacrifice that the homeland required.[24]

Finally, one of the most influential members of the Lombardian lobby, Father Gemelli, came up with another of his radical declarations. In the magazine *Vita e Pensiero* he visited the question of the mandate of military chaplains, one of whom was Father Giuliani. Despite being well aware that they were not allowed by the Catholic Church to bear arms, Gemelli exhorted the chaplains to assume a more active role than their official mandate permitted, entrusting to them the task not just of ministering to the rank and file, but actively 'fighting the new heretics'.[25]

Both before and after the pope's August 1935 speech to the nurses, it was Cardinal Pacelli's voice that indicated Holy See sympathy, and eventually approval, for the invasion. So, did Pacelli quietly give Cardinal Schuster and his Lombardy lobby the green light to lead a nationwide call for a holy war, and launch a campaign against the Ethiopians and their Church to facilitate it? The archbishop was certainly strongly pro-Fascist; he was said to lack 'only a black shirt'.[26] Gemelli had also long been a Fascist supporter, and spoke much of the need for sacrifice by the Italian military. 'Sacrifice' in the attack on Ethiopia, he declared, again echoing the notion of a holy war, was 'an offering to God'.[27]

The Great Mobilisation was a resounding success; by 1936 the number of volunteer Blackshirts under arms had risen from 20,000 to 115,000, of which the troop carriers from Genoa and Naples had shipped 97,500, forming seven divisions, to join the regular conscripts in Ethiopia.[28]

For the Sanctity of the Cause

The invasion of Ethiopia would hold the record for the resources mobilised for a holy war. In fact, the invasion force was so massive, and the groundwork so extensive, that it almost bankrupted Italy, and severely limited the country's ability to fight the further wars that Mussolini had planned. Traditionally much of the money for crusades would come from special taxes, and that was the solution chosen by Mussolini. The time had come for the *Duce* to cash in on the religious zeal for the invasion that the bishops had generated for him among the populace. But the dictator went further than that. He was clever enough to devise an event which he called 'the Day of Faith', an ingenious scheme to help finance the slaughter in Ethiopia, while at the same time further strengthening the spiritual and psychological commitment of Italians to it. Once again, the plan required the active participation of the bishops, who obliged by urging all Italian couples to donate their gold wedding rings to the 'holy cause' on 18 December, in return for which they would receive steel rings.

The institution of marriage in Roman Catholicism being a sacrament, the support and active involvement of the clergy were critical to the success of the idea, and they did not disappoint. Postcards were published promoting the event and making it clear that the invasion had the support of Christ himself. The image depicted a heavenly Jesus hovering over two hands in blessing. One hand was removing a wedding ring from the other, while above was the caption 'For the sanctity of the cause'. As with all the paraphernalia sanctifying the invasion, there appears to be no record of the Vatican ever censuring or denouncing the manufacture and distribution of these postcards.

In September the League of Nations had warned that if Italy invaded Ethiopia, it would face economic sanctions, and in November they came into effect. Albeit not such as to reduce Italy's ability to continue the war in Ethiopia, they were seized upon enthusiastically by Mussolini's propaganda as proof of an international conspiracy and a reason to intensify the war effort. The League's sanctions were actually of considerable benefit to Mussolini in rallying Italians to his cause in the name of patriotism. The Catholic episcopate was also of great service in this respect, for, following Fascist logic, the bishops actually succeeded in representing the war of invasion to the Italian public as a struggle between good (the Italians and their righteous intentions in Ethiopia) and evil (the League of Nations and its sanctions). On other occasions the evil was the Ethiopian Church.[29]

On 23 November the archbishop of Bologna made it known that all priests of his diocese 'desirous of giving gold to the Fatherland' might send it to him, and he would 'personally present it to the Leader of Fascism in Rome'.[30] The senior clerics were in a state of near hysteria. Joining the chorus, Francesco Petronelli, bishop of

Avellino in southern Italy, confirmed that the invading troops were doing God's work, writing in his pastoral letter four days later, 'While our heroic soldiers carry the glorious flag of victorious Italy in East Africa, marked by the Cross, our gaze is turned to the sky and our hands are raised upwards. *Auxilium meum a domino* ['My help [comes] from the Lord'].'[31]

There was clearly no doubt in the minds of Pius XI's own clergy that he supported the invasion; indeed, one of their most spectacular acts involved Santina Mangaria, bishop of Civita Castellana, a diocese near Rome, who was subject directly to the pope. On 8 December, at a public function in the presence of Mussolini, the bishop spoke glowingly of the invasion of Ethiopia, thanking God for allowing him to see 'these days of epic grandeur'. Approaching the *Duce*, the bishop slipped off his gold pastoral chain and handed it to him with the Fascist salute.[32] Then the bishop of San Miniato in the province of Pisa, Tuscany, stepped forward, telling Mussolini that 'for the victory of Italy [in Ethiopia] the Italian clergy are ready to melt down the gold of the churches and the bronze of the bells'.[33]

There was no apparent end to the rhetoric; Monsignor Navarra, bishop of Terracina, near Rome, and, like Santina Mangaria, subject to the pope as bishop of Rome, was recorded in *Il Popolo d'Italia* as proclaiming, 'God bless you, O Duce! Let Him sustain you in your daily, titanic work, and ensure victory for the Italian armies.'[34] And Mario Taccabelli, archbishop of Siena, publicly donated his gold pectoral cross.[35]

Not surprisingly, most of Cardinal Schuster's bishops in Lombardy excelled themselves in their donations. Cazzani contributed several artefacts, including three pastoral rings of solid gold. Adriano Bernareggi, bishop of Bergamo, and Alessandro Macchi, Bishop of Como, were two of the many bishops who encouraged their priests to donate and to persuade the faithful to do so. And Giacinto Tredici, bishop of Brescia, reported in the *Bolletino* of his curia how enthusiastically the citizens of his diocese were making their offerings.[36]

In the same month, Ledóchowski's *La Civiltà Cattolica* came up with yet another article on Ethiopian Orthodoxy, this time branding it 'Pharisaism in all respects' and 'a monstrous mixture'.[37]

Emanating from such high-level Church authorities, the rhetoric was largely responsible for the dehumanisation of the Ethiopians in the eyes of the invading armies, thus greatly facilitating, and indeed encouraging, the behaviour that came to characterise the conduct of the Italian military and even Italian civilians during the invasion and occupation.

The Day of Faith

Not surprisingly, following so much rabble-rousing by the Italian Catholic clergy, the Day of Faith met with great success; thousands of Italians lined up to donate their wedding rings. As if possessed, the ever-zealous Cardinal Schuster blessed twenty-five thousand replacement steel rings, and one parish priest in the archdiocese of Siena requested permission from his bishop to melt down the church bells to support the war.[38]

In Rome's Piazza Venezia, forty-five thousand gold rings were donated, and the great success of the day, as Christopher Duggan observed, was due as much to the Catholic Church as the propaganda of the state.[39]

Vatican Reactions

Regarding the political antics of the Italian episcopate and even of some of his own clergy over the Day of Faith, Pius XI had little to say. He did send an emissary to ask the bishops, orally, to be 'cautious', and not to 'express judgement as to the right and justice of the Abyssinian campaign'—a half-hearted message that not surprisingly was ignored.[40] Despite being the primate of Italy, and having previously denounced what he called 'state worship' and 'exaggerated nationalism', the pope made no serious attempt to constrain his war-mongering prelates.

Just one voice from the Vatican is on record as being disturbed by the stridency of the clergy: Monsignor Domenico Tardini, a senior official in the Secretariat of State, who expressed his concern that the clergy were not encouraging restraint or reflection; they were uniformly 'shrill' or 'bellicose', the bishops being 'the most inflamed of all'.[41] However, the pope maintained his silence.

After the pope's August 1935 speech, in which he seemed to be opposed to the forthcoming invasion, Emperor Haile Selassie had written him a letter of thanks.[42] Thus, mystified by the papal silence later in the year, the sovereign requested his envoy in Paris, *Blattén Géta* Welde-Maryam Ayele, to write to Pacelli: 'It was observed that some cardinals and bishops are donating their valuables to the war effort in addition to their preaching in their respective churches that the Fascists are fighting for a good cause in Ethiopia. I am instructed by Emperor Haile Selassie to ascertain the position of the Vatican on this issue.'[43]

The secretary of state's reply attempted to distance the Holy See and the Vatican from the Italian Catholic Church, stating that 'the speeches of some cardinals and their support for the war do not represent the Vatican and its leader Pius XI', and that the actions of the clergy arose from their own individual decisions.[44] Pacelli did not, however, answer the emperor's question, which remained unaddressed: What was the pope's position? Did he disagree with what the cardinals were doing? Was he ambivalent? Was he somewhat in favour? Pacelli did not say.

Lucia Ceci attributes the pope's silence to the degree of pressure exerted on him by the Italian government. Speaking of the pontiff buckling under 'the diktat of silence on the Fascist war of conquest imposed on him by Mussolini', she points out that when he wanted to express his hopes for peace in December 1935 (two months into the war of invasion), the Italian ambassador to the Holy See told Secretary of State Pacelli that such a statement would be regarded as 'a hostile act' by the Fascist government and the country'. 'Then nothing more will be said of the matter,' replied Cardinal Pacelli.[45]

Lucia Ceci's argument could well explain why the pope would avoid a head-on confrontation with Mussolini that would have followed a complete denunciation of the invasion, but one cannot help wondering why the normally outspoken and strident representative of Christ on earth—if seriously committed to the cause of peace— would have felt the need for permission from the Italian ambassador to make such an innocuous statement as an expression of hope for peace. One can detect a certain eagerness in Cardinal Pacelli's acceptance of the ambassador's negative response, which of course would not have come as a surprise.

It must be said, however, that Pius did respond to an attempt to bring the war to an end, albeit in Italy's favour. In December there was a joint proposal by the British and French foreign ministers to partition Ethiopia, awarding part of it to Italy, together with an economic monopoly over another part. Although the proposed partition was entirely at Ethiopia's expense, and was developed without reference to the emperor, Pius XI supported the proposals, and attempted to get Mussolini to accept the terms before it was too late. In doing so, as Jacques Kornberg puts it, the pontiff 'counseled appeasement signaling to aggressors that they could proceed with impunity'.[46]

However, Mussolini prevaricated, and in any case, when the proposal went public following a leak to the media, Emperor Haile Selassie was outraged and complained bitterly to the League of Nations that instead of enforcing the position of the League, its two most powerful members had betrayed the principles of collective security on which the League was based. The storm of criticism in Britain, where popular opinion was that Ethiopia had been betrayed in favour of appeasing Mussolini, led to the resignation of the British foreign minister and the collapse of the proposals. By 18 December the scheme was a dead letter.[47]

The pope had made a serious error of judgement in backing a plan that was almost certainly doomed to failure. Once again, the impression is gained that, far from being neutral, he was viewing the situation through Italian eyes.

Churches under Attack

Traditionally Ethiopian churches were regarded as untouchable and, indeed, as places of refuge, as they had once been in Europe. Thus, early on in the war the Italian army, advancing through the northern province of Tigray, had often been met by groups of Ethiopian priests prudently greeting the alien force that had appeared in their parish, clearly hoping that confronting the invaders in a civil manner would be a better survival strategy—for both them and the Church—than taking to their heels. However, the Ethiopians, who had expected a reputedly Christian country such as Italy to respect their Christian traditions, soon learned otherwise. Realising that Ethiopian churches were the lifeblood of the communities and embodied the national spirit, the Italians, doubtless with Cardinal Schuster's words ringing in their ears, started attacking churches, and the Italian Royal Air Force was soon having a field day doing so.

In the north—first Tigray and later Begémdir—and particularly in the south-east where Graziani was advancing, churches were singled out as targets. For the pilots of the Regia Aeronautica, the distinctive and unmistakable sign of the circular rural parish church in a clearing surrounded by the dark-green foliage of ancient trees typically provided the first visible sign of human settlement. Thus, in the course of the 'softening up' flights of the Air Force ahead of the advance of ground troops during the invasion of the Christian highlands, Ethiopia's churches suffered extensively from incendiary bombs and machine-gunning. Then, during the military operations that followed the invasion, being the centres of socio-economic and cultural life, these rural churches and monasteries suffered direct attacks aimed at suppressing local support for the Ethiopian defence forces. Thirdly—and particularly in the south-east where the invaders were under the command of Rodolfo Graziani—the churches were attractive and lucrative targets for pillage during 'reprisals' by ground troops against defenceless civilians, a favourite form of exemplary repression.

In November–December 1935 fighting on the northern war front was very intense, involving the slaughter of thousands of Ethiopian defenders at virtually all battle sites. Meanwhile, the Regia Aeronautica was bombing houses and churches, including— to take but one example—the church of the Archangel Gabriel in the market town of Dabat, territory of the military commander *Dejazmach* Ayalew Birru. The Air Force bombed the area, targeting the church, at the beginning of December, as commander *Ras* Imru was approaching Dabat (Map 9) with a defence force. The church of Dabat St Gabriel, with its beautiful paintings of the Blessed Virgin and the saints, was destroyed.[48]

The 14th-century Debre Abbay was another example of a rural monastery and church deliberately bombed in the early months of the invasion. Located in a forested area in Tigray region on the northern edge of the deep gorge of the river Tekkezé, Debre Abbay was one of the monasteries of the ancient complex of Waldibba, a well-known monastic centre located on the other side of the gorge (Map 9). According to Ethiopian Church traditions, Debre Abbay was founded in 1388 by Father Samuél of Waldibba, whose remains were said to be preserved in the monastery's church of Bethlehem.

In a remote and sparsely populated part of the countryside, but benefiting from extensive gardens where fruit and vegetables were grown, the monastery was well endowed. At the time of the Italian invasion the monks were following the rule of St Tekle Haymanot, and Debre Abbay had long been a centre for traditional Church education, especially the eucharistic liturgy, in which its senior monks were considered the Church's highest authority.[49]

In the 16th century many of the monks had been massacred in the *jihad* of Ahmed Grañ. However, the monastery had recovered, and suffered no further disasters until it was bombed by the Italians on 22 December 1935, an action that completely destroyed the monastery church.[50]

The principal monastery building was also destroyed, with seven other buildings in the monastery complex suffering direct hits. The monastery normally had several hundred clergy and students in residence; fortunately most of them were able to seek cover and hide from the air raid. Nonetheless, two monks died in the attack.[51]

It should, however, be noted that at the outset not all Italy's military commanders prioritised the crusade against the Ethiopian Church. Although ruthless and having no hesitation in gassing civilians, the supreme commander of the armed forces during the invasion, Marshal Pietro Badoglio, was concerned that the deliberate desecration and pillaging of churches would make it difficult for Italy to rule Ethiopia in the future. Thus, in late 1935, already looking ahead to a post-invasion situation, he created a precedent by ordering measures to be taken against ground-troops who physically attacked churches. While the Air Force was bombing Debre Abbay, he was reporting to Rome the case of nineteen infantrymen who had been punished after desecrating the church of Enda Sillassé ('The Holy Trinity') in Tigray, and another case in which soldiers had burned the timbers of three other churches. His complaint was that such acts would 'hinder the work of pacification' and confirm the impressions that Ethiopians might have 'that accuse us of being enemies of their religion and desecrators of churches' (which, nonetheless, he dismissed as propaganda).[52] However, as we shall see, this policy was short-lived; Badoglio would not remain in Ethiopia long enough to discover whether his pacification strategy was effective. He would soon be replaced by Graziani, whose approach to the Ethiopian Church, and to the task of pacification, was entirely different.

Meanwhile, in the south, as the emperor recalled in his memoirs, while pursuing the armies of his son-in-law *Ras* Desta, under Graziani's command the Italian Air Force attacked the village and church of Negellé (Map 5) with incendiary bombs, setting them on fire, then followed up with an attack on the settlement of Wadara.[53]

Slaughter in Wag

Wag, a small but historically important area in north Wello immediately on the border with Tigray, is believed to have been Christianised by the 13th century, and was traditionally ruled by *wagshums*, a bloodline with a strong tradition of descent from the biblical king Solomon.[54] Fighting in the area was intense from the beginning of the invasion, since civilians in Wag were some of the first to join the Ethiopian military in trying to defend their homeland, particularly in the face of aerial bombardment of their towns in November 1935.

On 2 January 1936 the Regia Aeronautica delivered another onslaught, destroying residents, churches and houses in the towns of Seqota (the capital of Wag) and Amdewerq, in a terrifying barrage of incendiary and high-explosive bombs. But worse was to come; the Air Force followed up the bombardment with no less than 28 C-500T yperite bombs, each containing a quarter of a ton of yperite sprayed from aerial explosion—one of the heaviest recorded discharges of poisonous gases in a single day in the entire invasion and occupation. Before the unfortunate residents could flee the onslaught, they were drenched in toxic chemicals.[55]

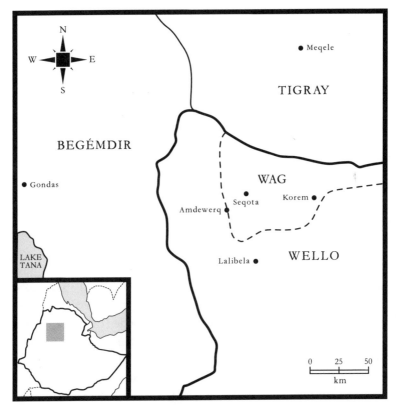

Map 3: Wag and Wello (based on *Encyclopaedia Aethiopica*, vol. 4, map 'Wag')

Vatican Support

The horrors of the new year were met by a hardening of the Holy See's stance; it was then that after months of wavering, followed by his ill-fated attempt to support the British–French proposals for partitioning Ethiopia, Pius XI finally came round to publicly supporting the invasion. Forty-eight hours after the carnage in Wag, concerned that Americans were generally opposed to the war, he advised Mussolini to strengthen his pro-war propaganda in the United States in line with an anti-sanctions campaign being conducted jointly by the Italian government and the Vatican.[56]

89

Clearly the pope knew that his clergy should not have been supporting the invasion; a seasoned Polish diplomat reported that Pius XI 'has looked on with embarrassment and even annoyance at the patriotic actions of bishops and clergy which have contributed to … and facilitated military operations in Africa'. However, the pontiff had apparently decided that to protect the position of the Church, he would accept the war as a necessary evil: 'Nonetheless, because of the necessity of maintaining the clergy's popularity with the Italian population, the Vatican cannot oppose their actions.'[57]

A few days later, as the slaughter in Ethiopia intensified, Luigi Cardinal Lavitrano, archbishop of Palermo, who had voted for the Fascist Party in 1929, announced that Providence had made Italy 'Queen of the Mediterranean, in order that she might the more easily diffuse abroad the benefits of Christian civilization of which Rome was the trustee'.[58] And signalling that the Holy See was now openly supporting the invasion as a holy war, Cardinal Pacelli also took the opportunity to weigh in, speaking of 'the sacred destiny of Rome' and 'Rome's *holy conquests*' (emphasis added).[59]

The fact is that whatever Pius XI's private thoughts or regrets, the endorsement of the war by Secretary of State Pacelli and the inflammatory speeches of the senior Italian Catholic clergy certainly 'legitimised the support of many people and encouraged the hesitant'.[60] As David Kertzer remarks, 'Not since the days when popes ruled the papal states had the Catholic Church been so closely identified with the government', and 'Not since the time of the crusades had it played such a central role in urging Catholics to foreign conquest'.[61]

The message received by the people of Italy and Catholics around the world was now unequivocal: the *fasces* and the Cross were as one, and by early 1936 support for the ongoing invasion was virtually universal throughout Italy. Indeed, it is difficult to overstate the popularity of the war at that time; thousands of Blackshirt volunteers embarking for Ethiopia filled the ports of Genoa and Naples as far as the eye could see. The Church had served Mussolini well.

Crusader frenzy in Italy reached a new height during the first quarter of 1936. Early in January, while Pacelli was cheerleading his holy conquistadors, Archbishop Ascalesi of Naples was presiding over a ceremony to bless an enormous force of Blackshirts departing for Ethiopia, with a number of Fascist officials, 'for the glory and honour of the country', as the prelate announced in his benediction.

As they set sail, the archbishop resurrected yet another tradition from the medieval crusades: the troops were accompanied by a statue of the Virgin Mary to support and guide them to their sacred destiny.[62] The Mother of Christ had again been brought in to champion the holy war.

The Consolata missionaries decided to add fuel to the fire by publishing in their periodical *Missioni Consolata* articles once again branding Ethiopian Christians as heretics. In January, the article 'The Heretical Clergy of Abyssinia' described the Ethiopian Church as a 'member cut off from the only true plant of life', which, 'detached from Rome, had only a form of Pharisaic religion, a weak, narrow, superficial Christianity without deep roots'. The article dismissed the Ethiopian clergy as 'venal, fanatic, ignorant, corrupt and hypocritical' and, the author apparently being aware that elderly widows in Ethiopia traditionally retreated to convents to end their days in prayer, spoke disingenuously of 'nuns without virginity'.[63]

Meanwhile, in Ethiopia, Emperor Haile Selassie was setting out from his temporary headquarters at Dessie to Korem, Tigray, as 'bombs rained down upon us'. In his memoirs he recalled his shock and bewilderment at the actions of the invading forces:

> the Italians were aware that the Ethiopian people were firm in their Christianity and so, as every Sunday priests and monks, men and women, old and young flocked to hear Holy Mass, they lay in wait for them, and set out to exterminate them with bombs. For this reason many churches were set on fire ...
>
> Apart from killing Christian people and from setting fire to Christian churches, their burning of ancient *Gi'iz* manuscripts, which, written on parchment, had long been preserved in many churches and represented sources of knowledge and wisdom, caused much distress not only to the Ethiopian people but to scholars all over the world who were researching into this kind of knowledge and learning.[64]

HOLY WAR

Death of an Icon

Despite being a chaplain, the ultra-nationalist Padre Reginaldo Giuliani, captivated by the mystic alliance that he believed linked the Cross and the Fascist war machine, and entranced by what he called 'the music of cannons and artillery',[65] exhorted the troops forward with the zeal of a commander. The fighting was bitter, for, unlike the Ethiopians, who forty years earlier had allowed the Italian soldiers under siege in their fort at Meqelé to leave unhindered, and had sent two thousand Italian prisoners of war back to Italy unharmed after the Battle of Adwa, the Italians followed the policy of killing all prisoners of war, including military commanders and soldiers who had surrendered.

It was during those frantic early weeks of 1936, when the struggle for Ethiopia was particularly intense, that Father Giuliani was killed in the heat of battle, at the age of 48. His death occurred on 21 January, the first day of a major three-day engagement in Tigray (see Map 2), generally known by historians as the First Battle of Tembien, and termed by the Italians the Battle of Uarieu Pass.

The Ethiopian defenders fought tenaciously to gain control of the pass, which, had they done so, would have meant a major strategic setback for the Italians in their efforts to penetrate further into Ethiopia. In the process, faced with modern weaponry including tanks and machine guns, around eight thousand Ethiopians, most of whom were only lightly armed, lost their lives. A measure of their bravery and effectiveness is that half the officers of the Blackshirt battalions and more than a thousand well-armed Italian and Eritrean soldiers also died in the battle. While the Ethiopians failed to take the pass, neither side could be said to have won the battle, despite the Italian Air Force relentlessly gassing the Ethiopians in the rear.

When the news of Giuliani's demise became public in Italy, the crusader frenzy was driven to new extremes. In death the chaplain went from being a renowned Italian patriot to a national martyr, elevated in the eyes of his fellow countrymen almost to sainthood. The citation for his gold medal read, 'A blow of a scimitar, brandished by a barbarian hand, cut short his terrestrial existence: ending the life of an apostle and beginning that of a martyr'.[66]

The various representations of Father Giuliani's death showing him holding a cross, and being killed by half-naked men referred to variously as 'savages' and 'barbarians', accompanied by narratives referring to the chaplain as a Christian martyr, delivered a misleading and indeed dishonest message. Giuliani was not killed because of his faith—far from it. Unlike the Ethiopian clergy, who would be singled out by the Italians and killed *because* they were clergy of the Ethiopian Church, Giuliani was killed because, and *only* because, he was a member of a heavily armed alien force illegally invading the sovereign state of Ethiopia and killing thousands of its citizens— innocent and defenceless men, women and children—in the process. There were many Catholic Italians who had been working in Ethiopia for years, and who had never been harmed or threatened by the Ethiopians. Furthermore, most of the Ethiopians defending their country against the Italian onslaught were Christians, and some were themselves Catholic, as were several members of Haile Selassie's government. Nonetheless, the image of Padre Reginaldo Giuliani as the perfect Christian sacrificing his life for a supposedly sacred cause would continue to inspire the Italian troops long after the First Battle of Tembien.[67]

Schismatics and Infidels

In Italy the crusader spirit was still riding high among the clergy. There was the occasional dissenting voice, such as that of Evasio Colli, bishop of Parma, in northern Italy, who bravely warned against 'waves of collective hatred, organized lies, and prejudices of every kind',[68] but his pleas were drowned out by the majority, who concurred with the position taken by Ferdinando Bernardi, archbishop of the southern Italian city of Taranto. On 23 February 1936, far from calling for restraint on the part of the invading forces, and expressing concern for the Ethiopians who were dying trying to defend their families and their homes, he denounced the victims, echoing *La Civiltà Cattolica* in branding them 'schismatics'.

Bernardi was following Cardinal Schuster in proclaiming the invasion a holy war. In addition, significantly, he referred to Ethiopian Muslims as infidels.[69] This was one of the first public references by the rabble-rousing prelates to Ethiopian Muslims, implying that as infidels they should be dealt with by the crusaders in time-honoured manner. The difference, however, was that while the medieval crusades were aimed at recovering the Holy Land from the Muslims, the Muslims of Ethiopia had never raised a hand against the Catholic Church, and neither had they taken possession of any part of the Holy Land. On the contrary, they had allowed Bishop Jarosseau's Catholic mission to operate unhindered within their holy city of Harar. As we shall see, this denigration of Ethiopian Muslims was not only inappropriate; it was one of a series of miscalculations by the Italian episcopate in its alliance with the Italian military.

For those who looked to the Holy See for reassurance that the Roman Church might nonetheless be following the principles of Christian charity rather than the policies of Fascism, there would have been disappointment, for the Holy See was now clearly committed to the invasion. On the very day that Bernardi was proclaiming a crusade, the secretary of state at the Vatican added his voice to the chorus. Leaving no room for misunderstanding, he told an audience of high Catholic officials, including four cardinals of the Curia, 'Rome gives the world the example of conciliation between Church and State; from Rome come the words of life which spur on to holy conquests',[70] adding, 'No State shall resist the power of Rome.'[71]

This is the first occasion on which cardinals—including members of the Curia—are specifically mentioned as having been participants at a gathering at which such statements were made. But more would follow; Gaetano Salvemini counted no less than fifteen cardinals, from both the Curia and the Italian Church, taking part in pro-war demonstrations during the invasion, and remarked, 'So many cardinals, especially cardinals in the immediate entourage of the Pope, could not, we may be sure, have been acting against his wishes.'[72]

More Madonnas

It was just three days later, on 26 February 1936, that Archbishop Ascalesi was again preaching the Cross in Pompei, and leading a tumultuous procession of the icon of the Madonna of the Rosary of

Pompei to embark at the port of Naples for the voyage to Ethiopia in the *Conte Grande*, which set sail on 3 March.[73] For this event Ascalesi had clearly been given a free hand, and he pulled out all the stops. The miraculous image was preceded not only by clergy, but also by war veterans, disabled ex-soldiers, and mothers and widows of those fallen in the First World War, as well as political dignitaries. Over 'the interminable procession' flew 'swarms of aeroplanes' throwing out flowers, and flyers glorifying the Holy Virgin and the invasion of Ethiopia. As Lucia Ceci noted, the effectiveness of the 'fusion of traditional religious *motifs* and political messages' was amplified by the aeroplanes as symbols of 'the virile and war-like modernism of Fascism'.[74]

Furthermore, the presence of the Madonna ensured that through the 'good hearts' of the invading Italians, their 'strong muscles', their 'heroism', and 'because it is inevitable, even through their weapons', Catholic Christian civilisation and 'the soul and glory of Italy, as a new sun', would 'penetrate and radiate in the lands of Ethiopia'.[75]

The framing of the invasion of Ethiopia as a holy war against a population branded by Pius XI as heretics, schismatics, pagans and infidels led to an unprecedented outpouring of religious devotion across Italy. It was as if the clerics in every diocese were not only hand in glove with the Fascist military, but were determined to outdo their peers, as literally hundreds of images and statues of the Madonna were dispatched to Ethiopia to ensure victory and protect the invaders.[76] In Italy, the fear of death, family problems and insecurities linked to war had long been addressed by Marian devotion, particularly during the First World War. But these traditional cults were now embedded within the militaristic values of Fascism. In a well-orchestrated campaign requiring a high degree of coordination between the bishops, statues of the Holy Virgin carried to Ethiopia were sometimes placed at the head of the marching legions, to give the soldiers 'an aura of invincibility'. The Mother of Christ was no longer present just to bless the oppressed and provide succour to the fearful, but, in her capacity as 'the Queen of Victories', she was to lead the crusaders to 'complete Italian' victory.[77]

Well-known Marian statues and icons that left the Italian shores to inspire and empower the 'holy warriors' included the celebrated

Madonna dell'Oltremare, an image that sailed for Ethiopia in March 1936. Donated by the city of Faenza in Ravenna, it arrived at Naples on a military truck carrying the national flag, escorted by a great crowd including uniformed *carabinieri* and soldiers with fixed bayonets.[78] Also taken to Ethiopia was the famous Madonna Immacolata di Don Placido, the Madonna del Divino Amore, and a Madonna dell'Arco.[79]

The icon of the Madonna di Montevergine—or rather, no doubt, a consecrated copy of it—was also sent to the battle front, and this is of particular interest, because the Madonna of the abbey of Montevergine is often known in Italy as the 'Black Madonna'. With her flesh painted in a dark shade of pink, the face of the Holy Virgin is thought to be the work of a 5th-century Palestinian artist, and is said to have been fitted into a large icon in Byzantium in the 13th century. Thus, like most images of the Madonna sent overseas by Italian clerics to champion the destruction of the 'schismatics', the Madonna of Montevergine was itself the work of 'schismatics', the iconography of Byzantium being considerably more developed and sophisticated than the religious art of contemporary Rome. It is thus ironic that an Orthodox icon should be so venerated by Catholics as to be used to champion an attack on one of the world's oldest Orthodox Churches, and all the more ironic that it should be the image of a Black Madonna.

The Mother of God in Ethiopia

There was another striking irony in the Italian clergy's use of Marian imagery to rally support for the crusade against Ethiopia: it would be difficult to find any national Church with greater veneration of the Holy Virgin than the Ethiopian Church. The fact that Pius XI was well aware of this presumably explains his continued silence in the face of his clergy's abuse of Marian images; as he had now thrown in his lot with the Fascists so far as the invasion was concerned, his was most likely the silence of embarrassment.

The mother church of Ethiopia is the cathedral dedicated to Mary of Zion at the empire's original capital of Aksum. The oldest-surviving church in Ethiopia, and one of the oldest in the world, it is thought to have been founded by Emperor Ezana in the 4th century.[80] Since she received the title Theotokos (Mother of God), veneration of the Holy Virgin has been central to Ethiopian theology, and in fact the Marian cults that emerged in Italy in the 20th century, with its secular and semi-pagan overtones—not to mention the Madonna of the Manganello—would certainly have been regarded by the Ethiopian Church as blasphemous.

No sanctuary is more beloved of the clergy of Ethiopia's holy city of Lalibela (Map 3) than the monolithic church of the House of Mary, which attracts more pilgrims on Ethiopia's Marian holy days than any other church in the rock-hewn complex. Excavated underground, this ancient edifice, which has been in continuous use since its foundation, is a fully developed basilica with narthex, nave, aisles, galleries and a domed sanctuary with sacristies. In the nave, coloured bas-reliefs decorate the columns, capitals, corbels and arches. No greater evidence of the sustained devotion of the Ethiopians to the Mother of God since ancient times could ever be sought than this great subterranean cathedral, which holds a position of pre-eminence at Lalibela, a complex long regarded as one of the wonders of the world.[81]

Carnage in the Holy War

The Ethiopian defence forces continued to meet the invasion with determined resistance, but by mid-March 1936, under an onslaught of bombing and torching of villages, and the poisoning of water sources with toxic gases, tens of thousands of Ethiopian soldiers and civilians died in a rout that 'turned into something approaching genocide'.[82] Meanwhile, apparently oblivious to the carnage, Cardinal Schuster was granting his benediction to his 'missionaries of the Cross'.[83] A few days later the defenders experienced a critical setback in Tigray at the Battle of Maychew, where, on 31 March 1936, after the emperor and his army were drenched in asphyxiating gases, the tenacious Ethiopians faced inevitable defeat. Fighting spirit and frontal attacks were no match for machine guns, bombers and gas.[84]

While the war in the north was being pursued by Badoglio, Graziani's troops were rampaging through south-eastern Ethiopia,

HOLY WAR

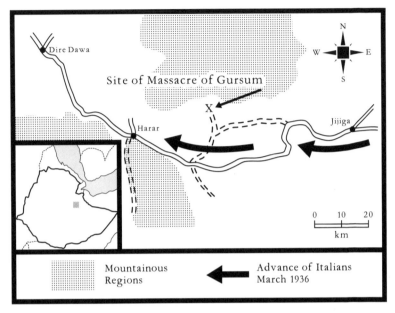

Map 4: Eastern Ethiopia: Dire Dawa, Harar and Jijiga (based on *Guida dell'Africa Orientale Italiana*, map, p. 448)

leaving a trail of destruction in their wake. As his army approached the urban centres of Jijiga and Harar, bombers of the Regia Aeronautica flew ahead to 'soften up' the population.

Many members of the minority Christian population of the predominantly Muslim city of Harar (population then about 45,000[85]), which ranks as Islam's fourth-holiest city, were slaughtered between March and July 1936. In the face of the invasion, Harar had been declared a defenceless 'open city', but this designation was not respected by the Italians.

The sufferings of Harar were appalling. One detailed testimony appears in a letter written to Dr Werqineh Isheté, the Ethiopian envoy in London known as Dr Charles Martin. The author was a reliable Muslim eyewitness whom Dr Martin knew, and whom he had employed previously when he was governor of Chercher Province, near Harar. Smuggled out to London via Djibouti and passed to Dr Martin's confidante Sylvia Pankhurst for publication in September, the letter contained reports concerning events in

Harar. The ambassador's former employee began, 'Before the Italians reached Jigjiga, Harar and Dire Dawa [see Map 4], all the strong men left for the high mountains. Some said they would wait to hear from the Emperor Haile Selassie because they believed their Christian brothers abroad would give them help.' He went on:

> There remained in the cities only old men, women and children who thought they would be spared the bombs and poison gas because they took no part in hostilities. The religious men, who had devoted all their lives to the worship of Christ, also remained, believing that so long as they had the Bible in their hands, no-one would injure them, and that this war was only a matter between two earthly governments.[86]

Although the existence of a Catholic mission in Harar was regarded by the Muslim residents as something of an anomaly, the fathers were held by the inhabitants in considerable esteem, and they provided medical services and education facilities for both boys and girls. Indeed, Emperor Haile Selassie as a boy had himself attended the mission school, run by his tutor, the highly respected Monsignor Jarosseau, who had become a legend in his own lifetime. The Orthodox priests and monks of Harar had presumably heard that Italy was a Christian country, and were almost certainly unaware that the Catholic Church had proclaimed a crusade against the Ethiopian Church. Indeed, they expected the Italians to have the same qualities of piety and Christian charity as their French Catholic counterparts.

Unfortunately, that trust was misplaced. The invading Italians had very little in common with the caring Catholic clergy of Bishop Jarosseau. The assault began with an aerial attack on 22 March, and this was followed by a much more devastating onslaught by two squadrons of bombers on 29 March. Even the principal mosque, the cathedral where Emperor Haile Selassie's father was buried, the Ethiopian Red Cross and the French Catholic mission suffered direct hits from incendiary bombs. Although most of the residents had fled to the hills, leaving only a few hundred in the city, one source reported approximately 40 deaths and 120 wounded, in addition to thousands made homeless.[87] Bishop Jarosseau packed his bags and took shelter from the bombing in a cave outside the city.[88]

Monsignor Jarosseau later resumed his work at the Harar mission, but the French prelate who had spent 55 years of his life ministering to Ethiopians was not what Rome had in mind for the 'schismatics, heretics and infidels'. In due course Pius XI had Jarosseau and his dedicated international Catholic team unceremoniously deported from Ethiopia and replaced by Italians.[89] The much-vaunted Vatican policy of neutrality towards the national Catholic Churches had once more been waived; for the Holy See, Italian nationalism was clearly the order of the day.

A Cry for Justice

Although Ethiopian armies under commanders such as *Ras* Desta, Aberra Kassa, Wendwessen Kassa and Asfawessen Kassa were still heavily engaged on the battlefield, the Ethiopian Crown Council realised that Addis Ababa would soon fall to the invaders, and that the capture or death of the emperor at the hands of the Italians could spell the end of Ethiopia as a sovereign state. Thus it was agreed that the emperor should seek assistance from the League of Nations in Geneva.

So it was that on 2 May 1936 Haile Selassie left Ethiopia in desperation to plead the nation's cause at the League, in which he still—surprisingly—placed great faith. It was agreed that the Egyptian archbishop Qérillos (Cyril) and the four Ethiopian bishops, Peter, Michael, Isaac and John, would remain in Ethiopia to maintain the integrity of the Ethiopian Church. Accompanied by an entourage that included *Ichegé* Gebre-Giyorgis and *Ras* Kassa Haylu, the emperor went first to Jerusalem—an emotional visit. His first destination was Golgotha, and on the following day he visited the Ethiopian monastery of Debre Genet, accommodating 'monks and nuns who have come from Ethiopia having renounced the world'. In the emperor's own words:

> But when they heard of the entry into Addis Ababa, Our capital city, of our aggressive enemy, and when they saw our arrival in a foreign country as an exile from Our own, and in particular when we told them that in the Italian war many churches and monasteries had been burnt and that monks and priests, women and children as well

as the aged had perished through poison gas and bombs, they began bursting into tears.[90]

The distraught emperor then went on to Britain.

Arriving at Addis Ababa on 5 May, triumphant at the head of a military convoy of some two thousand vehicles, General Badoglio drew to a halt outside the city. Mounting a stallion, he entered on horseback, striking the pose of the conquering crusader. In Rome, Mussolini announced to a vast crowd in a state of near delirium that the war was over. It wasn't; the invaders had simply reached the capital. In fact, hostilities were entering a new phase of intensity, but it suited the *Duce* to give the impression that they had come to an end. The Italian tricolour fluttered over Haile Selassie's palace, which now served as Badoglio's administrative headquarters—the Governo Generale—but Italian control was actually limited for the most part to a few towns and principal highways.

Nonetheless, the *Duce*'s ploy succeeded: his claim that the war was over diverted attention from Ethiopia, and the international spotlight swung instead towards the civil war that was erupting in Spain. Within a few days he would issue written instructions for the establishment of a reign of terror in Ethiopia and atrocities would escalate. Ethiopia would become a garrison state, and the war would continue.

But what would be the posture of the Holy See? Now that Mussolini had apparently got what he wanted, the pressure on the pope lifted. If Pius XI's acquiescence in the invasion had been achieved under duress, now was the opportunity for him to shake off the image he was acquiring of Fascist sympathiser and Italian ultra-nationalist. However, it would soon become clear that that was not his chosen course of action.

5

A HAPPY TRIUMPH

> 'When I saw the wholesale massacre of Christians by Christians,
> I stood and thanked God that he had not made me a Christian,
> though I know that the sin did not lie with Christ.'
>
> Muslim eyewitness of Italian atrocities,
> Harar, September 1936

On 6 May 1936, while Pietro Badoglio's jubilant forces were still pouring into Addis Ababa, Pietro Tacchi Venturi, the pope's Jesuit private emissary between the Holy See and Mussolini, sent the *Duce* a letter of congratulations, throwing to the winds any remaining pretence of neutrality: 'The hearts of all good Italian Catholics beg God to continue to give you his divine aid to ensure that the fruits of victory are truly those that one has the right to expect of a victorious apostolic Roman Catholic nation.'[1]

The Catholic media were ecstatic. The 'schismatics, heretics, pagans and infidels' had apparently been vanquished. Two days later the diocesan weekly of Turin, *L'Armonia*, and the Catholic newspaper of the province of Alexandria, in a burst of religious fervour, were pointing out the providential nature of the 'conquest' falling in May, the month dedicated by Catholics to the Mother of Christ, referring to her as the Queen of Victories.[2]

The next day, when Mussolini proclaimed the existence of a new 'Roman Empire', Italians were euphoric. Badoglio, now ensconced in the former Italian legation in Addis Ababa, was appointed viceroy of Italian East Africa (something of a misnomer, since his orders came from Mussolini, not from the king), and General Rodolfo Graziani, who was still commanding on the southern war front, was promoted to marshal. Monsignor Elia Dalla Costa, archbishop of Florence, was so excited about Italy's apparent victory in her holy war, and so certain of the divinity of the invaders, that he branded the attempts by Ethiopians to defend their homeland as a 'mask concealing the war against God'.[3]

On 12 May, Pius XI finally spoke out on the subject of the invasion. If his earlier reservations had been sincere, and still reflected his thinking, his speech would presumably have been one of solemn reflection, shame and remorse for the savagery of the Italians in Ethiopia, and solace for the quarter of a million innocent Ethiopians killed during the invasion. It would also have been one of caution and sage advice to the military to avoid the excesses of the victor. But, on the contrary, the pontiff was apparently now utterly convinced of the righteousness of the holy war. He spoke enthusiastically and publicly of a 'happy triumph by a great and good people', the church bells of Rome were rung with jubilation, and across Italy the clergy organised religious processions to celebrate the victory.[4]

The international community was aghast. Just the day before, the Anglican bishop of Liverpool had read from his pulpit reports of Italian atrocities in Ethiopia,[5] and after hearing the pope's speech, the Anglican bishop of Southwark broke diplomatic protocol by declaring his outrage that 'a victory won by flagrant breaking of covenants, by bombs deliberately flung on Red Cross hospitals, by mustard gas scattered to torture defenceless non-combatants' had been hailed as 'the happy triumph of a great and good people'. 'In the name of Christ', he declared in an extraordinarily blunt reprimand to the pope, 'we most clearly dissociate ourselves from such an utterance.'[6]

Daniel Binchy goes to some length to explain the pope's speech, pointing out that the pontiff was celebrating the triumph as a prelude to world peace, and suggesting that it was 'the Italian in him' that prompted his indiscreet words.[7] However, it must be said that it requires a considerable stretch of the imagination to suppose that conducting an aggressive war in defiance of the League of Nations could in any circumstance be a prelude to world peace. Furthermore, Binchy goes on to defeat his own argument that Pius's words were a momentary indiscretion, when he admits that the pontiff's speech was not extempore, the choice of words clearly being deliberate.[8]

Delighted by the pope's acceptance of the invasion and his endorsement of its apparent success, Mussolini could not resist telling Giuseppe Bottai, a long-standing member of the Fascist Grand Council, 'I want to make a cynical declaration to you: in international relations there is only one morality—success. We were immoral, they said, when we attacked the Negus [Emperor Haile Selassie]. We won, and then we became moral, completely moral.'[9]

The invasion of Ethiopia had achieved its short-term objective of providing the *Duce* with what he could present to the Italians as a glittering military victory. In the longer term, once 'pacified', and with the help of infrastructure to be built across the land, Ethiopia's role as a powerhouse to serve the Italian military in further foreign conquests would also, he expected, be achieved. Thus the military adventure had served its immediate purpose, Italians now considered their army invincible, and Mussolini was riding high on the crest of a wave of adulation. His attention would now turn to interventions on behalf of General Franco's rebels in Spain, and the prospects of advancing his agenda of conquest and expansion through closer cooperation with Nazi Germany.

As for Ethiopia, as far as Mussolini was concerned, the viceroy's job was straightforward: 'pacification', which meant dismantling the existing polity, executing the ruling classes and the intelligentsia, and putting down resistance using the techniques of counter-insurgency that the Italians had developed in Libya. As far as the Catholic clergy—and, indeed, the Holy See—were concerned, the 'gates of Ethiopia' were now presumed to have been opened, the 'obstacle' of the Orthodox clergy had been dealt with, and the Catholic clerics and missionaries who were on stand-by could now be sent forth to Ethiopia to do their duty. The prelates were beside themselves with joy; the holy war was over—or so they had been led to believe.

Singing the hymn of praise to the Almighty known as the *Te Deum*, they rejoiced in 'the success of Roman and Christian civilisation over barbarity'.[10]

Taking Mussolini's 'war is over' speech at face value, most observers, including the Italians at home, assumed that the war was over when the *Duce* said it was. However, at the time, the declaration had little significance in Ethiopia; indeed, few Ethiopians even knew that such a declaration had been made. The event that triggered the announcement was the arrival of Italian troops in the capital in early May 1936, but for the defence forces still fighting in the field, with strong local loyalties and only a nominal interest in the affairs of the centre, the presence of Italian soldiers in the city was not a critical factor. In any case, the Italian military was still heavily engaged in battle and in some areas was actually stepping up its attacks on not only the Ethiopian military, but also civilians.

Holy War, Graziani-Style

War on the civilian population was particularly evident in Harar, the first city encountered by Rodolfo Graziani's invading troops that housed a significant Christian minority. The general was already implementing Mussolini's policy of creating a bulwark against the Ethiopian Church by favouring Ethiopian Muslims—the military's first departure from the policy of the Roman Church, which expected the army to regard both Orthodox Christians and Muslims as enemies.

We do not know if Father Giuliani fulfilled his desire to participate directly in targeted attacks on Ethiopian Christians, but the soldiers he inspired with his belligerent speeches certainly did, for the Christians who had survived the bombing now found that, far from protecting them, their faith made them prime targets. Dr Martin's correspondent reported:

> The first order given to the Italian armies was to kill everyone carrying the cross. I saw a man pick up a gold cross in the street, and whilst he had it in his hands an Italian soldier killed him because he thought he was a Christian ... When I saw the wholesale massacre

of Christians by other Christians, I stood and thanked God that he had not made me a Christian, though I know that the sin did not lie with Christ.[11]

This witness, who as a Muslim had nothing to gain from denouncing the abuse of Christians by the Italians, was explicit in his account: 'When the Italian armies arrived in the city of Harar on Thursday, May 6th, they killed between that day and Sunday 509 of the people remaining there, without even exchanging a word with any of them.'[12]

When the Italian military massacred civilians, the carnage was often followed for days or weeks afterwards by slaughter carried out by roving bands of Blackshirts. This was also the pattern in Harar, which fell within the Italian military's southern sector, in which the 6th 'Tevere' Division was at that time the principal Blackshirt force. They were the militiamen who had been blessed by Archbishop Ascalesi in Naples and had sailed from Italy reinforced by the presence of the holy Madonna of the Rosary of Pompei. The report by the shocked Muslim continued:

> One Sunday I saw some Italian white soldiers enter an Ethiopian church and ring the bells. Sixteen old men thought it was time for prayer, but before they could enter the church the Italians killed them. I heard the words of these poor men: '*Egziabher Yasywo*' (May God open your eyes to the truth!) I could not help crying, but the Italians were laughing. The dead bodies lay for two days on the steps of the church.
>
> I saw an old man sitting in his house, his Bible in one hand and a white flag in the other. Two white soldiers and five Somalis [*askaris* from Italian Somaliland fighting under Italian command] entered and asked the Ethiopian for his money. He replied that he was only a poor man and had only three *thalers*, which he offered them. They fired three bullets at once and he lay dead.
>
> I saw an old woman, who had a daughter of 15 or 16 years of age. They killed the old woman and took her daughter away. The Italians asked the Amhara people for money and where the money of the Ethiopian government and the ammunition were to be found.
>
> The massacre of poor old people and children lasted for 18 days and nights, and then stopped for a while. When news of it reached

the strong men who had gone to the mountains, they gave battle at Gara Mulata, Fiamboro, and other places [see Map 5].'[13]

A New Viceroy

Within a few days of Badoglio's appointment as viceroy, his proposals for running Ethiopia through traditional local leaders had been rejected by the minister for the colonies, Alessandro Lessona, in Rome and replaced by a strategy based on the Fascist policy of direct totalitarian rule. Badoglio resigned, and on 21 May Marshal Graziani, who was quickly summoned to Addis Ababa from the southern war front, was appointed viceroy in his place. From that moment on, Badoglio's attempts to restrain the troops from attacking and plundering churches were forgotten.

In Italy the new viceroy was viewed as the classic hero. Born in 1882, Graziani had originally planned to be a Catholic priest, but then decided to go to law school instead. However, he abandoned his studies and joined the military.[14] Tall and of striking appearance, he was proud of his reputation as Mussolini's strongman.[15] During the First World War he had fought in the Italian colony of Libya and became the nation's youngest colonel. In 1921 he returned to Libya and stayed for twelve years, achieving considerable notoriety as military commander there. In 1935 he was appointed governor of the colony of Italian Somaliland. By the time he became viceroy of Italian East Africa, Graziani's infamy in ruthlessly suppressing civilians had already earned him the appellations Butcher of Tripoli and Hyena of Libya.

Two weeks before being appointed viceroy, Graziani was in the small, predominantly Muslim town of Jijiga, which had been largely reduced to 'a mass of ruins' by the Italian Air Force in March.[16] On an official visit to a bombed church there on 7 May, he had fallen into a deep hole which he was convinced had been deliberately concealed to trap him. The historian Anthony Mockler attributes to that incident what he terms Graziani's 'paranoic hatred' of, and suspicion towards, the Ethiopian clergy.[17] This could, of course, only exacerbate the already strongly anti-Orthodox stance of the Italian army.

A HAPPY TRIUMPH

We have already seen that despite Italy being a signatory to the Geneva Conventions, during the invasion the Italians had taken very few prisoners of war; virtually all prisoners were executed, whether or not they had surrendered.[18] Graziani now made this policy official, by ordering that any Ethiopian soldier who continued to fight after the Italians had reached Addis Ababa in early May, and any civilian who resisted the invaders in any way, or was even suspected of not wanting to submit to Italian overlordship, should be branded a 'rebel' and shot. With Ethiopian and Italian battalions still engaged in battle in the field, and still fighting under their respective military commands, this policy led to the cold-blooded slaughter of thousands of Ethiopian soldiers taken prisoner during battle.

Dr Charles Martin, the outspoken Ethiopian minister in London, was outraged. He protested bitterly, complaining, 'General Graziani has declared all Ethiopians still fighting for their country as "brigands" to be shot immediately, not combatants to be treated as prisoners of war. Against this illegal conduct, I make the strongest possible protest.'[19] Aware that the Italians had carried out terrible atrocities in Libya, Martin was explicit in his fears for Ethiopia: 'judging from the horrible events of the war in Tripoli ..., repetition of wholesale massacres of unarmed men, women and children is likely, only too likely, to occur.'[20]

The Ethiopian envoy's predictions turned out to have been well founded. Although both Badoglio and Graziani were professional soldiers, under their command not only the buccaneering Blackshirts but also the regular military continued the tradition of civilian abuse by routinely resorting to dishonourable conduct. Not only were the Ethiopian military and the civilians who joined them executed when taken prisoner, but they were subjected to shocking barbarities.

As Haile Selassie's military commanders with their outdated strategies were vanquished during the course of 1936–7, their successors, principally civilian resistance fighters known as Patriots, began adopting guerrilla tactics. The most common method of fighting the Patriots was to blackmail them into surrender by terrorising the civilian population, which was accomplished largely by the bombing and aerial spraying of men, women, children, animals, crops and drinking water with toxic chemicals provided by the Chemical Warfare Service known by the Italians as 'Section K'. When the invasion began, an extensive chemical weapons facility covering twelve and a half hectares had already been established near Mogadishu in neighbouring Italian Somaliland, with facilities for preparing liquids and gases for the invasion. It contained no less than seventeen warehouses for storage, together with 35,000 gas masks and decontamination materials for the protection of Italians.[21]

Crusaders in the Service of the Duce

Upon the Italians assuming control of Addis Ababa, any pretence that they were on a 'civilising mission' evaporated overnight. Henceforth there would be no parliament; having no use for democratic institutions, Graziani commandeered the parliament building and handed it over to the Fascist military High Command for their headquarters. And far from 'building schools', as Mussolini's propaganda machine had promised, the schools were actually closed, and all secondary education for Ethiopians was banned. The renowned Menelik II School, which Haile Selassie had attended as a child, was closed and commandeered as the headquarters of the Italian Air Force. The prestigious Teferi Mekonnin School was closed, and the crusading zeal engendered by the Italian Catholic clergy that had helped to drive the forces of invasion was now harnessed to carry out mass executions in cold blood of educated Ethiopians, community leaders, and clergy of the Ethiopian Church. Meanwhile, the fusion of Catholicism and Fascism, the quasi-religious iconography, and the incessant talk of a holy war continued to inculcate a sense of high mission among the invading troops.

However, as often was the case with their medieval forebears, the Italians' crusading zeal was typically devoid of Christian principles. On the contrary, 'Roman civilisation' involved some of the most brutal practices. The application of toxic gases was stepped up and refined in order to provide for high-volume discharge during low-flying aerial spraying—a technique intensified for use on civilians, crops, livestock and water sources. Other methods of terrorising civilians included the destruction of entire villages, and execution on the slightest pretext—most commonly by hanging in public, but also by burning families alive in their houses using oil-fuelled flamethrowers. Methods of dealing with the Patriots were particularly savage, including butchery, skinning alive, beheading followed by public displays of the severed head, and hanging by the wrists causing slow death from gangrene. The methods adopted are well chronicled, for the Italians left behind numerous photographs of such practices being carried out.

Piero Calamandrei, a law professor at Florence University who maintained a private diary, noted that one of his most brilliant students had confessed to him that Fascism had deprived his generation of any capacity to think. Calamandrei sensed that part of the problem was due to the unremitting emphasis placed on faith and obedience, which had restricted the bounds of discussion and left people insulated within a kind of emotional bubble, 'incapable of appreciating the force that certain moral principles, which they do not feel, have for others'.[22]

Persecution on the Southern Front

The disempowerment of what Graziani viewed as an Amhara elite, together with the suppression of the Ethiopian Christian clergy, particularly in predominantly Muslim areas, was well under way by the time the Italians reached Addis Ababa. The pope certainly knew what was going on in Ethiopia, for he spoke out on several occasions against Mussolini's decision to pose as the protector of Islam. However, no objections were heard from the Holy See concerning the suppression of the Ethiopian Church, which continued unabated through 1936 and 1937.

The approach to counter-insurgency adopted by the 6th 'Tevere' Blackshirt Division under Graziani in the south-east became a blueprint for the pattern of exemplary repression subsequently adopted by the Italians in Ethiopia throughout the occupation. Following action by the Ethiopian resistance, the Italians would turn their fury against unarmed civilians—men, women and children. The population would be massacred, the parish churches burned and looted, and the clergy slaughtered.

One early example, which was a prelude to what would follow, was the massacre of Gursum, a settlement east of Harar (see Map 5), which the Italians reached on 24 May 1936. Following a clash between the Italians and the Ethiopian resistance, in which casualties on both sides were heavy, in the sworn affidavit of a witness who was able to identify several of the massacre victims by name for the UN Italian War Crimes Commission:

> Next day, the Italians, instead of pursuing the Patriots, turned against the peaceful inhabitants of Gursum, who had surrendered their arms so as to live in peace, and began a cruel and systematic extermination of the population ... they tied five to eight persons together in a bundle at a time and shot them all. Their corpses were tied by their legs, dragged away like carcasses and thrown into a big trench dug for that purpose ... the number of persons who were executed wantonly by the Italians was 150.[23]

Gursum church also attracted the attention of the invaders. The witness continued: 'The Italians broke into the church at Gursum and plundered everything found therein. The church remained unrepaired for a long time and the population suffered a great deal.' And neither did the Italians spare the surrounding communities: 'On the next day after the massacre the Italians, suspecting that the inhabitants living in the neighbourhood might have been supplying the Patriots with provisions, burned their houses and plundered their property ...'[24]

The massacre of Gursum stands as one of the many war crimes perpetrated by the Italians in Ethiopia that have largely escaped the attention of historians. No one was ever held to account, and the victims have long been forgotten. Taking place only two weeks after Mussolini announced that the war was over, it established a pattern of behaviour that would prevail throughout much of the occupation.

On 9 June 1936 Viceroy Graziani ordered the 'Tevere' Blackshirts to move to Addis Ababa to help defend the Italian occupation of the city, by which time he had appointed General Guglielmo Nasi governor and military commander of the Governorate of Harar.[25] Dr Martin's Muslim eyewitness described how the Italian army in that governorate reacted when the Ethiopian defence forces fought back—another pattern of behaviour that would come to characterise the Italian mode of occupation:

> Whenever the Ethiopian soldiers killed some of the Italians, the poor people in the hands of the Italians were made to suffer. For example, the Italians sent 40,000 soldiers and 50 aeroplanes to attack the Ethiopians in the mountains ... Fighting lasted from June 10 to July 23, and whenever reports came through of heavy Italian casualties, especially of the white soldiers, the Italians got wild and fell upon the Ethiopian defenceless non-combatants in the towns, killing them without restraint. There was a general order that from July 16 to July 20 5,000 Ethiopians must be killed because of the fighting at Fiamboro in the mountains and along the railway.... Instead of going to fight the strong men, they obeyed the order by just killing the children, women and old men.[26]

The Massacre of Hagere Maryam

For months the Italians were struggling to gain control of the southern reaches below Addis Ababa, particularly the lowlands where the Rift Valley with its necklace of lakes links Kenya's northern districts with the great triangle of the Danakil Depression. The armies of *Ras* Desta proved very difficult to dislodge, and in order to strengthen the Italian position vis-à-vis the Ethiopian forces, who were often given succour by the local communities, the Italian strategy was to attempt to neutralise the cultural influence of the Ethiopian Church. In this respect, the actions of the Italians in the small market town of Hagere Maryam (population recorded as 400 in 1938;[27] renamed Alghe by the Italians to remove reference to the Ethiopian Church, and now known as Bule Hora) serve as an example of what was happening in settlements in many of Ethiopia's rural areas.

The 'Laghi' Division of the Italian forces occupied Hagere Maryam on 22 July 1936.[28] The Hungarian physician Dr Ladislas Shashka, who was in Ethiopia at that time, spoke the local languages, and had himself been based with his wife in the nearby town of Yirga Alem, recorded the terrifying developments.

The church of St Mary at Hagere Maryam had been built in the early 1900s; Dr Shashka noted that with 'an old convent and

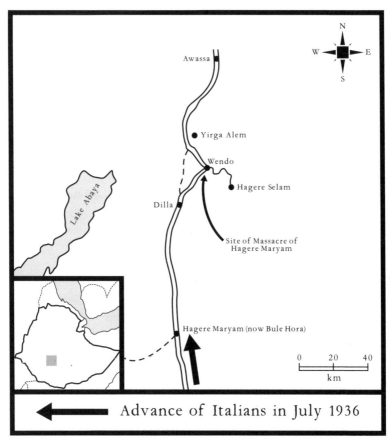

Map 5: Southern Ethiopia: Yirga Alem and Hagere Maryam
(© Ian Campbell)

theological school' in the town, there were many clergy present. He explained that, before the Italians arrived, the younger priests had left the town to live among the resistance forces in the forests and plains. 'These priests did not fight, but they considered it their duty to be with their people, to share the dangers of the struggle and help by their prayers and consultations.'

The physician reported,

> Only the older priests remained in Hagere Maryam when the Italians arrived. They were priests—that was enough; any position entitling

a man to authority or leadership among his people brought a death sentence. To execute this death sentence on the old priests some precautions were necessary, as their death would have provoked the vengeance of the neighbouring people. The priests were therefore transported to Wendo [a small town about a hundred kilometres north of Hagere Maryam; see Map 5], where their execution took place by machine guns.

One of them asked the Italian commanding officer to spare his brethren, old men who, being the servants of Jesus, would not have taken [up] arms even in their younger days. There was no answer; or rather, the answer was a thrust with the butt of a rifle, forward to the place of execution. A machine gun was erected before the old priests and set going. In a few minutes the bloody work was done. The aged men died on their knees, with a last prayer.

At this point in his testimony a distraught Dr Shashka described how the bodies of 40 Ethiopian priests 'lying in their own blood, with faces upturned to heaven, testified to the exalted character of Fascist civilisation—that Roman civilisation which was blessed even by the Christian priests of Rome!'[29]

Repression in the Lake District

In mid-1936 atrocities against the civilian population were particularly severe, the house-burning campaigns of Northern Shewa being replicated on a large scale among the lakes of the Rift Valley.

Evidence from victims of such atrocities is, of course, rare, but one example will suffice to give an idea of the horrors faced by thousands of families that lived in constant fear of this particular campaign. It was in July that a brigade under General Sebastiano Gallina (later listed as a UN war crimes suspect) was conducting what Graziani termed 'repressions' in Ethiopia's Rift Valley, in an attempt to keep the Addis Ababa–Djibouti railway free from attacks by the resistance.[30]

In the village of Oddo Becho, in Ada district, near the lakeside town of Debre Zét (Map 6), the Orthodox Christian family of Kassa Habte-Maryam was at home. The rural homestead consisted of a large compound with a main house, a smaller house, and a number of outbuildings. Kassa himself was not at home, but his wife, Shewareged Habte-Gebriél, was there in the smaller house with two daughters and Seifu, a baby boy. Meanwhile, her sons, Yeshitila and Grum, and daughters, Elfinesh, Aselefech and Mamitu, were in the main house.

Suddenly, without warning, Italian soldiers burst into the compound, looking for Kassa. Carrying out a search and finding he was not at home, they sealed the main house from the outside, locking the five children inside. Then, using flaming torches, some of the soldiers set fire to the eaves, while others stood around waiting with their guns to shoot anyone who might try to escape. Shewareged could hear the screams from the boys and girls as the roof of the main house collapsed in flames and the home became an inferno. But surrounded by armed soldiers, the terrified mother could do nothing. All five of Seifu's brothers and sisters were burned to death; all that remained was the jawbone of one of his sisters. Gallina's soldiers then moved on to the next homestead on their list.

Later in life Seifu emigrated to America, where in 2016, much older but still distraught as he recalled the horror that befell his family, he tearfully told his story to a stunned audience in Texas.[31]

The Martyrdom of Bishop Pétros

During 1936 the war was raging not only in the Rift Valley, but also in the central region of Shewa, in Wello, and in Begémdir in the north (see Map 1), where the principal Ethiopian military commanders were the three sons of *Li'ul-Ras* Kassa. The *Ras* himself, as noted earlier, had left the country with the emperor and was currently in Jerusalem.

The forces of his eldest son, military commander *Dejazmach* Wendwessen, headquartered at the holy city of Lalibela, were continuing the fight, spearheading the resistance in the surrounding region of Lasta. Meanwhile Aberra, the best-known of the Kassa brothers, was with his battalions at the Kassa stronghold of Fiché, the capital of Selalé, near the monastery of Debre Libanos. Likewise, Asfawessen continued to command the Begémdir army, headquartered in the town of Debre Tabor. However, in due course he came down to Shewa and joined forces with Aberra.[32]

A HAPPY TRIUMPH

The Italians had managed to win some degree of cooperation from the Egyptian archbishop (who was empowered to ordain Ethiopian priests under an arrangement with the Egyptian Orthodox Church dating back more than a thousand years), albeit with limited enthusiasm on his part. However, Graziani was aware that his acquiescence counted for little, for Qérillos was a relative newcomer to the Ethiopian Church, and in real terms had little authority. Of the senior Ethiopian clergy still in Ethiopia the most influential was Bishop Pétros (Peter).

Highly respected as a man of God, the bishop was known for his honesty and piety. Born Hayle Maryam in 1882 in Fiché, Bishop Pétros received traditional Church education at the monastery of Debre Libanos, where he became a monk at the age of 24.[33] He lived and taught in various monasteries in Ethiopia until 1927, when he became *memhir* of the church of Marqos (St Mark), Addis Ababa, in the palace compound of the future emperor Haile Selassie, of whom he was father confessor. In 1928 he was appointed bishop of Eastern Ethiopia, based in the town of Dessie.

Dr Shashka knew Bishop Pétros as 'an example of wisdom, of patriotism and Christian virtue'.[34] The prelate had fearlessly denounced the Italian invasion and the indiscriminate killing of civilians. Furthermore, despite being requested by the Italians to endorse the military occupation in return for a comfortable life in Addis Ababa, he had refused, preferring to remain in fasting and prayer at Debre Libanos.

On 26 July, as several resistance armies under a combination of military and Patriot commanders invaded Addis Ababa in a daring attempt to recapture the city from the Italians, Bishop Pétros appeared in the city to help Aberra and Asfawessen rally the Ethiopians. Aberra sent his men to bring the cleric back to safety. However, shrugging them off and saying that in any case he had come to die, Pétros walked into the city centre in his robes, where, carrying his cross, the brave bishop strode directly in front of the cathedral of St George where the Italian forces were massed.[35] The Ethiopian attackers were repulsed, and the attempt failed. Aberra and Asfawessen managed to escape, but Bishop Pétros was arrested.

Graziani was furious, for the attempt to recapture Addis Ababa shook the Italians, who were always worried about their vulnerability to attack, since the topography of the city and its surroundings made it difficult to defend. The only Ethiopian of any significance in his hands after the flight of the commanders was Bishop Pétros, so the viceroy had him interrogated and charged with treason.

Adopting tactics he had tried several years before with the Libyan resistance leader Omar Mokhtar, Graziani gave the bishop an ultimatum: he should collaborate with the Italians, and in return for accepting Italian hegemony and denouncing the Patriots as bandits, he would be allowed to live in comfort at the expense of Italy. However, the viceroy was no more successful with Pétros than he had been with Omar Mokhtar, for the fearless bishop refused: 'The cry of my countrymen who died due to your nerve-gas and terror machinery will never allow my conscience to accept your ultimatum. How can I face my God if I turn a blind eye to such a crime?'[36]

Dr Shashka, who was in Addis Ababa at the time, noted that the address of the fettered bishop at the tribunal, which was held in public, deeply impressed the Italian officers, and even Graziani himself. 'His accusations were as grave as the dignity with which he knowingly faced immediate death.'[37] Ciro Poggiali, the Italian correspondent based in Ethiopia for *Corriere della Sera*, could also not help admiring the prelate's calm and dignified stance, noting in his secret diary, 'He defended himself well, bravely, before a tribunal [consisting of members] clearly inferior to himself.'[38]

Giovanni Gebre-Iyesus, an Ethiopian educated in Italy and now working for the Italians as secretary of the Special Court in Addis Ababa, actually refused to act as translator in the bishop's tribunal, pointing out that Pétros was only following the principles of his religious beliefs and thus should not be executed. He also warned that the death of such a venerated figure would inevitably backfire on the Italians.[39]

According to Haile Selassie's Russian military adviser Fyodor Konovalov, Graziani sent an officer from the offices of the Governo Generale in Addis Ababa to tell the tribunal to shoot the bishop, to which the tribunal lawyer replied that the case was still proceeding, and that so far he had found no legal grounds for execution. However, it was not long before a curt response arrived from the viceroy: 'Shoot the Abun [Bishop] at once.'[40]

A HAPPY TRIUMPH

Thus it was that on 30 July 1936, in front of a stunned and silent crowd, the death sentence was passed, and Bishop Pétros was paraded before a firing squad of eight *carabinieri*.[41] The imposing ascetic, 'with no sign of emotion and with great dignity', raised his cross to bless 'first his judges then the crowd'.[42] Tradition has it that his last words asked God to give his people the strength to resist the Italian invaders. Bishop Pétros died before a horrified public, his speech cut short by a hail of bullets.

Graziani proudly reported the bishop's execution to Rome, taking the opportunity to assure Minister Lessona that the policy of summary execution of captives was being vigorously enforced: 'All prisoners have been shot.'[43]

The impact on Ethiopians of the execution in cold blood of such a distinguished and revered prelate was massive—in some ways eclipsing even the horrors of the invasion. The Italians had created the nation's first 20th-century martyr, and throughout Ethiopia Graziani's name would live in infamy. The shock of the execution of Bishop Pétros did more to expand and strengthen resistance to the Italian occupation than anything the Patriot leaders could have done.

It comes therefore as no surprise that, in his seminal work on the resistance in the province of Gojjam, the Ethiopian scholar Sultene Seyoum found that by mid-1936 there were Ethiopian clergy actively promoting the ideology of the resistance. In response to the Italian High Command referring to the Ethiopian resistance as *shiftas*, i.e., bandits, one Tigrayan monk, Father Tesfa-Maryam, spoke out against the Italians. Echoing the sentiments of Bishop Pétros, he said, 'One who is called a *shifta* is one who plunders, kills and sheds Christian blood. The Ethiopian people cannot be called *shifta*. It is you who have left your country and shed Christian blood who are *shiftas*.'[44] It is not known for certain what became of Father Tesfa-Maryam, but according to one notable source, *Dejazmach* Mengesha, soon after this speech the Italians buried him alive.[45]

Desecration in the South-East

In August and September 1936, centres of Christianity in the districts around Harar continued to be subjected to wanton abuse and destruction. Reports reaching England from Harar indicated that Jijiga (see Map 4) was receiving particularly rough treatment: 'The Ethiopian church at Jijiga has become a lodging house for white soldiers, and people see the native women dragged in there by force at night. The graveyard, which is near the church, has been destroyed by the Italian soldiers and covered with sand.'[46]

This was the church where Graziani had fallen into a well in early May—an incident said to have exacerbated his hatred for the Ethiopian clergy. Perhaps that experience, in the context of the role of the Ethiopian Church as the official religion of Ethiopia, and thus its inevitable identification with the national spirit, made that church a particular target for persecution. In any case, according to accounts reaching London from the Ethiopian consulate in Djibouti, 'At Jigjiga no Ethiopian can pray because the Italians believe their prayers are for the kingdom of Ethiopia.'[47]

By late September it was being reported that the Italians had converted the Ethiopian church at the market centre of Dagabour in Harar diocese into a customs house.[48]

An Apostolic Visitor

By the end of July 1936 Viceroy Graziani was reassuring Rome that civilians suspected of being non-compliant were still being shot: 'Inexorable repressive measures have been effected against all population guilty, if not of complicity, at least absence of reaction [to the Ethiopian attempt to re-take Addis Ababa].'[49] He was also intensifying his attacks on communities he viewed as actual or potential obstacles to annexation of the Ethiopian state: the 'Amhara aristocracy', educated Ethiopians, and the Ethiopian Church, which he claimed harboured soothsayers who wielded great influence on the general public, with their predictions about the impending demise of the Italian administration.

Graziani's persecution of the Ethiopian Church not only played into the hands of the senior Italian clergy; it also commanded the attention of the Holy See. Apparently assuming that the 'obstacle' of the Ethiopian clergy was now being taken care of, the pope chose that moment—early September 1936—to make a critical decision.

He would send an apostolic visitor on a follow-up mission to Ethiopia for the next step: to 'ascertain on the spot the spiritual needs of the peoples and to work out a practical programme' of evangelisation by Italian Catholic clerics.

It has been suggested that despite his infamous public celebration of Mussolini's apparent victory, Pope Pius XI was actually still unhappy and uncomfortable with the attack on Ethiopia. If, as primate of Italy, he was indeed concerned about the brutality of the invasion that his senior clergy had so enthusiastically supported, and the death of hundreds of thousands of Ethiopians in the process, and if he was really beginning to regret his alliance with Mussolini, this was another opportunity for him to make a measured response. He could have selected a moderate cleric—at least one not overtly Fascist—in order to show some degree of compassion and to distance the universal Catholic Church as far as possible from the swash-buckling Blackshirts. However, his choice was the pro-Fascist Cardinal Archbishop Giovanni Maria Emilio Castellani,[50] who was charged with drawing up a plan for what the Vatican referred to as 'the new missionary enterprise under the new circumstances', and with convincing the Fascists that the Catholic Church would give them its enthusiastic support.[51] It is clear that Castellani was to play a critical role in ensuring the success of the crusade, for he would be the only person in Addis Ababa in a position to ensure the maintenance of the alliance between Fascism and the Catholic Church. As it turned out, Archbishop Castellani would perform that task with consummate skill.

Monsignor Castellani was born in 1888 in the village of Civitella near Todi, Umbria. In 1910 he became a Catholic priest and by 1929 had been appointed archbishop of Rhodes.[52] However, any lingering notion that the pontiff's apostolic visitor would be an impartial assessor and rapporteur on the situation in Ethiopia and the spiritual needs of its peoples evaporated the moment he touched down in Addis Ababa. No sooner had he arrived than he started behaving as if he had been appointed archbishop of Fascism International.

Stepping onto the runway in Addis Ababa on 13 October, Castellani gave the Fascist salute to the welcoming guard of honour, and just two days later the American minister in Addis Ababa,

Cornelius Engert, an astute observer, made the following comments to the US secretary of state:

> Having made his peace with the Pope the Duce—following the example of France—will be quick to use the Church for the strengthening of Italian political influence abroad ... And after the serious setbacks the Roman Catholic Church has recently suffered in Spain and Malta it may be assumed that it will eagerly welcome a chance for expansion elsewhere. As a significant indication of the spirit animating the collaboration between the spiritual and secular powers in Ethiopia the following utterance by Mgr Castellani may be quoted: 'Italy is the country God has designated to bring to the world an ever higher civilization which will also redound to the glory of the Church. That is why God is always on our side, for he knows that Italy is worthy of assuming such a lofty mission. It will be the Empire of Rome that will carry the Cross of Christ thanks to the stupendous work of the man with that wonderful personality—the *Duce*.'[53]

In no time at all Castellani was playing a key role for Mussolini. Not only was he cooperating with the Fascist administration; he was demonstrating the total support of the Catholic Church for the ongoing military operations in Ethiopia. He was also turning a blind eye to the atrocities, and instead providing Rome with glowing reports of peace and tranquillity. Celebrating a Pontifical Mass on 26 October, the apostolic visitor again gave thanks for 'the magnificent work of Mussolini, who combines the calmest balance with the daring of a hero' in ensuring that 'it will be the Roman Empire which will carry the cross of Christ into the world'.[54]

Graziani was delighted, and the prelate wasted no time in ingratiating himself in the corridors of power in Addis Ababa, where he enjoyed all the pomp and glory befitting a member of the Fascist High Command. Across Italy cinema audiences were regaled with Mussolini's propaganda agency Film Luce's newsreels of Castellani with Graziani; Castellani at official opening ceremonies; Castellani with the local Fascist Party leader Guido Cortese; Castellani making speeches; Castellani reviewing the troops; Castellani with the Blackshirts. The archbishop of Rhodes had never received so much attention. Working hand in glove with the Fascists, he was discharging his duties to the hilt, and was having a field day enjoying Venturi's 'fruits of victory'. It did not take him long to conclude that what Africa Orientale Italiana needed was Giovanni Castellani. The apostolic visitor was in his element, and was clearly intending to stay.

6

CIVILISING ACTIONS

'I assure you nothing will happen to you.'
Marshal Graziani, addressing Aberra and
Asfawessen Kassa before their surrender and execution

By September 1936, Graziani was sowing such terror that he seemed to be finally getting the upper hand. However, all three Kassa brothers and their battalions were still holding out. Wendwessen, who had distinguished himself as a military commander during the invasion, was being subjected to incessant attacks in the district of Lasta, in the vicinity of the holy city of Lalibela. He had been sought by the Italians for months, and his army had suffered some of the worst chemical weapons bombardment that any fighting force has ever had to endure. But still the Ethiopians stood firm.

By 11 September an exasperated Graziani was insisting that General Alessandro Pirzio Biroli,[1] who had been appointed governor of the Ethiopian province designated Amhara by the Italians, step up the pressure with more ruthless measures: 'Today in the daytime the Air Force will carry out reprisals with asphyxiating gas of whatever type, on the zone in which it is probable that Wendwessen has led his armed forces, without distinction between those who have submitted and those who have not submitted.'[2]

Still not satisfied, the raging viceroy followed up with even more vitriolic orders later the same day, leaving no doubt as to what he required: 'reprisals without mercy should be effected against all districts of Lasta ... the villages must be systematically destroyed in order that the people be convinced of the inevitable necessity of abandoning their leaders ... the goal can be attained by use of all means of destruction from the air day after day, mainly using asphyxiating gases.'[3] The level of impunity in the use of chemical weapons to gas civilians was stunning. Making no attempt to hide it from the record, the day after receiving Graziani's directive, General Pirzio Biroli, a relative of Lessona with a well-earned reputation for harsh treatment of civilians, reported that seven aeroplanes had successfully carried out the required mission. He wrote, 'I have given orders ... that tomorrow morning all aircraft at the airport of Asmara should carry out bombing with *yperite* on four zones indicated as the refuge of armed men and leaders of the Lalibela and Bilbala Giyorgis garrisons.'[4]

Righteousness and Impunity

As the war continued, the atrocities carried out by the Italians went from bad to worse. Grotesque forms of torture and murder such as decapitation, skinning alive, burning heaps of wounded soldiers and civilians with flame-throwers, and tying up victims followed by suspension until they died of gangrene, were commonplace during the invasion, but after May 1936 they were carried out on a wider scale.

One of the most disturbing aspects of the war was the degree of impunity with which the Italians behaved. Smiling gleefully into the camera, they were captured by military photographers while conducting the most bestial of atrocities. Thereafter, the blood hardly dry on their hands, they would return to base to attend Holy Mass in churches such as the one they had built at the heart of their garrison at Debre Birhan.

Considering that the majority of the conscripts were young men who had never killed anyone in their life before being drafted, one can only conclude that the level of impunity they exhibited can be put down—at least to a considerable extent—to the constant refrain from the Catholic clergy that they were doing the righteous work of God. The blending of Fascism with Catholicism was intense throughout 1936. As David Kertzer puts it, 'In Italy, faith in the *Duce* was rivaling faith in Jesus Christ.' In August, shortly after the execution of Bishop Pétros, the Fascist Federation of the central Italian town of Ascoli Piceno recommended in its periodical: 'All that the *Duce* affirms is true ... After reciting the "Credo" in God every morning, recite the "Credo" in Mussolini.'[5]

Meanwhile, in Rome, Pius XI, whose secretary of state Eugenio Pacelli was presumably well informed of what was going on in Ethiopia, did not speak out against the abandonment by Graziani and his military of any vestige of Christian principles. The sustained silence of both the Holy See and the Vatican as one war crime was followed by another gave the inevitable impression that neither the excesses of the Italians nor the sufferings of the Ethiopians making their last-ditch stand to defend their homeland and their families were of any concern.

From other parts of Christendom the plight of the Ethiopians was met with more sympathy, though little tangible support. In a visit to the head of the Anglican Church, Archbishop Cosmo Lang, Emperor Haile Selassie said, 'The reason for leaving our country and the crimes being committed daily against our people even after our exile, are not, I trust, unknown to you. We seek God's guidance in our search for true justice. In this, we beg you not to forget us in your prayers.' 'After we had requested this audience with you', the sovereign went on, 'we heard that the Pope of Rome had declared [the war's] legitimacy and recognised the Italian occupation of Ethiopia.'

The archbishop offered a diplomatic response, suggesting that the Vatican was not aware of the situation in Ethiopia: 'The truth has eluded the pope, because of intense propaganda activities by the regime.' Equally diplomatically, the emperor chose not to challenge the archbishop on that score, but reflected, 'For the last 3,000 years Ethiopia has been struggling against paganism. It is a sad commentary that today it is denied its own freedom by another Christian people.' At that point the archbishop's diplomacy turned to embarrassment:

'That is a question which has deeply affected my conscience. I beg you not to rub salt into it.'[6]

The House of Abo

Back in Ethiopia, not only was Graziani conducting exemplary repression against Ethiopian civilians; he was also extending his pogrom against the Ethiopian Church. As noted earlier, after St Tekle Haymanot, the most venerated Ethiopian saint was, and still is, *Abba* (Father) Gebre Menfes Qiddus ('Servant of the Holy Spirit'), also known affectionately as Abo.

Thought to have arrived in Ethiopia in the early medieval period, this saintly monk acquired a reputation for living in harmony with the wild animals of the forest, and was much sought after as a healer of the sick. His reputation is a reminder of the emphasis traditionally placed by the Ethiopian Church on caring for the environment.

Gebre Menfes Qiddus lived in relative isolation in two separate elevated locations: a well-wooded hill named Midr Kebd north-west of Lake Zway, one of the great lakes of the Rift Valley, and a site some fifty kilometres to the north at the top of Ziqwala mountain, an extinct volcano surmounted by a crater lake that is regarded as one of Ethiopia's most sacred sites, and which featured on the world map drawn by Fra Mauro between 1448 and 1459. In both locations are ancient monasteries and churches consecrated to the saint (see Map 6).

At the monastery of Midr Kebd, the Italians conducted one of the Italian occupation's first systematic and large-scale attacks on a major institution of the Ethiopian Church. Father Mikaél (Michael), a 30-year-old monk at Midr Kebd at the time, was walking near the monastery when he saw hundreds of soldiers heading for the monastery, led by three Italian officers on horseback.

Sufficiently quick-witted to melt away into the undergrowth near the road, Father Michael was able to avoid being seen and make good his escape. The soldiers, who were members of a Somali or Libyan Muslim battalion under Italian command, invaded the monastery grounds and attacked the monks while they were at prayer in the monastery church of Gebre Menfes Qiddus.[7] They burst into the

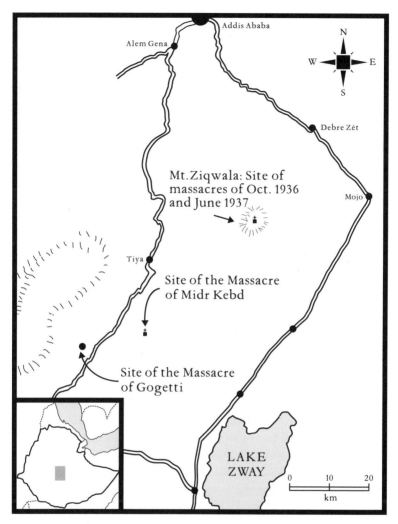

Map 6: Lake Zway, Mount Ziqwala and Midr Kebd (based on *Ethiopia: Around Ziquala*, map)

church, where they killed the elderly monks, who, in the words of Father Mikaél, 'were not young enough to be able to jump out of the windows'.[8]

As we shall see, for the purposes of massacring Ethiopian Christian clergy, Graziani's strategy was generally to employ Muslim soldiers, both irregulars and regulars, and the attack at Midr Kebd was no exception. Indeed, in predominantly Muslim areas the Italian military also often encouraged Muslim civilians to attack Christian settlements. However, the next major attack on the House of Abo would be carried out by the Italian Air Force in an even greater onslaught.

The principal church of Gebre Menfes Qiddus, which typically accommodated around 200 monks and 100 nuns, was situated at the monastery of Mount Ziqwala (see Map 6). The first attack on that monastery on the mountain, in another case of exemplary repression, is well known to have been carried out by the Regia Aeronautica, and Viceroy Graziani made no attempt to hide it from Rome. In a report on 21 October 1936 he stated that he had ordered 'reprisals' on 'the line of villages' from Mount Ziqwala across the plain in a north-easterly direction to the Mojo–Adama railway line (which the Italians had commandeered), and that the attack on the monastery of Ziqwala, which included gassing the inhabitants, was a collective punishment for clergymen having given succour to the Ethiopian defence forces:

> Twenty-five airplanes took part in the action, amongst which were ten bombers. Villages were destroyed first with explosive and incendiary bombs and then with yperite. Particularly two large villages, one situated at the top [the monastery of Ziqwala] and the other half-way up Mt Ziqwala [the church of Menber Maryam] were almost destroyed by the action of the bombers. In those villages are the two well-known monasteries whose prior some days ago presented himself at Mojo with several hundred priests to make a solemn act of submission, but during the recent attacks they have given asylum to the rebels.[9]

Graziani was as good as his word, for the Air Force did not limit itself to explosive and incendiary bombs in its onslaught. On 21 October, the 44th Group of the Regia Aeronautica dropped on the villages of Ziqwala no less than four C-500T bombs, each loaded with the chemical agent yperite, producing a total of some 850 kg of the substance, which rained down corrosive drops that penetrated clothing and produced potentially fatal internal lesions.[10]

The bombing destroyed numerous homesteads, the explosions and the gas indiscriminately killing men, women and children.

Dr Mikre-Sellassie Gebre-Ammanuel quotes an eyewitness who claimed that as many as 1,800 people died in the attacks on the Ziqwala settlements in October 1936.[11]

Reactions in Rome

By October 1936 the war was one year old, albeit that six months earlier Mussolini had announced to the world that hostilities in Ethiopia had come to an end. Although the Ethiopian armies had been reduced in size and effectiveness, the war was still being prosecuted on multiple fronts, and the Regia Aeronautica was operating on an even larger scale, with more aeroplanes than before. The persecution of Ethiopian civilians, particularly the clergy, had escalated beyond previous levels, and outrages were being committed by the Italians on a daily basis. Thus the question inevitably arises: What was the reaction of the Roman Catholic Church to these developments? Did the Italian episcopate begin to have second thoughts about its support for the military adventure that had led to such carnage?

There were no second thoughts; on the contrary, the reaction of the senior clergy was calm and positive. Since Archbishop Schuster's declaration twelve months before that the invasion was an assignment from God, and that the 'gallant' Italian army was 'opening the gates of Ethiopia to the Catholic faith and Roman civilisation',[12] there had been no abatement of the rhetoric. Since January 1936 the Holy See had fallen in line with the Italian episcopate, a contemporary commentator writing that Pius XI 'has thrown his weight on the side of the totalitarian leaders, and he has felt that the imperial policy of Italy must mean an advance for his own Church in the conquered territories'.[13]

Eugène Cardinal Tisserant, a Vatican official and an old friend of the pope, who had been appointed head of the Congregation for the Oriental Churches,[14] was now sufficiently confident to specify more precisely what Cardinal Schuster's reference to 'opening the gates' actually meant: 'With the conquest of the empire a vast field is opening to Catholic Missions whose work has hitherto been hampered in Abyssinia by the unyielding opposition of the Monophysite clergy ... The work of the Catholic missionary will nobly go hand in hand with the civilising actions which Italy, under the Fascist government, has already begun.'[15] But Tisserant's assumption that the obstacle of Ethiopia's 'unyielding' clergy had been removed was premature. Although Graziani still had the Ethiopian Church in his sights, and hundreds of churches had been destroyed or damaged, the clergy were not yet liquidated; the 'civilising actions' referred to by Cardinal Tisserant had yet to run their course.

The 'civilising actions' were, however, having a profound impact, for as one resistance leader was shot and replaced by another, the enthusiasm of Graziani's troops in impressing upon the Ethiopians the merits of 'Italian civilisation' during the second half of 1936 knew no bounds. Summary executions were held daily, the Regia Aeronautica bombed and strafed the countryside, and, when not being bombed, the villages were sprayed with poison gas. 'Burn and destroy all that is possible to burn and destroy,' the viceroy had instructed his generals in writing at the beginning of 1936,[16] and by late October, amidst an orgy of chemical weapons bombardment, the Italian military was depopulating extensive tracts of land in highland Ethiopia, as Graziani exhorted his forces, 'We must continue the inexorable work of destruction of everything.'[17]

The Martyrdom of Bishop Mikaél

Bishop Pétros was not the only senior Ethiopian cleric to suffer the wrath of the occupying forces for his strict adherence to his faith. On 3 December 1936, in another chilling case of exemplary repression, the Italians executed Mikaél (Michael), the second of Ethiopia's four bishops, in Gore, the principal town of the province of Illubabor in the west of Ethiopia (Map 7).[18]

Bishop Mikaél, who was born in Gondar, and known as *Papas ZeAzéb* of Ethiopia, was a distinguished and popular ecclesiastic of the Ethiopian Church. When the nation's four bishops were appointed, some seven years before the invasion, Bishop Mikaél had been assigned to western Ethiopia, covering Illubabor, Wellega and part of Kaffa. When he arrived in Gore two years later, he was warmly received, and the five years he spent there endeared him to the local population.[19]

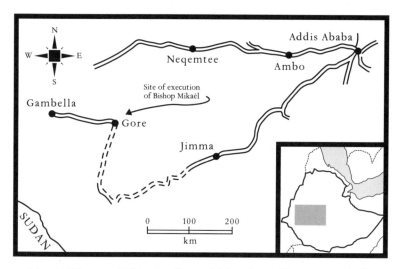

Map 7: Western Ethiopia: Gore, Addis Alem (© Ian Campbell)

When the Italians attacked Ethiopia, the bishop, who by then was quite elderly, spoke publicly against the invasion, and advocated resistance. When the military commander *Ras* Imru arrived in Gore to reorganise his forces for a fresh attack on the Italians, Bishop Mikaél reportedly wanted to join him, but was persuaded to stay behind. Eventually the Italian army arrived at Gore and Bishop Mikaél was arrested by the commander, Colonel (later, General) Giuseppe Malta, on Tuesday, 24 November 1936, and imprisoned.[20]

Despite the residents of Gore pleading for his release, Malta insisted that the bishop cooperate with the invading forces and persuade the local people to submit to the Italians. After a week in prison, he refused to cooperate and instead publicly exhorted the population to resist, following which he was subjected to a hasty trial at which he was charged with refusing to submit to the occupying forces and with excommunicating Ethiopians who went over to the Italians. He was then taken out and shot near the church of St George.[21]

'I Assure You Nothing Will Happen to You'

On 10 December, military commander Wendwessen Kassa, cornered in a cave by enemy forces, finally surrendered. However, the Italian terms of surrender proved to be hollow promises for a few hours later General Pirzio Biroli telegraphed Graziani announcing with characteristic 'lively satisfaction' that Wendwessen had been shot in cold blood at 2.30 am.[22]

Graziani had been negotiating the surrender of Aberra and Asfawessen Kassa, and following the execution of their brother Wendwessen, the cunning viceroy, pretending that Wendwessen was still alive, wrote to Aberra from Addis Ababa, guaranteeing him safe passage:

> Now I tell you to surrender and I assure you nothing will happen to you. You have fought for your country, and for this no-one will condemn you ... I have sent a message to your brother Wendwessen to come here. As you know he has already surrendered at Lalibela. After a few days he will be here. I will write to you when he arrives. Then you should come to Addis Ababa without delay.[23]

This was followed by an equally enticing offer from the much-feared General Ruggero Tracchia, one of Graziani's right-hand men and commander of the 2nd Eritrean Brigade in Aberra's fiefdom of Selalé, the district of Debre Libanos: 'I was glad to see from a message sent by you about your having concluded an agreement with Graziani. If you are really a peaceful man, assemble your soldiers at Fiché and receive me at a peaceful parade; and if you comply with this, I assure you on behalf of my Government that your life will be spared.'[24]

Astonishingly, despite the knowledge that the Italians normally executed Ethiopian soldiers after they had surrendered, Aberra, clearly unaware of Wendwessen's fate, took the Italian generals on their honour. Knowing he could not defeat them at that time, and worried about the inevitable slaughter of the civilian population resident in the vicinity if he continued fighting, he made the painful decision to surrender, and Asfawessen followed suit.

The two brothers were taken to Tracchia's camp at Shinkurt, on the plain near Debre Libanos, where the general invited them into his tent, offered them chairs and served them coffee. But no sooner had Tracchia stepped outside than *carabinieri* came and took them back to nearby Fiché. At 7 pm, in the town centre, military commanders Aberra and Asfawessen Kassa were executed by firing squad.[25]

Graziani was happy to claim full responsibility. 'In pursuance of my orders they were shot at dusk in the square of Fiché,' he announced proudly to Lessona. 'Selalé situation liquidated.'[26]

The execution of military commanders of the stature of the Kassa brothers had a devastating impact, for it showed beyond doubt that the Ethiopians would gain nothing by submitting. They took the view that if they were going to be killed anyway, they might as well die fighting. Thus the enduring effect of Graziani's policy of unrestrained terror was an escalation of the resistance—a rod for his own back, and one that would eventually lead to his removal. Nonetheless, in the short term, with more troops arriving to reinforce the battalions guarding Addis Ababa, the Italians assumed that the policy of exemplary repression was working. And on the international front, the emperor was losing support at Geneva; member states of the League of Nations were beginning to recognise Italian hegemony over Ethiopia.

Although the Kassa brothers had been executed and *Ras* Imru captured, Ethiopian battalions under the command of *Ras* Desta Damtew, the emperor's son-in-law, still faced the enemy on several different fronts in the lakes region, south of Addis Ababa. Having sent several commanders to surround *Ras* Desta, Graziani now turned his attention to his unarmed targets: the clergy of the Ethiopian Church and what he called its 'wizards and soothsayers'. The Italian rank and file, conditioned as they were by the barrage of propaganda denigrating the Ethiopians, were only too happy to oblige by doing all they could to liquidate the 'heretics'.

The Apostolic Visitor Returns to Rome

By the end of December 1936 Archbishop Castellani was packing his bags as he wound up his assignment, and in January he arrived back in Rome. Given his enthusiastic involvement in the affairs of the Governo Generale and the Fascist Party throughout his sojourn in Addis Ababa, and his clear intention to return, it comes as no surprise that he painted a very positive picture of the situation in Ethiopia. In the presence of several cardinals. including the secretary of the Congregation for the Propagation of the Faith, he reported: 'In the

HOLY WAR

missionary aspect there is now true freedom, great peace, a beautiful conquest. Ethiopia now elevates its eyes to heaven in the hope of a holy future. This was bound to come, for it had been predetermined by Holy Providence.' He seems not to have mentioned the massacres of the Ethiopian clergy, or the murder of Bishop Mikaél, which had taken place on his watch. However, he made an indirect reference to their elimination, stating that although the Ethiopian clergy had represented in the past 'an impassable obstacle' to the evangelisation of Ethiopia, he now expected that with 'the changed circumstances' the future 'will fulfil our hopes'.[27]

The archbishop had fulfilled his terms of reference. His reports had sanitised and sacralised the outrages of the Italian military: all was sweetness and light. Yet the fact is that around a quarter of a million Ethiopians had been slaughtered during the 'take no prisoners' war of invasion (see Appendix I), and thousands more were now dying in the war of occupation, in what Graziani himself called 'reprisals without mercy'. In addition, as we have seen, while Castellani was in Ethiopia, a high-ranking Ethiopian military commander was gassed out of his redoubt, promised safe passage, then executed; two more commanders were tricked into surrendering after being promised safe passage in the name of the king of Italy, then executed in public in cold blood; two of the four bishops of the Ethiopian Church were executed in public for refusing to endorse Italian hegemony; and in the south the war was still raging, with several of Graziani's battalions heavily engaged with *Ras* Desta's armies.

In addition, numerous attacks on the Ethiopian Church were under way during Castellani's visit, including massacres of the clergy at several important religious centres, and yet, despite deploying more than a hundred thousand soldiers in Ethiopia, the Italians were at that time in control of no more than a fraction of the country. Nonetheless, the archbishop was clearly endorsing the invasion, the occupation and the elimination of the Ethiopian clergy as the fruits of a sacred mission. He was also preparing the ground for his own appointment as apostolic delegate for Italian East Africa.

It is not altogether surprising that Castellani remained tight-lipped about the war raging in Ethiopia, for Mussolini had managed to perpetuate the myth that it had ended on 5 May 1936, and his propaganda office was determined to maintain that illusion. On 3 February 1937, the same day that information came through about a battle in which several Italian officers and more than two hundred of their troops had been killed, a dispatch arrived in Addis Ababa from Rome requiring every journalist to sign a declaration saying they would not transmit anything that might suggest that fighting was continuing, since, as Christopher Duggan remarks, 'the official line in Italy was that "the war is over"'.[28]

In any case, Castellani's strategy worked. Three months later, he would be back in Ethiopia as apostolic delegate, accompanied by a large contingent of missionaries.[29]

Meanwhile, Graziani was not satisfied with the pogrom against the Ethiopian Church, for at the heart of that Church lay one of her most illustrious institutions, as yet untouched: Debre Libanos. The viceroy had eliminated the monastery's principal supporters in the form of Bishop Pétros and the Kassa brothers, who had also been three of Ethiopia's most senior military commanders, but the monastery's associations with the national spirit and the imperial establishment remained, along with the clergy and the 'wizards and soothsayers' whom the viceroy had in his sights. The execution of the bishops, the destruction of churches and monasteries, and the operations against the clergy had not succeeded in terrorising the majority of the Ethiopian episcopate and their flock into submission; in fact, in many cases it had strengthened their resolve. Thus, 'It was necessary to pull off a coup to lead to their submission.'[30] And that coup would be the decapitation of the Ethiopian Church through the destruction of the monastery of Debre Libanos.

However, even Graziani did not have an entirely free hand. He needed a reason to go to such an extreme, because Lessona was looking for an excuse to have him removed, and any erratic or outrageous behaviour on the viceroy's part that could be seen to be inflaming the resistance rather than reducing it would have played into the minister's hands. Thus Graziani needed to come up with a convincing reason for destroying Debre Libanos, which would mean the slaughter of a large number of defenceless civilians. Unfortunately, that excuse was not long in coming.

7

TERROR IN THE CAPITAL

'He who seeks to strike terror in others is himself more in fear.'
Claudius Claudianus, Latin poet, AD 370–404

In December 1936 a group of Ethiopian government officials in the emperor's entourage in exile in England were seeking activists to publicly strike against the occupying forces.[1] The position of Emperor Haile Selassie in the League of Nations was precarious, for, as noted earlier, several countries were beginning to recognise the Italian military occupation as annexation. Indeed, the sovereign's men expected a public attack on the Italian High Command to convince wavering members of the League that the war was not over, and that the Italians were not in control of Ethiopia.

Three of the exiles were at the heart of the plot: Lorenzo Ta'izaz, an Eritrean lawyer who was the emperor's right-hand man; his foreign minister, Hiruy Welde-Sillassé; and *Blattén Géta* Éfrém Tewelde-Medhin, who had previously served as consul in London, and had been relocated to Paris after the arrival of the emperor in London. *Bejirond* Letyibelu Gebré, a wealthy and well-connected former courtier and military commander who had fought at the Battle of Maychew, and who had remained in Ethiopia, was chosen to be the local coordinator.

Simi'on Adefris, a young Catholic Ethiopian businessman in Addis Ababa, played a critical role in introducing to Letyibelu a small group of young radicals who had been plotting for some time to strike against the Governo Generale. This group of urban intellectuals—a Catholic, an Orthodox Christian, a Protestant and a Baha'i, most likely assisted by an Armenian who had fought in the resistance against the Turks during the Armenian genocide—typified the small but increasingly well-educated sector of Ethiopian society sponsored and encouraged by the emperor, who believed that his programme of modernisation could be achieved only by bringing into the civil service meritocrats to offset the power of the feudal lords.

Years ahead of their time, the multi-cultural group of Simi'on Adefris and his friends were shocked by the apartheid system being introduced into Ethiopia, and the barbaric behaviour of the Italian military, which was so gross that even young Ethiopians who might otherwise have attempted to come to terms with the invaders often ended up joining the resistance.

Two Eritrean members of the group, named Moges Asgedom and Abriha Deboch, were recruited by Letyibelu to lead the attack on the High Command. As Italian colonial subjects, they were working for Graziani at the Governo Generale, but Moges was actually an Ethiopian loyalist, and Abriha was a disgruntled employee who, owing to Rome's increasingly harsh racial policies, had turned against his employers. Unbeknown to them, he had become a double agent.

The Massacre of Addis Ababa

The opportunity for the plotters to make the strike came on Friday, 19 February 1937 (Yekatit 12 in the Ethiopian calendar), at a public alms-giving ceremony conducted by Graziani to commemorate the birth of the Prince of Naples. The event, to which Ethiopians deemed to be poor and deserving were invited, was held at the seat of the Governo Generale: the former emperor's palace in the Sidist Kilo area of Addis Ababa.

During the ceremony, while Graziani was addressing the crowd, the two young Eritreans, who were on duty as members of Graziani's entourage, left the dais and threw several hand grenades at their Italian employers, with the support of a number of accomplices. No senior officials of the Governo Generale died, although a few, including Graziani, were seriously injured. Despite his injuries, which triggered the temporary appointment of his deputy, Graziani remained as viceroy. But the Italians slaughtered almost all of the 3,000 Ethiopians at the ceremony, including many clergymen.[2] Shortly afterwards the Fascist Party authorised further reprisals in which thousands more innocent Ethiopians died, including a substantial proportion of the most highly educated Ethiopians, and thousands more were injured, or died in prison. In the evening of 19 February, the Fascist Party federal secretary, Guido Cortese, unleashed the Blackshirts of the 6th 'Tevere' Division, joined by Italian civilians, for a repeat performance of the three-day massacre of Tripoli, which they carried out with a terrible zeal. They were given carte blanche—the medieval three days of unrestricted murder and pillage—and were even told which areas of the city they should destroy. Over several days more than 4,000 houses were looted and burned, while those residents fortunate enough not to be locked inside were hunted through the streets and beaten, shot, bayoneted or clubbed to death, thrown over bridges or dragged to their deaths behind vehicles. It is estimated that a total of around 19,000 Ethiopian civilians died in the massacre of Addis Ababa, an event known thereafter as *Yekatit 12*.[3]

No families, regardless of their religion, were allowed to bury, or even attend to, their dead; most of the bodies were incinerated by the Italians in public; others were thrown into rivers or drinking-water wells. Thousands more civilians were rounded up and held in detention camps and prisons in and around the city, in which many died.

The massacre of Addis Ababa, which was authorised by the Italian administration, was the largest single crime against humanity committed by the Italians in Ethiopia, and would never be forgotten. Carried out with an almost total disregard for human life, it was also the deadliest onslaught by invaders under Catholic command on the capital city of an Orthodox Christian country since the sack of Constantinople during the Fourth Crusade of 1204.

While the massacre of Addis Ababa was under way, the Italians killed unknown numbers of Ethiopians in parallel massacres in the nation's secondary towns, wherever Blackshirts were garrisoned.

They also interned several thousand men, women and children in concentration camps in Italian Somaliland and Eritrea.

The Burning of St George's Cathedral

One of the most spectacular events during the massacre of Addis Ababa, which at the time was largely overshadowed by the scale and horror of the slaughter, was the attempt by the Italians to burn down St George's Cathedral. The burning was organised by the Italian authorities and the aim was to destroy a symbol of the spirit of the nation and the very heart of the monarchy. The Orthodox cathedral was a magnificent edifice. Founded by Emperor Menelik and rebuilt by his daughter, the Empress Zewditu, St George's was truly a royal church, for this was where Emperor Haile Selassie had been crowned in 1930 with great pomp and pageantry before representatives of several of the world's heads of state.

In an act of homage to his revered predecessor, Emperor Haile Selassie had had an equestrian statue of Emperor Menelik cast and mounted on a plinth in the centre of the piazza in front of the cathedral, creating a magnificent focal point for the city centre.

The demolition of the statue, carried out by order of the Italian minister for the colonies, Alessandro Lessona, had already outraged the Ethiopians, but that desecration would pale beside the destruction of the cathedral, which would symbolise the end of the supremacy of the Ethiopian Church and its embodiment of the spirit of national resistance to the invaders. The Blackshirts of the 6th 'Tevere' Division, who had sailed from Italy with the great icon of the Mother of Christ, were determined to witness the end of St George's. Thus, in the evening of Friday, 19 February 1937, at the height of the massacre of Addis Ababa, an eager and excited crowd of militiamen, regular soldiers, *carabinieri* and Italian civilians waited expectantly to witness the spectacle of Menelik's great church being turned into a flaming torch.

There was, however, another reason for the hysteria of the Italians, and particularly for the older generation: defiling the cathedral and razing it to the ground would also help to bring closure to Italy's open wound, for they knew that it had been built to give thanks for the Ethiopian victory against the previous unprovoked invasion by the Italian army four decades before, at the Battle of Adwa, in 1896. Whenever Italians passed Menelik Square, they were reminded of the shame of that battle—their bête noire.

Furthermore, the cathedral had been consecrated to St George, the patron saint of Ethiopian sovereigns, on whose commemoration day the battle had taken place. And the paintings adorning the interior included a depiction of the battle, overseen by the saint, together with portraits of Emperor Menelik and the Empress Taytu. Finally, and ironically, the engineer employed to oversee the construction had been an Italian, Sebastino Castagna, who had been taken prisoner after the battle, but liked Ethiopia so much that he chose to stay on in the service of the sovereign, and married into the Ethiopian royal family.

However, before the ritual destruction, the Italians had business to conduct: pillage. This was normal Italian practice before destroying churches, and the procedure was well established. They had discovered that in addition to the artefacts to be seen in the cathedral itself, in the crypt below was a collection of valuable works of art, codices and other treasures.[4] That night was *carta bianca*, so, surging forward, the mob crossed the portals to run amok inside, seizing whatever they could get their hands on, while others organised military trucks to transport the plunder. The loot was enormous; Dr Shashka reported that they needed seven or eight trucks 'to carry the silver and gold vessels, the precious crosses, the prelate's staves and the valuable religious paintings and manuscripts'.[5]

Meanwhile, other trucks arrived loaded with drums of petrol. Some were carried into the church and stacked up against the walls; the soldiers opened the others and splashed the contents over the inner and outer walls. Finally, the crowd made way for the most important dignitary to arrive: the Fascist Party federal secretary, who swept into the scene in an open car with his entourage. It was time for the fire to be ceremoniously lit. The signal was given, as testified by Ciro Poggiali, 'by the order, and in the presence, of *Federale* Cortese',[6] and a group of Blackshirts standing by with incendiary bombs hurled them at the edifice.[7]

Whether any of the Italians present, who were overwhelmingly Catholic, felt a tinge of regret or shame at what they were doing, we will probably never know, but it seems unlikely, for the crowd was ecstatic. Yelling and cheering, they watched the roaring flames leap upwards, lighting the night sky. The temple of the 'schismatics and heretics' was about to fall.

Across the road from the cathedral of St George was the city's Municipality Building, situated in a large compound which the Italian authorities had turned into a detention camp earlier in the day. Full of Ethiopians who had been rounded up after the announcement of a curfew in the afternoon, it afforded a clear view of the conflagration at the cathedral. For the inmates, the desecration heightened their feeling that something unimaginable was happening. One of the detainees, who later became a well-known newspaper editor, wrote that the burning cathedral 'looked like a sunset in the west'.[8]

Inside St George's the flames were fierce, and one by one, the great windows burst outwards from the intense heat. However, as the petrol burned itself out, the flames died down, and the cheering stopped. The Italians fell silent; the attempt had failed. The sacred wall paintings were destroyed, the interior fittings were damaged, and parts of the outer walls were blackened by the flames. However, the building survived, structurally unscathed.

Guido Cortese's reaction to the fiasco at the cathedral is not on record, but we can be sure that he was driven off in a fury at the incompetence of his Blackshirts—fury that was to be exacerbated by the humiliation of seeing the job of destroying the edifice being assigned the next day to a more competent arm of the military: the Regia Aeronautica.

Did anyone die in the flames? Ciro Poggiali, who was well connected with both the Italian civil administration and the military, noted in his diary that a colonel of the Grenadiers saved the lives of fifty deacons who had been tied up with the intention of burning them alive inside the building. Whether the colonel managed to persuade the Blackshirts to release them, or ordered his regulars to do so, Poggiali does not say, but this was one of the few occasions on which a regular commander reportedly intervened to counter the actions of the Blackshirts.[9] The 65th Infantry Division of the regular army, known as the Grenadiers of Savoy, was unusual in having attached to it a Blackshirt unit—the 11th Blackshirt Battalion—so this could explain how a Grenadier colonel was in a position to restrain a Blackshirt company.

There are unconfirmed reports that during the attack on the cathedral some of the clergy of St George's *were* burned to death. The British acting consul general, who seemed to be satisfied that the story came from a credible source, informed London that he had heard from 'an Italian officer of standing' that some priests 'were left to burn in St George's Cathedral'.[10] We cannot, however, be certain that clergymen died in the fire, for the British envoy's report might refer to the deacons who actually received a last-minute reprieve, as reported by Poggiali.

Presumably concerned that news of the massacre of Addis Ababa was reaching the world's press, thus giving the impression that the Italians were not actually in control of Ethiopia, and thereby revealing that the war had not yet come to an end, Mussolini ordered the massacre to be terminated before the three days of *carta bianca* had run their course. Instructions were thus received from Rome that the 'reprisals that had been authorised' should be brought to an end at midday on Sunday, 21 February, which was 24 hours earlier than planned.[11] By that time the Regia Aeronautica had not yet carried out the previous day's orders to bomb the cathedral, and the orders were cancelled before the bombers had taken off. Although the Blackshirts continued their rampage unofficially for several more days, the Air Force obeyed the termination order, and St George's Cathedral survived.[12] Nonetheless, the Ethiopian clergy continued to be hunted down; on Sunday, 21 February, the day he ordered termination of the massacre, Mussolini instructed Graziani to make sure that 'all civil and religious suspects' were shot 'without delay'.[13]

Other City Churches: Desecration and Abuse

While control of the rural areas largely eluded the Italian military during the five years of its presence in Ethiopia, the principal urban centres—Addis Ababa and secondary towns such as Dire Dawa, Gondar and Jimma—were for the most part under Italian control.

For Graziani tight security in Addis Ababa was essential, as there were thousands of Italians now based there, and the numbers were increasing. He was always nervous about the armed Patriots in the hills around the city, and attempted to maintain the fragile peace in the capital with spies and informers. The incident of *Yekatit 12* took the Italians by surprise, and the massacre that followed demonstrated not only the barbarity of the occupiers, but also how nervous they were, behind the mask of Fascist implacability.

As Lessona discovered when Graziani had earlier resisted his instructions to demolish symbols of Ethiopian national sovereignty such as the statue of Emperor Menelik opposite St George's Cathedral, the viceroy was concerned not to do anything to trigger an uprising in Addis Ababa. He feared that he had insufficient troops to contain such a situation, which could result in extensive loss of Italian lives.

Principally for these reasons, Graziani's policy was to maintain tight control, law and order in the city, which generally precluded aerial bombing, the use of artillery within the city perimeter, and anything likely to provoke mass insurrection. This policy reflected the fact that the Ethiopians were still living in areas scattered throughout the city; the geographic aspect of the Italian apartheid policy, which would soon drive all Ethiopians to the west of their capital city, had not yet come into force.

However, although the churches of Addis Ababa were generally spared aerial attack and machine-gunning during the occupation, they suffered in a variety of ways, for political, military or historical reasons. For example, the attempt by the Blackshirts to burn down the cathedral of St George arose from its association with the Ethiopian monarchy and with the Ethiopian victory at the Battle of Adwa, and the pillage of the same edifice was part of the general looting of the city carried out by the Italians under the three days of *carta bianca*.

In fact, most, if not all, of Addis Ababa's churches, numbering approximately 25, were affected to some extent during the massacre of February 1937. Many were looted and also lost clergy to the slaughter at the palace or the pogrom that followed. A typical example is that of the church of Kidane Mihret ('Covenant of Mercy'), which adjoined the royal church of Ta'eka Negest Be'ata LeMaryam ('Seat of the King: The Entry of Mary'), commonly shortened to Be'ata Maryam, but also known as the Menelik Mausoleum, because the crypt contained the tomb of Emperor Menelik. The 23-year-old *Dyakon* Dawit (David) Gebre-Mesqel was serving both churches, which were situated within the periphery of Emperor Menelik's original palace compound, now taken over as the headquarters of the Italian regular army. Thus David, who lived in a nearby church house, was dwelling on the perimeter of a sensitive area exempted from attack.

Dyakon David was also fortunate in that not only was his church located outside the area earmarked later in the day for destruction; he had also decided not to go to the alms-giving ceremony at the Governo Generale. The clergy had been invited, and being attached to one of the most important churches of the city, he and his colleagues were expected to attend. However, David, who related his story in detail to the present author while still in the same house he lived in during the Italian occupation, was due to lead Holy Mass beginning at noon, together with two other deacons. The decision not to go to the Governo Generale saved his life.[14]

Mass was actually to be conducted at the adjoining church of Kidane Mihret, for during the invasion the emperor had arranged for the church of Be'ata Maryam to be surrounded and reinforced with stones or concrete to help protect it against possible attack, so it was not in regular use.

At the church of Kidane Mihret, David and his fellow deacons went ahead with the Mass, and David was not aware that there were disturbances in the city until he heard the sound of gunshots, at around 2 pm. The slaughter had not yet reached as far south as the Menelik palace, but unbeknown to David, the Italians had announced a curfew and were closing down shops, churches and other institutions across the city.

While Mass was in progress, David was suddenly aware of a disturbance, and watched in horror as a squadron of Blackshirts burst into the church. Brandishing guns and daggers, they started evicting the congregation, while one group forced their way into the sanctuary and ordered out the three senior priests. In the pandemonium David and his two fellow deacons were chased out at gunpoint, and ordered to stand in a corner of the churchyard.[15]

David and his colleagues stood in the compound as ordered, until half past three. Then they were told to walk across to David's house, which was a distance of about a hundred metres. It was only on leaving the compound that David learned that people were being attacked: 'On Friday afternoon there were massacres in the streets. Vehicles were driven deliberately over people, and there was shooting.'[16] The priests in the sanctuary, who had been told to stay there when the soldiers invaded the church, were sent home. Among them was Father Welde Samiyat, the highly respected head priest of Be'ata Maryam.

On Saturday night the repression squads raided the neighbourhood east of the Menelik *gibbi*, not far from David's house. There Father Welde Samiyat was upstairs in his two-storey residence when he heard a commotion outside. Opening the window, he was shocked to see that Italians had arrived and set his neighbour's house on fire. But no sooner had the prelate shown his face than he was shot— for no reason—by an Italian soldier, and fell to the floor. So died the venerable head priest of Emperor Menelik's imperial church of Be'ata Maryam. The atrocity affected *Dyakon* David deeply; seven decades later he recalled it with undiminished horror.

* * *

The massacre also had terrible impacts on the Orthodox church of St Peter and St Paul in the city's northern suburb of Gulelé, for it was outside that church's cemetery walls that thousands of corpses were unceremoniously incinerated over a period of many days, the remains being buried in mass graves. The Italians prohibited the burial of massacre victims inside the cemetery, for there were far too many bodies, and in any case part of the cemetery was used for the burial of Italian soldiers.

However, on the other side of the road was the church of St Peter and St Paul itself, and there, at the very gate of the church, the Italians were dumping dead and dying victims of the massacre, as well as regularly using the area as an execution site throughout the occupation. Burial rites were not allowed for those executed, or for massacre victims, and such policies by the Italians never ceased to shock the Ethiopians. In 1963, a clergyman who had begun serving the church in 1909/10, at the time of Emperor Menelik, and who was there during the Italian occupation, recalled how one evening during the massacre the Italians brought 26 bodies and threw them into the field around the church. The following day only 16 were found; the others had been consumed by hyenas.[17]

The church of St Rufael in Gulelé, founded at the time of Emperor Menelik, was also desecrated during the occupation.[18] During the abortive attempt by a combination of defence forces and Patriots to retake the city at the end of July 1936, some of the attackers had by chance passed by the church on their way into the city. Following the attempt, in which the Italian military managed to rout the attackers, Italian soldiers went to the church and threw hand grenades at the unsuspecting clergy, killing several of them. The military then took over the church and secured it with armed guards, some of whom threw cigarette butts into the church store, burning it down.[19]

As in the case of the church of St Peter and St Paul, during the massacre of Addis Ababa the Italians brought truck-loads of corpses to the church of St Rufael, where they forced priests to dig mass graves, each accommodating ten bodies.[20]

* * *

The military surrounded the church of Lideta St Mary, in the south-western quadrant of Addis Ababa, and closed it down. They planned to demolish it, presumably to utilise the land for some other purpose. However, by the time of liberation in 1941 their plans had not materialised, and the church survived.[21]

The church of Yeka Mikaél (St Michael), to the north-east of the city, was also closed. One of Addis Ababa's earliest churches, it was founded around the 15th century in the form of an underground rock-cut basilica.[22] The present church nearby was constructed in octagonal 'Menelik' style in 1926–7 by Menelik's daughter, the pious Empress Zewditu. During the occupation, the Italians closed the church and deported several of the priests to Mogadishu, Italian Somaliland, where they were imprisoned.[23]

The well-known church of Intotto Maryam (St Mary), where Emperor Menelik was crowned in 1889, and which is actually a few kilometres outside the city, was partially looted by the Italians, who stole Menelik's coronation crown and also removed a large cannon that he had captured during the Battle of Adwa.[24]

Being a royal church, Be'ata Maryam also attracted the unwanted attention of the Italians, particularly as it housed the tombs of Emperor Menelik, Empress Taytu, Empress Zewditu and Archbishop Matéwos, who had crowned Emperor Menelik and remained a faithful ally of the royal family until his death in 1926.[25] In addition, the wall paintings in the interior depicted not only Menelik's coronation, but also, as in St George's Cathedral, the Ethiopian victory at the Battle of Adwa.[26]

To avoid an urban uprising, Graziani did not destroy the church of Be'ata Maryam. However, he exercised tight control over it by appointing a collaborator as head of the church, which enabled the Italian authorities to neutralise its image as a symbol of the monarchy. This involved prohibiting its regular use as a church, removing the golden crown that capped the pinnacle of the dome, robbing the church of its treasures, and prohibiting visits to the royal tombs.[27]

Wilful attacks on Orthodox clergy with no conceivable military objective continued long after the massacre of Addis Ababa. Dr Shashka, the Hungarian physician, described the fate of an elderly priest who had survived the massacre, but 'against whom Fascist daggers were aimed':

> When Italian authorities became aware that he [the elderly priest] was still alive, Cortese convoked the murderers [i.e. Blackshirts] to the seat of the Fascio. Order was given to Gallini, one of the most able dagger-men, to stab the Coptic [Ethiopian] prelate. The priest was surprised in his house where some twenty or twenty-five Abyssinians, mostly women, were assembled after the massacre to offer up a devout prayer ... While the prelate was kneeling in prayer, Gallini stabbed him with the dagger from behind, and retired with the satisfaction of one who had done his job.[28]

The Vatican Reacts

News of the attack on Graziani at the Governo Generale on 19 February 1937 was reported in the Italian press within hours of the event, and on the same day Guido Cortese in Addis Ababa received authority from Rome for the reprisals. Soon, news of the carnage in Addis Ababa and the burning of St George's Cathedral appeared in the world's press, from New York to London, from Paris to Melbourne. However, international observers expecting a strong response from the Holy See to the shocking news were disappointed. The pope was silent on the issue. Indeed, his interest in Ethiopia at that time was focused on publicly recognising King Victor Emmanuel III as emperor of Ethiopia, despite the traditional papal policy of recognising such changes in wartime only after an international peace conference. Seemingly in a hurry demonstrate his loyalty, the pontiff was the second head of state to do so after Adolf Hitler, signalling that the Holy See considered Italy's actions in Ethiopia legitimate.[29]

Confident now to plan for the future in Ethiopia, as if that nation was a sea of calm, the pontiff appointed a special commission to develop a strategy. The outcome was a two-pronged approach: the Congregation for the Oriental Churches would address the issue of the 'schismatics', while the Congregation for the Propagation of the Faith would focus on converting the 'pagans'.[30]

Another Christian Enemy

Although the Italian episcopate considered the Ethiopian Church the most significant obstacle hindering the expansion of the Catholic Church in Ethiopia, the Orthodox Ethiopians were not the only Christians to be persecuted by the Italian administration in Addis Ababa. During the 1930s there was a common belief among the Catholic hierarchy that the greatest dangers to the Catholic Church were Protestantism, Judaism, Freemasonry, democracy and individual freedom of expression and conscience. Pius XI was particularly concerned about the dangers to Catholicism posed by Protestants, despite the fact that they constituted only a tiny minority of the Italian population, and in 1928 he had actually forbidden

Catholics to take part in groups that encouraged inter-faith dialogue. Thus, given the element of religious persecution embedded in the invasion and attempted annexation of Ethiopia, as well as the fear of any non-Italian influences, it is not altogether surprising that within a few months of the war of invasion becoming a war of occupation, the Governo Generale in Addis Ababa introduced a policy of closure of all non-Italian Protestant missions in Ethiopia (except for the German Hermannsburg Mission) and deportation of the missionaries.

Alfred Buxton, a well-known British Protestant missionary, was an unusual case. He had entered Ethiopia for the first time from Kenya in 1931, not long after the coronation of Emperor Haile Selassie, and stayed for four months. During that visit he was impressed with the longevity, ubiquity and size of the Ethiopian Church, and was convinced that it had great potential for evangelisation throughout the nation. He saw a parallel between the Ethiopian Church and the Christendom of pre-Reformation Europe in the priestly adherence to the dead language of Gi'iz (which was incomprehensible to the majority of Ethiopians), and their disinclination to preach or evangelise. He was thus unique among the Protestant missionaries in Ethiopia in wanting to strengthen the Ethiopian Church rather than compete with it. He received support for his unusual plans from important dignitaries such as *Ras* Kassa; Foreign Minister *Blattén Géta* Hiruy; Dr Charles Martin, the future Ethiopian minister in London; and ultimately the emperor himself.

Buxton even went to the greatest seat of Orthodoxy in Ethiopia, the monastery of Debre Libanos, where, despite the Italian propaganda about barbaric heretics, he was pleasantly surprised to find friendly and supportive clergy. His companion on that occasion, the Swedish Protestant missionary Per Stjärne, who spoke Amharic, had been equally surprised: 'Well, my impression of Debre Libanos is entirely altered. I thought it was full of bigoted monks where we could do nothing. But [now] I think it is quite otherwise.'[31]

Buxton received warm support from the emperor for a Bible school for the clergy that would lead to an Amharic translation of the Bible by the Ethiopians, and managed to recruit a number of students. By late 1934 he was back in Ethiopia again, by which time some Bible Churchmen's Missionary Society (BCMS) missionaries had settled in missions there as a result of his earlier visit. His local protégés, whom he had recruited with assistance from the emperor, were four educated young Ethiopians who gave up well-paid employment to become preachers of the Gospel: Hayle-Gebriél (who had been deputy governor of the province of Harar), and Werqu, Abeba and Temesgen Gebré, the son of a priest from Gojjam. All four were devout and committed teachers. Hayle-Gebriél is said to have gained the distinction of being the first Ethiopian to read a passage of scripture in Amharic (rather than Gi'iz) in the cathedral in Addis Ababa, and in the following week Temesgen preached in Amharic to a congregation of three hundred in the cathedral compound.[32] The year 1935 saw the four preachers going from strength to strength throughout the country, while Buxton remained in the background.[33]

But by May 1936 the invader was at the gates of the city, as Buxton's biographer put it, and soon everything would unravel. Hayle-Gebriél found a compound suitable for the Ethiopian preachers, and Buxton—either astonishingly naive or trusting entirely in Providence—went to see Graziani to request clearance for their mission. The Englishman's plans were, of course, totally unacceptable to the viceroy. A British Protestant asking permission to evangelise in Italian East Africa was bad enough, but supporting and strengthening the Ethiopian Church, the very institution that the Italians regarded as their enemy? The request was outrageous. Graziani's hatred for both the Ethiopian clergy and erudite foreign-educated Ethiopians was well known, and the suggestion that the latter should infiltrate the former to strengthen the hold of the highly nationalistic Ethiopian Church on the population that he was trying to bring under Italian control was anathema to the viceroy. From that moment on, Hayle-Gebriél, Werqu, Abeba and Temesgen were in double jeopardy, for not only were they Protestants, but they had now been identified as posing a potential danger to the Italian administration. They were thus now living on borrowed time.

Needless to say, no sooner had Buxton been assured by Graziani that religious freedom had been proclaimed than Hayle-Gebriél, Werqu and Temesgen were arrested and imprisoned on trumped-up charges.[34]

Buxton returned to England, having bid three of his four protégés farewell in prison. Fortunately for them, despite being under suspicion, they were in due course released—most likely following intervention by the British legation. Although anti-Protestant feeling among the Italians was simmering for political reasons—mainly due to the British, French or Swedish nationalities of the missionaries, who were gradually being deported—it had not yet reached crisis levels, and the Ethiopian converts were not yet in Graziani's sights.

But that was to change. Following expulsion of the foreign missionaries, Ethiopian Protestants had been allowed to continue to practise their faith and in some cases even to take over mission buildings. However, after the attempt on Graziani of 19 February 1937, the Italians had launched an anti-Protestant pogrom in which many Ethiopian Protestants were sent to concentration camps.[35] In the security clampdown that accompanied the massacre of Addis Ababa, Italian security forces raided the BCMS Bible school, and arrested the entire community of some fifty teachers, evangelists and students, of whom one in three would die in prison in tropical Mogadishu, in 'a beastly place below sea-level'.[36]

During the raid, the Italians found records of visits to the countryside by Hayle-Gebriél, Werqu, Temesgen and another preacher named Beyene. Hayle-Gebriél and Temesgen were not present in Addis Ababa, but Werqu and Beyene were arrested, together with a young man named Tageni, who was mistaken for Temesgen owing to the similarity of their names. That night the Italians killed the two evangelists Werqu and Beyene, as well as the unfortunate Tageni. Abeba, one of the original four preachers, was imprisoned. Graziani had the remaining BCMS missionaries deported, and Hayle-Gebriél disappeared.[37]

Buxton's biographer thought that Temesgen was out of town, but he wasn't. He was actually at the Governo Generale during the attempt on Graziani of *Yekatit 12* when the grenades were thrown, and was one of the few to survive the machine-gunning of the crowd that followed. Arrested by the military immediately afterwards, he ended up in the squalid detention camp at the Municipality Building in the city's Arada district, from where he was moved to the overcrowded Central Prison. Having been imprisoned by the Italians previously, he guessed, correctly, that his name would be on the 'wanted' list, and was astute enough to adopt a false name.[38]

Four days after his arrest, and still detained in brutal conditions in the compound of the Central Police Station, Temesgen, who survived the Italian occupation and after liberation became a well-respected newspaper editor and writer, described a disturbing incident he witnessed in which Italian Catholic clergy arrived at the prison with a list of Ethiopian Catholic prisoners to be freed: 'Then Catholic clergymen who had come in with the officer started looking [among the prisoners] for fellow Catholics. They called out their names from a list and had them released.'[39]

But that was not all; the Italians started pulling out the Protestants pointed out by collaborators, following which they were taken away and shot: 'Those suspected to be Protestants and identified as such by informants were taken and killed with a machine gun at the gate of the prison.' The executions terrified the detainees, and from that moment onwards, no one wanted to be known as a Protestant:

> For a few hours they asked [us] questions about religion. Then they asked each prisoner to name [his or her] religion. All the prisoners claimed to be either Catholic or Muslim. There was no-one who claimed to be Protestant, with the exception of *Ato* [Mr] Ar'aya, *aleqa* [head] of [the church of] Medhané Alem ['Saviour of the World'], who was a courageous and devout Christian.[40]

Temesgen, with a history of close relations with non-Italian Protestants, was distraught, writing rhetorically, 'The missionaries who were in Addis Ababa, Ethiopia, knew *Ato* Ar'aya. What did they [the Italians] do to him? How did they kill him?'

Ar'aya refused to renounce his faith, and the clergymen watched as the innocent *aleqa* was dragged to a military truck: 'After the three days of rampaging in the town, Fascist beasts who had returned from Holetta with a truck tied the legs of *Ato* Ar'aya to the back of the truck.' Before the vehicle moved, Father Ar'aya sang a mission hymn: 'Heaven is opening for me to enter; I will see Jesus there!' The response from the Blackshirts was that it would be better for him to listen to their song, and they chanted their 'war cry': '*Du-ce! Du-ce!*'

Temesgen was horrified by the behaviour of the Catholic clergymen, who just watched:

> They did not oppose the death-penalty ... Each Italian Fascist behaved like a king, and the Catholic monks,[41] with their ropes around their waist, were standing and watching when it was decided to kill *Ato* Ar'aya, and while he was being killed. [Their only reaction was that] they were not impressed with his singing, because *Ato* Ar'aya's voice was weak from hunger and thirst.[42]

The truck sped away, dragging Father Ar'aya behind it. Meanwhile, the Catholic clergymen left the prison with their freed Catholic prisoners.

The Reverend Guy Playfair, a British field director for the Sudan Interior Mission, who was sent on a tour of inspection in Ethiopia after the 1941 liberation, was shocked to learn about the persecution of Protestants during the occupation. He reported that in one incident, apparently in 1940, infuriated that the Ethiopian Protestant community continued to flourish after the deportation of the foreign missionaries, the Italians arrested and imprisoned fifty Ethiopian Protestants. They were each given up to one hundred lashes, one unfortunate man receiving four hundred. For months afterwards the badly lacerated victims, described as looking like 'raw meat', could not lie on their backs, three of them died, and others remained incarcerated. While they were in prison, Italian Catholic priests came to visit them from time to time—not to bring them consolation or sustenance, but to try to persuade them to renounce their faith by kissing the crucifix in order to gain immediate freedom.[43] Such accounts might be difficult to believe were it not for the fact that similar instances of 'conversion by coercion' on the part of Catholic priests were reported by former prisoners of the Ustashe in Croatia under the notorious clerico-Fascist regime of Ante Pavelić.

8

A BUNGLED MISSION

'Demoralise the enemy from within by surprise, terror, sabotage, assassination. This is the war of the future.'

Adolf Hitler

On the day following the strike against Graziani's entourage at the Governo Generale, the young Ethiopian Catholic Simi'on Adefris drove the two putative assassins Moges and Abriha to the monastery of Debre Libanos to meet Abriha's wife, Taddesech, who was staying with her mother in the vicinity. Moges and Abriha moved on to join the Patriots in Northern Shewa, and Simi'on decided to run the risk of returning to Addis Ababa. But he was stopped, his motor car was impounded, and Graziani had him interrogated under torture and killed. His family managed to take possession of his body, which they buried secretly at the Catholic cemetery in Addis Ababa's northern suburb of Gulelé.[1]

For the Ethiopians the attack of *Yekatit 12* at the Governo Generale certainly announced that they had not yet been conquered, and that the Italians were not really in control. However, it also gave Graziani the excuse he sought to destroy his perceived enemies once and for all. The viceroy already had the monastery of Debre Libanos in his sights. Moges and Abriha were in the vicinity only fleetingly, but given the viceroy's state of mind, and his obsessive hatred for the Ethiopian Church, the news that they had passed through the monastery lands was all he needed. He would claim that the clergy of Debre Libanos had been involved in a secret plot against his High Command and would have them all killed.

Although he was still in hospital, Graziani was fully conscious by Sunday, and by the following day, 22 February, he had made sure that General Pietro Maletti, who had replaced General Ruggero Tracchia as military commander for Northern Shewa, based in Debre Birhan (see Map 14), had made his first move against the monastery. Maletti dispatched a search party to Debre Libanos charged with finding Moges and Abriha.[2]

Apart from the monastery church, monastic energies at Debre Libanos have never been expended in building edifices. Thus, the visitor sees the lands surrounding the monastery in their natural state, much as Tekle Haymanot himself saw them in the 13th century. In those days the normal access to the monastery was on foot, from above. His disciples would follow him along the plateau and down

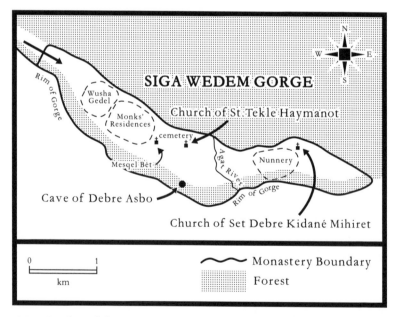

Map 8: Plan of the monastery of Debre Libanos (© Ian Campbell)

a narrow rocky path cut into the steep cliff above the cave of Debre Asbo. However, Emperor Menelik, who took the holy waters of Debre Libanos when he was ailing in his old age, would make his way with his entourage down the mule track which followed a gentler decline into the gorge over the four-kilometre stretch from Chagel, and it was this approach, which passes through the monastery village of Wusha Gedel, that became the principal access to the monastery in modern times (see Map 8).

Reconnaissance

The residents of Chagel, where pilgrims turn off the Fiché road to reach Debre Libanos, were surprised to see ten uniformed Italian military officers on mules and a squadron of *askaris* making their way down to the monastery.[3] The monastery had—and still has—no walls and no gate. The monks live at one with their environment, monastic rules prohibit the unnecessary felling of trees, and the security of the community is left to Mother Nature, the surrounding escarpments, and the conviction that the monastery is under the protection of the Almighty.

Accompanied by soldiers of the 2nd Eritrean Battalion, the officers questioned the priests and monks they met, and searched the monastery grounds, the monks' residences, the cemetery, and the nunnery beyond the sacred Agat River. But the monastery is surrounded by rocky crags, steep escarpments, deep valleys and caves in which it would be quite impossible to find anyone in hiding. In any case, Abriha, Moges and Taddesech had already gone their separate ways, and so, having achieved nothing, the soldiers wound up their mission and set out for their camp at Fiché.

The incident brought great excitement at the monastery to a day already filled with anticipation, for the following day would be the annual celebration of Kidane Mihret, 'The Covenant of Mercy', believed in Ethiopian Orthodoxy to have been entered into between Christ and his Mother, according to which Mary acts as intercessor between the faithful and her son.

HOLY WAR

Sacrilege at the Covenant of Mercy

The twelve-year-old Tibebe Kassa, whom the present author interviewed on several occasions in later years, was fast asleep in the monastery village of Wusha Gedel that night, when he was awakened by the noise of vehicles, people shouting, and then the sound of distant gunfire. Running outside, he discovered that a number of Italian officers and many *askaris* had arrived at the monastery unannounced in the darkness. But this time the 'Taliyans', as they were called by the Ethiopians, had arrived in military trucks: the dreaded heavy-duty khaki-coloured Fiat Trenta Quattros that under their dark canvas awnings were usually full of anywhere between fifteen and twenty-five menacing armed men—whether regulars, Blackshirts with their guns and daggers, or *askaris* with their rifles and swords or sabres. And if not full of soldiers, they would often be transporting Ethiopians who had been rounded up, delivering them to some unknown destination from which they would most likely never return. Aklilu Gebré, a friend of Tibebe's who was an eleven-year-old deacon of the church of St Tekle Haymanot at the time, recalled counting six truck-loads of soldiers, and seeing the vehicles parked within the monastery grounds, at the foot of the escarpment.[4]

For the Ethiopian clergy it was disrespectful for anyone to enter the monastery in uniform and on horseback, but it was even worse for military trucks to be driven into the holy places. Until the Italian occupation, trucks were almost unknown at the monastery; their appearance now on hallowed ground was regarded by the monks as sacrilegious.

By the time Tibebe arrived, the Italians had already opened fire on the church of St Tekle Haymanot, apparently expecting the monks and priests to be inside.[5] Fortunately, few, if any, of the clergy were in the church, and so far as is known, none were hit by the gunfire. But everyone knew about the military onslaught that had put Northern Shewa in a state of siege for months—the burning, the shooting and the gassing—and no one wanted to hang around when they saw the trucks and heard the sound of gunfire. So, streaming out of their homes, and accompanied by *Tsebaté* Tekle-Giyorgis and *Meggabi* Gebre-Mikaél, many managed to scramble down the steep

Figure 1: In 1540, papal confidants Father Tesfa Seyon of the monastery of Debre Libanos and Filippo Archinto, Vicar-General of Rome, stand behind the throne of Pope Paul III, who is receiving from Ignatius of Loyola legal documents founding the Society of Jesus.

Figure 2: The centre panel of a 15th-century Ethiopian triptych, depicting the Seven Archangels (holding swords) surrounding the Virgin Mary, the Christ Child, St. Peter and St. Paul. The theme of the Seven Archangels was, and still is, canonical only in the Ethiopian Orthodox Church.

Figure 3: Tesfa Seyon of Debre Libanos was one of the founders of Italy's cavernous state church, the basilica of Santa Maria degli Angeli e dei Martiri, which was designed and built by Michelangelo in the ruined frigidarium of the Baths of Diocletian, Rome. Above the main altar is mounted the basilica's most important painting, depicting the Seven Archangels.

Figure 4: This wall painting of the Holy Virgin with the Seven Archangels painted in 18th-century Ethiopian style can be seen today in the church of St Tekle Haymanot at Azezo, Gondar, to which the monastery of Debre Libanos temporarily relocated in the 16th century.

Figure 5: The church of St Tekle Haymanot at Debre Libanos built by Emperor Menelik over the tomb of the Saint, and seen here before the Italian invasion, had long been one of Ethiopia's most revered pilgrimage sites. In May 1937 Marshal Graziani would order the massacre of the clergy and congregation of the monastery church.

Figure 6: The Catholic Cathedral of the Nativity of the Blessed Virgin Mary, completed in 1933 with the encouragement and direct support of the Ethiopian government, bears witness to the high standing of the Catholic Church in Ethiopia before the Italian invasion.

Figure 7: In the summer of 1935, Pius XI, who was on the papal throne before and during the invasion of Ethiopia, declared Ethiopian Orthodox Christians to be heretics, thus designating them Enemies of the Faith. Although shortly afterwards he suggested that the planned attack might not be a 'Just War', he made no serious efforts to moderate pro-Fascist Italian clergy who were actively promoting the invasion.

Figure 8: Crusaders under divine protection: The publication of picture-postcards of Christ hovering above the invading forces to guide them into Ethiopia reinforced the message that the invasion had the blessing of the Catholic Church, and would take Italians to their 'promised land'.

LA MADONNA DEL MANGANELLO
protettrice dei Fascisti

Figure 9: The Mother of Christ in the service of Fascism: Installed in a number of Italian churches, the popular Madonna of the Manganello, wielding the Fascist club, or bludgeon, was named 'Patroness of the Squadristi'.

Figure 10: Father Reginaldo Giuliani, a well known Catholic priest seen here in his Blackshirt uniform, was an ardent Fascist who held the Ethiopian Church in contempt. Regarded almost as a saint after his death in action with a Blackshirt battalion during the war of invasion, the Italian administration of occupied Addis Ababa would name a street after him.

Figure 11: Shortly before the October 1935 invasion of Ethiopia, Emperor Haile Selassie (in white, right) leaves the cathedral of St. George in Addis Ababa after attending prayers for peace.

Figure 12: During the invasión, *Li'ul*-Ras Kassa Haylu, a distinguished member of the royal family and sacristan of the monastery of Debre Libanos, was in command of Ethiopia's armies at the northern war-front.

Figure 13: The Italian troops frequently displayed impunity in photographing their atrocities and distributing the photographs widely during the invasion and occupation of Ethiopia.

Figure 14: In October 1935 Ildefonso Cardinal Schuster, the influential Archbishop of Milan, announced that God had assigned the Italians to invade Ethiopia, and that the invading troops were Missionaries of the Gospel "carrying the cross of Christ". His statements being unchallenged by the Vatican, he was widely seen in Italy as having placed a divine seal of approval on the war.

Figure 15: Far from "carrying the cross of Christ", Cardinal Schuster's Missionaries of the Gospel were better known for carrying the heads they had severed from the Ethiopians they encountered.

Figure 16: The Day of Faith: To help finance the invasion of Ethiopia, the Italian Catholic clergy exhorted Italian civilians to line up in their thousands to donate their gold wedding rings. Cardinal Schuster personally blessed 25,000 of the steel rings provided as replacements.

Figure 17: Alessio Cardinal Ascalesi, Archbishop of Naples, arrives at the port city at the head of a procession from Pompei bearing the holy icon, Our Lady of the Rosary of Pompei, now known as 'Patron of the Italian Army Invading Eastern Africa'. As the Italian Royal Airforce flew ceremoniously overhead, the icon was joined on board by several thousand Blackshirts bound for what was now widely regarded by Catholic Italy as a Holy War.

Figure 18: "Catholic Christian Civilisation" was to "penetrate and radiate in the lands of Ethiopia", bringing "equity, charity and fraternity". In reality, the invading Italian forces met the slightest suspicion of resistance with public hangings, a form of exemplary repression that they perfected and implemented widely during both the invasion and occupation.

Figure 19: In a ceremony traditional in Catholic Italy, a priest – most likely a military chaplain – among Graziani's troops en route to Harar in April 1936 blesses machine-guns to be deployed against the Ethiopians.

Figure 20: When the invading army reached Addis Ababa in May 1936, the Italian Catholic clergy organised victory parades across the nation. Here the pro-Fascist Giuseppe Nogara, Metropolitan Archbishop of the archdiocese of Udine, preceded by his bishops, celebrates the reported conquest by leading a procession conveying the miraculous icon of the Madonna delle Gracie, ironically, a 14th-century Orthodox Christian painting from Udine's Sanctuary-Basilica of the Beata Vergine delle Gracie.

Figure 21: Marshal Rodolfo Graziani was a professional soldier. Having fought in Libya and Europe during the 1st World War, he went on to achieve notoriety as military commander in Libya. Following eighteen months as Viceroy and head of a ruthless administration in Ethiopia, he would be one of the few military commanders to remain loyal to Mussolini until the end of the Fascist era.

Figure 22: Victory for the crucified Christ and an assured place in heaven: The Italian Catholic clergy and their published propaganda imbued the forces of occupation in Ethiopia with a sense of divine mission.

Figure 23: A picture for the family: Under the protection of Mother Italy in her role of *Magna Mater* - a pagan deity wearing a turreted Crown symbolising Rome - a devout Fascist soldier in occupied Ethiopia pictures himself writing a letter to his mother while sitting at a table supported by *fasces*.

Figure 24: Graziani had the highly revered Bishop Pétros shot in public in Addis Ababa in 1936 for opposing Italian hegemony and refusing to denounce the Patriots. Celebrated as one of the greatest martyrs of the Italian occupation, he would be canonised by the Ethiopian Orthodox Church in 2009.

Figure 25: Bestowing a mantle of righteousness: As soon as he arrived in Addis Ababa, Pope Pius XI's Apostolic Visitor, Cardinal Archbishop Giovanni Castellani, ingratiated himself with the Fascist administration. Here he leads the party hierarchy in prayer to bless the reconstruction of the city's Kevorkoff building as Casa del Littorio, an annex of the party headquarters, in November 1936. To his left stands party supremo Guido Cortese, who would be responsible for the massacre of Addis Ababa; to his immediate right is General Italo Gariboldi. Marshal Graziani stands at the far left of the photograph.

Figure 26: Seen here in 1997, the church of Gebre Menfes-Qiddus at the monastery of Midr Kebd, where the medieval saint is believed to have lived, was the site of a massacre of Orthodox clergy by soldiers under Italian command in 1936. While monks inside the church were being slaughtered, some of the younger ones managed to escape through the windows.

Figure 27: One of only three remaining bishops of the Ethiopian Orthodox Church following the execution of Bishop Pétros, Bishop Mikaél of the western town of Goré was imprisoned by Colonel Giuseppe Malta in late November 1936. A few days later Malta had him shot in public for not submitting to the Italian administration and refusing to excommunicate the Patriots. In 2016 the Ethiopian Orthodox Church would canonise Bishop Mikaél as a Martyr Saint.

Figure 28: Babies and small children who crawled out through the burning walls of their houses during the massacre of Addis Ababa were thrown by Italian Blackshirts back into the flames, as depicted in this graphic bas relief on the city's Martyrs Monument.

A BUNGLED MISSION

escarpment to Kateba Maryam (St Mary), a church founded in the 15th century and built just above the lower terrace of the gorge.⁶

Some of the monks clambered further down to Kora, a place of sanctuary at the bottom of the gorge at the confluence of the Siga Wedem and the sacred Agat River. There they would be on holy ground, at one of the earliest and most secluded monasteries associated with the saint. Among the silence of caves and lonely hermits, where sacred artefacts had once been hidden from the *jihad* of Ahmed Grañ, Kora St Tekle Haymanot was regarded by the faithful as inviolate.

A Narrow Escape

Meanwhile, on the upper terrace it was becoming clear that the officers' mission actually went far beyond looking for Moges and Abriha. They were rounding up whomever they could find— clergy, the elderly, deacons who were little more than children— for execution. Totalling around fifty, they were forced to walk to a forested area known as Gubrazel, near the monastery cemetery, and a firing squad of *askaris* was prepared. However, Tibebe, who was there, and who had picked up a little Italian over the previous few months, understood some of the officers' conversation: they were having second thoughts. If they shot these prisoners, the rest of the clergy would not return to the monastery, and would probably disappear from view. They were afraid that Graziani, who presumably wanted the entire clergy eliminated, would be furious at the botched mission.

Sensing their hesitation, one of the local onlookers told the Italians that the people they had rounded up were 'not so important', and advised them that if they wanted more victims, they should choose 'a better day', when all the clergy would be present. Whether this intervention was a ploy to get the captives released, or the work of a collaborator—or both—is not clear, but it saved the day for the terrified captives. The officers decided that for now, they would pretend that they had no ill will towards the Debre Libanos community. Then they would return at a later date. 'We have no problem with you,' they told the hapless group, 'We were looking for Abebe Aregay'—a reference to the well-known Patriot leader. 'We were told he would be in the church.'[7] The *askaris* let the detainees go, and they quickly melted into the night.

Death at Kateba St Mary

In the darkness at Kateba St Mary, some of the officers and several *askaris* had followed the monks and started rounding them up at gunpoint. The Italians were in an angry, vengeful mood. Their quarry had eluded them, so they seemed to feel they needed to execute at least a few of the clergy. Outside the church they lined up some elderly monks. These were the ones Graziani hated the most—he called them 'soothsayers', believing that they went around predicting the demise of his administration. The order to fire was given, and the sound of gunfire echoed off the escarpment walls. When a messenger from Gubrazel reached the church, he found the bodies of three elderly monks, together with several others wounded.[8]

Although little information about the incident on 22 February at the monastery and Kateba St Mary reached the rest of the country, it was well known to the monks, and in 2015 was mentioned to the Awen Films crew by the elderly *Meggabi* Welde-Tinsa'e of Debre Libanos. He said that after the attack of *Yekatit 12* in Addis Ababa, when the Italians were searching for Moges and Abriha, the military 'brought many machine guns and started firing into the forest, at the houses, and everything else. There were huge losses, with many dead and wounded. Then the commanding officer ordered them to stop.'[9]

In his testimony for the UN War Crimes Commission, the resistance leader *Ras* Abebe Aregay also included a reference to the incident: 'To show that they knew who made the attempt, the Italians went to Debre Libanos Monastery. When they could not find Abriha's wife because, on his way to me, he had passed through Debra Libanos to warn his wife to escape, they murdered three monks.'[10]

Tsebaté Tekle-Giyorgis never returned to the monastery. He reportedly went to Menz, where he joined the resistance. The Italians replaced him with an Italian appointee named *Abba* Gebre-Maryam. *Meggabi* Gebre-Mikaél, apparently more trusting of the Italians, returned to Debre Libanos and, in doing so, sealed his fate, for even greater horrors were yet to be visited upon the monastery.

9

A BEAUTIFUL CONQUEST

'No State shall resist the power of Rome.'
Eugenio Cardinal Pacelli, Vatican secretary
of state, 23 February 1936

Lying in hospital in Addis Ababa, the viceroy was an angry man. In considerable pain, he was nonetheless able to dictate a telegram that would achieve infamy as evidence for the UN war crimes trials. Addressed to General Nasi, it began by reiterating the policy of killing prisoners of war: '[Concerning] the surrender of numerous Amhara notables and ex-army officers. I order that they all be shot immediately according to the direction of the Duce repeated a thousand times and yet little observed by many. It is time to put an end to it.'

Moving on to the subject of the attack at the Governo Generale, he widened the net from the 'Amhara' to 'Abyssinian chiefs and notables' in general: 'Keep in mind also that here I have already aimed at the total destruction of Abyssinian chiefs and notables and that similar measures should be carried out in your territories.' Then, in a telling passage that made it clear that he planned to use the attack as an excuse for an expanded pogrom, he added, 'A better opportunity could not be found to get rid of them.'[1]

The following day Nasi passed on Graziani's instructions to his subordinates, widening the net still further: 'I give you orders to shoot all—I say all—rebels, notables, chiefs, followers either captured in action or giving themselves up ... or cunning elements hiding among the local populations.'[2]

By 20 March, Mussolini himself had thrown his full support behind Graziani's pogrom: 'Approve of your action re soothsayers, storytellers and witch doctors. Vital extirpate dangerous elements and maintain absolute law and order.'[3] The northern Italy evening edition of *Secolo la Sera* interpreted the order with a hypocritical perspective, echoing the crusading spirit of the Italian clerics: 'Italy will continue unperturbed her work of civilisation and of redemption of the people liberated from the tyranny and barbarism of the Negus.'[4]

Thus it was that a campaign of death and destruction was unleashed against Ethiopian civilians of any standing, particularly priests, community leaders and elders. The South African journalist George Steer reported, 'Orders were sent out from Addis Ababa to shoot all the surviving Amhara chiefs in southern and western Abyssinia, and to cleanse with machine-gun the most important of the national monasteries.'[5]

Much of the offensive against the Ethiopian Church was conducted under these directives, which brought the pogroms of the Italian occupation close to genocide. Numerous military 'tribunals' embarked on a macabre tour of the countryside, carrying with them portable gallows, rounding up and hanging notables in public, in village after village, town after town. Thousands of innocents died in the slaughter, which would continue for much of 1937.[6]

Onslaught in the North

Tigray had been the first diocese to be penetrated by the Italians when they crossed the Eritrean border in October 1935. It was an almost surreal situation, for Emperor Haile Selassie had held back from moving his troops to the border, keen as he was to show the League of Nations that Ethiopia was not the aggressor. Thus the Italians had at first encountered virtually no resistance. However, the situation had changed dramatically since then. By 1937 northern Ethiopia was suffering bombardments of both civilians and the military, was now fully engaged in the war, and its churches were falling victim to Graziani's persecutions. Many churches and monasteries were attacked; here we mention just a few of those that suffered.

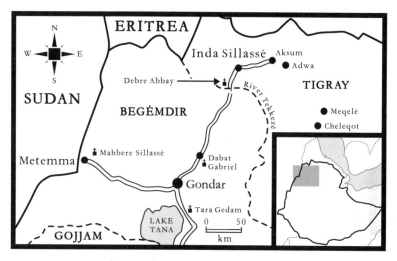

Map 9: Northern Ethiopia: Begémdir and Western Tigray
(© Ian Campbell)

In the diocese of Begémdir, south-west of Tigray and close to the border with the Sudan, near Metemma, lies Mahbere Sillassé, an ancient monastery whose foundation is traditionally ascribed to kings Abriha and Atsbiha, who are revered in the Ethiopian Church as 4th-century Christian sovereigns. St Frumentius is believed to have had a vision of the Holy Trinity at the site of the monastery, the plan of which forms a circle. The monks, who live in simple thatched houses around the monastery church, follow the rules of a 17th-century monk named Amde Sillassé. These rules constitute one of the world's strictest monastic orders, prescribing a community-oriented form of asceticism forbidding any form of private property.[7]

One of the monasteries of Begémdir targeted by the Italians, Mahbere Sillassé had been richly endowed by the 17th-century Emperor Fasiledes. On 24 March 1937 the Regia Aeronautica bombed the monastery, destroying the monastery church of the Holy Trinity and killing between 24 and 50 monks.[8]

On the same day the nearby 14th-century monastery of Debre Abbay on the northern banks of the Tekkezé River, which had been bombed during the invasion, was raided by ground troops.[9] Diocesan records show that on this occasion the Italians sought out and shot dead the head of the monastery, *Meggabi* Gebre-Maryam, who was in hiding. The killing was carried out by Eritrean *askaris* from Keren, which indicates that they were almost certainly members of one of Graziani's Muslim battalions. When Father Gebre-Maryam was shot, one of the bullets passed through his body, killing one of the soldiers.[10]

In the bombing attacks and the raid of 1937 many of the monastery's rare artefacts were destroyed or looted. However, a 14th-century illustrated parchment prayer book—one of the community's most valuable treasures, which was apparently hidden—survived, and can be seen at the monastery today.

An Apostolic Delegate

Archbishop Castellani's strategy to ensure his own rapid return to Addis Ababa bore fruit. On 25 March 1937, apparently confident that the coast would soon be clear for a programme of evangelisation and proselytisation, Pope Pius XI appointed the pro-Fascist cleric as apostolic delegate for what the Italian government now called Italian East Africa. This was the prelate who had ingratiated himself with Graziani and the Fascist Party officials in Addis Ababa during his earlier trip to Ethiopia, following which he had announced that the Italians had achieved a beautiful conquest, referring to the clergy of the Ethiopian Church as a previously 'impassable obstacle' for the Roman Church—a problem that would now be resolved as a result of 'the changed circumstances'.

Castellani embarked for Ethiopia with a large contingent of Catholic personnel.[11] By that time Mussolini's 'reprisals without mercy' had been stepped up, military commander *Ras* Desta had been captured and executed, 20,000–30,000 civilians had been slaughtered with impunity in the February 1937 massacres in Addis Ababa and the secondary towns, and thousands of religious and community leaders were being hanged in public in towns and villages across Ethiopia.

A BEAUTIFUL CONQUEST

During the first half of 1937, Italian military actions against civilians were focused principally on Northern Shewa. Though still in hospital, Graziani was able to assure Mussolini that through these 'police operations', as he called them, he had succeeded in unleashing terror on a massive scale. On the very day that Monsignor Castellani was preparing for his journey to the reportedly tranquil land of Ethiopia, following Italy's 'beautiful conquest', the viceroy was reassuring Rome that his troops were busy, day after day, depopulating Northern Shewa, leaving desolation in their wake:

> News March 25th: Tegulet has received the treatment it deserved ... we proceeded with fire and sword. For more than 25 kilometres not a stone remained. More than 40 villages destroyed, more than 4,000 tukuls [thatched cottages] burned; our losses—killed 31, wounded 38. Enemy losses: killed in battle 212, shot 396 ... On the 24th in the Fiché sector ... Tullu village, which had supported the rebels, has been razed to the ground.[12]

Meanwhile, the apostolic delegate was met by an enthusiastic Fascist reception committee, and was granted one of the finest houses in town. The former American legation building, a villa built in classical Greek revival style standing in extensive parkland in a western suburb of the city, had been built by Emperor Menelik's prime minister and minister of war, *Fitawrari* Habte-Giyorgis.

Martyrs of Gojjam

In Gojjam, north of Shewa, which is enclosed by the great bend of the Blue Nile, the Italians were attacking many of the thousands of churches located in that diocese. The Italians came to refer to the 'Gojjam revolt' as having begun in the second half of 1937, but in fact reprisals and attacks of exemplary repression were common months before then in this ancient region of Ethiopian Christendom.[13]

Although it was Tigray where Ethiopian Christian monasticism first proliferated, it was Gojjam that became in many ways the cultural heartland of the Ethiopian Church before the Ahmed Grañ *jihad* of the early 16th century. Here arose the great scriptoria and royal churches of the medieval period, and many aspects of the ancient Christian culture of Gojjam have proved remarkably resilient. Indeed, Gojjam is today perhaps the only place in the world where monks and priests can still be found producing Christian parchment manuscripts in the time-honoured manner.

Under the ruthless General Alessandro Pirzio-Biroli, the Italian Governorate of Amhara, which incorporated Gojjam, was the scene of brutal repression during late 1936 and early 1937, as the Italians struggled to gain control over the inhabitants. Entire villages were destroyed by flame and sword.

Mertule Maryam, a well-known monastery with strong historical connections with Ethiopian royalty, and with origins reaching back to the 14th century, lies inside the bend of the Abbay (the Blue Nile) as it turns south to begin its encirclement of Gojjam (Map 10). Empress Iléni founded a royal monastery on the site between 1490 and 1522, and had a beautifully ornamented church built there. The edifice was, however, destroyed by the troops of Ahmed Grañ in 1535–6, in the same *jihad* that spurred Father Tesfa Siyon and his compatriots to move to Rome.

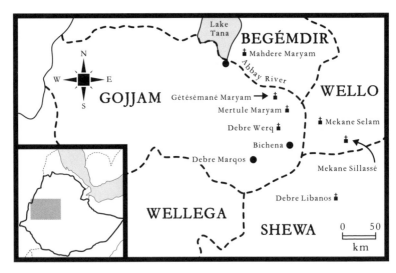

Map 10: Gojjam and the Blue Nile (© Ian Campbell)

Nonetheless, under Emperor Susinyos in the early 17th century a group of Italian Jesuits under the direction of Father Bruno

Bruni set out to replace the ruins of Empress Iléni's church with a magnificent basilica on the same site.[14] Unfortunately the project, which involved craftsmanship of outstanding quality and probably incorporated some of the material from the earlier church, was never completed, leaving the monastery dominated by massive imposing but unfinished masonry.

Seltene Seyoum identifies Mertule Maryam as one of the religious centres where clerics were massacred by the Italians in the pogroms that followed the attack on Graziani in February 1937.[15] This is confirmed by Father Kefyalew Mehari, who found that on 26 and 28 April 1937 the Italians killed a total of no less than 363 priests at the churches of Mertule Maryam and Tedbabe Maryam (see below).[16] It seems that the clergy at Mertule Maryam hid their treasures from the Italians, for most of the artefacts survived. The Italians did, however, steal some ancient manuscripts.[17]

It was ironic that the Italians should strike at Mertule Maryam, for that magnificent edifice, though unfinished, was one of a number of great monuments to the history of collaboration between the Ethiopian and Roman Churches.

* * *

Another historic institution that lost many of its clergy to the Italian onslaught is the church of Tedbabe Maryam, across the Blue Nile gorge from Mertule Maryam (see Map 10). Founded by Emperor Claudius (Gelawdéwos) in 1552, it stands in splendid isolation, almost inaccessible to any but the most intrepid pilgrims, on the summit of a remote flat-topped mountain, or *amba*. During the reign of Emperor Susinyos the clergy adopted the Latin rite, and maintained it until the restoration of Orthodoxy in 1633.[18]

* * *

One of Gojjam's most illustrious monasteries is Debre Werq ('Mount of Gold'), built on a low hill overlooking the town of the same name in East Gojjam, on the western side of the Blue Nile gorge (see Map 10). The monastery is generally believed to have been founded in the 15th century, though there are indications that it may date back to the 11th century.[19]

HOLY WAR

The monastery church, devoted to the Mother of Christ, was regarded by the Jesuits in the early 17th century as one of Ethiopia's most important churches.[20] It was a traditional circular, three-division church consisting of two concentric ambulatories with the holy of holies, or *meqdes*, in the centre.

The Italians, who established a garrison near Debre Werq town, positioned artillery on one of the hills nearby, and fired a mortar bomb to burn the church down. Clearly visible across the valley, the church of Debre Werq Maryam was an easy target. The bomb penetrated the outer wall, passed through the ambulatory, and continued through the wall of the inner aisle, lodging itself in the wall of the inner sanctum. Although the walls suffered considerable damage, the bomb reportedly failed to explode.

Present at the time was a member of the church, Father Igwale Jenberu, who later became a renowned teacher of *Digwa*, the liturgical book of the Ethiopian Church containing the hymns and troparies for the Divine Office,[21] earning himself the title of *YeDigwa Merigéta*. In due course Father Igwale shared his testimony with Father Bi'isé Tiruneh, a monk of Debre Werq with the title of *aqqabé*, who recounted the incident for the benefit of the present author.[22]

The church continued in use with the damaged section cordoned off until reconstruction following a visit to the church by the emperor in 1969–70.

Fortunately, it appears that no one was killed in the attack on Debre Werq Maryam. Had the bomb exploded, a significant part of the patrimony of the Ethiopian Church might have been lost. Whether any of the artefacts had been hidden we do not know, but in the possession of the church was—and fortunately still is—a rich collection of treasures, including an icon attributed to St Luke, and a Gospel book with images by the Venetian Nicoló Brancaleon, who was employed as a herald and painter by the imperial Ethiopian court in the 15th and early 16th centuries.[23] Today the remains of the bomb are preserved at the church.

Following the attack on the Governo Generale in February 1937 there were also massacres of unknown numbers of Ethiopian clergy north of the Blue Nile in Begémdir at the 16th-century churches of Qworata and Mahdere Maryam (see Map 10).[24]

PART THREE

A STRIKE AT THE HEART

10

PREPARING THE KILLING FIELDS

> *'Executions in consequence of mentioned attempt are made at isolated places so that nobody—I say nobody—can witness them.'*
> Viceroy Rodolfo Graziani, 19 March 1937

Although by the end of the first quarter of 1937 the Italians had already slaughtered the clergy of several notable churches and monasteries, there is no question that for them the crowning achievement in the war on the Ethiopian Church would be the destruction of the monastery of Debre Libanos. Graziani knew that the massacre of that community—a strike at the very heart of the Ethiopian Church—would create shock and terror across the land, and might even sound the death knell of the Church as a national institution.

But the timing had to be right. Following the abortive attack on the monastery in February, Graziani did his homework, and bided his time. He would wait until the biggest event of the year, which would attract the greatest number of clergy and pilgrims: 20 May. As inscribed in the Ethiopian *Synaxarium*, the Lives of the Saints, this is the day in 1370 when the monks of Tekle Haymanot's original monastery of Debre Asbo moved their Holy Father's remains from the cave where he died to Elam, a site nestling among trees in the wooded escarpment high above the present church of St Tekle Haymanot.[1] Ever since, 20 May has been the best-attended day of the year for the monastery of Debre Libanos. Furthermore, 20 May is also the monthly celebration for St Michael, who is said in the hagiography of St Tekle Haymanot to have rescued the saint's mother from a terrible fate. Thus, on that day the congregation of the church of St Tekle Haymanot would be supplemented by devotees of St Michael.

Graziani's choice of this important date would ensure the presence of not only the clergy and monks normally resident at Debre Libanos, numbering around one thousand, but also at least a thousand additional visitors. Indeed, in his proposals for the massacre, General Maletti would in due course inform Graziani that he expected the event of 20 May to attract a total of two to three thousand 'clergy, servants, mendicants and pilgrims'.[2]

By early March Graziani had made his decision and selected the date, and on the 7th of that month he made it clear to General Tracchia that the time had come for the destruction of the monastery. A week later, on receiving a report on the monastery by Major Mario Quercia, the viceroy wrote across the top of the first page of the report, 'Inform General Maletti that he must proceed to the total liquidation of the monastery in May 1937' (see Appendix III).[3] No stone would be left unturned, and every step would be covered by carefully worded reports to Rome. In due course a case would be framed against the monastery to justify the slaughter. But that would come later. Graziani got his secretary to open a new file. There was no mistaking the objective of the project now under way: 'Liquidation of the monastery of Debre Libanos'.

A Machiavellian Plan

The viceroy planned the operation carefully. If the Debre Libanos community was to be enticed into the monastery and captured, it was essential that this time the military presence should raise no suspicions. *Carabinieri* would move into Debre Libanos as an apparent gesture of goodwill. They would develop personal relationships with the monks and the priests, and convince them that they were there to support them. When the day scheduled for the massacre arrived, the presence of the military would be accepted as normal, and the community would be enticed into the monastery church. Then the word would be given, and the clergy and congregation of the House of St Tekle Haymanot would be rounded up and shot.

Thus, in March a group of *carabinieri* established itself in *Ras* Kassa's house in the monastery village of Wusha Gedel, and were in due course more or less accepted by the community. They gave food and money to the monks, and established a degree of local influence.[4] However, some of the clergy knew that the *carabinieri* were also seeking informants,[5] for *Meggabi* Welde-Tinsa'e revealed that they were asking questions about Moges Asgedom and Abriha Deboch, and threatened some of the monks with execution if they didn't talk.[6]

Nonetheless, Graziani's strategy was quite effective, and as the appointed day approached, arrangements were made for a celebration of unprecedented proportions. A proclamation was read out by collaborator Gebre-Maryam, the Italians' new appointee as *tsebaté*, before a crowd at the monastery, announcing that on 20 May the *ichegé* (a collaborator appointee) would attend, all members of the Debre Libanos community and their family and friends should be present, and Italian dignitaries would distribute gifts.[7] He also announced that anyone who failed to attend would henceforth be barred from the monastery—for devotees of St Tekle Haymanot, an edict almost equivalent to excommunication.

Seeking a Rationale

Meanwhile, Italian Military Intelligence personnel were at work in Addis Ababa suggesting possible links between the monastery and 'the attempt',[8] as Graziani used to refer to the February attack on the Italian High Command, or what the Ethiopians called *Yekatit 12*. These were being prepared at the office of the royal military advocate, Major Giuseppe Franceschino, in preparation for an explanatory telegram to be transmitted to Rome after the massacre. The case against the monastery was put together using fragments of circumstantial evidence.[9] In case the rationale turned out to be unconvincing, Graziani was reassured by the compliant military advocate, who advised him, 'We cannot trust anyone, neither the clergy nor the notables. The feelings of rebellion are latent in all of them.'[10]

If the connection between *Yekatit 12* and the Patriots was tenuous, its connection with Debre Libanos was equally speculative, relying as it did on hearsay and anecdotal evidence. Nonetheless, Franceschino drew his conclusions with great confidence: 'One must with a clear conscience conclude that one cannot speak only of the complicity of the monks of Debre Libanos, but of the much graver hypothesis of their share in the guilt.'[11]

The report also incriminated the former *tsebaté*, Tekle-Giyorgis, and Graziani seemed to be content not to demand more convincing evidence. He probably realised that if Franceschino had gone further with a genuine trial, the viceroy's plan would most likely have failed, since by definition a clandestine conspiracy would have involved few people, providing no basis for mass executions. Thus, terminating the inquiry before too many facts emerged would ensure that the viceroy was unchallenged in claiming that the 'secret' plot had involved all the clergy of Debre Libanos. It is not surprising that the suspects were never charged.[12]

A Faithful General

The district in which the monastery of Debre Libanos stood fell under the military jurisdiction of a commander well known to Graziani and trusted by him: General Pietro Maletti, commander of the north-east sector of Shewa, with headquarters at Debre Birhan.[13] Born in 1880, and having attended a prestigious military school, Maletti was enjoying a career as a professional soldier. Like Graziani, he had fought in the First World War, where he was known as a harsh disciplinarian with a 'punitive' approach, employing 'coercion rather than persuasion'. These being qualities sought by his superiors, he was assigned to Libya, where he commanded Eritrean battalions. In 1935 he was transferred to East Africa, and by 1937, having fought under Graziani in the southern front of the invasion of Ethiopia, had become one of the viceroy's most trusted generals.[14]

For the first phase of the liquidation of Debre Libanos, Maletti sought a suitable execution site near the monastery. The location

PREPARING THE KILLING FIELDS

needed to be accessible by motor vehicles but invisible to anyone not actually on site, in accordance with Graziani's assurance to Lessona that 'executions ordered in consequence of mentioned attempt are made at isolated places and that nobody—I say nobody—can witness them'.[15]

The general was provided with a knowledgeable local collaborator, who recommended Laga Weldé, a site on the plain near the edge of the gorge where a seasonal stream, or *laga*, known as the Fincha Wenz, meandered eastwards into the gorge (see Map 11). So long as the locals were kept to the other side of the surrounding hills, there would be no witnesses.[16] The execution site was easily accessible from the Addis Ababa–Fiché road, between two hills known as Gobola and Tsebaté.

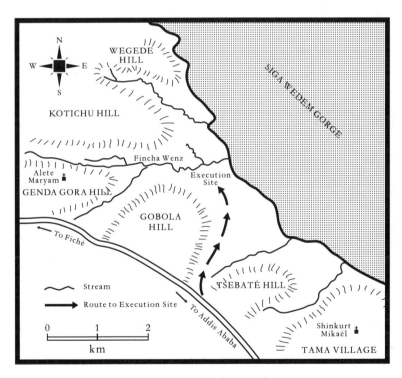

Map 11: The massacre of Debre Libanos: the execution site at Laga Weldé (© Ian Campbell)

A Secret Site

While Maletti was preparing for the executions at Laga Weldé,[17] another, more secluded site was being sought for the elimination of people other than Debre Libanos clergy. While Graziani would later issue orders for the execution of the monks and priests of Debre Libanos to be broadcast as a warning to others, it was important that the second set of executions, which would involve under-age victims as well as pilgrims and clergy from other churches, should not be made public.

As in the case of Laga Weldé, local knowledge for the site selection was required, and in this instance Maletti was assisted by the Italian *residente*. Some seven kilometres from Debre Birhan town, the site lay among the rolling hills of the highland plateau, on the way to where the former Shewan capital of Ankober formed the gateway to the old caravan route across the lowlands to the Red Sea.

In a sparsely populated area known as Ingécha, this second execution site, referred to locally as Borale, was near the Debre Birhan–Ankober road but hidden from it (see Map 12).[18] The site lay in a shallow valley of the seasonal Borale River, surrounded by hills crowned with rocky outcrops, while on the lower slopes cattle grazed and crops were grown by a few scattered subsistence-farming families. The execution site was adjacent to the river, which for much of the year was no more than a small stream around which cattle would find dry-season grazing.

Overlooking the site were two homesteads. On one on the northern slopes, a young boy named Letarge lived with his parents, brothers and sisters; on the southern slopes was the homestead of *Ato* Yirgu and his family.

Borale was less than three kilometres from an Italian military camp at Awsene Amba.[19] It was also easily accessible by vehicle from the garrison town of Debre Birhan, but provided the seclusion necessary to fulfil the viceroy's assurance to Rome regarding secrecy. The requirement was convenient for Graziani, for it facilitated secret executions—secret even from Rome—without the risk that the news would leak out. In any case, since Northern Shewa was aflame with exemplary repression, the burning of dwellings, and the use

PREPARING THE KILLING FIELDS

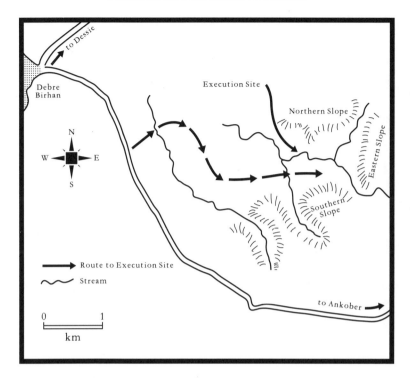

Map 12: The massacre of Debre Libanos: the execution site at Borale, Ingécha (© Ian Campbell)

of poison gas, the massacre at Borale could go virtually unnoticed amidst the carnage.

11

ENCIRCLEMENT AND CAPTIVITY

> *'One must be cunning and wicked in this world.'*
> Leo Tolstoy

All set to deal with Debre Libanos, General Maletti was elated, for his troops had just successfully conducted scorched-earth 'punitive action' in the nearby district of Menz. Apparently annoyed that not a single person had presented themselves 'in homage' to his invading forces, he reported that after entering the district on 6 May, his men had managed to kill 2,523 Ethiopians and destroy 115,422 'tukuls'. They had also destroyed three churches, and slaughtered the monks of the monastery of Gultené St Michael before burning it to the ground.[1]

The onslaught of Maletti's troops in Northern Shewa, which had been maintained at fever pitch since mid-April, was a death march of wanton slaughter and 'destruction of everything', just as Graziani had ordered.[2] Indeed, the viceroy's programme of repression was reaching a climax. By 17 May the viceroy's orders were explicit: 'What I recommend is to quell without mercy and eliminate rebel leaders and followers.'[3] And the following day:

> News 18th May. Debre Birhan sector. Menz region has got the hard necessary lesson it deserved … The repression …. displaying

merciless rigour against those hostile towards us ... rebels pursued and finally surrounded in the valley by our strong and fast columns suffered very serious losses and have found that ditches and precipices thought to offer secure shelter inaccessible to us do not hinder our repression ... Rebels killed: 2,491 ... 15,302 tukuls burnt.[4]

Assembling the Troops

Maletti had planned to complete his assignment in Menz before moving on to deal with Debre Libanos on Tekle Haymanot Day, 20 May. However, while embroiled in Menz, he was informed that the saint's day was 18 May (10 Ginbot). This was two days earlier than he had thought, so he changed his plans. Leaving his troops 'to complete the ongoing punitive action' in Menz, he left on 15 May, then went on to Addis Ababa, having ordered his 20th and 4th Colonial Battalions to move towards an area he called Gurenié,[5] and to reinforce his battalions at Fiché. At that point, he reported, none of his forces knew the purpose of these manoeuvres, because 'for the encircling [of Debre Libanos] to succeed, it was necessary to maintain absolute secrecy until the last moment'.[6]

Thus, on Monday, 17 May, Maletti went up to Fiché for the long-awaited attack on Debre Libanos. Apart from his own military command of the north-eastern Shewa sector, which included the infamous 45th Colonial (Muslim) Battalion as well as the 20th Eritrean Colonial Battalion, the general had assembled a formidable array of Italy's colonial troops. These included the 12th Colonial Brigade, the 51st, 52nd and 56th Colonial Battalions, and the 23rd Colonial Battery. In addition, he had also brought in *carabinieri* normally stationed at Debre Birhan and Fiché.[7]

Altogether, to attack unarmed priests, pilgrims and elderly monks, Maletti had put in place an army of more than 6,000—a massive fighting force such as would normally have been deployed to face a heavily armed and resolute enemy.

If Maletti's objective was limited to executing only some of the elderly monks (as he eventually reported), a single platoon would have been more than sufficient for the task. But Maletti was launching a massive operation involving a widespread dragnet in which no one was to be allowed to escape.

Each of the military units had its function, and one of the first tasks was allocated to the 51st Colonial Battalion, a highly trained group of soldiers. Specialising in negotiating the type of rugged terrain found around Debre Libanos, they would be deployed to control access to and from the monastery.

Ferocious Castrators

The company at the heart of the army taken to Debre Libanos by General Maletti to implement the next phase in Italy's holy war was the 45th Colonial (Muslim) Battalion. Created by Graziani following the defection to Kenya of more than 700 Christian Eritrean *askaris* from the Royal Corps of Colonial Troops, the purpose of creating the 45th was to ensure that he would have at his disposal a force willing to carry out attacks on Ethiopian Christian clergy and civilians that Eritrean Christian *askaris*, most of whom were members of the same Orthodox faith as their Ethiopian cousins, might refuse to do.

Formed in February 1936 from Muslim colonial Eritrean, Libyan and Somali troops already on active service in Ethiopia in other battalions taking part in the invasion, the 45th had distinguished itself at the southern war front, and now constituted one of Maletti's crack colonial battalions. Graziani had certainly groomed the men of the 45th Battalion as a merciless fighting force. The Libyan battalions fighting under Italian command already had a notorious reputation for taking no prisoners, but General Maletti regarded the 45th as a unit like no other, proudly referring to them as 'ferocious castrators' when 'unleashed'. He described them as '1,500 men armed with daggers, spears and rifles ... agile as monkeys', guided by what he called 'their infallible instinct'.[8]

Delaying Tactics

At 8 am on the morning of Tuesday, 18 May, Maletti ordered his men to proceed from Fiché to Debre Libanos under the command of Colonel Garelli, who set about encircling the monastery. Some soldiers were ordered to occupy the sacred ground around the church of St Tekle Haymanot; others were deployed in and around the cemetery, and at the monastery village of Wusha Gedel. Some were even sent to the nunnery, beyond the church of St Tekle Haymanot and across the holy waters of the Agat River (see Map 8).[9] One battalion surrounded the lands beyond Debre Libanos, some of the men taking up positions along the edge of the plateau on the escarpment above the monastery, while others patrolled the edge of the terrace where it overlooks the Siga Wedem gorge. Maletti would report that by 2 pm 'the entire gorge was blockaded',[10] a 'complete surprise [to the monastery], and perfectly successful'.[11]

Dressed in their traditional attire, the faithful started appearing on the track leading eastwards from Chagel to the monastery—priests with their white turbans, monks in their coloured cloaks, groups of women head-to-foot in white, the sick and the lame hobbling along the rough track hoping for relief at the holy waters of the saint, the occasional lone bare-footed hermit with his gaunt, long-staffed iron cross, and traders carrying bamboo umbrellas, food, wax tapers and other artefacts for sale at the market that always sprang up below the escarpment on holy days.

However, when they reached the church, the pilgrims got their first shock. Muslim soldiers had not been seen at Debre Libanos since the massacre of 1531. But now here they were, swarming over the monastery grounds. The soldiers checked on each person as they entered. While at first the operation had the appearance of a regular security exercise, it took on a more ominous character when the visitors spotted troops up on the escarpment above. New arrivals were screened and ushered into the church, which was gradually filling up under the watchful eyes of the *askaris*.

By the afternoon, several of those locked in the church had realised that they were captives, and in danger. Many could be heard thanking God that if they were to die at Debre Libanos, they would go to heaven.[12]

While the captives at Debre Libanos were facing the prospect of an early death, General Maletti discovered that he had been misinformed. This was not Tekle Haymanot Day at all; he had sent in the military two days too soon. He could not cancel the operation;

things had gone too far for that. Yet if he had the captive clergy and pilgrims shot, those expected to arrive over the following two days would hear about it and would stay away. He decided to play for time. He pretended that he was there to reorganise the monastery. He would distract and calm the senior clergy with a discussion on the future of Debre Libanos, then would move the captives out of the monastery early in the morning to a location where they would not be seen by the new arrivals. But for the time being they would remain in the church.[13]

At 4 pm the great doors of the church were closed, and Maletti had some seventy clergy seized and checked by the *carabinieri*. From these he selected 'Vice Prior' *Abba* Gebre-Maryam Welde-Giyorgis and *Meggabi* Welde-Mikaél Chaffa, who duly presented themselves to be interviewed by the general and his aide-de-camp in his command tent.[14]

Maletti shared his apparent concerns with the two senior clergymen, diligently acquainted himself with the day-to-day details of the running of the monastery, and appointed senior monks and priests to various positions of responsibility. A strange meeting, it was actually a charade. The clergy were asked about the nuns of Debre Libanos, well known for caring for the sick and the dying. Their refuge, known as Bét Selihom ('The House of Selihom'), had been named after the pool of Siloam at Jerusalem, where Jesus is said to have healed a blind man. They told Maletti that there were about one hundred nuns, of which 71 were fit enough to look after the invalids, who were about 50 in number.

The general even recorded the rations given to the infirm of the monastery: 'a flat loaf of barley' or 'a soup made of either broad beans or chickpeas'.[15] Thus the charade proceeded, with Maletti discussing minutiae of Bét Selihom such as the serving of chickpea soup, while the congregation of the monastery, locked in the church without food or water, awaited the death sentence. The general then reached the topic of specialised monastery services, for which, after a seemingly diligent study of the matter, he decided 'to nominate a certain number of treasurers, conservationists, librarians, etc., to keep, maintain and ensure the functioning of certain essential services: in total four monks'.[16]

Why was General Maletti's report so detailed and apparently sympathetic to Debre Libanos? Why did he go into such depth into the future operations of the monastery that he was about to annihilate? And what was the point of writing such a report two days *after* the massacre? Although a delaying tactic, the meeting may not have been staged for the monks alone. His account was an official report, not a telegram to his friend Graziani. Written as if he had actually intended to implement those plans at the time, the report gives the impression that Maletti was unaware that his orders were to destroy the monastery. Indeed, in his preliminary report, in which he had estimated that two to three thousand people would be at the monastery, he had not suggested that they were to come to any harm. Even two days *after* the massacre, the opening sentence of his report stated merely that he was ordered to proceed with the 'setting straight [*risanamento*]' of the monastery, with no hint of its impending destruction. Perhaps Maletti was aware of Mussolini's decision to replace Graziani, and may have been, so to speak, playing safe, signalling to Rome that he had no intention of executing anyone unless ordered to do so; he was not executing defenceless civilians of his own accord.

Meanwhile, one of those inside the church was young Tibebe Kassa, who had watched the operation with fascination from the beginning, and had gone to the church to see what was happening. His friends had told him that if he said he was a deacon, the soldiers would leave him alone. But that had proved to be the worst possible advice, because Tibebe, who in fact held no position in the Church, had been seized by *askaris* and pushed inside, and now, as darkness fell, he too realised that he was now a captive. In the gloom, he could see that those around him were bewildered but calm. They were being led in prayer by elderly members of the clergy. A bearded priest reached for the ancient tome of *The Contendings of St Tekle Haymanot*, the holy man whose mortal remains lay beneath their feet, and the congregation prayed for the miracle that would save them.[17]

Detention

Wednesday, 19 May, hardly features in Maletti's report—a lacuna possibly explained by the fact that on that day one of his troops' principal tasks seems to have been pillage.[18] The only event mentioned was the refusal of the monks and deacons still in their huts and cottages to follow his orders to turn themselves in. 'I ordered their immediate arrest', he wrote, 'and, at 6.00 am, the number of them arrested reached 325.'[19]

Nonetheless, from eyewitness accounts it is clear that Wednesday was a busy day. As dawn broke, the clergy were dragged from their beds, and the great doors of the church of St Tekle Haymanot were swung open. Ordered to leave in single file, the captives emerged into the daylight to find that they were required to give their details: name, place of birth, age and occupation.[20]

The first 30 or 40 captives to have completed the identity check were assembled near the bell-tower, and were made to climb unceremoniously at gunpoint onto a military truck, which took them up the rough track through Wusha Gedel, onto the Fiché road. It continued its journey a short distance to a heavily guarded field known as Mesqel Massaya,[21] on the western side of the road, where the prisoners were offloaded. Then a second group climbed aboard another truck, which was also dispatched to Mesqel Massaya, in a cycle that would continue for the rest of the day.

At around 5 pm, Tibebe had to join the line. He gave his details, again thinking that if he pretended to be a deacon, he would be safe. But he found himself being ordered onto one of the trucks, to join the adults, many of whom were monks and priests. Tibebe was confused. Why were they arresting the clergy? As the truck passed his home in Wusha Gedel, he wondered when he would see his parents again.[22]

Arriving at Mesqel Massaya, Tibebe recognised several of his friends who had been there since the previous day, as well as pilgrims who had been captured at Chagel en route to the monastery. By 6 pm, several hundred captives had been transferred from the church of St Tekle Haymanot to Mesqel Massaya.[23]

That evening at Fiché, General Maletti received the telegram he had been expecting, stating that Royal Military Advocate Franceschino had 'gathered absolute proof of the complicity of monks of Debra Libanos monastery together with the authors of the attempt'.[24] In fact, the report contained no absolute proof; it actually consisted principally of hearsay. It indicated that Abriha Deboch was close to the *tsebaté* and a few of the senior monks, which was not surprising, given his mother-in-law's connections with the *gebez* of the monastery, and the fact that she lived in the vicinity. At most, the investigations suggested that some of the monks might have been tipped off that there could be trouble in Addis Ababa in the near future, which again was not surprising, given that ten days before the attack on the High Command, Abriha had taken his wife, Taddesech, to the safety of the monastery, to stay with her mother. There was no evidence that the clergy as a body had any involvement in, or even knowledge of, the forthcoming attack on the High Command. Nonetheless, the viceroy apparently felt that the outcome of the investigations was sufficient to enable him to present the liquidation of the monastery as punishment for a crime, rather than an act of exemplary repression designed to terrorise the Ethiopian Church into submission and presumably to satisfy his own paranoia.

The attack of 19 February having given Graziani the excuse he needed to eliminate his enemies, real or imagined, his telegram went on: 'Therefore execute summarily all monks without distinction, including vice-prior. Please assure me this has been done by informing me of the number of them.'[25]

12

DEATH IN THE AFTERNOON

'We are going to pay the ultimate price, but fear not them that kill the body, but are unable to kill the soul.'
Father Tesfa of Debre Libanos, 21 May 1937

The Day of the Saint

Although 20 May 1937 was the holy day of both St Tekle Haymanot and the Archangel Michael, there was nothing holy about the behaviour of the Italian military in Ethiopia's Christian highlands. Captain Corvo, the *residente* in Bahir Dar, Gojjam, was that very day writing a chilling order to one of his subordinates—one of several documents later submitted to the United Nations as evidence of Italian war crimes: 'You are to punish without pity all persons found in possession of arms and ammunition. I instruct you to burn not only their houses, but also the persons themselves.'[1] Under their policy of exemplary repression, when the Italians burned houses it was common practice to burn the occupants to death in the process. However, since this was not normally admitted in writing, Corvo's written instruction reflects the level of impunity reached by Cardinal Schuster's 'missionaries of the Cross' by May 1937.

Early in the morning Maletti arrived at Debre Libanos with commanders Colonel Marenco and Dr Barca, as well as more troops from Fiché.² The great bell—a gift to the monastery from co-religionist Tsar Nicholas II of Russia in happier times—clanged a welcome from the bell-tower, and the Italians were greeted ceremoniously by the clergy. However, the greetings were not reciprocated. Instead, Maletti feigned anger at finding so few people. Pretending to be unaware of the hundreds of faithful already imprisoned at Mesqel Massaya, he made great play of his apparent annoyance, and went on to use his 'disappointment' at finding such a small crowd as a reason for locking up the visitors who had just arrived. 'As I was informed, you used to be about 700, but now I see only 300 of you. Now, as I want to punish those who did not welcome me [i.e., those who had not yet arrived], you must stay in the church so that you may not be mixed with them.'³

More pilgrims continued to turn up, only to find that the monastery had become a trap; they were never to return. In due course the official welcoming ceremony was completed, and that was when Maletti's charade came to an end, as it was followed by the arrest of the very monks that he had just put in charge of the monastery.⁴

The first to fall to the bullets of the general's *askaris* were the elderly, the sick and the dying, who were traditionally cared for by the nuns. Unable or unwilling to climb onto the trucks, the Italians had them shot on the spot. Others were shot as they tried to run away.⁵ Monks unable to leave their cottages were shot where they lay; others were rounded up and executed. Some disabled victims were shot on the banks of the monastery's River Qonjit, where their bodies tumbled down onto the stones below.⁶

Later that morning the military started removing people from the church. Since most of the resident clergy had already been moved to Mesqel Massaya, the captives of 20 May included many visitors, including priests and monks from other churches and monasteries. As the monastery grounds swarmed with *askaris*, the captives were ordered to sit on the ground in groups in the open space between the bell-tower and the House of the Cross, until they were ordered onto the trucks. Once full, the trucks drove off, returning empty for a new load.

In this way the prisoner convoy to Mesqel Massaya was resumed, further swelling the numbers there. While the fate of the monks and priests was sealed, that of the deacons—several of whom were little more than children—was still in the balance. Maletti was being cautious about shooting them, and at 2.15 pm he telegraphed Graziani for his instructions: 'Please notify me urgently if the deacons are to be set free, or imprisoned, or shot.'[7] The elimination of the deacons, as we shall see, had already been planned in considerable detail. Graziani did not want them killed at Laga Weldé; the executions would be carried out secretly at Borale.

By 3 pm the convoy to Mesqel Massaya had stopped running, and the prisoners there were being divided into groups. Then the captives at the monastery were taken in four trucks to spend the night at another site, close to the church of the Saviour of the World at Chagel.[8] It was most likely at this moment, when the captives were waiting to be transported to the new holding ground at Chagel, that a photograph was taken. The 26-year-old *Tenente* (Lieutenant) Virgilio Cozzani, a commander of the 45th Battalion,[9] was apparently a keen photographer and, despite Graziani's assurance to Mussolini that executions would be kept secret, the young officer captured the moment for posterity. Judging from the shadows, his photograph was most likely taken at around 4 pm.

The photograph shows several groups of captive Ethiopians sitting on the ground guarded by *askaris*, and waiting to be loaded onto four large trucks with their tailgates open, drawn up below the escarpment in the background. The bed of each truck is covered with a canvas awning. A fifth truck stands nearby, and a sixth is parked in a different position, closer to the church of St Tekle Haymanot, which is out of the picture, to the left. On the back of the photograph Cozzani wrote the date (20 May), noting that the captives wearing a headdress were believed (by the Italians) to be priests.[10]

Some of the Ethiopians on the ground in the photograph are wearing turbans, and are clearly priests, and a few seem to be wearing monks' caps. However, while several are almost certainly male pilgrims, those in white with their heads covered could be women. This would be consistent with the fact that most of the monks and priests belonging to Debre Libanos had been relocated to Mesqel Massaya the day before.[11]

It was 10.03 pm when Graziani responded to Maletti's telegram. During the afternoon he seems to have been trying to frame a case against the deacons but had not yet managed to do so, so he was not yet ready to have them shot. For now, they would have to be held captive. Concerned that Maletti should not overstep the mark, the viceroy was explicit: 'They must be imprisoned,' he pencilled in at the bottom of Maletti's message, presumably for his secretary's attention. Just to be sure, he repeated, 'I say imprisoned.' Then, yet again, 'Assure with the word "imprisoned".'[12]

In his report of 22 May, Maletti described the capture of about a thousand people found 'hiding' in the Siga Wedem gorge. He wrote that the operation of identifying and listing them took the entire night of the 20th, and the morning of the 21st. Among the thousand people arrested, he identified 297 monks, 155 deacons and 'hundreds' of servants, gardeners, workers, pilgrims, craftsmen and labourers, 23 of whom he suspected were 'messengers of the monastery to and from the periphery' while 'pretending to be pilgrims'.[13] This section of Maletti's report is tantamount to fiction, for it would have taken not one day but several weeks for a detachment of soldiers to comb the entire Siga Wedem gorge. No doubt some of the *askaris* went down into the gorge, but in one day they would not have reached much further than Kora, at the bottom of the gorge below Debre Libanos. Nonetheless, they would have come across many people. Anyone in Rome reading Maletti's report about people 'hiding in the gorge' would probably visualise people crouching down in some sort of crevice to avoid capture. However, the gorge is a vast cultural landscape of more than two hundred square kilometres, and since the 13th century—if not earlier—there have been thousands of people not 'hiding' but living within the gorge. In fact, there were, and still are, more than 56 villages established on the terraces in the gorge, each with its own church, as well as a number of monasteries. There are also anchorites, hermits and monks living in caves, and a number of ancient rock-hewn churches.

Maletti wrote that some people had gone into hiding when his troops made an appearance, 'clear evidence of the propaganda of the monastery hostile to us'. However, the atrocities, bombing and use of poison gas in Northern Shewa were so well known that anyone with their wits about them would have gone into hiding on spotting the Italian military. Moreover, there is nothing unusual or suspicious about finding people in isolated locations in the Siga Wedem gorge. For centuries the residents of the gorge have included some of the world's most ascetic communities, many still following the strict monastic rule of St Anthony.

However, none of this was explained to Rome. The impression was given that anyone found in the gorge must be 'suspicious' or 'hiding' and thus 'hostile' and subject to arrest. But the viceroy must have been gratified, for his scheme was unfolding as planned. The number of captives had reached four figures, and was still climbing.

'Fear Not Them That Kill the Body'

General Maletti took personal charge of the operations on Friday, 21 May; Graziani was to report later in the day, in a chilling turn of phrase, that the general had been at Debre Libanos 'to settle the question of this monastery'.[14] The viceroy was anxious to know exactly what was happening as it unfolded, for he urged Maletti, 'Please notify me of the progress of the mission. I wish to be kept informed frequently.'[15]

As the sun was rising, under the command of Italian officers, *askaris* of the dreaded 45th Colonial Battalion made their way from Fiché to the plain of Laga Weldé. They disembarked and took up positions in semicircular formation around the plain, adopting vantage points on the slopes of the five hills: Wagede, Kotichu, Gobola, Tsebaté and Shinkurt.

Curious and frightened villagers from the settlements at Shinkurt, and Alete Maryam on the hill of Genda Gora, watched from afar. They knew about the prison camp at Mesqel Massaya, and sensed that something terrible was happening.

Behind the line of armed men, a fifteen-year-old boy named Zelleqe and his father, from Tama village near Shinkurt, managed to find a viewpoint near Tsebaté hill from which they could see much of what was going on, albeit from a considerable distance. They were to stay there, transfixed by what was unfolding before their eyes, for the entire day.[16]

At around 9 am, the captives at Mesqel Massaya were assembled, inspected, questioned and once again divided into two groups: clergy and pilgrims with connections with Debre Libanos; and laity with no direct link with the monastery.[17] Anyone wearing a hat was deemed by the Italians a monk or priest, and was put in the first group.[18] At 10 am, Maletti, clearly delighted with the way things were developing, telegraphed Graziani reassuringly, 'Everything is proceeding normally just as if Your Excellency was on the spot.'[19]

Eventually Tibebe concluded that pretending to be a deacon might not be such a good idea after all. So he refrained from his earlier claim and, fortunately, being a 'bare-head', was told to join the 'non-clergy' group, where there were several other boys.

In the early afternoon, empty military trucks started arriving at the transit camp at Mesqel Massaya. Tibebe watched as the first group of captives standing in the 'clergy' section were put onto the first truck. As the vehicle pulled away, Tibebe noted that it contained 30 to 40 prisoners.[20] An armed guard sat in the passenger seat beside the driver, and another in the back, watching over the captives. The vehicle turned north towards Fiché and gradually disappeared from view.[21]

Zelleqe caught sight of the truck on the Fiché road as it came into view near Tsebaté hill. He watched as it turned off the road, to the north-east, and lumbered along the grassy lower slopes of Gobola, swaying with its heavy load across the undulations. Passing through the cordon of *askaris*, it turned north-west as it approached the edge of the precipice and came to a halt at the Fincha Wenz, a small, meandering stream that had cut a shallow gulley into the plateau of Laga Weldé for about two hundred metres before plunging into the gorge. During the long rains from June to September the Fincha Wenz would overflow its banks, creating a marshy floodplain, and for this reason the execution site is also known locally as Chafé, meaning 'wetland'.

Trained soldiers of the 45th Colonial Battalion who had taken up position along the Fincha Wenz now swung rapidly into action. Without further ado, the victims were pulled off the truck. On one side was the edge of the gorge; the other three sides of the plain were ringed with armed *askaris*. There were Italian officers milling around and several *askaris*, two of whom were manning Breda machine guns set up on tripods, facing the Fincha Wenz.

The Italians lined up a group of prisoners with their backs to the guns. Many elderly, and some tottering without their prayer sticks for support, the captives were made to squat in a line near the edge of the southern bank of the stream, which, being seasonal, was quite dry at this time of year. Then the soldiers produced a long narrow black cloth, which they draped across the victims, like a narrow tent, forming a hood over the head of each captive.

At this moment a voice rang out. It was one of the captives—a monk named *Abba* Tesfa, a teacher in one of the schools at Debre Libanos—the namesake of his forebear whose portrait graced Italy's state church of Santa Maria degli Angeli. Quoting Matthew 10:28—a reassuring biblical message that would long be remembered in the annals of the monastery—he cried, 'My Brothers, Martyrs, we are going to pay the ultimate price, but fear not them that kill the body, but are unable to kill the soul. So do not be afraid of those who would destroy your body, for you will all go to heaven!' The theme was then taken up by two other senior clergymen, *Aleqa* Mekbib-Haylé (a monk engaged in charitable work at the monastery) and *Aleqa* Wedajéneh, a senior scholar, who added, 'Even if we lose our worldly life, we will now live in heaven.'[22]

However, the Italians had hundreds more captives to execute before dark, and so, eager to get on with the business in hand, the Italian commander[23] gave the order to shoot. At around 1 pm, as the staccato of machine-gun fire echoed from the hills across the plain, some of the most renowned clergy and theologians of the Ethiopian Orthodox Church fell forwards into the gulley, their backs riddled with bullets. *Askaris* stepped forward to remove the cloth, and a junior officer delivered a final pistol shot to the temple of each victim.[24] Meanwhile, the empty truck, which had been driven back to Mesqel Massaya to collect more victims, was soon replaced by another vehicle with a similar load. The same black cloth, now wet with blood, was used again, the guns spoke, and another line of clergymen met their end.

All the available eyewitnesses state that the victims at Laga Weldé were made to sit in a line with their heads covered by a long narrow black cloth. Furthermore, both the eyewitnesses and the monastery authorities state that the shooting was carried out by machine guns. However, it appears that during the course of the afternoon, after several loads of captives had been shot, there was a change in the procedures at the execution site. A photograph of the massacre taken by *Tenente* Cozzani in the possession of Luigi Panella shows a firing squad of Muslim *askaris* shooting the clergy with hand-held weapons, and possibly without the black cloth. And another of Cozzani's photographs, perhaps taken later in the day, shows a shocking scene of considerable disorder—almost pandemonium—at the execution site. Dead or dying Ethiopians are sprawled over the ground—some inside the shallow gulley, some having partly fallen into it, and others on the banks of the stream. Excited *askaris* are running around wildly like bandits, dressed in a motley assortment of ragged 'uniforms', few of which look like regulation attire.

Although Maletti's report makes no mention of irregulars under his command at the time, the chaotic scene in this photograph suggests the possibility that some might have been deployed at Laga Weldé. However, Luigi Panella is of the opinion that the soldiers concerned were all members of the 45th Colonial Battalion.[25] In this same photograph the senior officer, Major Castellano, can be seen facing directly into the camera, amidst the carnage, as well as Captain Ragazzoni and Captain Aliotta, all seemingly quite happy to be photographed, despite Graziani's solemn assurance to Mussolini that such executions were held in secret.[26] The same spirit of jingoism that pervaded the Italians during the massacre is also reflected in a trite but revealing comment written—apparently by Cozzani himself—on the back of one of the photographs: 'Monks, cheerio!'[27]

From his view at Mesqel Massaya, Tibebe, who made a point of counting the captives, reckoned that approximately 600 monks, priests, deacons and visitors were taken to Laga Weldé, although it was only later that he learned where they had gone. He noted that it took about 30 minutes for each truck to cover a complete cycle, and that each turnaround was marked by radio or telegraph messages sent from Laga Weldé to Mesqel Massaya, instructing the *askaris* there to prepare the next load of prisoners. According to Tibebe, the process came to a halt at around 3 pm.

Based on Tibebe's information, each of the four or five trucks made an average of four deliveries, totalling around eighteen truckloads.[28] Thus, with an average of 35 prisoners per vehicle, this would have been equivalent to about 630 prisoners executed at Laga Weldé by 3 pm, which is consistent with Tibebe's figure of about 600.

By about 3.30 pm, the movement of prisoners from Mesqel Massaya to Laga Weldé had ceased, but many captives still remained in the camp. Tibebe now found himself being loaded onto one of the trucks together with the other boys and several other prisoners, and driven off. But when they reached the main road, instead of turning north to Laga Weldé, the vehicle swung south, towards Addis Ababa. The captives did not know what to think. Fearful of what was to befall them, he and his companions, who were deacons, students, visitors to the monastery and young boys like himself, sat terrified in the lorry as it made its way towards the capital. Stowed in the back were clothes, prayer books and prayer sticks belonging to the monks and priests who had just met their death.

Meanwhile, at the monastery the air was full of the shouts of officers and troops; no one was spared, and no mercy shown. *Askaris* rounded up anyone who had stayed away from the church or was too old or feeble to have reached it. Some of the victims would by now have realised their fate, but many of these unfortunate monks would have had no idea what was going on, as they were hauled out of their homes by gangs of armed soldiers. According to the monastery, the Italians sent two more trucks to Debre Libanos on 21 May to collect these remaining prisoners for execution.[29]

The execution of those who baulked at climbing onto the trucks was one of several episodes that went unreported to Rome, thus contributing to the disparities between the actual number killed in the massacre and the figures in the Italian telegrams hitherto quoted by historians. In this case, thanks to the research of diplomat-writer Birhanu Denqé, we have some details. The shooting of those who either refused to board or tried to run away, we are told, was carried out by the *carabinieri* under the command of a certain *Shum-bashi* Abriha, apparently Eritrean. Highly thought of by the Italians because he 'shared their ideas', he was 'assigned to kill as many people as he could'.[30] The actual number killed was recorded: 'Monks who refused to leave were machine-gunned in the church compound near the Weyra tree. Those killed were thirty, except *Abba* Habtu, who survived.'[31]

Zelleqe, who was still stationed at his vantage point, saw truck-loads of prisoners continuing to arrive at the execution site of Laga Weldé until the convoy finally ceased at around six. By the time the exercise came to an end, no less than 39 truck-loads had discharged their human cargo.[32] With between 30 and 40 victims in each vehicle, a total of some 1,200 to 1,600 clergy and pilgrims were that day executed on the plain of Laga Weldé.[33]

The viceroy's telegram to Rome in the evening after the massacre made no mention of nuns, but in a sworn affidavit *Ras* Abebe Aregay testified that nuns were executed: 'The Italians returned [to Debre Libanos monastery] in the month of Ginbot and exterminated all the monks and nuns of the monastery.'[34] The monastery authorities are in no doubt that nuns of Debre Libanos were among those killed, for the plaque at the monastery erected in 1973 refers to the slaughter as having been of 'monks and nuns'.[35]

Apparently delighted with the outcome of the day's work, Maletti telegraphed the news to Graziani in Addis Ababa, but mentioned only the execution of 297 monks and 23 'suspects'—a total of 320 dead. Of these, 260 may be accounted for by a handwritten note on the back of one of Cozzani's photographs, indicating the shooting of '260 monks'. Maletti's report of the executions was very curt, stating only that troops had shot the victims 'in a valley near Fiché', the executions being carried out 'in successive groups'.[36]

Having received Maletti's confirmation that all had gone according to plan, Graziani now proceeded to write a long telegram to Lessona in Rome, spelling out Franceschino's reasons for linking the monastery with the attempted assassination. He went on to report, 'In consequence of my orders, General Maletti today at 13 o'clock has ordered to the firing party two hundred and ninety-seven monks, including vice prior and twenty-three others also deemed guilty of complicity.'[37]

As noted earlier, by the end of the previous day, Maletti had reportedly captured 'around one thousand' people earmarked as 'hostile', which meant that they were liable to be executed, and many more were captured on 21 May. However, the general's telegram of that day reported a total of just 320 monks and 'suspects' executed, with 155 deacons held pending a decision on their fate.[38] That telegram made no mention of the 'hundreds of other people' people'—a reference to numerous non-clergy who had been arrested. Yet they were certainly not released, because there is no evidence of anyone reappearing after being held at Chagel, apart from the 30 young boys, who were imprisoned.[39] However, a separate telegram sent the following day (see Appendix IV) indicates that those people had, without exception, been 'definitely resolved'—meaning they were executed. No one will ever know the precise number, but notwithstanding the margins of estimating error, there is no doubt that General Maletti executed far more people at Laga Weldé than was reported in Graziani's telegram to Rome.

13

MASSACRE AT BORALE RIVER

> 'The whole history of Christianity proves that she has indeed little to fear from persecution as a foe, but much to fear from persecution as an ally.'
>
> Lord Macaulay

The Gravediggers

As the convoy carrying Tibebe and his compatriots made its way through the night of Friday, 21 May, few, if any, of the captives managed to sleep. The ride was rough and noisy, and the passengers were terrified. Apart from boys such as Tibebe, the group consisted of deacons, visitors to Debre Libanos, and students. Unbeknown to them, their fate had already been decided for a clandestine operation was under way. Early that morning, even before the selection of victims at Chagel had begun, soldiers carrying shovels had arrived at Ingécha. Watched by a few local children, they had started digging along the bottom of the shallow valley where the narrow Borale River meanders westwards.

Meanwhile, by 3 pm the convoy had arrived at Debre Birhan, where the vehicles came to a halt, and the captives alighted. Although Graziani reported that the prisoners were held in churches,[1] this is incorrect. They were actually imprisoned in a former *carabinieri* camp in the town of Debre Birhan near the cathedral of Debre Birhan Sillassé.[2]

As the prisoners walked to the detention camp, Tibebe started counting, and reckoned that they totalled around 280, including himself and the other boys. Arriving at the camp, they found that it was already occupied by around 120 other prisoners who had been visiting Debre Libanos when the Italian military arrived, and thought they had been spared execution. That brought the total number of detainees at the camp to about 400.

It was on this day that Maletti sent his report to Graziani in which he described having captured 155 deacons and 'hundreds' of other people whom he described as servants, peasants and pilgrims—a description confirmed by Tibebe.[3] At the time, Maletti was not certain whether he was expected to kill them, for he telegraphed Graziani asking the viceroy to confirm that everyone 'without distinction' was to be 'definitively resolved', i.e., executed.[4] Maletti's report stated that following Graziani's instructions, the deacons were 'incarcerated for now at Debre Birhan'. In fact, not all of the 155 'deacons' were actually deacons. Thirty of them had already been identified as schoolboys with no formal connection with the Church, and one member of this group was Tibebe.

On Monday, 24 May, Graziani finally made up his mind, ordering Maletti to immediately execute 'all the deacons of Debre Libanos, excepting boys. Confirm with words "Complete Liquidation"' (see Appendix V).[5]

This left the question of the hundreds of students, teachers, pilgrims and visitors from other churches. It is clear that even given Graziani's appetite for executions, the only captives whom he could possibly incriminate in the attempted assassination were those connected directly with the monastery of Debre Libanos. Ever since the attack of *Yekatit 12* and the massacre of Addis Ababa, Minister Lessona had been trying to get Graziani ousted from the position of viceroy. He had complained to Mussolini that Graziani was of unsound mind, and was dragging the Italian administration into disrepute. So, with Lessona looking over his shoulder, watching for any excuse to claim that the viceroy had taken leave of his senses, Graziani could not risk ordering in writing the cold-blooded execution of such large numbers of civilians with no conceivable connection with the attempt on his life.

Thus, in the absence of any other written orders from Graziani, how did Maletti know on 21 May that further executions were to be carried out at Borale, leading him to authorise the gravediggers to begin their work on the same day? And how did he know the numbers to be executed? For many years, as we shall see, this would remain a mystery.

From the time the group of captives arrived at Debre Birhan, the non-Debre Libanos prisoners, teachers and pilgrims—'people without distinction'—disappear from the Italian records. Only the deacons (who *were* connected with Debre Libanos monastery) and the boys are mentioned in Graziani's communications.

On 25 May officers and *askaris* ordered the 400 prisoners to assemble, and started singling out the 30 boys who were not deacons. They were ordered to stand to one side and were escorted out of the camp, with no time to say farewell to their older companions. They were then moved to a *bande militari* camp in the town centre.[6]

Meanwhile, in the Borale valley the soldiers had returned with their spades and resumed digging. In all, they dug for five days. By Tuesday evening three large trenches had been completed along the shallow riverbed, each around ten metres long, three metres wide and one and a half metres deep. One of the children who watched the men at work was fifteen-year-old Feqyibelu Yirgu, who lived in the cottage overlooking the site from the south. After the soldiers had left, he jumped inside the trenches. Asked in his old age how deep they were, his response was, 'Up to my chin!' None of the children knew what the trenches were for, although his older sister Mulatwa, who was 25 years old and married with four children, had her suspicions.[7]

Martyrs for the Church

Early in the morning of Wednesday, 26 May, the solitude of the Borale valley was disturbed by the arrival of several hundred soldiers.[8] Running out of their cottages to watch the goings-on, the local children saw some of the soldiers checking the excavations, while the others started walking up the surrounding slopes, clearing away the few people and livestock in the vicinity. The fifteen-year-old Feleqe Asress ran up the hillside and heard the rest of the day's events from a safe distance, but saw little.[9] Another was seven-year-old Derbi Tsegé, who also fled in the face of the advancing soldiers.[10] Young Letarge, who lived in his father's house on the northern slope of the valley, was watching, together with two little boys named Gebre Gonete and Negash Yirgu, the nephew of Feqyibelu.[11]

In *Ato* Yirgu's house on the southern slope, his daughter Mulatwa was watching the proceedings. For some reason no soldiers came to the house, or if they did, they failed to realise that Mulatwa was there. Outside the house Feqyibelu was crouching in the undergrowth, about 200 yards from the trenches.

The soldiers now took up positions around the site, preventing anyone from entering the valley. Then at about 11 am, local residents some distance to the west of the valley saw a convoy of trucks approaching,[12] which stopped a few hundred metres from the Borale River.[13] In each truck were many prisoners, tied together. In addition, there were three passenger vehicles carrying several Italian officers.

The commander, his officers and several soldiers drove to the Borale River in the valley near the excavations, and had machine guns set up on steel tripods. Then one of the trucks left the convoy and proceeded along the valley, coming to a halt at the western end of the southern slope, not far from *Ato* Yirgu's house. Feqyibelu saw that the truck was packed full with about 70 people, and that several of them were young.[14]

Negash described the offloading as a noisy affair, 'with a lot of pushing and shouting'.[15] After some of the prisoners had been ordered down from the truck, Feqyibelu could see that the ropes were being adjusted so that the prisoners were now tied together in batches of five or six. The prisoners were all male—a mixture of old and young, clergy, deacons, and many laity with no direct connection with the Church. Feqyibelu estimated that around a third of the total were deacons. Approximately half of the victims wore clerical vestments, and several wore a cross on a leather necklace and carried a holy book in a traditional leather case. The victims' outer garments were removed and piled up near *Ato* Yirgu's house, following which *askaris* tied each prisoner's wrists together with wire.[16] Escape was impossible. Officers then made the captives walk to the execution site, where they were lined up along two of the trenches. Unlike what happened in the executions at Laga Weldé, no cloth or cover was placed over the victims' heads.

Without further ado, the machine guns opened fire, and the captives crumpled and fell. Victims who still showed any sign of life were finished off by an officer with a pistol, and any bodies that had not fallen into the trenches were pushed in.[17]

Negash Yirgu, who in 2015 was still living in the same family house overlooking the execution site, confirmed Mulatwa's and Feqyibelu's accounts in detail, re-enacting the executions on site for the benefit of a visiting group of researchers from the University of Debre Birhan and the University of Addis Ababa, together with the present author.[18]

Negash, like his neighbours, had no difficulty pointing out the precise shape and location of the mass graves, which extended over a total distance of around fifty metres, and recounting the details of the massacre: how the victims were made to stand and how they were shot, with their wrists tied together with wire, for his family had never forgotten the day in May 1937 when the normally tranquil valley just below his front door became a place of horror and death.[19]

Feleqe Asress, who watched the soldiers bring the prisoners to the execution site but was chased away out of sight before the killing began, recalled: 'I did not see the actual shooting, but I could hear the sound of the machine guns. The soldiers who did the shooting were *ferenjes* [Europeans] and *Hamasiens* [Eritreans].'[20]

Mulatwa, who watched the executions from her house in frozen horror, later recalled the sound of the captives in their last moments. She would never forget the way they burst forth in a joyful chorus: 'They were ululating with joy as they became martyrs for the Church.'

Feqyibelu watched transfixed as the next group of captives was brought to the trenches and shot, and so on until all of them had been executed. By that time Mulatwa had fled in terror from the house and disappeared over the hilltop, running from the scene as fast as she could.

In 1948, Baron Eric Leijonhufvud (1907–72), who had recently retired as Ethiopian advocate general and had been teaching at the Haile Selassie Military Academy in Addis Ababa,[21] published in his memoir a sketch captioned 'Massacre of monks from Debra Libanos' (Fig. 44).[22] Accredited to 'an Ethiopian artist', it depicts the execution of men in clerical clothes in a shallow valley encircled by a ring of soldiers.

The illustration shows two homesteads, planted with eucalyptus trees, standing on opposite slopes of the valley, a scene similar to the setting at Borale. Running along the bottom of the valley is a trench into which the bodies of priests or monks are falling, as they are shot by soldiers facing them across the trench and firing two tripod-mounted machine guns. Along the top of the slope behind the victims is a line of soldiers. In the foreground is a track on which can be seen, at the edge of the sketch, the front part of a vehicle. Supervising the proceedings is a uniformed Italian officer.

The degree of detail in the sketch suggests that it was drawn by an eyewitness, in which case the slopes and the homesteads shown may be drawn from the actual scene rather than from the artist's imagination.

There were no trees or homesteads in the immediate vicinity of Laga Weldé in 1937, no sloping ground around the site, and no track or pathway. On the other hand, all of these features were, and still are, present at Borale. Thus the sketch most likely shows the executions at Borale, and was probably the work of one of the soldiers.

Around midday the shooting stopped, by which time Feqyibelu estimated that around 500 victims had been shot. The soldiers then began to shovel soil on the bodies lying in heaps in the mass graves.

In 1958 the authors of the Amharic *History of Haile Selassie I Military Academy from 1927 to 1949* [EC] published an unidentified photograph taken during the occupation (Fig. 45).[23] The illustration, which is not cited in the text, is captioned, 'This photograph shows the cruelty of the Fascists'. Neither the location nor the date of the photograph is identified. Eight uniformed Italian soldiers—a combination of regulars and militarised labourers—pose nonchalantly with rifles and shovels along the edge of a shallow trench containing numerous corpses. They appear to be either waiting for more bodies to be thrown in or are about to shovel soil on top of the bodies. The shadows at the feet of the two soldiers on the right indicate an overhead midday sun. In the background, a featureless landscape slopes gently upwards to the crest of a low hill, which is planted with eucalyptus silhouetted against the skyline.

If one ignores the apparent slope of the landscape down to the left, which is created mainly by the tilt of the camera, the scene in the photograph is consistent with the landscape at Borale. Most likely it was taken either at Borale or at the site of a mass grave following another, similar massacre conducted in a similar setting. Although the digging of mass graves to bury massacre victims would become common under Italian occupation in the Balkans, it was less common in Ethiopia.[24] Furthermore, the deployment of Italians rather than the Eritrean *askaris* to do the digging of the trenches and the covering up of the bodies afterwards was unusual, and would be consistent with a desire on the part of the commanders to keep the executions and the location secret. For these reasons it is likely that this photograph shows a section of the mass grave at Borale. Another photograph (Fig. 46) could be either of the same trench or possibly the second trench. The victims can be seen to have their wrists tied together, as the eyewitnesses reported.

By 1 pm, according to the witnesses, the soldiers had left. The 30 boys in Debre Birhan were now the sole survivors of the congregation that had gathered at Debre Libanos on that ill-fated St Tekle Haymanot Day. Trembling with fear, the youngsters could scarcely eat their food, hungry though they were. Meanwhile, General Maletti was telegraphing his report to Graziani, putting it on record that he had had the deacons of Debre Libanos executed, as specified in Graziani's order.[25]

The Toll at Borale

Tibebe's evidence of the number of captives he saw suggests that the death toll at Borale was around 370. Yet eyewitnesses at Borale report a figure of 500 or more victims executed there.[26] The key to the difference is Feqyibelu's observation that many of the victims he watched being executed were wearing clerical vestments, and that some of them still had their neck crosses and prayer books when they arrived at the execution site. And Mulatwa made a special point of mentioning that their outer garments were removed and piled up outside her house while the executions were taking place. Yet Tibebe observed that not a single captive brought from Debre Libanos had been allowed to retain such clothes or to carry such artefacts.

Clearly, the 370 captives counted by Tibebe were augmented by around 130 other people belonging to other churches, who arrived at Debre Libanos during or after the executions at Laga Weldé. They must have been brought to Debre Birhan on 25 May, after the boys had been moved to make room for them. This would be consistent with the reports by eyewitnesses at Borale that only a few of the clergy executed there belonged to Debre Libanos. In fact, they recognised some of the victims, identified them by name, and knew to which churches they belonged. Furthermore, the bodies in the photographs generally appear to be adults. It thus becomes clear that Maletti's report mentioning only the shooting of the deacons did not tell the whole story.

Furthermore, given the dimensions provided by Feqyibelu, the volume of each trench was around 45 cubic metres. This suggests that the trenches dug at Borale could easily accommodate 500 bodies.[27] Clearly there was no need for the soldiers to excavate such large trenches if the intention was to bury 'only' 125 deacons.

The inevitable conclusion is that around 500 victims died at Borale, of which 125 were deacons belonging to the church of St Tekle Haymanot at Debre Libanos.[28] The 'hundreds of others', as Maletti referred to them, totalling around 375, consisted of pilgrims and clergy belonging to other churches who had been visiting Debre Libanos to celebrate the day of the saint.

14

TELLING THE STORY

> *'That a lie which is all a lie may be met and fought with outright,*
> *But a lie which is part a truth is a harder matter to fight.'*
> Alfred Lord Tennyson, 'The Grandmother'

'There Remains No Trace'

As we have seen, after the massacre of Debre Libanos Graziani confidently informed Rome that 'no trace' of the monastery remained. Since there had been around a thousand resident clergy, plus several hundred laymen and women, and at least another thousand or more regular visitors associated with the monastery, the only way of ensuring complete liquidation would have been to execute all these people, amounting to at least two thousand. The monastery confirms that around one thousand clergy were executed, as testified by all available eyewitnesses. Furthermore, based on the testimony of the eyewitnesses, an additional thousand or so visiting clergy and pilgrims were also executed, which is consistent with the monastery publication stating that the total death toll of the massacre was around two thousand. It is clear that the Debre Libanos community was, as planned, completely liquidated.

Had Maletti's intention been to execute 'only' 297 clergy, the most difficult time to do it would have been on a special saint's day, when more than two thousand other people would be crowding around, making the process almost impossible. And he certainly would not have made the exercise even more difficult by announcing that everybody should attend on that day, on pain of excommunication from the monastery. Rather, he would simply have sent one of his brigades unannounced, executed the first 297 clergy he came across, and then left. The only possible purpose of enticing the greatest possible number of people to the monastery would have been to include them as victims, thereby ensuring that no trace of the monastery would remain.

On 27 May the viceroy telegraphed the minister for the colonies, reporting the shooting of the deacons. He also stated that 'there are left alive only thirty schoolboys', which was true.[1] Judging from the behaviour of the Eritrean *askaris* at Borale—their having spared a young boy, and having turned a blind eye to Feqyibelu hiding as he watched the executions—it is apparent that some of them were reluctant, or unwilling, to shoot children. In fact, the Christian Eritreans had a reputation for mutinying when ordered to commit civilian atrocities. The 45th (Muslim) Colonial Battalion, which could have been relied on to carry out such executions, had moved on to the Mendida area,[2] and thus was no longer available for operations at Borale, which is why the executions there had to be carried out by a regular Eritrean company. Perhaps it was for that reason that Graziani did not order the boys to be shot.

Nonetheless, there was a snag: the full extent of the massacre at Borale had been kept secret not just from the Ethiopians, but also from Rome, and the viceroy could not afford to run the risk of the truth getting out. All witnesses had to be eliminated. He would have realised that the boys were most likely aware of the actual scale of the massacre, and so he could not risk them going home to Debre Libanos, for word would soon get about. For Graziani, that left only one solution—the method he usually employed when he wanted people out of circulation: concentration camps. Only a few weeks before, he had reported in breath-takingly light-hearted fashion how he had dispatched to Danane concentration camp 1,100 men, women and children 'who represent Amhara people of no particular importance, but who for the moment had better be prevented from roaming about'.[3]

TELLING THE STORY

For the 30 boys of Debre Libanos, that was the answer. For now they would be held at Debre Birhan, but eventually they would follow these unfortunates to the infamous concentration camp in far-away Italian Somaliland, from which they would most likely never return.[4]

However, that still left the problem of Lessona. The minister might well have used Graziani's decision to deport 30 innocent children to Danane—after he had told Rome that they had been spared—as further proof of his unsuitability for office. So the viceroy added to his previous lies with yet another, glibly reporting, 'there are left alive only 30 schoolboys, who have been sent to their native homes in the various districts of Shewa'.[5]

The Final Toll

The problem of Debre Libanos was now resolved. The congregation of Ethiopia's leading monastery had been exterminated, together with anyone else who had any involvement in its affairs.

We can conclude that between 1,800 and 2,200 Christians were executed in the massacre of Debre Libanos. The monastic community normally numbered at least 1,400 to 1,600, rising to over 2,300 on special occasions.[6] During the Italian occupation, when times were hard for the Ethiopians, the number would typically have been rather less, but given the importance of the celebrations of May 1937, when the community was told that anyone who did not attend would be barred in future, the congregation could hardly have numbered less than 2,000, and could have been more.[7] Thus it is not surprising that in his report of the executions, Graziani proudly informed Mussolini that the monastic community had been completely liquidated.[8]

The toll in Table 14.1 includes five deaths in the basement of the House of the Cross at Debre Libanos, which was erected by Emperor Menelik II in the early 20th century to house the cross of St Tekle Haymanot. Immediately after the massacre, Debre Libanos was deserted. Nonetheless, in late June 1937, one month after the massacre, someone forced open the door to the cellar of Mesqel Bét. As he entered, he was taken aback by a nauseous odour and, in the half-light was greeted by an awful sight. The children and servants of *Tsebaté* Gebre-Maryam, who had been locked inside for safety, had

211

died a terrible death by starvation. Unable to escape, and without food, their cries for help had been unheard in the deserted monastery.

It seems that the *tsebaté* himself, despite being a Fascist appointee, had locked up his charges in the hideaway. Whether he still had the key in his possession, or managed to hand it to someone else before disappearing, is unknown, but even if he did, by the time the door was opened it was too late. More than half a century later, this tragic episode is still spoken of in hushed tones by the old men and women of Chagel. It is one of the most poignant stories of the Italian occupation.

The best estimate that can now be made of the final death toll of Debre Libanos is set out in Table 14.1.

Table 14.1:
Number of Victims Killed in the Massacre of Debre Libanos

Date (1937)	Execution site	Types of victim	Number of victims
22 Feb.	Kateba Maryam, below Debre Libanos	Monks	3
20 May	Debre Libanos (at the Qonjit River)	Disabled and incapacitated elderly clergy	Unknown (est. 30 clergy)
	Chagel, during the night	Residents of either Chagel or the monastery who failed to board the trucks, and those shot while trying to run away	Est: 30 (half assumed to be clergy)
21 May	Laga Weldé, between Shinkurt Mikaél and Alete	Monks and priests of Debre Libanos	800
		Clergy from other churches, plus laymen, students, destitute and possibly nuns	400–800 (half clergy)
	At the church of St Tekle Haymanot	Monks who failed to board the trucks	30

25 May	Borale, in the area of Ingécha, near Debre Birhan	Deacons from Debre Libanos	125
		Non-Debre Libanos clergy, teachers, pilgrims	est. 375 (incl. 125 clergy)
29 May	Addis Ababa	Monks held in prison	3
Late June	House of the Cross, Debre Libanos	Children & servants of *Tsebaté* Gebre-Maryam starved to death	5
Total			1,801–2,201

A Secret Message

It is clear that the number of victims of the massacre of Debre Libanos as reported in Maletti's telegrams (320 monks and 129 deacons of Debre Libanos) is much lower than the actual total as indicated by both the eyewitness accounts and the monastery publication (both indicate the death of around 2,000 clergy and pilgrims). We also note that Maletti's figures are limited to the executions he was instructed by Graziani to carry out; the viceroy's telegrams did not instruct him to execute clergy from other churches, nor did they tell him to execute the pilgrims.

The question then arises: if Maletti received no order to execute all the other people he was holding captive, why did he do so? After all, his report suggests a cautious commander, his aim having been only to 'set the monastery straight', and it gives the impression that he carried out executions only when ordered to do so. So what induced such a cautious commander to exceed his mandate, far beyond his written instructions?

The answer most likely lies in an extraordinary incident not previously published, and unknown to the present author when he wrote *The Massacre of Debre Libanos*.[9] On 19 February, the same day that Graziani sent Maletti the telegram instructing him to execute the monks, he also sent him a personal and private message that was off the record. Classified as 'most urgent', the message was taken across to the Regia Aeronautica in Addis Ababa, on the instruction of the viceroy, to be carried in a clandestine manner by aeroplane and dropped at the monastery of Debre Libanos for Maletti. So far as is known, no carbon copy of this clandestine message was ever made, and as it was not telegraphed, no text was ever on file. After receiving it, later the same day, the Regia Aeronautica confirmed that the viceroy's 'most urgent' message would be delivered to Maletti by air as required.[10]

It is clear that the mission was accomplished as promised, for at 11.20 pm on the next day, 20 May, in a telegram to Graziani updating him on recent increases in the number of captives, Maletti informed the viceroy that he would ensure that the instructions in what he referred to as the viceroy's 'secret message' were implemented. 'I will carry out the order firmly,' he assured Graziani.[11]

It is difficult to imagine that Graziani's secret message dropped at the monastery for Maletti, being off the record, and delivered separately from the telegrams he was dispatching at the same time to the same general, could have been anything other than a supplementary order to execute all of the captives. This would explain why Maletti executed everyone he had rounded up, and it would also explain one of the greatest mysteries of the massacre: how it was that by the following day, 21 May, he had ordered a platoon to begin excavating three large mass graves at Borale capable of accommodating hundreds of bodies *three days before* he received the telegram instructing him to conduct the second set of executions.

The secrecy of this unofficial message would of course explain why neither Maletti nor Graziani reported the additional executions. But at the same time, the knowledge that Maletti had followed the instructions in the message would explain why the viceroy was confident enough to inform Rome that the monastery had been completely liquidated. In which case, Graziani knew more than he ever told Mussolini, and he and Maletti took their secret to the grave.[12]

'The Dogs Have Martyrs in Their Mouths'

Following the massacre, the Italians cordoned off the execution site at Laga Weldé. Nonetheless, a few brave souls ventured forth, one of whom was the fifteen-year-old local resident Zewdé Gebru, who saw the bodies there. As the site was still being guarded, how close he was able to get to the scene of carnage is not clear. Yet in the tv2000 documentary *Debre Libanos*, he states that he could see between 600 and 700 bodies, though doubtless only those on top of the piles of corpses in the gulley of the Fincha Wenz would have been visible.

Meanwhile, in the valley of the Borale River at Ingécha, silence reigned. For three days after the executions, soldiers returned to the site to check on the mass graves—presumably to ensure that the evidence was not being uncovered. But soon hyenas and vultures started appearing in the valley to get at the bodies. In some sections of the trenches, the corpses were piled up so high that they almost reached ground level. Mulatwa would recount with horror that 'dogs were seen with the bodies of the martyrs in their mouths', and as the days passed, the smell of death hung in the air. And Negash Yirgu recalled, 'For fifteen days the stench was terrible. Wild animals were getting at the bodies.'[13]

However, in June the 'long rains' arrived, washing topsoil from the slopes down into the Borale River gulley, covering the execution site. As each year passed, with increased cultivation of the surrounding countryside, environmental degradation increased, the gulley was filled in, and the shallow valley became a floodplain, leaving the corpses that had not been dragged away by wild animals deeper below the surface. None of the residents dared attempt to retrieve or interfere with the bodies, for fear of the risk of prison or death.

A Deafening Silence

When news of the cold-blooded murder of the clergy of one of Christendom's greatest and most revered monasteries reached the Vatican, what was the reaction? What was the response to the destruction of a venerable institution that had been known to the Holy See for centuries, and that had produced theologians whose work had laid the foundations of the Pontifical Ethiopian College and the national church of Italy, the basilica of Santa Maria degli Angeli? Was the pope outraged that the holy war was out of control? Did he conclude that the Vatican's marriage of convenience with Fascism had taken the faithful too far from the path of righteousness?

Amazingly, there was no reaction. No denunciation; no regret; not even a comment. The Vatican had not condemned the martyrdom of Bishops Pétros and Mikaél, the massacre of Addis Ababa, the burning and looting of St George's Cathedral, or the bombing of churches and monasteries, and those silences were in themselves telling. But how could the Holy See remain silent in the face of the carnage now being endured by the Ethiopian Church? Should there not have been at least an appearance of concern and compassion?

It might be argued that the silence of the pope in the face of atrocities during the invasion, and his infamous reference to Italy's 'happy triumph of a great and good people' in May 1936, arose from the fact that information about how that 'happy triumph' had been achieved had not reached Rome in the heat of battle. But the massacre of Debre Libanos, which took place later, during the occupation, was a complex operation. It had spanned several days, and had been reported in writing to Rome. Furthermore, at the time of the massacre there was a substantial Italian Catholic presence in Ethiopia, including a personal representative of the pontiff and numerous Catholic clergy. It is thus most unlikely that the Vatican could have been unaware of the carnage. In October 1936 the Holy See had dispatched to Ethiopia a group of missionaries from the Verona Institute under the Congregation for the Oriental Churches,[14] and there was an apostolic delegate in the country, supported by senior clerics and numerous priests, brothers and nuns. These clerics were certainly well aware of what was happening to the Ethiopian clergy, for they were engaging with them, as they themselves reported, 'put[ting] forth strenuous efforts to bring the Ethiopian Church under the influence of the Pope'.[15]

During the invasion and the first few months of the war of occupation, Pope Pius XI was quite unwell. However, by Easter 1937 he had recovered sufficiently to resume some of his duties. Moreover, the secretary of state, Eugenio Cardinal Pacelli, was in a position to intervene. He was, for example, well able to handle the situation when Archbishop George Mundelein in America delivered a speech containing a public attack on Adolf Hitler that achieved such notoriety that the German government demanded an apology from the Vatican. Pacelli lost no time in addressing that issue, and the slaughter at Debre Libanos took place in the very same week.[16]

On 31 May, his 80th birthday, Pope Pius was again unwell and had to cancel a public function.[17] So while we would not necessarily expect to find him *personally* denouncing atrocities, the Holy See was functioning quite normally. We would therefore expect the secretary of state to have ensured that the Holy See took a clear position on the massacre of Debre Libanos, particularly as he was a well-organised administrator, with under-secretaries supported by professional staff in touch with the media, a bevy of apostolic nuncios, and a vast network of informants, both official and unofficial. In fact, the secretary of state was meticulous. He had a prodigious memory, and insisted on being informed of everything. He met the pope every morning, and reserved two mornings a week to meet individually with each of the thirty ambassadors accredited to the Vatican.[18]

It is clear that being articulate, and in a position to speak for the ailing pontiff if necessary, Cardinal Pacelli would have been able to make informed judgements, speak out against the atrocities being carried out against the Ethiopian Church, and probably moderate Graziani's persecutions, had he wished to do so.

It appears, however, that he did not wish to do so, for the Italian episcopate seems to have been quite pleased with the situation in Ethiopia. The members of the Anti-Blasphemy Committee of Verona, for example, were so delighted that they made a proposal to erect a monument to Christ the King in Addis Ababa, 'as an act of gratitude to the God of Hosts for blessing Fascist Italy and its *Duce*, and for addressing the heretical blasphemies that for centuries kept these [Orthodox Christian] people backward, pagan, uncivilised and barbaric'.[19]

The Holy See itself continued to be silent about the level of barbarism employed to address the Ethiopians' 'heretical blasphemies'. But whatever the reasons for that silence, for the Italian military in Ethiopia it could once again only imply consent: a green light for them to carry on. In any case, embedded within the High Command in Addis Ababa was the pope's personal representative, Archbishop Castellani, who apparently saw only a beautiful peace. It is then not surprising that as soon as he had finished liquidating Debre Libanos, far from scaling down the suppression of the Ethiopian Church, the viceroy turned up the heat.

PART FOUR

ONWARD, CHRISTIAN SOLDIERS

15

PERSECUTION OF THE HOUSE OF TEKLE HAYMANOT

'Hatred is the coward's revenge for being intimidated.'
George Bernard Shaw

The massacre of Debre Libanos sent a shock wave through Ethiopian Christendom. The greatest sanctuary of the Church had been despoiled and pillaged, the holy places desecrated, and the monks and priests murdered. Yet Graziani's 'No trace remains' report to Rome did not mark the end of the suppression of the Debre Libanos community. The viceroy was on the warpath. Those who had survived the massacre owing to their absence on St Tekle Haymanot Day were imprisoned, along with many others.[1] He also had residents of nearby areas such as Chagel, with its close associations with *Ras* Kassa, dragged from their houses, never to return. Graziani's paranoia ensured a continuous programme, over several months, of harassment, repression, imprisonment and execution of those with even the remotest connection with Debre Libanos.

Next to be targeted were the families of anyone with land at Debre Libanos. Graziani had them rounded up, and around a hundred of them were imprisoned at Debre Birhan, where six died.[2]

While the viceroy was conducting his vendetta, his troops were carrying out his orders for 'terror and extermination' and 'the destruction of everything'. After the slaughter at Laga Weldé, General Maletti continued his pogrom through Northern Shewa. Moving on with the 20th and 45th Colonial Battalions, he resumed his scorched-earth policy with fire and sword en route to the rugged countryside of Moret, north-west of Debre Birhan (see Map 15).[3] And in nearby Denneba, where the Regia Aeronautica was having a field day, thousands of Ethiopians were suffering an onslaught far beyond anything they had suffered before Mussolini proclaimed 'War is over'. Apparently forgetting his plans to 'liberate Ethiopians from tyranny and barbarism', Graziani informed Lessona: 'Debre Brehan [sic] sector. From today the air force will hammer unceasingly the rebel stronghold in the Denneba zone in order to destroy, burn,

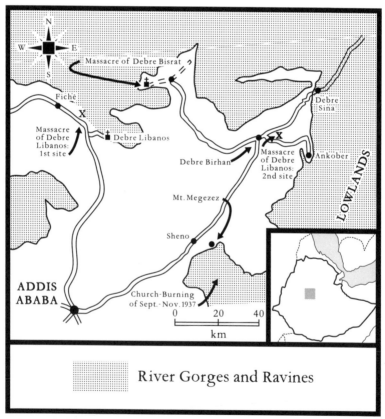

Map 13: Central Ethiopia: Northern Shewa (© Ian Campbell)

PERSECUTION OF THE HOUSE OF TEKLE HAYMANOT

terrorise. It will, moreover, study the possibility of flooding the stronghold with yperite.'[4]

As Professor Angelo Del Boca observes, following the massacre of Debre Libanos, the pursuit of the Orthodox clergy was extended to all parts of Ethiopia.[5] The next step in that escalation was to extend the persecution of the House of Tekle Haymanot beyond the Siga Wedem gorge. Tekle Haymanot was a leading monastic order, with rules followed by several monasteries throughout Ethiopia, and any devotees of the saint—even if they had never been to Debre Libanos or were situated far away—were now at risk of incarceration and death. Although some distance from the parent monastery, the parishes of Moret were very much within the spiritual compass of Debre Libanos.

The Massacre of Debre Bisrat

The district of Moret in the diocese of Shewa consists of a rocky escarpment surrounded by deep valleys. As the topography precluded motorable roads, the area was almost impenetrable to the average traveller, and the population lived largely in scattered and remote settlements. But hidden away on the terraces of the great gorges could be found churches of early foundation, one of the most notable being the 14th-century church of Zéna Marqos situated within the monastery of Debre Bisrat (see Map 13).

The monastery stood on a rocky eminence in a rugged environment that for centuries had kept the community inviolate. The founder of Debre Bisrat, a monk named Zéna Marqos, was a cousin of St Tekle Haymanot, and Zéna's mother had been buried at Debre Libanos alongside the tomb of the saint. As a young man Zéna had evangelised with his older relative in the wilds of Moret, and he had decided to build his church there.[6]

Debre Bisrat was in General Maletti's sights, for it was the second most important monastery of the House of Tekle Haymanot after Debre Libanos itself. Debre Libanos had been liquidated; now it was the turn of Debre Bisrat. Thus on 1 June 1937 the general dispatched his 'ferocious castrators'—the 45th Colonial Battalion, which had just carried out the massacre of Debre Libanos at Laga Weldé—

instructing them to 'destroy, burn and terrorise', as Graziani required, in Moret.[7]

On 5 June the officers and *askaris* of the 45th arrived at Debre Bisrat, which could only be reached by a three-hour walk along a narrow ridge from the town of Inawari. It seems that some of the monks or priests saw them coming, and managed to escape, for Graziani reported that those killed by his troops were 'the remaining monks'.[8]

When the Italians arrived with their *askaris*, Abbot Welde-Mikaél ('Son of St Michael') was conducting Mass in the monastery church of Zéna Marqos.[9] The marauding soldiers burst into the church, killed the abbot, and started rounding up the priests and monks, as other *askaris* began to drench the church with petrol. One 80-year-old priest named Welde-Ammanuel ('Son of Emanuel'), who was living in the churchyard as an anchorite, was murdered on the spot for refusing to move away from the fire.[10] In all, no less than 43 clergymen were reportedly slaughtered at this holiest of sites, and the valuable artefacts were either looted or burned with the church.[11]

The Destruction of Debre Assebot

Another important contribution to the suppression of the House of Tekle Haymanot was made by General Guglielmo Nasi, who had been appointed governor of Harar province. He discovered that one of the few Christian monasteries in his overwhelmingly Muslim province followed the order of Debre Libanos. Thus, hard on the heels of the atrocities at Zéna Marqos came the destruction of yet another celebrated foundation of the House of Tekle Haymanot: the monastery of Debre Assebot.

Also known as Assebot Sillassé Debre Wegeg ('Place of Wisdom and Light'),[12] Debre Assebot was some two hundred kilometres from Addis Ababa, about half-way between the capital city and Dire Dawa (see Map 14). Consisting of communities of both monks and nuns, each with their own church, it had been founded in the 14th century by the much-revered Father Samuél of Debre Wegeg, who, like Zéna Marqos, was a disciple of St Tekle Haymanot. Destroyed by

PERSECUTION OF THE HOUSE OF TEKLE HAYMANOT

the forces of Ahmed Grañ in the 16th century, the monks' church of the Holy Trinity had been recently restored under the patronage of Empress Zewditu.[13] There being no road, and as access was possible only by climbing for more than an hour up a forested mountainside, it was 'well isolated from noises and contacts with the world ... an oasis of asceticism and study'.[14]

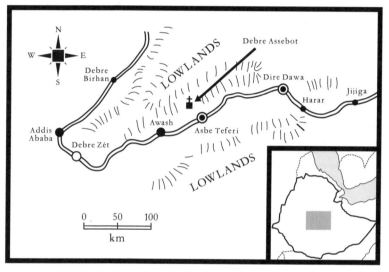

Map 14. Addis Ababa, Dire Dawa and Harar (© Ian Campbell)

On Wednesday, 2 June—only 24 hours after Maletti's burning of the church of Zéna Marqos at Debre Bisrat—Graziani was agreeing with General Nasi's recommendations for the liquidation of Debre Assebot. The delighted viceroy concurred without hesitation, saying that he fully approved 'adoption of this measure for the monastery of Assebot', and ordered him to hold the monks and deacons 'in confinement at Itala in Somalia'.[15]

Clearly proud of Nasi's initiative, and pleased that another of his commanders was now engaged in the quest to liquidate the Ethiopian Church's leading monastic order, the viceroy immediately telegraphed Minister Lessona in Rome, telling him that 'at the suggestion of General Nasi', the monastery of Assebot, 'belonging to the monastic order of Debre Libanos', was now closed, adding

225

that ten monks and forty deacons, representing what he called 'an *accolta* [bunch] of brigands and disruptors of public order', were on their way to incarceration in Somalia.[16]

It is difficult to imagine how a community of Christian ascetics living in such an isolated location inside an overwhelmingly Muslim area, surrounded by eleven thousand hectares of forests filled with wildlife including prowling lions, and with virtually no communication with the outside world, could have been disruptors of public order.

Nonetheless, the Italians carried out a large-scale massacre at the monastery, slaughtering 91 members of the community.[17] This has been confirmed by the head of the church of St Mary at Addis Alem, who had spent many years as a monk at Debre Assebot. He informed the present author that the Italians killed the majority of the community, and sent those remaining alive to a sweltering prison in Mogadishu, on the tropical Somali coast, where several of them subsequently died.[18] This is consistent with Graziani's report that by 2 June General Nasi's forces had raided the monastery and closed it down, and that ten monks and forty deacons who survived the massacre were to be imprisoned.

There were two churches at Debre Assebot: the church of the Holy Trinity, for the monks, and the original church of Father Samuél for the nuns. The Italians destroyed the church of the Holy Trinity, but the nuns' church survived intact.[19]

A Deadly Census

Weeks after the massacre of Debre Libanos, Graziani was still obsessed with the monastery. The 'nest of serpents' that he had targeted had been eliminated, but the viceroy was not satisfied. The next category of those to be hounded was anyone related to, or who had been friendly with, any of the victims of the massacre of Debre Libanos. Such people were more difficult to identify than those having membership of a monastic order, or farming land in a specific area. Consequently, house-to-house checks would have to be carried out to weed out the supposedly dangerous elements for whom the viceroy's heart was filled with hatred.

PERSECUTION OF THE HOUSE OF TEKLE HAYMANOT

However, by July 1937 there was also another factor coming into play. Lessona was actively trying to have Graziani removed from the viceroy's seat, and since *Yekatit 12* he had been making headway with Mussolini in that respect. Furthermore, not only were there plans afoot to replace the marshal, but there was also talk of a potential change in the stance of the Italian government towards the Ethiopian Church. Some of Mussolini's officials in Rome had realised that the viceroy's excesses were strengthening the resistance to the occupation, and they were contemplating a dramatic change of policy: to switch from attempting to destroy the Church, to supporting it, so as to be able to use its influence as a tool of Fascist propaganda. The proposal included rehabilitation of the destroyed churches and monasteries, including Debre Libanos. The very idea was, of course, anathema to the viceroy, obsessed as he was with vengeance against the monastery and all that it stood for, and having proudly announced only a few weeks before that it no longer existed. Furthermore, if the Governo Generale started bringing in 'new' monks to the monastery while relatives of the massacre victims were still around, the latter would meet the new arrivals, and word of the secret massacre at Borale and the full extent of the executions at Laga Weldé might get out. So the viceroy had reason to eliminate, or at least take out of circulation, all those with even the remotest connection with the victims at both execution sites. He had to work fast, and his actions had to maintain a low profile.

Consequently, in the early evening of 18 July, General Pietro Maletti, the staunch Graziani loyalist who had taken personal responsibility for the liquidation of the monastery of Debre Libanos, sent coded instructions from Debre Birhan via the Governo Generale, for onward transmission by air to Major Spinelli at Fiché, telling him of the decision to conduct a census of all those connected with the clergy executed in the massacre at the monastery. The elaborate precautions Maletti took to code the text, and to choose not to send the message through the normal channels, show that this was an undercover operation, to be hidden even from his own colleagues in the military. 'Include even monks and priests returning to Debre Libanos after the cleansing', Maletti instructed, noting that Hayle-Maryam Gazmu, who was working for the Italian military, had already been briefed verbally about the assignment while in Addis Ababa.[20]

It was an irregular arrangement, and was clearly to be carried out for the sake of Graziani alone, for the general ended his orders with the instructions, 'Proceed with swiftness, secrecy, and in a clandestine manner'.[21] Finally, the military were to report back with the code word '*censimento*' (census).

The exercise was apparently launched immediately, for, as we shall see, in addition to the people living near the monastery who had already been detained, hundreds of visitors to the Debre Libanos district, and relatives of the executed clergy, largely women and children, were tracked down, rounded up and imprisoned at Debre Birhan. This, however, turned out to be only a temporary arrangement. The unsuspecting victims were actually in transit, to a far more distant destination of which most of them knew nothing: Danane.

'For Purposes of Repression'

The Italians had built a prison camp at Akaki, on the outskirts of Addis Ababa, on the road heading south-east to the lakes of the Great Rift Valley. Under Commandant Stappacchetti, the occupying forces used Akaki both for political prisoners and as a transit camp for detainees en route to other concentration camps. After the attack on the Governo Generale, some 3,000 prisoners were held at Akaki in tents, cells and barracks surrounded by barbed wire, and the eyewitness accounts make horrifying reading. At 2 pm each day the Italians took detainees by truck for execution, and sometimes relatives who brought food for prisoners were seized and flogged.[22]

But it was Danane concentration camp that Graziani selected for the families and friends of the clergy of the House of Tekle Haymanot. The torrid, disease-infested concentration camp in the tropical coastal belt south of Mogadishu, the capital of Italian Somaliland, was the destination—and, in many cases, proved to be the final resting place—of hundreds of innocent men, women and children from the villages of the valleys, plains and gorges of Northern Shewa.[23]

Prisoners interned in Italy's concentration camps were typically forced to live in appalling conditions, with punishments, executions and death by starvation being daily occurrences. Explaining the principle that subject populations were expendable, Badoglio's rationale in the Italian colony of Libya had been:

> Above all a broad and clear territorial separation must be created between the rebel formation and the subject populations. I do not deny the extent and gravity of the decision which will amount to the ruin of the so-called subject population. But by now the path has been marked out and we must follow it to the end even if the whole population of Cyrenaica should perish.[24]

Graziani applied his experience as military commander in Libya to occupied Ethiopia, and in due course the same methods would be applied in the other countries Mussolini would decide to invade, notably Yugoslavia, where thousands would be brutally killed.

There were two categories of concentration camp in the Italian penal system. Danane was a camp *per scopi repressivi* ('for the purposes of repression'), as opposed to the somewhat milder category, *a scopo protettivo* ('for the purposes of protection').[25] Yet those sent from Debre Libanos to Danane were overwhelmingly neither combatants nor even activists; they were simply people whom Graziani did not want to be at liberty—typically for no particular reason. Indeed, a large proportion consisted of women and children. The Italians transported their prisoners to Danane in covered trucks, leaving Addis Ababa by night to avoid them being seen.[26] By the time they arrived, several captives in each truck had typically died of disease and hardships along the way.[27]

Although built to accommodate 400 prisoners, Danane, located on a coast road connecting it with Genale, a large commercial plantation, actually held between 1,500 and 6,500 at various times during the Italian occupation, in conditions of great inhumanity.[28] Accommodation was provided mainly in huts, with special buildings for interrogation and punishment.

Several officers of the Italian administration, which is well known to have been riddled with corruption, had extensive and lucrative banana and sugar-cane concessions at Genale, which they ran using forced labour from Danane. On Graziani's orders the prisoners were organised in gangs of 150 'to earn their food and lodgings', as he put it, thus introducing Ethiopians to industrial-scale slavery.[29]

For Ethiopians from the haven of Debre Libanos, accustomed to the mild climate of the highlands, the tropical conditions in the Danane–Genale complex were unbearable. They were kept barely alive by rations of dry biscuits infested with worms. According to the sworn testimony of surviving inmates, some 51 per cent of the prisoners at Danane died there. Malaria was endemic; almost everyone suffered from gastrointestinal disorders, and, in the absence of potable water, many were obliged to drink seawater.[30]

Those lucky enough to survive would never forget the horrors of Danane. Testimony provided in preparation for the UN War Crimes trials included the killing of sick prisoners and forced medical operations by the camp doctor.[31]

More Agony at the House of Abo

While the persecution of the House of Tekle Haymanot was proceeding at fever pitch, the hounding of members of Ethiopia's next most important monastic order—that of Gebre Menfes Qiddus, or Abo—continued. The reader may recall that the holy monk's first place of residence was Midr Kebd (see Map 6), where clergy were killed early in the occupation. On 11 June 1937 the Italians struck again, slaughtering 60 of the monks only a few days before the second bombing of the 'sister' monastery of Ziqwala.[32] It is thus possible that some of the monks were killed by aerial bombing, because, apart from the slaughter at the monastery, the Italian Air Force also bombed the general area around Midr Kebd, killing several people at the local market.[33]

On 19 June aerial bombardment at Ziqwala destroyed monastic buildings on the mountain, massacring monks and laypeople in the process.[34] One report claimed that no less than 211 monks who were in prayer at the time were killed.[35]

The present author was told that several of the survivors at Ziqwala who were removed from the monastery died later in custody, and this is confirmed in a 1950 affidavit submitted for the war crimes trials, in which *Blatta* Hayle Welde-Kidan, president of the Land Court of Ethiopia, testified: 'In the month of Hamlé, 1929 E.C. [July–August 1937], the Italians brought monks, nuns, aged, deacons and feeble persons by donkey from Ziqwala to Mojo [see Map 6]. There they were put in an enclosure near the river without shelter from the rain and on marshy ground. For this reason many of them died from sickness, and the rest were shot.'[36] The horrors of that tragic event are so ingrained in the institutional memory at Ziqwala that today they are still spoken of by the clergy.

* * *

During mid-1937 the Houses of Tekle Haymanot and Abo were being mercilessly persecuted. Yet while these horrors were being perpetrated, Maletti's forces were conducting another shocking campaign against the Ethiopian Church elsewhere in Northern Shewa.

16

AN ITALIAN JIHAD

'I don't know what effect these men will have upon the enemy, but, by God, they terrify me.'

Duke of Wellington

Throughout the Italian occupation, Northern Shewa remained a hotbed of resistance. Indeed, the first guerrilla attacks against the advancing Italians had taken place in this area, in April 1936.[1] The rugged landscape was ideal for guerrilla warfare, and being close to Addis Ababa it was the place of origin of many of the early residents of the city. In fact, after the massacre of February 1937 many people fled from Addis Ababa to join the Patriots in Northern Shewa.[2] The area also formed part of the Christian highlands, which had produced several members of the ruling classes largely responsible for the 19th-century expansion of the Ethiopian empire to the east, west and south, and was the birthplace of Emperor Menelik. Thus it became a natural focus of resistance to the Italians.

At its eastern perimeter, the Shewan plateau falls away in a steep escarpment towards the sweltering lowlands known as the Afar Depression and the ancient caravan routes to the Red Sea. At the end of a ten-kilometre peninsula of the high plateau stands the old Shewan capital of Ankober, perched far above the rugged countryside below, where in the 1930s the former customs office of Aliyu Amba still stood—a reminder of the times when traders would lead their camel caravans across the Muslim lowlands, pay their taxes, then begin the ascent into the kingdom of Shewa on the temperate plateau above.

The high plateau had long been settled by Christians. However, the eastern border area accommodated both Orthodox Christianity and Islam, as well as some pockets of Catholicism and ancient Judaism. Down in the forests of the valleys there were, and still are, monasteries of mixed Christian–Judaic heritage. Apart from the 16th-century *jihad* of Ahmed Grañ, which had been driven principally by Ottoman Turks, these religious communities had in recent centuries enjoyed a relatively harmonious coexistence, as was common in Ethiopia. But with the intrusion of the Italians, and their strategy of recruiting Muslim mercenaries, Ankober district with its religiously mixed population was particularly vulnerable to Graziani's policy of divide and rule. This policy had resulted in the arming of disaffected local groups to make deadly attacks on the emperor and his forces in retreat after the Battle of Maychew.[3] During the occupation, the initial challenges to the invading Italians came principally from highland Christian Amhara and some Oromo communities. Against these, the Italians were able to pitch Muslims with antipathy towards Emperor Haile Selassie, who had often ruled them with a heavy hand. Recruited from the nearby lowlands, some could be enticed with various favours, including the building of mosques. Overall, it was religion, rather than ethnicity, that was found by the Italians to be the most effective way to obtain local assistance in their attempts to crush the resistance to the occupation.[4]

The formation by the Italians of the 45th (Muslim) Colonial Battalion for deployment against Christian civilians has already been discussed, but their masterstroke in this regard was the cultivation of an alliance with the family of the elderly but widely influential *Sheikh* Sayed Raslan, who was based in the lowlands immediately east of the Shewan plateau. Sayed's energetic son, *Sheikh* Mohammed Sultan, became a powerful ally of General Maletti, and the relationship culminated in the creation of the Mohammed Sultan Group of irregulars, who would conduct a bizarre but deadly *jihad* under Italian command.

AN ITALIAN JIHAD

The sack of Addis Ababa and the massacre of the clergy of Debre Libanos had not only aroused anger across Ethiopia, it had also triggered the flight of thousands of men into the countryside to join the Patriots. In response, Maletti launched the Mohammed Sultan campaign to directly address the resistance that constituted a growing obstacle to Italian control of the Ethiopian highlands. Heavily armed companies under Lieutenant Colonel Giuseppe Costa, Lieutenant Colonel Quinico and Colonel Arduino Garelli, all under the command of General Maletti, had been battling resistance armies in various parts of Northern Shewa during May and early June 1937,[5] resulting in the deaths of not only many resistance fighters, but also numerous defenceless subsistence-farming families living in the vicinity. One Italian source reports that in Ankober district alone, between 5 May and 15 June, the Italians 'slaughtered and maimed no less than 15,000 innocent civilians'.[6]

In reality, the Mohammed Sultan irregulars would be focused on continuing this exemplary repression, terrorising the local population into rejecting and disowning the resistance. Based on research among local communities and eyewitnesses, Professor Ahmed Hassen, the leading authority on the history of Northern Shewa, describes how the Italians persuaded the *sheikh*, assisted by other *sheikhs* and chiefs, to declare a *jihad*, or holy war, against non-Muslims.[7] The *jihad* proved to be one of the bloodiest and most destructive confrontations of the entire occupation. Let loose in June, the forces of the *sheikh*—a coalition of various Muslim groups—were under the command of Italian officers whose active participation in the campaign still remains in the collective memory of the local communities, for it took the slaughter of Christians to a new level of horror.[8]

Into the Highlands

Ostensibly, the Maletti–Mohammed Sultan alliance sought to track down resistance leaders, but it was actually focused principally on mutilating and killing defenceless non-combatant Christians and looting and burning their churches. At the Italian military headquarters in the newly established garrison town of Debre

Sina, the force split into two fronts, each headed by senior Italian officers. One front headed westwards and the other, including *Sheikh* Mohammed himself, set out along the slopes of the escarpment through Aliyu Amba and across the Kasem River. The western section of the alliance divided into three companies. The Italians led one company north-west into the rugged district of Menz; the second aimed south-west towards the settlements of Sheno and Sendafa; the third separated from the second company at Debre Birhan, to head north-west for Moret and Merhabété (see Map 15).

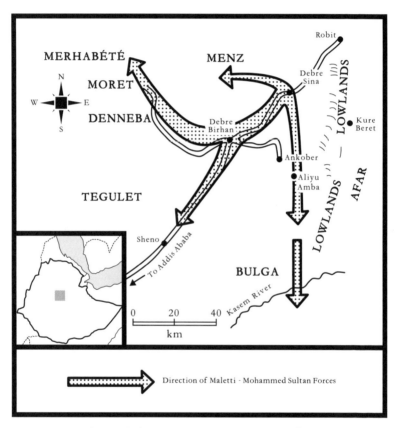

Map 15. Northern Shewa: the *jihad* of June 1937 (© Ian Campbell)

Following Graziani's written instructions, 'When in doubt always eliminate everyone without mercy', the campaign in Menz–

Merhabété, which lasted eight days, quickly gained the Maletti–Mohammed Sultan alliance a reputation for leaving behind them, in the words of an Italian military historian, 'a trail of blood and violence', in which 'they attack the villages, kill all the males over the age of three and emasculate the rest, kidnap the young women and seize the cattle'.[9] In each case the marauders maimed and slaughtered the local population, and destroyed their villages, churches and crops.[10]

The *jihadists* sent into Menz massacred numerous Christian communities, several of which were totally annihilated and as a result no longer exist. Only their memory lives on; speaking to postgraduate researchers from Addis Ababa University in the 1990s, local elders recalled from their youth some of the villages and churches that had fallen victim to the slaughter, with not a single soul surviving. These included Gedambo St George, Qeya St Gabriel, Gishe Robel, and Molalé Aradma Agancha Kidane Mihret ('The Covenant of Mercy').[11]

Down the Escarpment

The residents of the Ankober–Aliyu Amba area, who were victims of the group led by Mohammed Sultan himself, suffered horrors that elderly informants interviewed in the 1980s and early 1990s still shuddered to remember. The commanders had no compunction in unleashing their *jihadists* to run wild. As most able-bodied local men had either been killed in the war or joined the resistance, the militia burned entire villages, emasculating elderly men and boys, cutting off women's breasts, and publicly mutilating and butchering priests and monks, as they rampaged from church to church. Recounting the massacres fifty years later, surviving witnesses recalled their shock and amazement that the senior Italian commanders not only permitted but actually encouraged such excesses.[12] The Maletti–Mohammed Sultan irregulars surpassed even the general's 'ferocious castrators' of the 45th Colonial Battalion.[13]

Maletti's *jihadists* also killed members of the local Muslim Argobba community, who were either mistaken for Christians or, having coexisted peacefully for years with their Christian neighbours, were not supporting the campaign.[14] However, as Ahmed Hassen observes, these attacks eventually turned some Muslims away from the holy war: 'The Afar Muslim community took exception to the Italian-backed devastation being classified as a *jihad*', asking, after an attack on a local Muslim community: 'If the Italians sympathise with our religion [Islam] and the war they wage is a *jihad*, why do they devastate the village of Muslims like that of Mohammed Salih?'[15]

Father Satan

Realising that the campaign had done nothing to destroy the resistance, General Maletti announced that he was targeting Patriot leader Ayyele Haylé, who had been governor of Ankober under the emperor and who was regarded by Ethiopians as a hero of the Battle of Maychew. Ayyele had moved eastwards to the lowlands of Afar to lead the local resistance.[16]

Thus, in late June Maletti ordered the Mohammed Sultan Group to march again. However, while fanning out east and south-east of Debre Sina, far from pursuing Ayyele, the *jihadists* launched yet another reign of terror. Under the general's command they devastated numerous villages and ravaged the countryside along the escarpment with fire and sword. On this occasion the carnage was so horrific that the *sheikh* became known locally as Father Satan.

The upshot was that witnesses and survivors of the massacres of Northern Shewa, no longer willing to be sitting targets, decided to join the resistance. At the same time, the *jihad* began to lose steam. It was, in any case, an obvious travesty, for many of the district's Muslims had not been at loggerheads with the Christians, and had not agreed with the *jihad* in the first place, and others, as we have seen, were refusing to support what they no longer considered was a genuine *jihad*. Consequently, some of the locals banded together, armed themselves, and started fighting back. Eventually they managed to repel the attackers. In the process, in a conflagration known as the Battle of Kuré Wuha, at a settlement on the eastern escarpment named Kuré Beret (see Map 15), they finally managed to kill *Sheikh* Mohammed Sultan and three of his leading commanders, whereupon his surviving lieutenants fled eastwards, down into the lowlands.[17]

The Aftermath

With the death of Mohammed Sultan, the *jihad* of June–July 1937, which had lasted almost four weeks, was over. The campaign had destroyed and looted hundreds of churches, put the clergy to the sword, and slaughtered and maimed countless Christians and even Muslims in the process.[18] It also left so many unburied bodies in its wake that they created a public health emergency.[19]

For the Italians the pogrom achieved virtually nothing, other than to confirm their reputation for cruelty and barbarity against unarmed civilians. In fact, it intensified the resistance, bringing both Christian and Muslim communities that had been its victims into the Patriot movement.

There was never any reckoning of the death toll of the Maletti–Mohammed Sultan *jihad*. However, given that each of the four military columns, consisting of thousands of rampaging armed men, most likely killed hundreds of victims each day of the campaign, the typical combined daily death toll could have been in excess of a thousand, bringing the total death toll of the campaign into the tens of thousands, in addition to those who survived to suffer their injuries. This assessment is consistent with the view of Ahmed Hassen, who indicated to the present author that the scale and death toll of the Maletti–Mohammed Sultan campaign exceeded even that of the massacre of Addis Ababa, let alone the massacre of Debre Libanos.[20]

Such estimates are inevitably speculative, for, as Nicolas Virtue observes, throughout Maletti's 1937 campaign in Northern Shewa, details of the reprisals became barely worthy of mention in the telegrams from column commanders, who sometimes submitted vague reports such as 'Burned all villages and destroyed all crops'.[21] Considering that often no one was counting the victims, even one of Maletti's reports stating that his colonial troops together with five thousand irregulars had killed or executed 15,078 'rebels' and destroyed 56,865 dwellings must be regarded as only part of the story.[22] Indeed, even the official Italian statistics reporting 37,620 'rebels' killed during these campaigns must be regarded as a conservative figure.[23]

HOLY WAR

An Appeal to International Christendom

As news of the bloodbath in the Ethiopian highlands trickled across to Europe in mid-1937, Emperor Haile Selassie was outraged. Horrified by what he termed the 'merciless carnage', he sent a desperate appeal to the Christian Churches of the world from his exile in Bath, England. Stating that he believed that 'God's judgement will eventually visit the weak and the mighty alike, according to what each deserves', he charged the Italian army with ten 'barbarities', including 'a number of sacrilegious acts ... against the religious and spiritual practices of my people [and] of the Ethiopian Church', such as the massacre of Addis Ababa, which, he noted, had involved the killing of priests and Muslim *sheikhs* and the denial of Christian burial, 'the destruction of the ancient Church of the Monastery of Debre Libanos and other churches by deliberately setting them on fire by way of reprisal', the 'public execution of Abune (Bishop) Pétros', and 'the forcing of unmarried women and young widows in Addis Ababa and other towns into concentration camps and licensed brothels as prostitutes'.

The emperor also drew attention to the looting of the 4th-century monolithic Aksum obelisk—one of Ethiopia's greatest national treasures—and to the Italian practice of killing prisoners, concluding: 'I beseech the leaders and members of the international Christian community to denounce the iniquities perpetrated on my people. I also solicit your prayers for the ending of the despicable atrocities being committed on the orders and silent consent of the Italian government.'[24]

On 27 July the sovereign sent his letter to the Catholic archbishop Arthur Hinsley in Britain, for onward transmission to Pope Pius XI. Hinsley forwarded it to Pacelli. After sitting on the matter for several weeks, the secretary of state challenged the veracity of the emperor's report, despite the fact that most of atrocities were well known and were documented by the Italian military. Suggesting that the atrocities had not actually taken place, the Holy See decided not to 'go into the matter'. Once again, the pope, who had prayed to God to 'bless the land of Ethiopia, its kings and its people', chose to look the other way.[25]

17

THE HOLY WAR TURNS FULL CIRCLE

'Our country is going to be occupied by a heathen enemy!'
Orthodox clergy, Gojjam, 1937

Gojjam and Begémdir

The reign of terror prescribed by Mussolini led to yet another series of atrocities, this time by *residente* Captain Corvo, based in the lakeside town of Bahir Dar, Gojjam, in 1937. Matteo Dominioni reminds us that such excesses were not just the initiative of individuals; they reflected Italian policy as established by Mussolini and conveyed down the hierarchy to the lower levels of the Italian military—a claim that is undoubtedly correct, given the number of surviving documents instructing subordinates to commit atrocities. A case in point was the drowning of several community leaders suspected of being opposed to the Italian occupation, whom Corvo had unceremoniously thrown alive into Lake Tana with heavy boulders tied to their necks.[1]

Graziani's concurrence with such actions is exemplified by his response to Corvo's superior—the governor of Gojjam, General Pirzio-Biroli—following the public hanging in Bahir Dar in July 1937 of twenty people suspected of aiding the resistance. The fact that four Orthodox priests were also shot in the process delighted the viceroy, who made a point of commending Pirzio-Biroli, stating that the governor 'had done well to follow the example of [the massacre of] Debre Libanos', which for the Shewan clergy 'had been very healthy'.[2] It must be said that this was not the only occasion on which Graziani and his commanders used this turn of phrase, reminiscent of medieval crusaders presenting themselves not as persecutors, but, as Jonathan Kirsch puts it, 'a loving mother unwillingly inflicting wholesome chastisement on her unruly children'.[3]

The atrocities in Shewa and Gojjam, together with the massacre of Debre Libanos itself, which, as Anthony Mockler writes, was so shocking that at first the news was scarcely believed, contributed to a rapid escalation in the resistance. Italian garrisons and military camps across Gojjam and beyond became increasingly besieged.[4] Thus by July 1937 the resistance in Gojjam was becoming more coordinated, and was beginning to increase beyond the earlier levels. In the process, the Ethiopian Church once again became a target, but not by chance; as Paolo Borruso explains, by early August Graziani was more determined than ever to destroy the Ethiopian Church and its clergy.[5]

Mikre-Sellassie refers to the destruction of many churches in the dioceses of both Gojjam and Begémdir, remarking that these were examples of 'Italian actions of terrorism against the Orthodox Church designed to weaken its influence upon the people'.[6]

The capital of Begémdir was the ancient city of Gondar, which had also served as Ethiopia's capital in the 17th and 18th centuries. On 5 August, despite the emerging new policy towards the Ethiopian Church, ecclesiastical scholars of Gondar—of which there were many, given the number of churches and church schools in that city—were rounded up by the Italians 'and half of them were killed and the other half imprisoned'. Church historian Kefyalew Mehari comments, 'All these were the victims of the Romans, and the memory is still fresh in mind.'[7]

It is not known exactly how many churches in Gojjam were destroyed, but it was certainly a significant proportion of the total.[8] In one district alone—Yilmana Dénsa, which accounts for no more than five per cent of highland Gojjam—60 churches were burned down by the Italians or demolished by the Regia Aeronautica. One of the monasteries razed to the ground by aerial bombardment was the Saviour of the World at Adét, the capital of the district, some 35 km south-south-east of Bahir Dar. It was destroyed on 4 September. In the massacre that ensued, the religious administrator of the monastery church, Father Kassa Wasé, was martyred. And at the nearby monastery of Debre Mewi St Mary, a historic church where Emperor Menelik's wife, Empress Taytu, had been educated, the senior priest, *Liqetebebt* Boyale Gétahun, was among those slaughtered.[9]

By the time of Graziani's commendation to Pirzio-Biroli in Gojjam for following the 'very healthy' example of the massacre of Debre Libanos, it was finally becoming clear to the Ethiopian clergy that the Italian Church had sacralised the invasion and that they were suffering the consequences. Michael Lentakis, a notable member of the Greek community in Ethiopia, recalled in his memoirs that it was believed in Ethiopia at the time that the massacre of Debre Libanos was intended to 'break the spirit of the Ethiopian Orthodox Church, and at the same time the Fascist Party would ingratiate itself with the Vatican'.[10]

The Backlash

The realisation that the Italians were intent on destroying the Ethiopian Church, together with the appalling lesson of the massacres of Addis Ababa, Debre Libanos and Zéna Marqos—that Italian brutality and disrespect for the Church knew no bounds—convinced the Christian highlanders that they were being besieged by a diabolical force, an evil comparable to the 16th-century *jihad* of Ahmed Grañ. The reaction in Gojjam was dramatic. In effect, the Church in that province proclaimed holy war against the invaders, an action which of course strengthened the national solidarity of the Patriots and stiffened the resistance even further.

A powerful directive from senior Ethiopian Church leaders to the Patriots of both Gojjam and Begémdir addressed the fighters as 'Sons of Gojjam and Welette Israél!'—Welette Israél being a prominent member of the 18th-century Gondarine aristocracy who had acquired legendary status. The proclamation exhorted the resistance 'to fight for your souls, your property, your children, your livestock and your religion ... With the prayer of Christians and the will of God, we are fighting and winning for the freedom of our country and our religion.'[11] It is not altogether surprising that the last few months of 1937 saw some of the heaviest blows inflicted upon the Italians since the beginning of the war. Graziani marshalled thousands of soldiers to relieve Italian garrisons that were effectively under siege and, when that attempt failed, in October he brought up two more columns of another 5,500 men to face the Ethiopians. The upshot was that two of the Italian battalions were completely annihilated and some of the troops would remain under siege until January 1938.[12]

Thus, the campaign of terror against the Ethiopian Church provoked a massive backlash that helped to escalate the resistance. Rome's charges of heresy had finally recoiled, for the spectre of Catholic supremacy also evoked shadows from the past. The Ethiopian clergy—particularly in Gojjam—now increasingly urged their communities to fight the Italians not just because they were illegal invaders, but because 'the enemy ... has come to shed Christian blood, to alter our Christianity and to make us Catholic'. In a resurgence of the ancient role of the intellectual Orthodox guarding the true faith against European barbarians, the Ethiopian clerics cried, 'One who alters your religion has come; combat him!' and 'He [the enemy] has come from beyond the sea to detach you from your religion'. Some declared, 'He is heathen; his religion is different; our country is going to be occupied by a heathen enemy!' Yet others were moved to quote the Bible as they exhorted the public to resist the invaders: 'As David killed Goliath, go and strike him!'[13]

Thus late 1937 saw the inevitable outcome of Italy's holy war: it eventually forced the Ethiopian clergy to play an active, rather than a passive, role in the resistance. While originally they had been willing to greet the invading forces with civility, and limit their activities to providing succour to the defence forces, praying, and burying the dead, the savagery of the attacks against the Church eventually drew them directly into the war. Remaining in their churches as sitting targets was clearly an invitation to martyrdom, and so, with the very survival of the Ethiopian Church now threatened, they had nothing to lose by joining the Patriots. Thus it was that several clerics in Gojjam and Begémdir became important and influential resistance fighters. The Italians had—albeit unwittingly—managed to recruit the Ethiopian clergy in two of the country's most important provinces into the resistance; the holy war had come full circle.[14]

PART FIVE

AN IGNOMINIOUS END

18

A WIND OF CHANGE

'Oh how the good man smiles to see what a Rod we have made for our own Back!'

William Hughes, The Man of Sin

The reader will recall that during the second half of 1937, when the pogrom against the Ethiopian clergy escalated the resistance in Gojjam to a state of outright war, serious doubts were being expressed in Rome about Graziani's policies of terror and exemplary repression—even though they had been ordered by Mussolini.[1] Foreign Minister Count Galeazzo Ciano, the *Duce*'s son-in-law, was to note in his diary that Mussolini was 'annoyed' by what he termed 'the revolt in Gojjam', which was 'of a considerable size'.[2] The viceroy's policies were intensifying resistance to Italian rule and bringing the administration into disrepute. Contemporary Italian reports on the Graziani period published in later years would speak of excessive and arbitrary use of rigorous measures, and identified the Governo Generale with injustice, ill-treatment and oppression.

The result was a gradual but definite about-turn in policy, a process that actually began in mid-July and was gathering momentum by the end of August. During that month General Maletti was still sanitising the massacre of Debre Libanos as having been a highly successful operation: the slaughter had been 'quick and firm', 'opportune and salutary', and a powerful demonstration of strength and confidence to both friends and enemies.[3] But the reality was that the war was still being waged, and Graziani was beginning to be perceived by Rome as a liability.

In fact, not only were Graziani's methods being questioned, the entire Italian policy towards the Ethiopian Church was being turned around. The barbarity of the onslaught in the Christian heartlands of Gojjam, Begémdir and Shewa had drawn the Ethiopian clergy directly into the war. By October the Ethiopians were waging their own holy war against satanic forces—a war Mussolini had begun to realise he could never win. Since the devotion of the Ethiopians to their Church was apparently indestructible, the policy now emerging from Rome was that, instead of attempting to destroy the Ethiopian Church, the Italian administration in Addis Ababa should support whatever was left of it, with the intention of using it as a means of controlling, and thereby 'pacifying', the general populace and getting them to submit to Italian hegemony. The dissolution of the monasteries was to come to an end, and the surviving 'heretics and schismatics' were now to be embraced. This diametrically opposite strategy would involve the appointment of new senior Orthodox clergy selected by the Italians from their collaborators, and would call for the repair and rehabilitation of the monasteries and churches that had been destroyed.

The new policy inevitably represented a major setback for Pius XI, who had established a special commission to develop an action plan for proselytisation and evangelisation, on the assumption that the clauses in the Italian constitution making Catholicism the state religion in Italy would be applied in occupied Ethiopia.

The dramatic change also pulled the rug out from under the feet of the senior Italian Catholic clerics who had done so much to popularise the invasion and to ensure its success. In return they had been expecting the army and the air force to deal with what they referred to as the 'obstacle' of the Ethiopian Orthodox clergy. Instead, the holy war was out of control, and was consuming its protagonists. Finally, the reversal was a great disappointment for the hundreds of Catholic missionaries who had already been sent to Ethiopia, as well as those standing by expecting to embark any day.

Seeds of discord between Mussolini's administration and the Vatican over the policy in Ethiopia had actually been sown earlier, in 1936, when the *Duce*'s policy of showing favour to Islam first began to take effect. Daniel Binchy points out that by March 1937 a semi-official pamphlet entitled *The Islamic Policy of Italy* had been issued in Rome, stating, *inter alia*, that 'no attempt to convert Moslems to Christianity is authorised by the Italian government'.[4] This had put paid to the plans of the Congregation for the Propagation of the Faith to proselytise in Muslim areas; instead, they were confined to areas regarded as animist. This restriction was followed by a further narrowing of the scope of the Congregation, prohibiting Catholic missionaries from working in Orthodox Christian areas, thereby thwarting the very purpose of the crusade. Furthermore, the Italian government even rejected the Holy See's plan to establish Catholic institutions of higher education in Ethiopia.[5]

For the Italian military it was also a dangerous time, for while Maletti's soldiers were diligently scouring the countryside for Graziani's imaginary enemies from the House of Tekle Haymanot, attacks by the resistance had increased in scale and frequency, and were being carried out on a wider front than ever before.

Quite apart from the fact that his policies of exemplary repression were now being called into question, Graziani was said by Lessona to be suffering from 'persecution mania', spending his nights 'surrounded by barbed wire, machine guns, armoured cars and a battalion of guards'.[6] Clearly he would not be permitted to continue in that manner for much longer, and by late August 1937, although Graziani was still in overall command of the armed forces, telegrams from the Governo Generale were being signed by his deputy, General Petretti. The viceroy had been sent to Asmara to 'recuperate'.[7]

Confusion in the Governo Generale

After taking over Graziani's office in August, General Petretti had discovered that associates of the massacre victims in the Debre Libanos area were being detained and sent to Danane concentration camp. Why were these people being deported? The deputy viceroy, whom Graziani seems never to have taken into his confidence, had stumbled across some of his superior's machinations, now being implemented by Maletti following the viceroy's 'census'.

Petretti was clearly mystified by the absence of any orders for such internments. There was one telegram dated 22 June on file mentioning relatives of the massacre victims, but it contained no instructions for a widespread dragnet. Of Graziani's 'census', which had been launched on 18 July, and the undercover operation that followed it, there was probably no record, the viceroy having sent his messages, as noted above, by an alternative route.

Presumably reluctant to completely countermand instructions for a major operation that had Graziani's blessing, but realising that it ran counter to Rome's newly emerging policy towards the Ethiopian Church, the deputy viceroy ordered the *residente* at Fiché to limit the operation. He then wired Debre Birhan on 25 August, informing the commander of his instruction to Fiché, noting that the telegram of 22 June had not authorised such a widespread exercise.[8] Whether he liked it or not, Maletti had no choice but to pass on the instructions, telling his commanders to 'limit and restrict' the numbers.[9]

Had Petretti not taken over the Governo Generale, these deportations to Danane might never have come to light. But Graziani, who was fighting a rearguard action to preserve his position and his policies, was losing ground. In September, much to his discomfort, he was obliged to assure clergy of the Ethiopian Church that their religion, 'in accordance with the definite wish of the Great *Duce*, Benito Mussolini', was now the official religion, thereby arousing the anger of the Vatican.[10]

The new policy went public at Mesqel (the Ethiopian celebration of the finding of the True Cross by Helena, the mother of the 4th-century Emperor Constantine) in September, when Graziani himself attended the celebrations in Asmara. His speech on that occasion must have been one of the most painful of his career. Obliged to follow Rome's new policy line, he started backtracking, claiming that he had been misquoted in his statements about the Ethiopian Church: far from planning to 'wreck' it, he was actually permitting the churches to retain their lands. Even more surprisingly, he went on to do the unthinkable: he authorised the reconstitution of the monastery of Debre Libanos, which was to be accomplished by bringing in clergy from other churches.[11]

Yet while Petretti was following the new policy of appeasement towards the Ethiopian Church, Graziani and his commanders in Northern Shewa were still intent on adhering to fire and fury. Once he knew that the monastery of Debre Libanos was to be resurrected, thereby invalidating whatever he had accomplished through its liquidation, having to announce it was a bitter pill to swallow. Not only had his actions against the monastery been implicitly discredited, but the plans to repopulate it meant that the families of hundreds of people who had mysteriously gone missing during the massacre would start talking to the newcomers. The viceroy was in a tight corner. No longer based in Addis Ababa, his authority had for all practical purposes been curtailed. Orders were now being dispatched from Rome directly to Addis Ababa, to be implemented by Petretti, who was not a member of Graziani's inner circle.

Determined to silence all members of the House of Tekle Haymanot, and to eliminate anyone related to the victims of the massacre of Debre Libanos, the viceroy made his decision. While proponents of Rome's new policy were going around wooing the clergy and drawing up plans for renovating their churches, he would ensure the incarceration of the remaining innocents of Debre Libanos in the most hideous and faraway place possible, from which, hopefully, they would never return: Danane.

Graziani's Final Fling

By late October 1937, the final phase of Graziani's programme of repression against the House of Tekle Haymanot was well under way. Directing it from Asmara, he had telegrams sent anonymously from the Governo Generale with 'Graziani' written at the bottom by hand—presumably by one of his secretaries. The fact that he got this phase of the campaign moving at all is a reflection of the close relationship between Graziani based in Eritrea, his supporters in Addis Ababa, and General Maletti in Debre Birhan. But the result was a bizarre situation in which new clergy arriving at churches on the orders of Petretti's faction at the Governo Generale were doing so almost concurrently with the arrest of clergy and their relatives ordered by Graziani's faction, and their transportation by the truckload to the concentration camp at Danane.

Graziani's 'swansong' in his campaign against the House of Tekle Haymanot was to run for no more than two weeks before it was brought to an end, but Maletti's efficiency ensured that even in that brief period many were arrested, and considerable numbers deported from the prisons at Debre Birhan to Danane.

'Consider it an opportune moment to evacuate to Danane families of monks and priests of Debre Libanos,' said an explicit telegram sent on Graziani's behalf from the Governo Generale to Fiché on 27 October, requesting feedback on the date of transportation, the number of prisoners and the number of vehicles required, and then adding, by hand on the telegraph sheet, 'Urgent' (see Appendix VI).[12]

The following day, Cardinal Schuster was in Milan cathedral celebrating the fifteenth anniversary of the March on Rome, Fascism's most important celebration. Speaking at High Mass, far from expressing regrets or compassion for the thousands of Ethiopian Christians who were being slaughtered, he hailed the March on Rome as having 'prepared souls for the redemption of Ethiopia from the bondage of slavery and heresy and for the Christian renewal of the ancient empire of Rome'.[13] It is ironic that slavery was hailed as one of the purported sins of Haile Selassie's administration, for, as Schuster was speaking, innocent wives, siblings and children of the victims of the massacre of Debre Libanos were being sent into bondage in Danane concentration camp, where many of them would perish as slave labourers on the notorious Genale plantations. There was nothing secret about such projects; as late as 1940 General Nasi was ordering in writing that, instead of shooting resistance fighters who surrendered, 'these prisoners may supply us with precious forced labour'.[14]

As instructed, Maletti started rounding up relatives of the massacre victims for transport to the capital en route to Danane. However, since the government in Rome had already issued orders for the repopulation of Debre Libanos, Graziani's men in Addis Ababa were running out of time and were panicking. 'As soon as the families of monks and priests of Debre Libanos arrive in Addis Ababa they must be made to proceed to Danane in the usual manner', one of the viceroy's staff at the Governo Generale instructed the military command in haste, on 2 November, using a *fonogramma a mano* to save time, adding that if the limited time available proved insufficient, the families should be 'confined to the concentration camp of Akaki'.[15]

A telegram signed on Graziani's behalf was sent on the same day from Addis Ababa to Debre Birhan, demanding confirmation of the evacuation of Debre Libanos within three days, the third day being marked as 'ultimatum', or within four days at the very latest. However, clearly under pressure, the writer was obliged to acknowledge that a new strategy was now in place, for he continued, 'On day six will be brought to Debre Libanos the *ichegé*, to take possession of the monastery, bringing with him fifteen monks destined [to remain] there'. Under the new policy, imprisonment of the clergy had become a thing of the past, apparently replaced by generosity and magnanimity.[16]

In spite of the last-minute panic, Graziani managed to send another large group of prisoners to Danane. On 5 November 1937, he had the 94 Debre Libanos residents being held at Debre Birhan imprisoned at Nefasit, near the Eritrean capital of Asmara. There they spent two weeks, followed by deportation by military trucks to Danane.[17]

Included among these unfortunate captives were the 30 boys belonging to Debre Libanos families, who Graziani misinformed Rome had been sent home to their parents. They would have to be disposed of, and so it was that in November, young Tibebe found himself once again a victim of Graziani's fury. One of the last of the community of Debre Libanos to be sent to Danane, he was transported there in a military truck, along with the other 29 youngsters.

When they arrived, following the long, harrowing journey to the sweltering Somali coast, the bewildered thirteen-year-old Tibebe was in a state of shock, for conditions at Danane were far worse than those of the *bande* camp at Debre Birhan. This was a world of horrors—of intense heat and the smell of death. He was put in a section where the prisoners were languishing in six tents, each accommodating some 150 or 160 inmates.[18]

The young boys were put together with the women, some of whom had been visiting Debre Libanos on St Michael's Day with their families, and had ended up being imprisoned with their children. While the adults were given heavy duties such as cutting trees, Tibebe had to wash the floors where the women were living; other children cleared rubbish.

Many of the prisoners Tibebe met turned out to be people he knew from Debre Libanos. Several were relatives of the executed clergy, who had been rounded up in Maletti's 'census', and transferred to Danane in late October, typically after passing through transit camps.

In all, a total of around 360 prisoners were deported to Danane from prisons at Debre Birhan during Graziani's panic in late October and early November. Several had been arrested in the vicinity of the monastery or because they were considered to be connected with it in some way. They also included a few *debteras* and priests, but the majority had been visitors or passers-by. Others, as we have seen, were relatives of the victims of the massacre, already grieving and now faced with new horrors.

Danane was a death camp in all but name, for inmates were lucky to survive more than a few months. In fact, 16 of the 30 boys had already died there by the time they were transferred to other prisons less than a year later. Few of the 14 survivors returned to the monastery; in 1998 Tibebe thought that he might be the only one still alive.[19] Based on this death rate, which is consistent with the rate of around fifty per cent reported by the Ethiopian Ministry of Justice official Mikaél Tessema (who was a prisoner in Danane at the time), it is likely that at least half of the 360 prisoners from Debre Libanos died at Danane.[20]

These 360 prisoners were only the *last* of those associated with the monastery to be interned. They joined those who had arrived between June and October. We do not know how many were interned in these earlier months, but the numbers were large enough for Petretti to be alarmed. Thus, just how many men, women and children associated with Debre Libanos or its clergy were sent to Danane after May 1937 is unknown, but it probably exceeded a thousand. Furthermore, it would have increased beyond this level had the pogrom not been brought to an end by the departure of Rodolfo Graziani.

19

MORE CLERGY TO THE SWORD

> *'There is no wrong men have not been ready to commit when they thought it could serve religious purposes.'*
> Lord Acton, *Selected Works of Lord Acton*

By September 1937 Rome's new strategy of rapprochement with the Ethiopian Church was definitely in place and was in the process of being implemented. In the major towns Italian commanders and governors were attending Church holidays such as Mesqel, Timqat and Easter, together with the Ethiopian clergy. They were even observing the holy days of saints such as Tekle Haymanot and Gebre Menfes Qiddus with great pomp—much, no doubt, to Graziani's annoyance, who, still exiled in Asmara, was having to watch from the sidelines.[1]

However, even though Petretti had taken over the viceroy's office at the Governo Generale, Graziani was still the *de jure* viceroy, and his friend Maletti was still willing to do his bidding in the remoter reaches of Northern Shewa, away from the prying eyes of Petretti.

Church Burning at Ankober

On Tuesday, 26 October 1937, a convoy of military trucks emerged from the Italian garrison at Tebassi, on the southern outskirts of Debre Birhan, and turned left to head north, passing through the town. Turning right a few kilometres beyond the city, they headed for the eastern perimeter of the Shewan plateau, for, as noted earlier, the rugged countryside at the edge of the plateau harboured resistance fighters. The numerous churches here (each parish typically served less than a hundred subsistence-farming households—one of the world's highest church densities) would be targets for Graziani's continued exemplary repression.

The area had already suffered from the depredations of the *jihad* of June–July, but burning any surviving churches and slaughtering the remaining priests would, Graziani presumably believed, destroy any lingering desire by the despised Orthodox inhabitants to support or shelter the resistance. Furthermore, pillaging would provide an added incentive for both the Italians and their *askaris*. The viceroy evidently thought there was a sufficient number of clergy left alive, and enough valuables remaining in the church treasuries, to make the campaign worthwhile.[2]

The convoy made its way along the stony tracks, past the site where just five months before, the deacons and pilgrims of Debre Libanos had been slaughtered. In the front of each vehicle were Italian officers armed with pistols and behind, under the canvas awnings, were around twenty Eritrean Muslim *askari* infantrymen, armed with rifles and sabres.

At Kundi, where the grassy plains began to fall away towards the escarpment, the road took a series of sharp turns and the trucks turned off to the north. Two kilometres later the convoy stopped at a site known locally as Kundi Fort (see Map 16), where a fort had been built by one of Shewa's 19th-century rulers. This was the end of the road and the beginning of yet another campaign targeting the Ethiopian clergy.[3]

The *askaris* leapt down from the trucks and started scrambling down the rocky slopes towards their first target: the parish church of Mescha St John (see Map 16).[4]

With the help of collaborators familiar with the area, the Italian officers and their infantrymen descended along four kilometres of mule tracks and thick undergrowth, and burst into the clearing where the church of St John stood, surrounded by a circular stone wall. As the officers barked out orders, the *askaris*, who knew the

MORE CLERGY TO THE SWORD

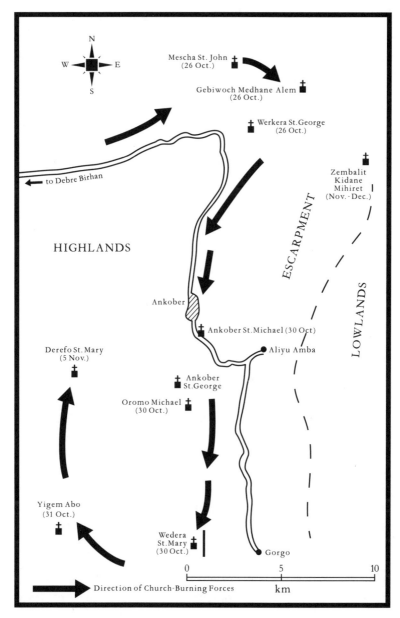

Map 16. Ankober district: church burning of October–November 1937 (© Ian Campbell)

routine, split up into groups. One group kicked open the wooden gate and ran to the church, while another fanned out to look for the clergy. A third group started splashing the outside of the church with benzine, while a fourth went in search of the treasury.

The *askaris* at the church emerged with carpets, silver-topped prayer sticks used by elderly members of the congregation for leaning on during the long services, and the holy *tabot* they had seized from the inner sanctum. Other valuables were taken from the treasury: icons, parchment manuscripts, ecclesiastical umbrellas, a silver-cased ceremonial drum and an ecclesiastical crown.

The officers ordered the plunder to be carried back to the vehicles, and the church was set ablaze, the flames shooting high up through the roof with a roar. Taken by surprise, people from the surrounding area screamed and ran out of their cottages, as *askaris* appeared, dragging with them the unsuspecting clergymen they had rounded up. There was not a moment to lose. A group of *askaris* knelt down to form a firing squad, and an officer gave the orders to shoot. Five priests raised their hands in prayer and, as shots rang out, crumpled to the ground: Father Belachew, Father Amenshewa, Father Teshome Belachew, Father Weldeyes, and Father Dirafu Shewa. Two monks were also executed: Father Habte-Maryam and Father Tekle-Weld, along with a scholar, *Debtera* Gebre-Sillassé.[5]

While smoke blew across the village, the roar of the flames, and the shouts and cries of the villagers and families of the clergy, created a cacophony as the Italians ordered the *askaris* on to their next target: the church of Gebiwoch Medhané Alem ('Saviour of the World') (see Map 16). Leaving behind them a scene of devastation and carnage where only moments before peace and tranquillity had reigned, the Italians moved on, for there were many more churches to deal with before dark.

At the Saviour of the World, a few kilometres from Mescha St John, the scenario was the same. The church was burned, sacred manuscripts were looted from the treasury, and four clergymen were dragged from their homes and shot: Father Mogesé, Father Kelkilé, Father Tsenebet, and a scholar, *Debtera* Daniél Gizaw.[6]

We do not know how many more churches were burned and clergy killed, but we do know that before the day was over the raiders had reached the parish church of Werqera St George (see Map 16), quite close to where they had left their vehicles. There they burned the church and killed the three priests they found: Father Moges, Father Hayle-Mesqel ('Power of the Cross') and Father Subsibé, as well as *Debtera* Werqineh.[7] By nightfall the soldiers were back in their trucks, heading southwards to resume their caravan of death.

By Saturday, 30 October, the military had burned and killed their way to the town of Ankober itself, some eighteen kilometres from Kundi Fort. The five churches of Ankober were actually all south of the town, and it is likely that as they were on or close to the main highway, their clergy had heard of the campaign, for when the soldiers reached the church of Ankober St Michael, there seem to have been no priests there to kill, and so the Italians had to make do with looting the treasury.[8]

After pillaging Ankober St Michael, the trucks turned off the main road, once again heading for churches where the clergy would not have been tipped off about the raid. Reaching the church of Oromo St Michael, they had a notable success, killing four priests and one monk: Father Desta Gebre-Iyesus, Father Aychiluhim Wibé, Father Taddesse Dilnasew, Father Hayle Welde-Maryam and Father Degife Gebre-Hiwet. In addition, they managed to loot the church of all its codices and other treasures.[9]

They staged another deadly attack at the church of Hehef St Michael near Ankober, where they put to death a further four priests and two scholars: Father Qirqos, Father Yegwala Ishet, Father Abbebe Ayu, Father Birhanu, *Debtera* Asrat, and *Debtera* Welde-Maryam.[10]

Astonishingly, the column still found time to attack yet another church before the end of the day: Wedera St Mary (see Map 16), where they were able to pillage all of the church properties, burn the church to the ground, and slaughter the two priests they encountered, Father Hayle and Father Wenderad Sema'at, as well as two Church scholars, *Debtera* Tsigé Neway and *Debtera* Kidane.[11]

By the next day, Sunday, 31 October, the raiding party had managed to move west across the Ayraka River—easily forded at that time of year—to reach the remote church of Yigem Abo (see Map 16). We have no details of the pillage, but we know that they

261

killed the head of the church, a priest named *Aleqa* Gebre-Hanna, whom they cut down with a sword.[12]

There is no record of how many churches were devastated during the next few days, but by 5 November the marauding soldiers had reached the parish church of Derefo St Mary (see Map 16), where they looted the treasury and slaughtered all five priests: Father Welde-Tsadiq Mengistu, Father Tesfa Welde-Tsadiq, Father Gebre-Maryam, Father Tamré-Beyene, and Father Asrat.[13]

By the time the convoy reached the garrison at Tebassi, the trucks were weighed down with loot, for the eleven-day campaign had gathered a rich harvest. Many churches had been reduced to smouldering pyres. And thousands of Orthodox faithful of Ankober district were grieving for their loved ones. The military had fulfilled the *Duce*'s orders for 'a reign of terror', and the 'schismatics and heretics' had paid the ultimate price.

Destruction in Bulga

In late 1937 Bulga, south of Ankober district (see Map 15), was a focus of attention for the Italians. It had for some time been a centre of resistance, and had already been devastated by Graziani's policy of exemplary repression. Describing a terrifying Italian raid on his grandmother's house when he was a young boy, eyewitness Gétachew Beqele, who later rose to high office in Haile Selassie's government, and accompanied the present author in his research in Bulga, recalled: 'The Italians followed a scorched earth policy, burning everything in sight and killing anybody they found. The Italians behaved badly, which provoked the Ethiopians to retaliate. The sort of atrocities the Italians committed included cutting off of heads and displaying them. They would burn down houses with civilians inside.'[14]

But in September 1937 an incident in Bulga struck fear into the Italians. In the absence of Emperor Haile Selassie, who was in exile in England, several Patriot leaders, wanting to unite and strengthen the fragmented resistance armies, enthroned a substitute. They decided to crown a young man named Melake-Tsehay Iyyasu, great-grandson of Emperor Menelik. He was a son of *Lij* Iyyasu, whom Menelik had named as his heir apparent and who had been the de facto ruler of Ethiopia from 1910 to 1916, but had been outmanoeuvred by politicians supporting *Ras* Teferi (the future emperor Haile Selassie).

Melake-Tsehay was anointed by the head of the monastery of Abiyyé Gedam at the church of Wegfelé Michael in Bulga. Crowned on 2 September, he announced, 'I have ascended to the throne of my father. People of Ethiopia, be united and fight your enemy!' Drums were beaten, and the Ethiopian flag was raised.[15]

Fitawrari Welde-Tsadiq Zewdé, a key figure in bringing about this dramatic new development, was the uncle of Gétachew Beqele, who testified: 'The news spread like wildfire and resistance leaders from every corner of the country flocked into Bulga. A government was organised and established and all the leaders who were gathered there were given traditional titles and appointed governors of the area from where they came.'[16]

This new development posed a serious threat to Graziani's administration; unification of the various factions of the resistance was what he dreaded most of all. The precarious survival of the Italians within their besieged garrisons depended largely on their policy of divide and rule: dividing the resistance among themselves, and dividing the Patriots from both the local communities and the Orthodox Church. Now the entire fabric of Italian hegemony was at risk. When Graziani found out what had happened, his reaction was harsh and swift. Mobilising his Eritrean and Somali Muslim battalions to surround the heartland of Bulga in a desperate effort to root out the resistance and eliminate its potential supporters, he launched wave after wave of exemplary repression, in which a great number of churches were razed to the ground.[17]

Some 44 km due south of Ankober lies Berehet district in the wider administrative unit of Bulga. The district consists principally of rocky enclaves and densely treed river gorges, interspersed with tiny settlements each clustered around a church, far below the plateau. These gorges were first settled by Christian Amhara in the 10th century, whereas the plateau came to be settled later by Oromo, who arrived in the area in the 16th century.[18] Thus many of the churches and monasteries dotted across the broken countryside of Bulga were of ancient foundation, and by the 1930s life for the conservative Christian communities in these valleys had in many respects changed little since medieval times. It was in Berehet district, in late November 1937, that the Italians organised yet another church-burning programme.

As in the case of Ankober district, we will never know the full extent of the carnage, the total death toll, and the number of churches burned and pillaged in Berehet. However, in some parishes the surviving residents were able to file their stories. One such case involved the church of Indode St Michael, situated in a deep valley just above a tributary of the Menso River that flows eastwards into the arid lowlands.

The latest campaign of exemplary repression was concentrated in this area because a few kilometres to the west of Indode St Michael, on the edge of the plateau, stood the great mountain of Megezez (see Map 13), and it was in the caves and crevices surrounding that mountain that *Ras* Abebe Aregay, the most renowned of Ethiopia's resistance leaders, had one of his camps. Thus the settlements in striking distance of Megezez, which could be reached from the main Addis Ababa–Debre Birhan road by military vehicles, became targets. The viceroy was still convinced that terrorism and destruction striking at the heart of the Christian communities of Northern Shewa would dissuade them from supporting the resistance. In fact, as we have seen, the effect was the opposite. But Graziani's hatred for the Ethiopian Church was visceral, and he would not be deflected.

There were many parish churches below the plateau and within a few kilometres of Megezez. Just how many of them were razed to the ground in the Bulga campaign of November 1937, and how many of their clergy died, is not recorded, but it is certain that most, if not all, of the churches were attacked and at least looted. One eyewitness, *Memhir* Demissé Abiyyé, who was himself with the Patriots in the area throughout the time of Melake-Tsehay, reported in 1988 that no less than 485 churches were destroyed.[19]

The attack on Indode St Michael was one of the few to be documented. Soldiers under Italian command reached the church on 24 November, looted it of its treasures, and killed the church's five priests: Father Zelleqe, Father Hayle-Maryam, Father Fisseha, Father Mekonnin, and Father ZeSillassé.[20] The nearby church of

Werqele St Michael was also burned down, and all its manuscripts and other artefacts were stolen. However, the fate of the priests remains unknown.[21]

Three days later, another church in the vicinity of Megezez—the church of Werqa St Michael—was attacked, looted of all of its treasures, and burned to the ground.[22] The fate of the clergy is unknown. The fact that the church appears never to have been reconstructed suggests that the entire community may have been annihilated.

Meanwhile, the onslaught in neighbouring Ankober district continued. As noted earlier, the records that survive cover only a fraction of the churches attacked. In some cases, documentation exists but is incomplete. For example, it is on record that on 8 November the church of Hagere St Mary was burned down while two of the priests were inside, and that, unable to escape, they were burned to death. However, their names are not recorded.[23]

By the Ethiopian month of Hidar (10 November to 9 December) the devastation had moved further east, with the burning of the church of Zembabit Kidane Mihret ('The Covenant of Mercy'), in which the Italians massacred five priests and a monk: Father Tedla, Father Tekle-Giyorgis, Father Mamo Qetsela, Father Mukriya, Father Welde-Maryam, and Father Bantiyirgu.[24]

In summary, the church-burning campaigns in Northern Shewa and Bulga between June and December 1937 were so extensive that some entire villages were depopulated and disappeared for ever. Thousands of clergy and their parishioners were slaughtered, of whom only a few can be identified today by location and name. The majority lie in unmarked graves.

More Devastation in Wag

Meanwhile, by September 1937, desperate to contain the rapidly growing resistance in the north, the High Command aimed its forces at a Patriot leader who had led a surprise attack on the Italians at Korem (see Map 3): *Dejazmach* Haylu Kebede, son and heir of the hereditary ruler of the ancient Christian region of Wag, a royal bloodline dating back to the 13th century. Arming collaborating mercenaries from Wello, the Italians ravaged Wag in an onslaught in which several churches were burned, including Tiya Kidane-Mihret and Weleh St Mary.

Following one of the battles, in which 5,000 resistance fighters were reportedly massacred on Graziani's orders to 'show no mercy', mutilation of prisoners by units under Italian command was widespread. In a horrific re-enactment of the Maletti–Mohammed Sultan *jihad* of Northern Shewa, Christian Wag was bathed in blood. One Italian officer described the savagery of his own troops as 'horrendous'.

Dejazmach Haylu was captured, mutilated, decapitated, and his head displayed publicly by the Italians for several days, mounted on top of a long pole. The Italians even executed several Ethiopian military commanders who attempted to give the rest of his body a Christian burial.[25]

The Italian army went on to devastate the region. Despite, or perhaps because of, the fact that the people of Wag had long considered themselves protectors of Orthodox Christianity, the atrocities included the burning of numerous churches. In one district alone (Dehna *wereda*, the other district of Wag being Ziqwala[26] *wereda*), the invaders razed no less than eleven churches to the ground: Biwel Arba'itu Insisa ('The Four Beasts of the Apocalypse'), Tibanzba St Gabriel, Amdewerq Qirqos (St Quiricus), Debre Zeyit St Mary, Gur-Amba St George, Adeljan St Michael, Abam Abo, Abmata St Libanos, Misqa St Mary, Bachi St Mary, and Chir Arba'itu Insisa.[27]

Slaughter at Addis Alem

In 1900 Emperor Menelik had founded the town of Addis Alem ('New World') some forty kilometres west of Addis Ababa (see Map 7), with the intention of moving the capital there. The plan was eventually abandoned, but the throne room of the palace being built at Addis Alem for the emperor, which was decorated both inside and outside, was converted into the church of St Mary. A historically important and architecturally interesting building, today the church, together with an adjoining museum, is frequently visited by tourists.

However, Addis Alem was not always a happy place, for during the occupation it fell victim to the Italians. On 3 December 1937 the Italian administration accused the priests at the church of sheltering Patriots. They dispatched to the church a company of soldiers, who killed seven clergymen. They also imprisoned ten priests, who were reportedly then starved of food and water.[28] As the new year dawned, the Italians had resumed their campaign in Bulga, where they were burning and looting the church of Akrimit St Michael, some twelve kilometres south-south-west of Indode St Michael.[29]

Unlike the attacks on well-known churches and monasteries such as Debre Libanos and Debre Bisrat and those on Mount Ziqwala, which were documented in reports to Rome, General Maletti's church-burning campaigns, which continued in remote areas long after the change of policy, seem not to have been documented. For that reason, they have remained largely unknown outside the villages and hamlets concerned. However, the escalation in the resistance that the attacks generated inevitably came to Mussolini's attention, confirming his view that the holy war had become counterproductive.

20

KISSING THE CROSS

'An evil soul producing holy witness is like a villain with a smiling cheek.'
William Shakespeare, *The Merchant of Venice*

General Maletti's church-burning campaigns had been conducted for several months in the face of Rome's new policy of embracing and rehabilitating the Ethiopian Church. Although Graziani would have been entirely aware of it—indeed, Maletti was doubtless following his instructions—we do not know the extent to which Mussolini was aware. However, the upshot was that on 10 November 1937 the *Duce* relieved Graziani of his position of viceroy. Although he did not leave for Rome immediately, he was described by Lessona as showing signs of derangement, and was replaced by the courtly and more even-handed Duke of Aosta. The ruthless Pirzio-Biroli and the notorious Captain Corvo were also removed from Ethiopia.

Graziani fought bitterly to stay on as commander-in-chief of the troops in Italian East Africa. He was allowed to return to Addis Ababa and stay on in that capacity just for a few weeks. Sent back to Italy in January 1938, he was replaced as commander-in-chief of the armed forces by General Ugo Cavallero.

Graziani certainly never concurred with Rome's change of policy towards the Ethiopian Church, as may be judged from the way he was to write proudly of the massacre of Debre Libanos as a highly successful instrument of terror, and as one of his greatest accomplishments, which had 'made the entire clergy tremble with fear, from the bishop to the last of the priests and monks'.[1]

Although deportations to Danane authorised by Graziani were to continue until late November 1937, the new viceroy soon began to implement new, more subtle policies, using the Ethiopian Church as a tool to help gain support for the Italian administration, rather than trying to destroy it. Having successfully courted and made use of the Catholic episcopate, and having raised their expectations in order to get the Vatican and the Holy See to turn a blind eye to his homicidal adventure in Ethiopia, Mussolini had now done the unthinkable: his administration was now to be hand in glove with the 'heretics and schismatics'. In his Ethiopian adventure the *Duce* had no further use for the Catholic episcopate, for he was bringing Italy's holy war to an ignominious end.

Fighting Alexandria

Official implementation of the new policy meant that the Church of Ethiopia would fall directly under the control of the Fascist administration. This also meant, of course, that the ancient ties that linked the Ethiopian Church with the Coptic Patriarchate of Alexandria would have to be cut. However, the Holy See saw its opportunity for a consolation prize. Even if the plans of the Congregation for the Propagation of the Faith had been largely thwarted, the Holy See might still be able to bring the Ethiopian Church under the umbrella of the Catholic Church. After all, as the historian Peter Kent pointed out, the Catholic Church 'had given the Italian government active support in its war effort, believing that it would be given as privileged a role in the empire as it held in Italy proper and, thus, that its missionary work would serve as a fitting complement to the "civilising mission" of the Italians in East Africa'.[2]

However, having promised the Ethiopian clergy independence from the Copts, there was no way the Italian authorities in Addis Ababa were going to tell them that they were now to be subservient to the Catholic Church. So, like bank robbers quarrelling over their loot, the Italian government and the Holy See were now at loggerheads. The marriage of convenience was coming apart at the seams.

At the end of November 1937, the Governo Generale in Addis Ababa asked the Egyptian archbishop Qérillos, who had earlier been taken on a visit to Rome, to take over the spiritual aspects of the Ethiopian Church on Italy's behalf, severed from Alexandria, with administration in the hands of the Italian-appointed *ichegé*. However, the archbishop refused, and returned to Cairo.

Graziani, who had not yet returned to Italy, was looking around for a suitable Ethiopian replacement for Qérillos. Having executed the energetic Bishops Pétros and Mikaél, there were only two Ethiopian bishops left alive, and of those he settled for the elderly and partially blind Bishop Abraham.[3] Informed of this on 2 December, the outraged Alexandrian patriarch launched intense discussions with the Italian government, only to learn on 8 December that Abraham had been appointed patriarch of the Ethiopian Church and that he had already consecrated three archbishops and three bishops. By the end of December the furious Coptic patriarch had excommunicated the hapless Abraham and declared his consecrations null and void. Nonetheless, the Italian government insisted on continuing with the new arrangements and went ahead regardless. As far as they were concerned, the Ethiopian Church was now independent of the Alexandrian Patriarchate.[4]

Repair and Restoration

Ethiopian churches—at least in the towns where the Italians were in control—were, at least in theory, now exempt from attack or desecration, and it was at this time, in mid-December 1937, that an example was made of Italian soldiers who were doing what had been routine since 1935. Two groups of three soldiers were arrested after entering the well-known Addis Ababa churches of Intotto Maryam and Tekle Haymanot, where, armed with rifles, they had threatened to kill the priests and had robbed the churches of money and sacred artefacts. Graziani, who was coming to the end of the extension of his tenure in Ethiopia, reported that he had instructed the court to proceed against the men with the utmost rigour.[5]

On 16 December, Abraham, who had submitted to the Italians, made a public proclamation on behalf of the Italian administration, promising that it would protect the churches, rebuild those that had been destroyed, and restore the property and estates that the Ethiopian Church had previously owned. Work began almost immediately on the burned-out cathedral of St George in Addis Ababa. The Italian government, Abraham assured his audience, was full of compassion.[6] Almost overnight, far from being a warning to other clergy who might consider opposing the might of the occupying forces, the slaughter of countless Orthodox clergy and their families across Ethiopian Christendom for more than two years had become unmentionable—an embarrassment to be forgotten, and eventually denied.

The collaborating bishop also addressed the Patriots, his speech leaving no doubt that the objective of the Italian church-burning campaign and the massacres that accompanied it had been to blackmail the Patriots into surrendering:

> God has chosen Italy to govern Ethiopia. And you, rebels, who live in the bush and the mountains, if, on account of you the churches are burnt and the old people, women and children are massacred, if the country is destroyed, God will hear their cries and see their blood and will punish you. But if you cease to do wrong, we will obtain pardon for your faults in the past.[7]

Abraham even announced excommunication of the Patriots, but many priests, including the entire clergy of Gojjam, never recognised him, and refused to attend his synods.[8]

A Christmas Message

On 25 December, having received more than a thousand letters and Christmas cards from America, Emperor Haile Selassie broadcast a radio message from London to the American people: 'Shame on those of us who are Christians and do not follow the ways of the Saviour of the World, whose life was filled with kindness, humility and martyrdom! If we lived by the laws he gave us and were worthy of being called Christians, peace would have reigned on this earth.'

Despairing of the behaviour of the Italians, he went on: 'the spirit of the wicked continues to cast its shadow on this world. The arrogant are seen visibly leading their people into crime and destruction. The laws of the League of Nations are constantly violated.'

Echoing his earlier remarks at Geneva ('Today it is us; tomorrow it will be you'), the emperor foresaw the horrors of Fascism that would shortly be visited upon the world, for he continued: 'The two-thousand-year-old Christian civilisation is threatened with destruction. If this happens, there will be a return to the days of barbarism, when the mighty could realise their aspirations at will.' Finally, he pleaded with the American people to 'remember in your prayers all those weak and endangered peoples who look to the flags of the free nations with confidence, hoping to discern the star which will announce their peace and future security'.[9]

A Masquerade

The year 1938 opened with feverish activity by the Italian administration in Addis Ababa. Now desperate to defuse the holy war and neutralise the Ethiopian Church as the symbol and rallying point of Ethiopian nationalism, the new viceroy ramped up the newly launched programme of repair and rehabilitation of churches and monasteries where some of the most egregious atrocities had taken place, and several of the Ethiopian clergy prudently played along. Entering into the spirit of the charade, they expressed homage in speeches extolling the goodness of Mussolini's government, and the Italian commanders would respond by kissing the Orthodox cross or Bible, and regale their audience with stories of the wonderful things they had done for the welfare of the Ethiopian Church.[10]

The Ethiopians were playing their part quite convincingly; it was perfect theatre, and it would continue throughout 1938. Calvin Shenk put it bluntly, pointing out that 'much of the forced subjection was merely superficial and Church leaders who praised the Italians did so quite insincerely as this seemed to be the option of greatest convenience'.[11] Indeed, the Orthodox prelates had decided that discretion was the better part of valour. In order to preserve what was left of their Church and the lives of the remaining clergy, they would accommodate the demands of the occupying forces; they would bide their time.

A Disaster

For Pius XI, the Addis Ababa administration's favouring of Islam was bad enough, and its failure to declare Catholicism the state religion in Ethiopia was a crushing disappointment. But Italy's embrace of the Ethiopian Church independent of Catholic control was the last straw, particularly as before the invasion the prospects for the Catholic Church under Haile Selassie had been relatively good—certainly far better than they had now become. Italy was clearly public enemy number one in Ethiopia, and Catholicism, now clearly identified with the enemy, had become as unpopular there as it had been after the religious wars of the early 17th century. For the Roman Church, the great crusade had been a disaster.

EPILOGUE

Rejoicings, Regret and Confusion

Pope Pius XI may not have expressed regret for the support for the invasion provided by the Italian episcopate and encouraged by many strident voices from within the Vatican, nor does he seem to have regretted turning a blind eye to the horrors of the occupation. Yet by late 1937 he had begun to regret his alliance with Fascism. We may never know the whole story, for Secretary of State Pacelli and his staff managed to shield much of the pontiff's growing disenchantment with Mussolini from public view. Nonetheless, that disenchantment would grow in intensity during the course of 1938. The conclusion drawn by David Kertzer from his study of the Vatican Secret Archives for the period is that, 'disillusioned and despondent', the pontiff 'worried that he had not been true to the sacred trust placed in him. He had let his patriotic sentiments as an Italian colour his judgement. He vowed to do all he could in the little time he had left to make amends.'[1]

Given the horrors of the invasion of Ethiopia, and the unholy alliance that facilitated it, the pontiff had good reason to worry that he had not been true to the sacred trust placed in him. However, even in the months that followed, he seems never to have condemned his cardinals for preaching the crusade and declaring the invasion a holy war.

And neither, apparently, did the average Italian cleric have such worries, for the clergy launched the New Year with great rejoicing.

HOLY WAR

On 9 January 1938, at a political celebration convened by Mussolini at Palazzo Venezia, sixty archbishops and some two thousand priests applauded a speech by Archbishop Giuseppe Nogara of Udine in which he asked for God's protection for Mussolini, 'so that He will help you to win all the battles which you so wisely and energetically are directing for the prosperity, the greatness and the glory of Christian Rome'.

The *Duce*, in turn, was effusive in his thanks to the clergy for their support for the invasion, replying that the collaboration between the Catholic Church and Fascism had borne great fruits for all. Under no illusions about the contribution of the Church, he expressed his gratitude for 'the efficient cooperation given by all of the clergy during the war against the Abyssinians ... remembering with particular sympathy the example of patriotism shown by the Italian bishops, who brought their gold to the local offices of the Fascist Party, while the parish priests were preaching to the Italians to resist and fight'. The hall resounded to the cries of '*Duce! Duce! Duce!*'[2]

But the rejoicing over the war in Ethiopia gradually gave way to a growing concern as the *Duce* increasingly mimicked Hitler. It seemed that the excesses of Italy's invasion of Ethiopia were soon to be experienced in Europe. The boot was now on the other foot, and the Holy See was outraged. Having not said a word when Mussolini's racial laws were passed in Ethiopia, the pope now condemned the prospect of such legislation in Italy. Denigrating Jews—including those who had converted to Catholicism—the laws were regarded by the pontiff as the 'new heresy', and the clerics followed suit. As Daniel Binchy put it, when Mussolini 'imported the racialist myth from Germany, and grafted it on to his own "doctrine", it was precisely those prelates who had hitherto stood highest in favour of his regime who echoed the Pope's condemnation in uncompromising language'.[3]

One of the strongest supporters of Fascism referred to by Binchy was, of course, Ildefonso Schuster, Milan's cardinal archbishop, who had proclaimed that the rampaging armies in Ethiopia were doing God's work. He was one of the first to change his tune when confronted with the realities of totalitarianism on his own doorstep, particularly when it seemed that the Catholic Church in Germany

EPILOGUE

might be about to suffer the same fate at the hands of Hitler that the Ethiopian Church had suffered at the hands of Mussolini.

On 12 March 1938 the German army invaded Austria, where it was warmly welcomed by the head of the Catholic Church, Cardinal Archbishop Innitzer, who issued a pro-Nazi statement to be delivered in all Austrian churches. Shocked, the pope suddenly found his voice. Forgetting his 'neutrality' towards the national Catholic Churches, and apparently discovering that he did, after all, have the authority to intervene and rein in their errant clerics, he had Innitzer reprimanded in a Vatican radio broadcast, and summoned him to Rome for a dressing-down.[4]

A few weeks later the ailing pontiff was confronted with another shock: a state visit to Rome by Adolf Hitler. All eyes were now on the Nazis, and the turmoil in Ethiopia was now conveniently forgotten. Indeed, Pius XI increasingly gave the impression of having entirely lost interest in the fate of Ethiopia. Nevertheless, he made an exception when events there concerned him. For example, the Vatican and the Fascist administration were still at loggerheads following the latter's move to sever the links between the Ethiopian Church and the Copts, and to declare the independence of the Ethiopian Church under the umbrella of the Italian administration. That did interest the pontiff, and in mid-1938, in a daring bid to resurrect the old plan of the Holy See to bring the Ethiopian Church under Rome, Archbishop Castellani was received by the pope at the pontifical palace of Castel Gandolfo. Castellani was seeking permission for the Ethiopian bishop Yohannis, a Fascist appointee, to visit Rome for a papal audience.

Furious, and fearing that the Ethiopian prelates would think that the office of the viceroy had supported the scheme, the Italian government informed the pope that Castellani would have to be replaced.[5] However, the Holy See, perfectly willing to resist Mussolini's instructions when it wished to do so, refused to remove the apostolic delegate. In fact, Pacelli complained of excessive government support for 'other religions' in Ethiopia, and that the government was hampering the construction of Catholic churches there, 'lamenting that even the Moslems in Ethiopia were better protected than the Catholic Church'.[6]

The Vatican was quite right about the status of Islam in Ethiopia. The Italians had built a large mosque in Addis Ababa, and their administration was winning the support of many Ethiopian Muslims. The fact is that for Mussolini, the alliance with the Catholic Church had served its purpose. He had got what he wanted, and now he had no need for Castellani. Thus, his response to Pius XI was that the archbishop could remain in Addis Ababa only if he fell in line with the policies of the Fascist administration.

Castellani had to make a choice, and he chose to side with the Fascists and remain in Addis Ababa.[7] Thus the dispute was resolved, but in the process the Holy See lost its final bid for control of the Ethiopian Church. For the Catholic Church, the holy war against the heretics, the righteous fury of the cardinals, the massacres of the Ethiopian clergy, the *jihad* and the church-burning campaigns had come to nothing.

Not surprisingly, Pius XI was displeased by the way in which the Catholic Church had been used by Mussolini and then, in effect, dumped when he no longer needed a holy war. In mid-1938, Tacchi Venturi, the pope's private emissary to the *Duce*, was bitterly reminding the dictator how essential the backing of the Church had been for him, that support having been 'not the least important reason for the Italian victory in Ethiopia'.[8] The war-mongering clerics themselves had little to say, the new policy in Ethiopia having taken the wind out of their sails. In any case, by 1938 most of their black-shirted 'missionaries of the Cross' had been sent to fight in the Spanish Civil War, where, having to contend with a well-armed enemy rather than defenceless civilians, many of them met their end.

Thus Archbishop Schuster's glorious campaign against Ethiopia's 'heretics and schismatics' was soon forgotten, and the rabble-rousing faded to an embarrassed silence. As regards the invasion, an acute case of collective amnesia was falling upon the Italian episcopate.

As for Pius XI, he had other things to worry about. Concerned that Hitler threatened the institution of the Catholic Church in Germany, on Christmas Eve 1938 he had no hesitation in personally delivering to his cardinals a denunciation of Mussolini's growing closeness to the Nazis, which had resulted in the *Duce*'s adoption of Hitler's anti-Semitic policies and the appearance of the swastika in

EPILOGUE

Rome. Once again, the pope's speech calls into question his claim of neutrality towards clergy of national Catholic Churches regarding political matters, which some scholars cite to explain his failure to restrain the Italian clerics and denounce Fascist excesses in Ethiopia.

A few weeks later, as the tenth anniversary of the Lateran Treaty which had sealed the alliance between the Church and the Fascist government grew near, Mussolini feared that the pontiff was about to deliver a stinging rebuke to his regime. However, the rebuke never came. On 10 February 1939 Pope Pius XI, whose clergy had sacralised the brutal invasion of Ethiopia, and who had turned a blind eye to the misdeeds of the invaders during the occupation that followed, died without having made amends. A speech he had prepared concerning the Church and Fascism lay beside his bed; the speech was never given, and Secretary of State Pacelli had all the printed copies destroyed.[9]

In 2006 the original document came to light. Not surprisingly, the pope's last thoughts were expressions of concern about the difficulties the Catholic Church might suffer under Fascism in the future. It was a sufficient critique of Mussolini's policies to have annoyed the *Duce*, and was clearly an attempt by a dying man to unburden his conscience. However, it was not the ringing denunciation of Fascism that some had expected, nor was it a powerful statement of pontifical regret or even confession of a mistaken or naive policy of the past. And it made no mention of Ethiopia.

Secretary of State Pacelli, whose enthusiasm for Fascism lasted longer than *Papa* Ratti's, and who had long managed to curtail some of the pope's more vehement outbursts against the actions of Mussolini's government, succeeded the pontiff as Pope Pius XII. The risk of an impending split between the Vatican and Fascism had now passed. Mussolini and Hitler would work together for foreign conquest, Hitler would invade Czechoslovakia and Poland, and the world would be engulfed by war. The Italians would invade Albania and Greece, and then, in concert with Nazi Germany, would invade and dismember Yugoslavia. Employing the same techniques of exemplary repression that they had tested and honed in Ethiopia— village burning, massacres, deportations and concentration camps— not infrequently under the direction of the very same military commanders, they would leave behind them a trail of suffering and death.

The War Continues

Although the crusade against the Ethiopian Church had officially been brought to an end by early 1938, the war continued much as before, with the policies of collective punishment and exemplary repression of civilians still in place. Commander Cavallero continued military attacks on churches and monasteries, but not on well-known or strategic targets. They were concentrated on smaller, lesser-known and more remote Christian centres that would not attract undue attention. In sworn testimony for the UN war crimes trials, an eyewitness of events in November 1938 in eastern Shewa, as the war entered its fourth year, reported: 'We saw those troops [Muslim *askaris* under Italian command] plundering all the property of the peasants and burning villages, including churches ... while bombing all the country all around there [Tamo], their infantry set on fire many famous churches by [flaming] torches'.[10]

The Italians continued to strike civilian as well as military targets; in the first quarter of 1939 in Bichena, Gojjam (see Map 10), under the command of Colonel Leopoldo Natale, churches and houses were still being attacked:

> The Italians burned two churches and then plundered and burned approximately 5,000 houses in Baranta District in Bichena ... This took place in the month of Yekatit 1931 EC (February 1939) ... The Italians first plundered and then burned all of the houses of Lamchow in Bichena, without leaving a single house standing, under the pretext that some of the natives of the country had become Patriots with *Dejazmach* Belay Zelleqe. The houses burned were approximately 200. Also three churches were burned down: Wasda St Michael, Ganaz St Mary and Sakala St Gabriel.[11]

However, over the course of 1939 international developments triggered doubts about the future of the Italian occupation of Ethiopia. There were expectations among Ethiopians that Italy would become embroiled in a European war, and that its enemies would come to their aid.[12] The day before his dismissal as viceroy, even Graziani had frankly admitted as much.

Thus the new viceroy had inherited a virtually impossible task. Resistance was again escalating, there was widespread corruption throughout the Italian administration and morale among the Italians was sinking. In addition, the Duke of Aosta had to deal with the aftermath and legacy of Graziani's tenure. While he maintained the death sentence for Ethiopians found in possession of arms, he saw no point in keeping innocent men, women and children in prison, and so he set about reviewing the situation of the thousands of Ethiopians serving life sentences in concentration camps and prisons in Ethiopia, Somalia, the Dahlak Islands and Italy.

At the age of thirteen, Tibebe Kassa of Debre Libanos was transferred from Danane concentration camp to a prison camp at Mogadishu, where he spent much of 1938. He was returned to Danane for a few months and was then transferred to Eritrea to be incarcerated in a prison at Nefasit. He was eventually released in February–March 1939, slightly less than two years after his capture at Debre Libanos.

By then the situation in Ethiopia was very tense, and there was something of a stalemate between the Patriots and the Italians, prompting the Duke of Aosta to warn Mussolini that a European war 'would bring on the high seas the task of pacifying the country and jeopardise the conquest itself'.[13]

Finally, the duke's fears came to pass. Following Hitler's invasion of Poland and Britain's declaration of war against Germany in September, and Germany's invasion of France in 1940, Mussolini, expecting a share of the fruits of what he perceived to be Hitler's inevitable victory, declared war on Britain and France.

Liberation

Italy's declaration of war against Britain triggered a sea change in British policy towards the war in Ethiopia. Italy was now Britain's enemy, and by mid-1940, with the Italo-Ethiopian war in its fifth year, forces under British command had arrived in Ethiopia to unite with the Ethiopian Patriots. In January 1941 three simultaneous attacks were launched on Italian East Africa, from Eritrea, Sudan and Kenya. Within three months a relatively small force of British, South African, Nigerian, Sudanese and Kenyan soldiers, fighting alongside the Ethiopian Patriots, had crushed the enemy, and the considerably larger Italian army in Addis Ababa had surrendered en masse. The British opened up Danane, freed the prisoners, and used the camp for incarcerating Italian prisoners of war. Emperor Haile Selassie, who had never lost his faith in God, and had regularly prayed in the church established in the greenhouse of his residence in England, was flown to the Sudan, finally arriving at Debre Marqos in central Ethiopia on 6 April 1941.

Reaching Fiché on 1 May, the sovereign went to give thanks at the monastery of Debre Libanos, where, received by Patriots, he found (in his words) only 'a few clergy'. In his memoirs the sovereign lamented, 'The monastery has been burned down by the Fascists, the clergy exterminated at the hands of the enemy, its treasures looted, and the entire vicinity abandoned and neglected. When We saw all this, We were extremely saddened and deeply moved.'[14]

The emperor returned to Fiché to see where military commanders Aberra and Asfawessen Kassa had been executed, and then made a triumphant entry into Addis Ababa on 5 May. At midday he raised the Ethiopian flag to a 21-gun salute, precisely five years after the Italian flag had first been raised on the same spot.[15]

Haile Selassie delivered a moving speech, outlining the background to the Italian invasion, and the horrors of the occupation. He shared the pain of those who had suffered during the massacre of *Yekatit 12*:

> How many are the young men, the women, the priests and monks whom the Italians pitilessly massacred during those years? ... The blood and bones of those who were killed with spades and pickaxes, of those who were split with axes and hammered to death, pierced with bayonets, clubbed and stoned, of those who were burned alive in their homes with their little children, of those who perished of hunger and thirst in prison, have been crying for justice.

Yet even in his hour of triumph, the emperor maintained his dignity and faith:

EPILOGUE

> When we say let us rejoice with our hearts, let not our rejoicing be in any other way but in the spirit of Christ. Do not return evil for evil. Do not indulge in the atrocities which the enemy has been practising in his usual way, even to the last. Take care not to spoil the good name of Ethiopia by acts which are worthy of the enemy.[16]

The Ethiopians followed their emperor's instruction not to repay evil with evil. The Italians were treated honourably, graciously and with Christian charity. The man whom Mussolini had denounced as a monstrous barbarian ensured that, despite the catalogue of atrocities the Italians had meted out to the Ethiopians, as Professor Del Boca observed, 'Not a hair of an Italian's head was harmed'.[17]

The 1940s

Following the entry of the British army into Addis Ababa on 6 April 1941, British Military Intelligence began closely watching the activities of the Catholic missions, and Archbishop Castellani in particular. The investigations revealed that in the papal legation in Addis Ababa a wireless transmitter of the latest Italian military type was being operated by nine Italian soldiers who had been demobilised just before the arrival of the British. These soldiers were in possession of passes signed by Castellani, who, however, did not communicate their presence to the British military command, although 'he was aware of the obvious irregularity of such an arrangement'. In addition, two other officials of the Italian government 'had been posted to the Legation in nebulous appointments under the express direction of Dr Franca' in his former position as director of the Italian Department of Political Affairs. Subsequent investigations found that 'various currencies and some bullion' had been transferred from the Banca d'Italia to the papal legation just prior to the arrival of the British. In addition, the legation was found to be transferring capital out of Ethiopia by receiving money from Italian residents and telegraphing instructions to Rome using 'the clandestine radio transmitter for the payment of the sums to the recipients by the Vatican'.[18]

More evidence of direct support by the Catholic Church for the Italian military was uncovered in the Consolata, San Vincenzo and

Capuchin missions. Arms and ammunition were discovered in May 1941 in the storehouse and the priests' quarters of the Capuchin mission in Dire Dawa, and 'the mission at Atsbi Teferi was found to be the depository for a large quantity of arms, ammunition, and hand grenades, which were found in the priests' rooms and even hidden in the altar canopy of the church itself'.[19]

British Intelligence concluded that the activities of the Italian Catholic missionaries in Ethiopia, including those of the apostolic delegate, were actively Fascist and subversive of peace and order. Brigadier Lush of the Occupied Territory Administration in Ethiopia informed Sir Philip Mitchell, the chief political officer in Nairobi:

> I am anxious to rid this country of an active and intelligent organisation, far more dangerous than the mediocre Fascists who have been removed by various purges which have taken place since our arrival here; but I realise the political and international complications of such drastic action. I would, however, strongly recommend that the Vatican be approached with a view to transferring Mgr Castellani to some other post and that I should be given a free hand to deport the majority of the Italian Catholic priests.[20]

After considerable diplomatic manoeuvring between Emperor Haile Selassie (who also wanted Castellani expelled), the British military in Ethiopia and the Foreign Office in London, the apostolic delegate was finally deported from Ethiopia on 29 November 1942, though he apparently retained his title until 13 December 1945.

It is worth noting that, whereas before the Italian invasion the Ethiopian government had welcomed—and, indeed, invited— Catholic missions into Ethiopia, after the war foreign Catholics frequently found themselves no longer trusted by the Ethiopians, because they were now identified with Italy and the invading forces. Even British attempts to get the emperor to agree to allow non-Italian Catholic clergy back into Ethiopia were initially met with considerable resistance.[21]

Archbishop Castellani would not be replaced until 1957, when Monsignor Joseph McGeough was installed in Addis Ababa as the new apostolic nuncio to Ethiopia.

EPILOGUE

The End of the Duce

In September 1943, by which time it was apparent that Germany would probably lose the war, Italy surrendered and joined the Allies. As a result, the Germans invaded Italy and occupied Rome for several months until the Allies swept up northwards through southern Italy. In the confusion, the Italians suffered what amounted to a civil war; the Fascist dreams of a 'new Italy' were shattered amidst poverty, food shortages, reprisals, public executions and social chaos. The Vatican was for a time virtually under siege, and in October the Germans rounded up Jews in Rome and deported them to the death camp at Auschwitz.

In April 1945 Mussolini and several other notable Fascists were executed by partisans. A few days later Hitler committed suicide as the Russian army closed in on Berlin, and by May Germany had surrendered. The Second World War was effectively over.

The moderation of the Italian strategy of terror and extermination in Ethiopia, and the radical change of policy towards the Ethiopian Church, both of which accompanied the replacement of Graziani by the Duke of Aosta in late 1937, brought the sacralisation of the war in Ethiopia largely to a close. It might be thought that this prevented the situation in Ethiopia reaching the acme of horror achieved by the Italian-supported clerico-Fascist regime of Ante Pavelić in Croatia, where the long-standing hostility of Croatian Catholics towards Orthodox Serbs would result in the cruel deaths of hundreds of thousands of Orthodox—sometimes at the hands of berobed Catholic clerics themselves. However, there was actually a remarkable parallel between the two pogroms, for the overall death toll of Ethiopians at the hands of the Italians was of the same order of magnitude as the death toll in Croatia—around three-quarters of a million (see Appendix I),[22] and both involved large-scale religious persecution encouraged by Catholic clergy, failure of the Vatican to denounce the war-mongering Catholic clergy, and the instigation of Muslims to commit atrocities against Orthodox Christians.

The Great Forgetting

Pius XI's secretary of state Eugenio Pacelli, who succeeded him as Pius XII in 1939, survived the war and continued to reign until his death in 1958. In 1945, looking back over the decade since the launch of the invasion of Ethiopia, which disempowered the League of Nations and took the nations of Europe on the slippery slope towards world war, Pacelli must have recalled how, while he was secretary of state, the Roman Church promoted the invasion as a holy war, thus sharing with Mussolini the awful responsibility for what followed.

Yet as Christopher Duggan observes, the Vatican encouraged the inclination on the part of Italians to 'quietly forget' about Fascism and their support for it, thus discouraging any systematic reckoning with the past. After the fall of the *Duce*, both the Holy See and the Italian Catholic Church lost no time in deflecting attention away from the Church's powerful support for Fascism. They announced that totalitarianism was incompatible with Christianity—a complete reversal of Pius XI's declaration that Fascism contained nothing incompatible with Christianity. The contrived argument was now that, owing to the incompatibility of the two doctrines, no Catholic could ever have been a Fascist.[23] Thus a veil was drawn over Fascism, and apart from a fleeting reference in Graziani's memoir, scarcely anything of Italy's brutal persecution of the Ethiopian Church would ever be published, or even mentioned. It was as if it had never happened.

The sufferings of the Italians when the Germans invaded Italy in 1943 facilitated the Great Forgetting. Having now themselves become victims of a ruthless totalitarian onslaught, they were only too ready to forget their support for the *Duce* and his genocidal cult. Indeed, the role of the Italian episcopate in the promotion of Fascism and the barbaric crusade in Ethiopia was not only forgotten, but denied. None of the prelates involved in the sacralisation of the invasion was ever held to account, and in due course proceedings were initiated to canonise Cardinals Pacelli and Schuster.

EPILOGUE

Justice Denied

In 1948, after the Paris Peace Conference had addressed the terms of settlement between Ethiopia and Italy, the issue of Italian war crimes in Ethiopia was raised by the Ethiopians before the UN War Crimes Commission. They drew up charges against 50 suspected Italian war criminals, from which, under severe time pressure, they selected just ten for trial. Their list was headed by Badoglio, Graziani and Lessona.[24] Graziani was charged with murder and systematic terrorism, deportation and internment of civilians, pillage and wanton destruction, use of gases and deliberate bombardment of hospitals, torture, and wanton destruction of religious buildings.[25]

The Ethiopian Ministry of Justice submitted a supporting portfolio of documentary evidence of war crimes to the commission, which included several incriminating telegrams issuing instructions to commit atrocities, Graziani's telegram to Lessona of 21 May 1937 reporting the execution of the monks of Debre Libanos at Laga Weldé, his telegram reporting the executions at Borale,[26] and an affidavit sworn by *Lij* Hayle-Maryam Gazmu describing briefly how General Maletti took control of the monastery and conducted the massacre.[27]

The Ethiopian submission was accompanied by a request that the defendants be tried 'in accordance with international practice for the trial of major war criminals', following principles of law and procedure 'in accordance with those of the Charter of the International Military Tribunal in Nuremberg'.[28]

The UN War Crimes Commission accepted prima facie war crimes charges against the eight military officials listed as suspects, but owing to political and bureaucratic difficulties and persistent obstruction by Britain, the Ethiopians had no choice but to reduce the number of defendants to just two; they chose Badoglio and Graziani.

Britain took the lead in blocking Ethiopia's attempts to bring the Italian suspects to justice. Britain—the very country that, while purporting to uphold the principles of collective responsibility at the League of Nations, had made Ethiopia its sacrificial lamb—once again betrayed its ally. The British government was opposed to committing to trial Badoglio, the leading defendant, because he had arranged for Italy's surrender and was considered a suitably right-wing leader who would keep Italy safely in the Western fold in the face of what was perceived to be a growing Communist threat. Furthermore, the British government had only limited interest in crimes committed against non-Europeans, and having recognised Mussolini's 'conquest' of Ethiopia, it was unwilling to acknowledge how it had been achieved. Nevertheless, the Ethiopian government stood its ground, publishing a two-volume set of documents entitled *La civilisation de l'Italie fasciste*, consisting of facsimiles and French translations of Italian telegrams ordering atrocities, and photographs of such atrocities being carried out.[29]

To put a gloss of legitimacy on its manoeuvrings, the British Foreign Office argued that Italy's invasion of Ethiopia had preceded, and thus was not a part of, the Second World War, which was deemed by the British government to have begun in September 1939, when Britain declared war on Germany. However, this was revised under pressure from the Chinese, who successfully demanded the trial of Japanese accused of invading China and committing atrocities against the Chinese well before Italy's invasion of Ethiopia. The commission's acquiescence showed the British argument to be without merit, but Ethiopia did not have the political leverage to prevail.

The Ethiopian attempts to file their submission met with yet further procedural obstructions by the British government. Thus, abandoned by the British and most of the Allies, Ethiopia was obliged to approach the Italian government directly to surrender Badoglio and Graziani as war criminals—a futile request. In September 1949, under intense political pressure, and fearful of losing British support for its claims to Eritrea, Ethiopia abandoned its efforts to bring the Italian war criminals to justice.[30]

Dramatis Personae

Rodolfo Graziani became chief of staff of the Italian Armed Forces and minister for war. He was the only marshal to stay loyal to Mussolini. Arrested in 1945 after Italy surrendered to the Allies, he was sentenced in Italy to nineteen years in prison in 1950 for continuing the collaboration with Adolf Hitler in the short-lived

EPILOGUE

Fascist Salò Republic. However, he was released after serving only a few months of his sentence. Graziani was never tried for war crimes in Libya or Ethiopia. He died of natural causes in Rome on 11 January 1955, and was buried at Affile, where he had lived.[31]

A monument constructed with public money in Affile in honour of Graziani in 2012 became the subject of international protests, leading to the successful prosecution of three Affile councillors—including mayor Ercole Viri—for the crime of 'apology of Fascism'. Nonetheless, the people of Affile re-elected Viri as mayor. However, in 2017 Ercole Viri was sentenced to eight months in prison, each of the other councillors being sentenced to six months. In 2019 the Court of Appeal upheld the sentences, but in September 2020 they were annulled by the Supreme Court.

The Duke of Aosta, Graziani's courtly successor as viceroy, was defeated during the liberation of Ethiopia, and was allowed by the British to surrender with full military honours. Well respected by his captors, he died of tuberculosis in a nursing home in Nairobi, Kenya.

General Pietro Maletti, who masterminded and oversaw numerous atrocities in Northern Shewa, including the massacre of Debre Libanos and the Maletti–Mohammed Sultan *jihad*, died in December 1940 while fighting the British in Italy's North Africa campaign. His responsibility for war crimes in Ethiopia was never acknowledged or addressed. On the contrary, he was memorialised in several Italian towns where streets are named after him.

General Alessandro Pirzio-Biroli, who carried out civilian massacres throughout the Amhara region of Ethiopia, gained further notoriety by perpetrating similar atrocities against civilians as governor of Montenegro in Italian-occupied Yugoslavia.

Cardinal Eugenio Pacelli, who became Pope Pius XII, died in 1958. Following public controversies about his conduct during the Holocaust, exacerbated by the publication of John Cornwell's book *Hitler's Pope* in 1999, the procedure for his canonisation ground to a halt. However, in 2009 he was declared Venerable.

The strongly pro-Fascist Cardinal Archbishop Schuster, who played a leading role in the sanctification of the invasion of Ethiopia and the Great Mobilisation to support it, was declared Venerable in 1994, was beatified in 1996, and is currently in line for sainthood.

Archbishop Giovanni Castellani, the pro-Fascist Catholic cleric who was appointed vicar apostolic of Addis Ababa in March 1937, became apostolic nuncio to Guatemala and El Salvador in 1945. Transferred to the office of the secretary of state in the Vatican in 1951, he died two years later.[32]

Recovery

Despite the slaughter of so many of the clergy and their parishioners, the destruction of churches and monasteries, and the loss of a great part of its cultural patrimony, the 'heresy' of Ethiopian Orthodoxy, declared as such by Pius XI and denounced so vociferously by the Italian episcopate, was not eradicated. On the contrary, the Ethiopian Orthodox Church recovered and flourished. Emperor Haile Selassie cancelled the Italian attempt to reconfigure the Church and to forcibly cut the link with the Egyptian Orthodox Church. He restored the relationship of mutual respect between the two Orthodox Churches, and resumed the negotiations with the Coptic Patriarchate that he had launched as regent in 1928, aimed at autonomy for the Ethiopian Church by mutual agreement. In May 1942 he sent a delegation to Cairo to request the return to Ethiopia of Archbishop Qérillos. Meanwhile, Bishop Gebre-Giyorgis Welde-Tsadiq was appointed *ichegé*. Qérillos did return to Ethiopia; by July 1948, five Ethiopian monks had been ordained as bishops, and *Ichegé* Gebre-Giyorgis was known henceforth as *Abune* Basilios, bishop of Shewa and abbot of Debre Libanos.

By June 1959 the Ethiopian and Egyptian Churches had reached an agreement regarding their future relationship under which the Ethiopian Church became autonomous, and *Abune* Basilios was appointed first patriarch of the Ethiopian Church.

The policy of tolerance towards other religions operating in Ethiopia, of which the Catholic Church was a principal beneficiary in the early 1930s, and which was brought to a brutal end by the Italian invasion, was restored after liberation. However, it would be more than two decades for the same spirit of religious tolerance to be introduced in Rome under Pope John XXIII.

EPILOGUE

The Ethiopian Church entered the 21st century with some 40 million members—the second largest Orthodox Church in the world after the Russian Orthodox Church.

Martyr Saints

Just as the horrors of the Italian invasion and occupation cannot be forgotten by those who lived through them and lost their relatives, friends and loved ones, or who were themselves scarred physically or mentally by the trauma of what they suffered, Ethiopians never forgot the martyrs who attempted to protect their flock from the horrors of the invading armies. The remains of Bishop Pétros were never found, but after liberation Emperor Haile Selassie had a statue of him erected in Addis Ababa near the spot where he was executed, marking recognition of the prelate as one of Ethiopia's most illustrious martyrs. In due course the statue was moved to the cathedral of St George, and another, larger statue raised in its place, which was, and still is, at the centre of a road junction known as Abune Petros Square.

On 9 May 2009, in Bishop Pétros's home town of Fiché, His Holiness *Abune* Pawlos, patriarch of the Ethiopian Orthodox Church, president of the World Council of Churches and honorary president of the World Conference of Religions for Peace, presided over the opening of a church and monastery complex consecrated in the bishop's name. Drawing aside a curtain, he revealed a tall marble obelisk inscribed 'Martyr Saint Bishop Pétros'. The prelate who refused to be part of Mussolini's terror machinery in return for a life of luxury had been canonised.

The words of His Holiness recalled the exemplary life and martyrdom of the bishop who had been shot for refusing to acquiesce in the invasion: 'His Grace *Abune* Pétros has become a great martyr in this world full of temptation. This obelisk erected in his name helps the current generation to remember the great deeds of His Grace Bishop Pétros.'

The patriarch returned to his seat, and the bishop of Northern Shewa, in whose grounds the throng had assembled, rose to say how glad he was to see the commemorative obelisk and the completion of the nearby church in the name of the martyr saint, as well as a new priests' training centre and a residence for monks.

In 1943 the residents of Gore were able to retrieve the body of Bishop Mikaél from where a small group of his followers had managed to bury him in December 1936. The remains were taken to St Mary's church, and a statue was erected in his memory at the site of his execution.[33]

In October 2016, under the patriarchate of His Holiness *Abune* Mathias, the Holy Synod in Addis Ababa canonised Bishop Mikaél, who had also been executed in public after refusing to endorse Italian hegemony over Ethiopia.

Two martyrs, who by being true to their holy vows fell victim to Italy's holy war, had ascended to sainthood.

A new statue of Martyr Saint Bishop Mikaél was erected in the town where he suffered martyrdom in public, his life cut short by a volley of bullets as he stood proudly as a beacon of hope for his fellow countrymen and women during the dark days of the occupation. There too a church was built in his name.

* * *

In the town of Cocquio-Trevisago in Lombardy, a street was named in memory of General Pietro Maletti. However, following the revelations of the tv2000 docu-film *Debre Libanos*[34] and the publication in Italy of *Debre Libanos 1937* by Professor Paolo Borruso,[35] the City Council of Cocquio-Trevisago decided on 10 February 2020 to honour the victims of the monastery of Debre Libanos by changing the street name from via Pietro Maletti Generale to via Martiri Cristiani—the Street of Christian Martyrs.

REFLECTIONS

The Crusader Spirit

One of the most remarkable aspects of the invasion and occupation of Ethiopia was that heresy—essentially a thought crime—should be used by Catholic prelates in the 20th century as justification for a holy war. And equally surprising was their success in sanctifying what had originated as purely secular violence with geopolitical objectives, thus rallying the citizens of Italy to support the invasion, inculcating a powerful sense of divine mission among the regular soldiers, and spurring the recruitment of tens of thousands of Blackshirt volunteers. The conviction that they were doing God's work almost certainly accounted for much of the sense of impunity with which young men, who had never before killed anyone, posed for photographs while performing the most shocking atrocities.

What is less easy to explain is the extent to which the Italians adopted medieval crusader practices: notably the customary three-day slaughter, pillage and burning of an invaded city (Addis Ababa) following attempted resistance by the inhabitants; decapitation, which was rife throughout the invasion and occupation; and the burning alive of captives.

The sack of Addis Ababa has already been briefly discussed, and the invading troops' obsession with the public display of the severed heads of their victims has also been noted as having been widespread and much photographed. The burning alive of Ethiopians in their houses has also been discussed—a practice that was common wherever exemplary repression was under way. Numerous Italian telegrams reported the burning of homesteads during these 'reprisals', but the official reports of the dead (usually referred to as 'rebels' and 'suspects') were generally limited to those shot or hanged; Graziani's reports make no specific reference to the numerous deaths by burning. However, the reader will recall the written instruction by Captain Corvo to his subordinates, indicating that it was an accepted practice: 'You are to punish without pity all persons found in possession of arms or ammunition. I instruct you to burn not only their houses, but also the persons themselves.'

So, what possessed these 20th-century Italian commanders, who were overwhelmingly Catholic, to institute these barbaric practices, all of which smacked of crusader zealotry? Were they consciously emulating their crusading forebears? Were they driven by a primeval instinct, or were they just following orders?

We may never know the answer, since none of those responsible, from Graziani downwards, were ever held accountable for their actions in Ethiopia. However, it appears that the enthusiasm for crusading had never completely died out, and that all that was needed in Rome for a revival of the crusader spirit was the expectation of a Promised Land, reinforced by the pope's talk of Ethiopian heretics and schismatics, and the bishops' constant refrain that the invasion was a holy war and that the soldiers were doing the work of the Almighty.[1]

Where Was the Holy Father?

This brings us to the question of what Pius XI was thinking, and doing, about the invasion. While these horrors were taking place, what was the reaction of the primate of Italy, whose clergy were using their churches and cathedrals to promote the invasion with such zeal?

We have seen that in the early 1930s, before the invasion, there was a positive and constructive relationship between the Catholic Church and Ethiopia; indeed, we have noted the direct assistance and encouragement given by the Ethiopian government to the Catholic Church's ongoing missions in Ethiopia. As far as Ethiopia was concerned, the Italian episcopate had nothing to complain about. We have also noted the pontiff's initial disapproval of Mussolini's plans for an aggressive war against Ethiopia. And we know that some of the most influential individuals such as Pacelli, Ledóchowski and Tardini either attenuated papal statements, or made it difficult for the pontiff to criticise Mussolini's actions as much as he would have liked, thereby contributing to the inconstancy of his responses. Yet despite his (albeit muddled) expression of concern in August 1935, no evidence has come to light to indicate that Pius XI subsequently made any serious effort to prevent Italy's attack on Ethiopia, although he had the opportunity to do so on several occasions.

Furthermore, and even more surprisingly, the pope chose not to condemn the vociferous campaign waged during 1935 and 1936 by a substantial proportion of the most senior and influential members of the episcopate of the Italian Catholic Church, even including those directly subordinate to him as bishop of Rome, to publicly garner human and material support for the invasion. He also stood by in silence when the same archbishops and bishops used their pulpits to dehumanise and denigrate the Ethiopians, brand Ethiopian Muslims as infidels, and promote the invasion as a holy war. Indeed, far from distancing the Holy See from the invasion, by early 1936 we find the secretary of state making it clear that as far as the Holy See was concerned, opponents of the invasion were, by definition, enemies of the Catholic Church, while the pope was putting his weight behind Mussolini in his fight against the League of Nations' anti-war sanctions.

So what are we to make of the pope's claim to be politically neutral? Pius XI claimed that he maintained neutrality so as to be in a position to mediate between nations in conflict. Yet when Emperor Haile Selassie put that claim to the test, the pontiff refused the request to mediate, stating that he 'would not treat with schismatics'.

It must be said that the claim of papal neutrality comes across as hollow, particularly in 1936. We have already noted several cases in which the Holy See threw its supposed neutrality to the winds when it chose to do so. The secretary of state was quick to discipline clergy of national Catholic Churches when they spoke *against* Fascism and the invasion of Ethiopia, insisting that clergy should not make political statements. However, he never disciplined clergy who made highly political public statements *in favour of* Fascism and the invasion. Another case concerns Monsignor Joseph Ciarrocchi, pastor of the Catholic church of Santa Maria in the archdiocese of Detroit, who spoke against the invasion, and published anti-Fascist articles. The response was a strongly worded letter from Pacelli ordering him in no uncertain terms to desist from writing on political matters, and threatening to withdraw his papal honours.[2] And this at a time when numerous Italian clerics and the editors of Italian Catholic Church newspapers and journals were publishing inflammatory political articles and making bellicose declarations in their churches and cathedrals in favour of Fascism and in favour of the war in Ethiopia, yet they were never disciplined.

Another well-documented case already mentioned is the alacrity with which Pius XI himself reined in Archbishop Innitzer of the Austrian Catholic Church, summoning him to Rome and giving him a dressing-down in April 1938 for delivering without Holy See approval a speech welcoming Hitler's invasion of Austria.[3] Yet Cardinal Archbishop Schuster of Milan had not been reprimanded after delivering a similar speech welcoming Mussolini's invasion of Ethiopia.

Whatever the private thoughts and intentions of Achille Ratti at the time, and whatever his difficulties, the inevitable conclusion is that his stance towards the clergy of the national Catholic Churches was in reality far from neutral, nor was it neutral towards the governments of Italy and Ethiopia before and during the invasion of Ethiopia. Consequently, the opportunity for the Holy See to make a difference was lost. As Gaetano Salvemini wrote, 'Had Pius XI instructed the Italian bishops to abstain from warlike propaganda, they must needs have done so.'[4]

An Eye on the East

The pope's meek acceptance of the Italian episcopate's sacralisation of the invasion and occupation becomes all the more surprising when we consider what had happened to the Russian Orthodox Church. A ferocious persecution of the Church by the Bolsheviks commencing in 1917 killed millions and led to Christian martyrdom on an unprecedented scale. By 1920, two-thirds of that nation's monasteries had been liquidated and some transformed into labour camps.[5] It was thus understandable that Achille Ratti, who had been raised to the papal throne in 1922 and who had a horror of Communism from his personal experiences in Poland, would do anything he could to avoid the Communists taking power in Italy. One might even forgive his infamous and much-quoted words that the *Duce* had been 'sent by Providence'.

But if Ratti was shaken and outraged by the barbaric destruction of the world's largest Orthodox Church, surely as Pope Pius XI he would not turn a blind eye to Catholic support for the destruction of the world's second-largest Orthodox Church. Philip Jenkins tells us that across Europe, Catholic clergy were aghast at how the large and powerful Russian Orthodox Church could be destroyed so rapidly by a 'ruthless regime with no compunction about inflicting violence and terror'.[6] If indeed the Italian clerics were aghast, one cannot help wondering why they campaigned so vociferously and energetically for Italy's military to do precisely the same thing in Ethiopia.

The Atrocities of 1937

As we have seen, 1937 was the peak year for Italian crimes against humanity in Ethiopia—crimes that foreshadowed what the Italians and Germans, either separately or jointly as the Axis, would go on to do in the other countries they would invade, such as Albania, Greece, Yugoslavia, Czechoslovakia, Poland and beyond.

Whereas the invasions carried out after Britain's declaration of war against Germany in September 1939 were extensively documented, those conducted before then are less well documented and not widely known. Thus it can be difficult for non-Ethiopian readers to realise, or even imagine, the impact on Ethiopian Christendom of atrocities such as the massacre of Debre Libanos. The sufferings of the Orthodox Church of Serbia under the Fascist regime of Ante Pavelić provide a point of comparison, but that episode is also surprisingly little known.

In fact, there are few well-known historical precedents to cite as a basis for comparison with the massacre of Debre Libanos. For British readers one could go back in time to the infamous Viking attack on the celebrated Christian monastery and church at Lindisfarne, Northumbria, in the year 793. In all material respects the attacks were similar. As in the case of Debre Libanos, the monastery of Lindisfarne was the most important sanctuary of Christian Britain, it was a remote monastery focused on theological study, it housed an important scriptorium producing parchment manuscripts, the attack was planned in advance, the invaders were heavily armed, the victims were defenceless, they were surprised and had no opportunity to fight back or flee, and the scene was one of desecration and carnage. It must be said that the attack at Debre Libanos was on a larger scale than that of Lindisfarne, and, unlike the attack on Lindisfarne, it left no clergy alive. Furthermore, unlike the Italians, the Vikings did not loot all the artefacts they encountered; they actually left several valuable items in place. In these respects, the incidents differed. Nonetheless, they bear comparison. They were both landmark events in the history and evolution of the national Church concerned, and in both cases the news, hardly believable, triggered shock and horror throughout the land.

Apart from the campaign against the Ethiopian Church, which is the subject of this book, the atrocities of 1937 also included the depopulation, with toxic gases, fire and sword, of large swathes of land across the Ethiopian highlands; the February massacres in Addis Ababa and several of Ethiopia's secondary towns; Mussolini's order for the execution of all the adult male residents of the village of Gogetti (see Map 6); the execution in cold blood of thousands of Ethiopian prisoners; the countrywide public hanging of community leaders; the liquidation of the educated elite; and widespread deportations to concentration camps and prisons, which by late 1937 were filled to overflowing. The question is: did these horrific events create alarm and debate within the Vatican, particularly in the office of the secretariat of state? And if so, what was the reaction?

With hundreds of Catholic clergy in occupied Ethiopia at the time, one would expect there to have been hundreds, if not thousands, of documents such as telegrams, reports, letters and memoranda flowing into the office of the secretary of state concerning the atrocities. Pius XI was well known to be outraged by the faintest suggestion of immorality on the part of Italians. So would the fastidious pontiff, who dispatched his agents to scour the villages and towns of Italy for offensive behaviour, plays or films, and who felt that immodestly dressed women—even on the beach—heralded severe moral decline, not have expressed outrage and shock at the moral decline of his Church's 'holy warriors'? Would he not have been prompted into action by the gassing of civilians, the severed heads, the massacres, the tortures, the dismemberments, the deaths by burning, the destruction of so many Christian churches and monasteries, and the murder of their clergy? These abominations, which were carried out as part of the campaign declared by his clergy to be God's work, were not required to prevent Italy from falling to the Communists; so why the silence?

It has been suggested that the pope was unaware of the atrocities in Ethiopia, owing to Archbishop Castellani's failure to keep him informed. However, the pontiff's strong personal interest in Ethiopians makes this most unlikely. It will be recalled that news of the massacre of Addis Ababa was broadcast in considerable detail by the European radio and press media within a few days of the event, and within weeks had appeared in detail on the front pages of newspapers worldwide. In addition, in March 1937 church services for the dead were held in England, and it is also on record that Monsignor Jarosseau personally submitted a report to Pope Pius XI on the ongoing atrocities. Furthermore, the monastery of Debre Libanos was not only of international repute, it was well known to the Vatican as Mons Libani, an institution with which the papacy had interacted in past centuries. Moreover, Pius XI had personally arranged for the reconstruction and expansion of the monastery church of St Stephen of the Abyssinians.[7] The massacre of Debre Libanos took place in May 1937, while Archbishop Castellani and hundreds of Catholic missionaries were on the ground in Ethiopia, and was reported in writing to Rome by both Graziani and Maletti, who was instructed by the viceroy to 'give publicity to these proceedings'. Finally, Graziani's report explicitly stated that 'no trace remained' of the monastery; by early June the slaughter had been made public in Sylvia Pankhurst's *New Times and Ethiopia News*; and in July, Emperor Haile Selassie personally broadcast an appeal to the Christian Churches of the world—including a specific appeal to Pope Pius XI—condemning the pogrom against the Ethiopian Church, in which he detailed several of the major atrocities.[8]

Given all this publicity and multiple channels of communication, it is inconceivable that either the pope or his secretary of state was unaware of the extent and intensity of the carnage in Ethiopia, even if Castellani was not reporting on the situation, Yet, so far as can be ascertained, the Holy See expressed not a word of concern, denunciation or even solace.

Outraged by the massacre of Addis Ababa, the American envoy in the city, Cornelius Engert, who could scarcely believe what he was witnessing, alerted Washington, stating, 'Not since the Armenian massacres have I seen such unbridled brutality and cowardice.'[9] It is a sad irony that whereas Pope Benedict XV personally intervened with Sultan Mohammed V in an attempt to bring an end to the massacres of the Armenian Orthodox,[10] his successor had nothing to say when the Ethiopian Orthodox were being massacred by his own countrymen and co-religionists.

A Disappointed Sovereign

Emperor Haile Selassie never forgot Pius XI's turn-around in his attitude towards the invasion. Interviewed in December 1973 by the then Ethiopian envoy in Rome, Ambassador Zewdé Reta, he recalled his state visit to the pontiff at the Vatican in 1924, and how solicitous Pius XI had been at that time:

> We remember how the pope received us and our delegation with respect and love. At the time we discussed the relationship between the Orthodox and Catholic Christians, and agreed to communicate through Bishop André [Jarosseau], the head of the Catholic mission in Harar and our French language tutor. [Later,] when Mussolini was preparing for war, using the Welwel conflict as a cover, we were making it clear that Ethiopia prefers a peaceful solution to the conflict. The pope was replying to our letters.[11]

Haile Selassie said that he was aware of the pope's speech of August 1935, in which the pontiff had 'declared that a war for territorial expansion was illegal'. In fact, he was so impressed and pleased that he had written to Pius XI, thanking him. However, his pleasure turned to dismay when 'the Vatican fell silent'.[12] Although by the time of his visit to Rome in 1973 Haile Selassie was anxious to reconcile with the Italian government of the day, the memory of Pius XI's change of heart never left him. He was shocked that the Holy Father had not said a single word about the massacre of Addis Ababa, the killing of Bishop Pétros and Bishop Mikaél, and the massacre of Debre Libanos. 'We were disappointed with the pope for remaining silent, knowing about these atrocities, which were incompatible with Christianity, humanity and civilization.'[13]

It was later suggested to Haile Selassie that the pope's silence was due to his fear of 'retaliation by Mussolini'. Whether he thought it appropriate for the representative of Christ on earth to be cowed by the *Duce* the emperor did not say, but he was certainly disappointed to have been let down by the pope, who had proved to be no more reliable than the League of Nations.

What Did Pius XI Really Think?

It is, of course, possible that Pius XI was appalled by the atrocities but was prevented from expressing his outrage in public. Many scholars expected that the Vatican Secret Archives would provide the answers to the mystery, for even if a policy of political neutrality or his fear of Mussolini falling from power had precluded him from speaking out, the archives must surely demonstrate that *Papa* Achille Ratti, a man generally considered pious, reflective and righteous, was personally distraught at the barbarity of the occupation. In September 2006 the sections of the Secret Archives for the period of Pius XI's reign were finally opened to scholars. But when Lucia Ceci examined those archives to find out how the Holy See had reacted to the massacres of the Ethiopian clergy, and specifically the massacre of Debre Libanos, she failed to find any such documents.[14]

We do not know, of course, whether such documents ever existed, or whether they have been removed. But whatever the explanation, how, in the absence of any primary written sources, do we explain the silence of the Holy See regarding the atrocities?

Certainly, the failure of the Holy See to react publicly to the atrocities in Ethiopia cannot be explained by the much-overworked 'neutrality' argument, nor by Pius XI's apparent fear of causing the Fascists to fall from power, since by 1937 Mussolini was losing interest in Ethiopia. In any case, scholars such as Daniel Binchy and Emma Fattorini have shown that Pius XI did not slavishly follow Mussolini's policies; there were plenty of issues which the outspoken and often overbearing pontiff was quick to raise with the Italian government whenever he felt that the *Duce* was stepping on Church prerogatives, or that the clergy of the national Catholic Churches were stepping out of line and not reflecting the stance of the Holy See.

The final nail in the coffin of the 'neutrality' argument must surely be Pius XI's reaction to the Spanish Civil War, which was concurrent with the Italian occupation of Ethiopia. Far from being silent, the Vatican sided with Franco, and the pontiff spoke out firmly and courageously in expressing his outrage over 'the horrible fratricide, the sacrilege, the horrible torment and destruction' perpetrated against the Spanish clergy, regretting that 'All that is most human, most divine; sacred persons, things, and institutions; invaluable and irreplaceable treasures of faith and Christian piety and of civilization and art ... indeed even the sacred and solemn silence of the tomb; all this has been attacked, disfigured and destroyed.'[15]

In his well-researched analysis, Daniel Binchy shows that neutrality was cast aside in the Vatican's unequivocal support for General Franco because of the 'brutal war on religion' that was being waged in Spain: 'In face of this threat to organised religion the Pope was bound to side with the insurgents ...'[16] In short, all the sentiments that 'neutrality' had allegedly prohibited in the case of the war on organised religion in Ethiopia poured forth from the Holy See when similar atrocities were carried out against organised religion in Spain. The inevitable conclusion is that the pontiff's decision not to speak out or intervene in the case of Ethiopia had nothing to do with political neutrality; it was presumably because the 'sacrilege, the horrible torment and destruction' was being inflicted by Italian Catholics, supported by the senior Italian Catholic clergy.

REFLECTIONS

Was the Pope a Racist?

It would also be tempting to assume that Pius XI shared the view common in 1930s Europe that standards applicable to Europeans were not appropriate for non-Europeans, who were generally considered genetically inferior, and whose sufferings were thus not to be equated with those of Europeans. Certainly, many—probably most—Africans believed that the invasion of Ethiopia was driven by a white-supremacy doctrine on the part of both the Catholic Church and the Italian government; indeed, the reputation and credibility of many Catholic missions on the continent suffered for several years afterwards as a result.[17] However, it is notable that by 1938 both the pope and Pacelli, to differing degrees, were expressing public concern when the anti-Semitism increasingly associated with both Nazism and Fascism began reaching alarming levels. At that time the pontiff reacted, publishing a powerful statement declaring, 'Let it suffice to say that racialism, as it has been dealt with by the Holy Father, does not constitute a political question, but a danger essentially spiritual, moral, and religious, to the whole human and Christian family, and thus a suitable subject for his paternal solicitude.'[18] On the other hand, such solicitude had been absent the year before, when Italy's racial laws introduced a draconian apartheid system in Ethiopia.

So was the pope what we, with our modern sensibilities, would call a racist? Apparently not, for he had been a champion of the Ethiopian community in the Vatican, and was also well known to be strongly in favour of the promotion of non-European Catholic clergy. His encyclical *Rerum ecclesiae* of 1926, which was a plea for the development of indigenous clergy, condemned missionaries who practised racial discrimination, stating, 'Anyone who looks upon these natives as members of an inferior race or men of low mentality makes a grievous mistake.'[19]

Other Possibilities

There are other possible explanations for the papal silence, of which one has been suggested by several scholars. Did Pius XI's Italian nationality take precedence over his moral conscience?

One acknowledges of course that the Holy See, being the supreme organ of the universal Catholic Church, is technically a separate institution from the national Italian Catholic Church, and this fact is frequently highlighted by scholars wishing to absolve the Holy See of responsibility for the misdeeds of the Italian Church. Yet this distinction can seem to non-Catholics like splitting hairs. After all, Pius XI's apostolic nuncios were Italian, he selected Italians for the overwhelming majority of positions in the Vatican, and he certainly sided with Italy on most, if not all, issues, including condemnation of League of Nations sanctions in respect of the invasion of Ethiopia. Even the well-informed analyst Daniel Binchy, who was conducting his research in 1938–9—at the time of the events concerned—concluded that 'while theoretically the distinction may, and indeed must, be drawn, it cannot be maintained in practice. History as well as geography has intertwined the fortunes of the Holy See and the Italian Church so closely as to make them almost indistinguishable.'[20] We therefore cannot dismiss the possibility that the pope's nationality swayed his judgement.

Secondly, in joining the Italian government and general public in celebrating so vociferously the 'conquest' of Ethiopia, Pius XI went along with Mussolini's claim that the war had come to an end in May 1936, thereby becoming complicit—wittingly or unwittingly—in propagating that falsehood. Clearly, raising the issue of war crimes carried out after May 1936 and throughout 1937 would have exposed the falseness of the tale that the Italian public had been led to believe. This would have annoyed Mussolini, a risk the pope may have been unwilling to take.

Finally—and bearing in mind the speed with which he intervened in Spain where the clerical victims were Catholics—we cannot rule out the possibility that, although he had initial misgivings about the invasion of Ethiopia in 1935, the reason Pius XI came around to accepting—and even supporting—it in 1936 was that he did, in fact, consider it a holy war against 'heretics' and 'schismatics'—vocabulary that he himself had used publicly, and that had certainly contributed to the Great Mobilisation. He may have been supportive of the war once it was under way, but, being concerned with appearances, he did not want to be the one to say so. If so, one would then conclude that the pope was not really silent, for he spoke through his agencies: his secretary of state, his cardinals, his archbishops and the Italian episcopate, the majority of whom were promoting the war. And he anticipated that one day, when the slaughter was over, his missionaries would be able to proselytise or evangelise any Ethiopians left alive, thereby bringing them under the Church of Rome, the only source of salvation.

Perhaps the most likely explanation for the silence would be some elements of each of these three.

The Opportunity to Speak

With the dramatic change of Italian government policy towards the Ethiopian Church in late 1937, the prospects for significant expansion of the Catholic Church in Ethiopia along the lines originally hoped for by the Holy See evaporated almost overnight. The Ethiopian Church was now untouchable in its new role as a potential instrument of Italian Fascist government propaganda and control. Italy's Catholic clergy were now, so to speak, out of the picture, and their joint venture with the military had gained them almost nothing.

Thus, as that *annus horribilis* drew to a close, the pope had little, if anything, to lose by speaking out against the murderous campaign that had brought the Ethiopian Church to its knees. The new policy provided an opportunity for Pius XI to assess the effect of the green light he had either intentionally or inadvertently given to his foot soldiers in the holy war in Ethiopia, to reflect on where Mussolini's totalitarianism was leading, and to consider the consequences of having 'supped with the Devil'. This was the moment for the voice of the Vatican to ring out, loud and clear, in condemnation of the evil that had been done in the name of the Church of Rome.

> It was not against the Infidel, but against Christians that you drew your swords ... It was not heavenly riches upon which your minds were set, but earthly ones. Nothing has been sacred to you. You have violated married women, widows, even nuns. You have despoiled the very sanctuaries of God's church, stolen the sacred objects of altars, pillaged innumerable images and relics of saints.[21]

Outraged, the pontiff denounced the Catholic army with these forthright words. But not, however, in 1937, nor even in 1938. This furious denunciation was issued in 1204 by Pope Innocent III, appalled by the ungodly behaviour of the Catholic army of the Fourth Crusade, which had sacked the Orthodox Christian centre of Constantinople and desecrated its churches.

If the pope in 1204 was well informed, and morally outraged, about the behaviour of his flock in a distant land, how much better informed and more outraged a 20th-century pontiff would surely be in similar circumstances. However, by the end of 1937 Pius XI was in many ways drawing closer to the Fascist government. Far from concerning himself with the behaviour of the Italians in Ethiopia and the suffering of their victims, there were other matters that needed attention, and for which he needed Mussolini's assistance. The pontiff was focused on using the *Duce*'s relationship with Hitler to persuade the Führer to abandon his plans to put hundreds of German Catholic clergy on trial on charges of sexual perversion, and not to proceed with charges against the Jesuits for illegal exportation of funds.[22] Thus, for the Church of Ethiopia, unlike the 13th-century Church of Byzantium, the hour for the voice of the pope to ring out never struck.

Did the Pope Fulfil His Mandate?

It is clear that Pius XI should not be thought of as an anti-Fascist pope, which is how he has sometimes been characterised. On the contrary, for several years following the Concordat he continued to be complimentary towards and supportive of Fascism. Later, during the second half of the 1930s, he experienced increasing difficulty in trying to adhere to Christian principles while accommodating Fascism, frequently wavering from one side to the other. The only time he could be said to have been anti-Fascist was towards the end of his life. During his last few months he finally began to realise that demagogues such as Mussolini and Hitler posed a serious threat to world peace, but by then it was too late; the fires had been lit.

Today we find historians citing papal statements to demonstrate that Pius XI supported the invasion of Ethiopia, or that he opposed it, depending on which side of the argument they wish to promote. This paradox arises largely because, as we have seen, his stance changed over time. He was initially opposed to the war because he felt it was unjust and particularly because it would be damaging for the Catholic missions already operating in Ethiopia. By late 1935, even though he had concerns about the injustice of the ongoing invasion, the war was so popular with Mussolini's government and the general Italian public that he had decided to refrain from criticising the Catholic clergy for their vociferous support for it. By the first week of 1936, when it was looking likely that the Italian military would prevail, Secretary of State Pacelli was signalling tacit support for the war, and advising Mussolini to do something about the pro-sanctions lobby in the United States. And by mid-1936 Pius XI was congratulating the *Duce* and the Italian nation on their 'victory', and making plans for expanding the Catholic Church in Ethiopia in the wake of what he believed to have been a conquest.

Later, as Pope Pius XII, Eugenio Pacelli would face accusations similar to those faced by Pius XI in his relationship with Mussolini: having been too accommodating towards Hitler and remaining silent during the build-up to and implementation of the Holocaust. In this regard, Jacques Kornberg, who has analysed Pacelli's papacy in depth, makes a persuasive case for calculated acquiescence in evil, arguing that while Pius XII was not an accomplice to evil, he allowed evil to occur because of the need to ensure the 'barque of Peter' would come safely to harbour, so that the salvation of the faithful could be assured. It would be anomalous to judge Pius XII by the liberal and humanitarian values of today. He was not running a 21st-century human rights organisation; his overriding concern was the survival and expansion of the Catholic Church. The price of his success in fulfilling his mandate and achieving that goal, Kornberg argues, was moral failure.[23]

It is difficult to avoid concluding that in acquiescing in evil, Pius XII was simply continuing the policy of his predecessor, who regarded the invasion of Ethiopia as an unfortunate episode through which the 'barque of Peter' had to be carefully and safely manoeuvred, even at the cost of a loss of moral authority. In other words, when the Italian episcopate cast the invasion as a holy war, Pius XI's response of silence was, in his view, a necessary evil to ensure the Church of Rome would survive. The pontiff had, in effect—to use the words that he himself had spoken earlier—made a concordat with the Devil.

This would not be the first time that Pius XI 'allowed evil to happen' so long as the outcome was beneficial to the Church. In 1929, during the Great Depression, the Vatican was in financial straits—a situation relieved by the Lateran Treaty, under which the Italian government paid the Vatican some $90 million in compensation for the loss of assets such as the Papal States.[24] In order to ensure that the funds were invested wisely, Pius XI appointed a layperson, Bernardino Nogara (brother of Archbishop Giuseppe Nogara), as the Vatican's financial manager, reporting directly to himself.

Nogara accepted the position on condition that his investments and transactions would be free of doctrinal considerations. Pius XI agreed, and was delighted when, owing to Nogara's shrewd investments and currency speculations, the money started rolling in. Nogara's newly created agency, which would eventually become known as the Vatican Bank, soon owned shares in numerous successful companies. According to John Pollard, there was 'hardly a sector of the Italian economy in which the Vatican did not own a share-holding of some sort or another'.[25] The pontiff railed against 'the trustees and managing directors of investment funds which they administer according to their arbitrary will and pleasure', and declared that such people, 'addicted to excessive gain ... were and are in great part the cause of these evils ... The desire for money is the root of all evil.'[26] Meanwhile, the very same pope was only too happy for the Vatican to be prospering from the very activities that he was denouncing.

One does not have to look far to see another startling paradox: the Vatican now owned shares in Italy's largest manufacturer of contraceptives, and was thus promoting and profiting from a practice strictly incompatible with Church doctrine as promulgated by Pius XI himself.

These were not just cases of choosing the lesser of two evils; the Vatican was now actually profiting from what it regarded as evil, rather than just allowing evil to happen.

It may be argued that the invasion of Ethiopia was another case of allowing evil to happen while also benefiting from that evil—

the benefit being not only from the potential for expansion of the Catholic Church. As Binchy observed in 1941, 'Papal finances are not a promising subject for study, at least for those who seek to base their statements on fact.'[27] Nonetheless, despite the difficulty of establishing the details, it is well attested that Pius XI, to whom Nogara reported regularly, permitted the Vatican banker to acquire substantial holdings in Italy's major arms and munitions factories. According to one published source, Nogara acquired 'a munitions plant that supplied arms for the Italian army's invasion of Ethiopia'.[28] This is consistent with the findings of Gerald Posner, who discovered that the Vatican had stakes in Breda, Reggiane and Compagnia Nazionale Aeronautica (CNA).[29] Furthermore, concerned that the war should not drag down the Italian economy by going on too long, Nogara made it clear to Pius XI that the Vatican's 'huge investments' in Italian stocks and Mussolini's state-issued bonds meant that 'the Church's interests were best served by a brief and successful [military] campaign'. Posner also states that the Vatican granted a loan to the Fascist government to help finance the invasion.[30] So far as the present author is aware, this claim has not been substantiated. Nonetheless, there appears to be little doubt about the Vatican's financial interests in Italian arms manufacturers under Pius XI.

When the Vatican acquired substantial interest in a company, Nogara often placed a Vatican representative on the board. Sometimes this was Francesco Pacelli, the brother of Pius's secretary of state. In the case of CNA, the representative was the pope's nephew, Franco Ratti.[31] CNA was a major supplier of military hardware for the invasion of Ethiopia, in that the company manufactured Caproni bombers, which they sold to the Regia Aeronautica, and which accounted for the majority of the bombers used in the invasion.[32] These aircraft each carried a payload of up to 1,000 kg of bombs, frequently deploying the infamous C-500T and C-100P bombs armed with the chemical weapons yperite and phosgene.

Franco Ratti also represented the Vatican on the board of Reggiane, or, to give it its full name, Officine Meccaniche Reggiane.[33] This company produced, among other things, Piaggio aircraft engines fitted to aircraft such as the Romeo Ro. 37, of which 49 were deployed in Ethiopia, as well as Ca. 101 Caproni bombers.

As for Breda, apart from manufacturing ships and trains, this company was a major armaments manufacturer. It produced the machine guns used on the Caproni and Savoia-Marchetti bombers deployed in Ethiopia, as well as the ubiquitous Model 30 machine guns, the Model 35 mortars and the field guns used by the Italian artillery.

Today such arrangements would trigger a public debate on the rights or wrongs of a good cause relying on 'tainted money'; it is sufficient here to note that the evidence reviewed indicates that Pius XI was indeed open to 'allowing evil to happen' if it was ultimately to the benefit of the Catholic Church.

Unfortunately, despite Pius XI's apparent belief that the end justifies the means, the outcome of his 'concordat with the Devil' was far from being the 'prelude to peace' that he optimistically proclaimed. On the contrary, the attack on Ethiopia would turn out to be the prelude to the Second World War—a conflagration that would cause unprecedented suffering and would ultimately almost destroy Italy. As such, the pontiff's decision to go along with the invasion could be regarded as one of the greatest errors in the history of the papacy.

As for the victims of the invasion, it is true that in turning a blind eye and allowing the episcopate to freely sacralise Mussolini's military adventure, the pope temporarily appeased the demagogue, and the Roman Church survived and prospered. However, the Ethiopians and their Church paid a terrible price. At the end of the day, it was not the Catholic Church's 'holy warriors' who carried the cross of Christ; it was the Ethiopians who bore that cross and suffered and died for their faith. The invasion of Ethiopia was their Calvary.

APPENDIX I

THE FINAL TOLL

In 1946 the Ethiopian government submitted to the Paris Peace Conference the following Ethiopian death toll arising from the invasion and occupation, compiled by a joint team of Ethiopians and expatriates in Addis Ababa after the liberation.[1] The emperor thought that the actuals 'could not be less than the statistics revealed', and were probably 'far more than alleged'.[2] It should be noted that since neither the Ethiopians nor the Italians maintained systematic records of Ethiopian fatalities, such figures will always be no more than estimates.

Table A.1:
Ethiopian Death Toll Submitted at the Paris Peace Conference

Category	Death toll
Killed in action	275,000
Patriots killed in battle during five years of Fascist occupation	78,500
Children, women, old and infirm people killed by bombing during the occupation	17,800
Massacre of February 1937	30,000
People condemned to death by 'court martial'	24,000

Category	Death toll
Persons of both sexes who died in concentration camps from privation and maltreatment	35,000
People who died of privation owing to destruction of their villages during the five years' occupation	300,000[3]
Provisional estimate of total casualties	**760,300**

In 1945 the Ethiopian government had submitted to the Conference of Commonwealth Prime Ministers a total figure of 831,300 dead, incorporating a higher estimate of the civilian death toll,[4] and in 2001 a total of one million dead was suggested by Imani Kali-Nyah,[5] which has been adopted by the Global Alliance for Justice—The Ethiopian Cause.[6] However, the present author has not seen the breakdown or rationale for either of these two higher figures, and to date no published scholars appear to have seriously challenged the 1946 figures, and so they are taken here as a basis for this brief review.

In the absence of information on the assumptions and sources on which these estimates were based, it is difficult to judge their accuracy, and it is beyond the scope of the present volume to attempt an independent assessment of the death toll. All that can be done here is to assess whether the figures are credible.

The 'killed in action' figure of 275,000

This category is clearly meant to refer to the Ethiopian soldiers fighting under military command, as opposed to Patriots, who are addressed in other categories below.

At the time of the invasion, Italian Military Intelligence, which, having had the benefit of a long-standing embassy and several consulates in Ethiopia, was well informed, calculated that Emperor Haile Selassie could mobilise 200,000–250,000 soldiers in the north and some 80,000–100,000 in the south, bringing the total to 280,000–350,000 men.[7] Angelo Del Boca provides a figure of 350,000.[8] As for how many of them died in action, Alberto Sbacchi quotes a certain *Dejazmach* Birru Amedé declaring that those killed

APPENDIX I

in the war numbered 'at least 250,000',[9] and this is consistent with the figure of 275,000 dead in the 1946 submission.

Some Italian sources considered this estimate an exaggeration, suggesting that Ethiopian losses were 40,000–50,000 on the northern war front, and 15,000–20,000 on the southern front.[10] However, such figures are typically based on two incorrect assumptions: (i) that the war fought by the Ethiopian army ended in May 1936, and (ii) that the fighting was limited to the northern and southern fronts under Badoglio and Graziani respectively. In reality the fighting under military command continued well into 1937, and took place on a number of fronts, with very high casualties, the remaining Ethiopian military units in the field being virtually wiped out. Furthermore, Mussolini's instructions to his commanders were not just to defeat the Ethiopians, but to annihilate the Ethiopian army, which they did, sometimes by getting the Italian Air Force to gas the retreating Ethiopians and at other times sending in mercenaries to slaughter them—and sometimes both at the same time, as at Maychew. It should also be recalled that after the first few weeks of the war, the Italians generally killed all Ethiopians who surrendered as well as those whom they defeated.

The conclusion is that the figure of 275,000 Ethiopian soldiers killed in the war, though representing a high percentage of the number of fighting men (79 per cent, based on a total force of 350,000), is plausible.

Patriots killed in battle: 78,500

It would be very difficult, and probably impossible, now to independently estimate the total number of Patriots killed, because the size of the resistance armies fluctuated from one day to the next, and the resistance was not centrally coordinated. The movement received a major boost in February 1937, then surged again after the massacre of Debre Libanos in May, and yet again during the church-burning pogroms of the second half of 1937. It declined in 1938 under the more conciliatory policies of the Duke of Aosta, to be boosted again in 1939, and yet again during the war of liberation. Thus the situation was volatile. Furthermore, there were several different groups operating throughout the Ethiopian highlands augmented by others in outlying areas. They operated relatively independently, were typically based on local loyalties, and each group fluctuated in size from less than one hundred to several thousand at various times.[11] Finally, even if the figures for the number of Patriots were available on an annual basis, there would be no way of knowing how many were survivors from the previous year, and how many were new recruits.

So far as the present author is aware, the only published figure for the number of Patriot deaths is the Italian total of 76,907, which is based on monthly military statistics from 6 May 1936 to 10 June 1940. This figure is quite close to the estimate of 78,500 submitted by the Ethiopian expatriate team, and thus in the absence of any other published estimates, there appears to be no reason to reject this figure.

Civilians killed by bombing: 17,800

During the invasion the Italian Air Force typically flew ahead of the ground troops to bomb towns, villages and churches. Then during the occupation, after May 1936, Air Force operations were intensified, and military (as distinct from passenger-carrying) flights were focused mainly on the bombardment of civilian settlements during the exemplary repression of civilians (particularly in Northern Shewa and Gojjam), and the bombing of resistance fighters and adjacent civilian communities suspected of harbouring them. In both cases, a significant proportion of the bombs were gas-filled. Graziani's telegrams often reported the destruction of several thousands of 'tukuls' in a single bombing, and there were many such operations over the six years concerned. Since it is well attested that the 'tukuls' were frequently inhabited at the time, and since incidents such as the bombing of Ziqwala are known to have resulted in heavy loss of life, a total of 17,800 dead civilians from bombing over the six years is quite possible, and could well be too low.

Massacre of February 1937: 30,000

The present author's study of the massacre of Addis Ababa estimates that 18,000 to 20,500 people died over a period of several days.[12] But

APPENDIX I

there were also massacres at the same time in secondary towns—in fact wherever Blackshirts were garrisoned—such as Dessie, Jimma and Mojo. Therefore, although these secondary massacres have not been studied, it is possible that their cumulative death toll could close the gap between the Addis Ababa figure of around 18,000–20,500 and the grand total of 30,000 submitted by the Ethiopian government. Thus, the figure of 30,000 for all the February 1937 urban massacres is plausible.

Patriots condemned to death by 'court martial': 24,000

This category was most likely meant to include (i) the victims of the 'flying tribunals', which were at least partially documented, (ii) execution of young educated Ethiopians, and (iii) dignitaries and community leaders hanged in Graziani's widespread anti-Amhara pogrom that swept the countryside over several months in 1937.

Judging from Graziani's telegrams, the number executed by the 'flying tribunals' throughout the occupation reached the low thousands. The number of educated 'Young Ethiopians' executed has been estimated at between 400 and 600.[13] On the other hand, given the duration of the anti-Amhara campaign, which could be regarded as ethnic cleansing, and judging from the number of portable gallows utilised and the large number of photographs extant of victims hanged in rural towns, villages and settlements, it is more than likely that this pogrom resulted in the death of thousands, and possibly tens of thousands.

All that can be concluded without further data is that the overall estimate of 24,000 deaths in this category is plausible.

Persons who died in concentration camps from privation and maltreatment: 35,000

There were three penal institutions for Ethiopians classified by the Italian administration as concentration camps: Danane (in Italian Somaliland), Nocra (on the Dahlak Islands off the coast of Italian Eritrea) and Akaki (near Addis Ababa). The largest was Danane, through which an estimated 6,500 prisoners in total passed, with a death rate of around 50 per cent. Although Nocra was the most notorious penal institution, it was smaller than Danane, with a peak of 1,500 prisoners. Akaki was about half the size of Danane, but to avoid double-counting, it should be noted that Akaki was used largely—though not entirely—as a transit centre for Danane and other, smaller prisons.

Since no other category in the 1946 submission includes deaths in the other prisons, this category is presumably meant to include deaths in *all* detention camps and prisons. However, many of the victims in the temporary prisons in Addis Ababa died during the massacre in that city, and these have already been included in the figures for the 'Graziani massacres'. The other prisons were mainly in garrison towns such as Debre Birhan, with at least one prison in Mogadishu, in Italian Somaliland. All of the prisons were under-provisioned, and most were badly run, visiting distress, hunger and disease on the inmates. However, in terms of numbers incarcerated, the other prisons were relatively small, and those who died in them—although high in terms of proportion—generally numbered in the hundreds rather than the thousands. For this reason, the figure of 35,000 may well be too high for this category.

People who died of privation owing to the destruction of their villages during the five years' occupation: 300,000

This figure is the major imponderable of the 1946 submission. If the definition is meant to cover only deaths that were unintended by-products of the destruction of villages, i.e., not deliberate, then the figure is almost certainly too high. If, on the other hand, this category includes:

- victims of the 'reprisals', which were homicidal and extensive (particularly in the Christian highlands and the lakes section of the Rift Valley), in which some 500,000 homes were reported in the 1946 submission to have been burned, not infrequently including the occupants;
- civilians killed in the massacres of Northern Shewa (including the church-burning campaigns and the Maletti–Mohammed

Sultan *jihad*), exercises that are believed to have resulted in a total of more than 40,000 deaths;
- victims of the massacres conducted at specific churches and monasteries such as Debre Libanos, Debre Bisrat, Midr Kebd, Gursum, Hagere Maryam and Debre Assebot; and
- civilians killed by aerial spraying (not bombing) of yperite and arsine;

then a death toll of 300,000 over the five years is plausible.

Conclusion

Given the above, while some of the categories might be somewhat under- or over-estimated, there appears to be no obvious reason to reject the estimated overall death toll of 760,300 submitted at the Paris Peace Conference, particularly as the submission did not include the number of people injured, or rendered invalids, who died later from their injuries.

Demographic Check

In the context of the population of Ethiopia at the time of the invasion, which, if we rely on the well-informed Adrien Zervos, was around 15 million,[14] a death toll of 760,300 represents around 5 per cent of the population. Considering that (i) the majority of the population were concentrated in the highlands, where the Italians focused most of their fire-power, and since (ii) the overwhelming majority of highland Ethiopians were living in the rural areas, where it is common for households to report having lost at least one of their family members to military action during the invasion or occupation, a death rate of 5 per cent might be too low, in which case the emperor's opinion that the actual figures were probably 'far more than' the estimate of 760,300 may have been justified.

Proportion of Christians

In the Ethiopian military, and in the Patriot resistance that eventually took over their role, Christians represented a high proportion of the total. This is because, although at the time of mobilisation in 1935 many different ethnic groups, representing various religions and creeds from across the Ethiopian empire, responded to the call to arms, many Muslims were in due course persuaded to go over to the Italians and even to fight for them. Moreover, the evidence from written and oral testimonies indicates that Christian highlanders were the most numerous in the Patriot movement.

Given that exemplary repression was at its most intense in the Christian highlands, and that Graziani made a particular point of attempting to crush the Ethiopian Church, Christians also accounted for the majority of non-combatant victims.

It can then be concluded that the majority—though by no means all—of those killed were Christians, of which most were Orthodox.

The 1946 submission reported the burning down of 500,000 homes and other properties, and a total of 2,000 churches 'ransacked or ruined'.[15] Given the widespread church burning in Shewa and Gojjam, this figure, representing at most 20 per cent of the estimated total of at least 10,000 churches in Ethiopia at the time of the invasion, is certainly credible.

There appear to be no published estimates of the total number of Orthodox clergy (including monks) killed by the Italian forces during the invasion and occupation. However, as we have seen, more than 1,000 clergy died in the massacre of Debre Libanos alone,[16] and in many of the (estimated) 2,000 churches attacked, the clergy were slaughtered. Thus, since there were typically not less than five clergy in even the smallest parish church, the death toll for the Ethiopian clergy was certainly in the thousands.

APPENDIX II

SPOILS OF WAR

Crusaders were traditionally permitted, and indeed encouraged, to pillage, and Italy's crusade against Ethiopia continued the practice with a vengeance, despite the establishment of the Convention with Respect to the Laws and Customs of War on Land, which Italy had signed in 1899 at The Hague along with 23 other Europeans states. Renewed in 1907, the Convention, which was designed to bring to an end the looting that had been normal practice for European powers throughout the second half of the 19th century, made any form of pillage—and specifically the plundering of cultural artefacts from religious institutions—an illegal act.[1] However, the Italians share with their Axis partners the dubious distinction of ignoring the Convention and extending the tradition of 'to the victor go the spoils of war' well into the 20th century.

During the invasion and occupation of Ethiopia, looting of churches, houses and farms was de rigueur. Indeed, long after Mussolini claimed that the war had come to an end, Graziani, who acknowledged that the war was still being waged, was actually issuing written instructions to his subordinates to maintain the principle of war booty. On 27 October 1936 he instructed his military, 'We must continue the inexorable work of destruction of everything. It is superfluous to add that plunder, cattle or anything else of value belongs entirely to the detachments that carry out the raid.' These instructions remained in place in occupied Ethiopia until they were cancelled by the Duke of Aosta on 19 January 1940. On that occasion, 41 years after the Hague Convention was signed, the duke declared that 'raiding' by all regular and irregular military detachments, guards and police should cease, saying that 'recognizing and respecting the right of private ownership ..., it is time to put an end to the methods of the past'. The viceroy ordered in writing, 'All directions issued in the past by [provincial] governments in their respective territories and by the former *Intendenza* of the A.O.I. [Africa Orientale Italiana] ... regarding war booty, cease to be in force on the date of this circular [19 January 1940].'[2]

Thus until 1940 Italian forces were entitled to plunder whenever actions were being taken against civilians, including during the massacre of Addis Ababa, when pillage was widespread.[3]

In the countryside the most popular object of secular plunder was livestock; military telegrams frequently mention thousands of head of cattle being stolen by Italy's marauding *askaris*. In the urban areas the Italians generally looted cultural artefacts and personal possessions such as money and jewellery, although chickens were also popular as eggs were in short supply.

In addition, the Italian administration appropriated without compensation all fixed and movable assets belonging to anyone suspected of opposing the Italian administration, including those in prison or executed, leaving their families destitute. In Addis Ababa alone, this resulted in the confiscation of the land, houses, furniture and other personal property of hundreds of residents, including some of the city's finest properties, which were converted to Italian use.[4]

Lost Patrimony

No comprehensive study of the loss of Ethiopia's tangible cultural heritage during the invasion and occupation has ever been published, but it was certainly massive, spanning the entire spectrum from personal possessions to national treasures. Many of the stolen artefacts were religious, belonging to or associated with the Ethiopian Church. There is no doubt that during what is today known as the 'Italian

Figure 29: The piazza surrounding the equestrian statue of Emperor Menelik, seen here in 1935 before the invasion, was known as Menelik Square. With the iconic landmark of St. George's catedral in the background, the area was a popular destination for a family outing in the tranquility of pre-occupation Addis Ababa.

Figure 30: During the occupation the Italians desecrated the grounds of the Orthodox church of St. Peter and St. Paul in the suburb of Gulelé by using them as an execution site and a dumping ground for dead and dying ctims of the massacre of Addis Ababa in February 1937.

Figure 31: The church of Be'ata Maryam, also known as the Menelik Mausoleum, in November 1930, photographed at the time of the coronation of Emperor Haile Selassie. During the occupation, under Viceroy Graziani, the Italians closed the church, robbed it of many of its treasures, removed the Golden Crown from the pinnacle of the dome, and prohibited visits to the royal tombs.

Figure 32: In 2015 *Meggabi* Welde-Tinsa'e of the monastery of Debre Libanos describes the little-known Italian assault on the monastery of 23 February 1937 that preceded the massacre in May.

Figure 33: As part of the pogrom launched following the massacre of Addis Ababa, the Italian military carried numerous prefabricated portable gallows across Ethiopia to hang community leaders, Orthodox priests and notables.

Figure 34: Graziani gave his friend General Pietro Maletti responsibility for conducting the massacre of Debre Libanos. Pictured here with his troops in Northern Shewa, Maletti was a harsh disciplinarian who began his military career in the elite *Bersaglieri* infantry, and, like Graziani, fought in the 1st World War. Immediately behind him stands Lt-Colonel Carlo Marenco of the 2nd Colonial Brigade.

Figure 35: Borale, Ingécha, facing north-west, in 1997. Members of the local community, in discussion wuth Professor Richard Pankhurst (second from right), are standing at the execution site on the Borale valley floodplain.

Figure 36: Following defections of Eritrean Orthodox Christian *askaris* from the Italian army, Graziani created the 45th Colonial Muslim Battalion in the well-founded expectation that they would be more amenable to slaughtering Ethiopian Christians.

Figure 37: In the afternoon of 20 May 1937, overseen by *bande militari*, clergy of the church of St. Tekle Haymanot at the monastery of Debre Libanos are ordered to sit on the ground. They await their fate, as military trucks stand ready to take them away for execution. In the background is the heavily wooded escarpment that towers over the monastery.

Figure 38: Returning to the execution site at Laga Weldé in 1994, *Debtera* Zelleqe, an eye-witness of the massacre of Debre Libanos born in the nearby village of Tama, points out the shallow gulley of the Fincha Wenz into which the bodies of the massacre victims fell or were pushed.

Figure 39: Seen here in 1994, *Debtera* Zelleqe shows how the victims were made to sit on the ground, with their heads covered, before being shot in the back. The other figure in the photograph is eye-witness *Meggabi* Fiqre-Iyesus, After liberation in 1941, Zeleke and Fiqre-Iyesus would be among a group of boys and young men commissioned by the monastery to collect the bones of the victims for burial at the monastery

Figure 40: This photograph of Ethiopians massacred by the Italians may have been taken at a tributary of the Fincha Wenz at the execution site of Laga Weldé.

Figure 41: In 1997, Feqyibelu Yirgu, an eye-witness of the second massacre of clergy and congregation of the monastery of Debre Libanos, which took place at Borale, Ingécha, stands with his family and Professor Richard Pankhurst near the spot where the convoy of military trucks halted and discharged the prisoners to be executed in May 1937.

Figure 42: Feqyibelu Yirgu's nephew, Negash Yirgu, stands in March 2015 with Professor Shiferaw and Ian Campbell at the execution site of Borale, Ingécha, below the house from which Mulatwa Yirgu watched the executions.

Figure 43: *Weyzero* Mulatwa Yirgu was able to provide a detailed account of circumstances surrounding the massacre at Borale, which she witnessed at the age of 25 years: the digging of the mass graves, the carrying out of the executions, and the aftermath.

Figure 44: This contemporary sketch of the massacre of Debre Libanos, reportedly the work of an Ethiopian artist, was published in 1948 by advocate Baron Leijonhufvud, a former teacher at the Haile Selassie Military Academy in Addis Ababa. All of the features in the picture corresspond to the scene of the executions at Borale.

Figure 45: Italian military pause for a group photograph while filling a mass grave. Published after the liberation, this photograph was almost certainly taken in Northern Shewa, and probably after the massacre at Borale.

Figure 46: This photograph appears to be another view of the same, or adjoining, mass grave pictured in Fig. 45. It can be seen that the victims' wrists are tied together, as described by the eye-witnesses at Borale.

Figure 47: Eugenio Cardinal Pacelli, seen here after succeeding Pope Pius XI as Pius XII in 1939, was Secretary of State of the Vatican at the time of the Italian invasion and occupation of Ethiopia. Despite being well informed, he appears never to have spoken out against the persecution and massacres of the clergy of the Ethiopian Orthodox Church that resulted from the invasion strongly promoted and supported by the senior Italian Catholic clergy.

Figure 48: A section of the newly created Mohammed Sultan group, in a rare photograph taken in the Northern Shewan district of Merhabété in early June 1937 by Lieutenant Virgilio Cozzani. Armed with Italian-issued rifles or swords, these irregulars were used as assault troops against Ethiopia civilians, and rapidly acquired a reputation for atrocities against Orthodox Ethiopian Christians that shocked even some of their commanders.

Figure 49: The Italians publicly displayed the severed head of *Dejazmach* Haylu Kebede, son and heir of the hereditary ruler of the Christian región of Wag, a royal bloodline dating back to the 13th century. This image shows the front cover of Sylvia Pankhurst's 1944/45 pamphlet on Italian War Crimes.

Figure 50: The Holy Synod of the Ethiopian Orthodox Church in Addis Ababa on the occasion of the canonisation of Bishop Mikaél in October 2016.

Figure 51: Pride of place in the Graziani Room of the Museo Coloniale, Rome, at the museum's official opening in May 1939, was taken by a display case containing the crowns of the last four Ethiopian emperors, believed to have been looted from the monastery of Debre Libanos.

Figure 52: Partisan leaders General Raffaele Cadorna (left), and Walter Audisio (known as Colonel Valerio) who executed Mussolini in April 1945, pose beside a display of Ethiopian crowns that they found in the dictator's possession at Dongo, Northern Italy, while he was attempting to escape to Switzerland. Despite the Peace Treaty of 1947 that committed Italy to returning all such artefacts to Ethiopia, the crowns, described by Italian sources as the "most valuable part of the Dongo treasure", and which in this photograph appear to still carry their museum display cards, have never reappeared.

period', Ethiopia suffered its most extensive loss of patrimony since the Ottoman-backed *jihad* of the early 16th century.

It is not possible here to undertake a detailed analysis of the items involved, but some indications can be made of the nature and extent of the pillage.

The most important and best-known single item looted was the Aksum obelisk (or, more accurately, stela), which, though dating from Ethiopia's late pre-Christian era, constituted one of the nation's most celebrated items of tangible cultural heritage and an iconic symbol of its ancient civilisation. The second-largest carved stone monolith in the world (the largest being another of the stelae at Aksum), as high as a nine-storey building, carved with door and windows and weighing some 160 tons, the 4th-century granite monument was removed by the Italians in pieces. By March 1937 it had been shipped to Naples, following which it was transported to Rome, where it was re-erected in the Piazza di Porta Capena as a war trophy. In one of the many ironies surrounding the invasion of Ethiopia, the Italians were very proud to have made war against people capable of creating such a great monument of civilisation, during an invasion for which one of the purported reasons was their lack of civilisation. Whether the Roman public saw the irony is not known.

As the campaign against the Ethiopian Church intensified, particularly during 1936 and 1937, the number of churches and monasteries pillaged and burned reached the thousands, and the amount of loot reached a level where accounting for it is now all but impossible. The finest sacred items, such as Gospel books and psalteries in the form of luxury hand-crafted and illustrated parchment codices written in the liturgical language of Gi'iz, were popular with the Italians. These were expensive and time-consuming to produce; a large edition of, for example, *The Miracles of Mary*, could well require the skins of an entire flock of sheep. Such items would typically have been seized by the officers. Also much prized were large items such as the silver-bound drums, traditionally played by the *debteras*, and ornate processional crosses. Persian carpets if they were in good condition would only have appealed to the most senior commanders who had access to international transport for their loot. Items made of gold, silver or gilt, such as chalices, were sometimes taken from churches by low-ranking officers in the Colonial Battalions and fashioned into secular artefacts.

Ethiopia has a rich tradition of ecclesiastical wall paintings and manuscript miniatures, some dating back to the early centuries of Christianity. Between the 15th and 20th centuries the Ethiopian Church was also prolific in its production of icons. Usually diptychs and triptychs of considerable sophistication, and reflecting the more contemplative tradition of the Orthodox Church, they typically depicted the Virgin and Child, the Crucifixion, the Archangels Michael and Gabriel, and the Apostles, flanked by various saints, from both Ethiopia and elsewhere. These had a relatively high survival rate compared with the icons of most Orthodox Churches (partly because of the temperate climate of the Ethiopian highlands), though by the 1930s they were no longer being used in the liturgy, and Ethiopian church treasuries frequently contained a number of them. Some of these icons had survived only after being hidden in caves from the 16th-century *jihadists*, and would be attractive items of loot for 20th-century Italians.

Lesser but nonetheless valuable items included the hand crosses typically carried by priests and monks, which were usually made of silver, brass, iron or wood, small parchment prayer books contained in leather cases, and small personal icons hung from the neck.

Finally, since Ethiopian churches were traditionally used as safe deposits for royalty, the larger and more important churches in each region would contain, for example, royal crowns and state regalia which would be made available for use by the sovereign or other members of the royal family when visiting that district.

The Pillage of Debre Libanos

During the occupation the destruction and looting of churches became rife, and reached unprecedented levels in 1937, particularly during the massacre of Debre Libanos. The situation at the monastery was unusual—and possibly unique—in that the massacre during which the looting took place was ordered in writing by Graziani, and at least some of the many items removed from the treasury of the monastery church of St Tekle Haymanot and the House of the Cross were listed by the military in a two-page document (see Appendix VII).[5]

The monastery's most important and valuable treasures were reported by the few surviving monks, who happened to be absent during the massacre, to have been removed on the personal orders of General Maletti and taken to his military camp at nearby Fiché. These included a large illustrated 16th-century codex donated to the monastery by Emperor Gelawdéwos, which was 'decorated in gold' and is said to have required more than one man to carry; a large gold-bound drum; a gold chalice and dish; an ancient cross believed to be cast in gold; and a number of crowns, including those of Emperor Yohannis IV and Emperor Menelik II, as well as a crown of Emperor Haile Selassie, all thought to be made of gold.[6] None of these substantial items appear on the official list of artefacts removed by the Italians, which is limited to more common items of modest value.

The memorandum attached to the inventory in General Maletti's report of the massacre states that the items listed were to be delivered to an entity in Addis Ababa to be specified.[7] However, research conducted by the present author in the 1990s with the assistance of His Holiness Patriarch *Abune* Pawlos, failed to reveal the fate of any of these items, with the exception of the cross reputedly the property of St Tekle Haymanot himself, marked '(I)' by the Italians in the list in Appendix VII, page 2. *Fitawrari* Nebiyye-Li'ul, who at the time of the research was acting sacristan of Debre Libanos in place of his father-in-law *Li'ul-Ras* Kassa, showed evidence to the present author that this cross, which is highly venerated and of considerable renown, was at Debre Libanos when it was reopened by the Italians following the change of policy in late 1937, and is still there. It was most likely returned to Debre Libanos when the monastery was rehabilitated under the Duke of Aosta.

The Italian inventory states that 22 sacred books were removed from the church of St Tekle Haymanot, and 60 from the House of the Cross. Since this category apparently covers all books found (i.e. printed books as well as traditionally bound parchment manuscripts), this represents far too small a library for an important teaching institution such as Debre Libanos. The present author's research in the 1990s suggested that by the early 20th century the monastery church library at Debre Libanos consisted of more than 500 parchment manuscripts and printed books, which would be a realistic number for such a monastery church. The analysis concluded that the Italian list of items removed is incomplete, and estimated that around 400 books—the majority being parchment manuscripts—were most likely removed during the massacre but were omitted from the Italian inventory.[8] In 2018, sources in the Ethiopian Orthodox Church confirmed this figure, stating that Church records show that the Italians stole around 400 books from the Debre Libanos library.[9]

There is no doubt that this figure included many parchment manuscripts; in an affidavit sworn for the UN war crimes trials, *Lij Hayle-Maryam Gazmu*, who was in the company of Colonel Garelli at the monastery of Debre Libanos on 20 and 21 May 1937, testified:

> his [General Maletti's] soldiers plundered the property and wealth of the church. Also, as this church was the burial place of many nobles and dignitaries, the Italian soldiers broke open the tombs, hoping to find gold ... This church was one of the wealthiest of all the churches and monasteries of Ethiopia, and the Italian armies plundered the property of this church without leaving anything intact; *they took even the oldest books* [emphasis added].[10]

Also missing from the Italian inventory, as noted above, are the most valuable items, none of which ever reappeared at the monastery, such as the large illustrated 16th-century codex that reportedly required more than one man to carry, the large gold-bound drum, the gold chalice and dish, the ancient cross believed to be cast in gold, and the royal crowns of Emperors Yohannis IV, Menelik II and Haile Selassie.

Looting Countrywide

We have seen that apart from Debre Libanos, hundreds of churches were pillaged by the Italian military before being burned. To identify all the churches ransacked would be a vast undertaking, and would probably now be no longer possible. As we have seen, many were small parish churches, but some—particularly around the gorge of the Abbay (Blue Nile) River—were edifices of renown, with long-standing connections to royalty. Some instances of pillage of such churches have already been mentioned; others include the celebrated church of Mahdere Maryam in Begémdir, from which many sacred books were looted, and the late medieval church of Gétésémané Maryam in Gojjam (see Map 10).[11] The ancient church of Weyn Washa Teklehaymanot, together with its monastery known as Tara Gedam, in southern Begémdir (see Map 9), was also pillaged. There the Italians forced their way into the church and stole its entire tangible heritage including sacred books—a loss regretted by the priests to this day.[12]

While many churches were stripped of everything they possessed, in some cases the clergy hid their treasures in caves or underground. For example, at Debre Libanos, despite the apparent theft of every movable artefact that the Italians found, the two most important and priceless items were well hidden and thus survived the occupation. One was a holy relic: a foot of St Tekle Haymanot (said to have fallen off owing to his long period of confinement in a cave at the monastery) preserved in a gold reliquary. The other was the saint's own *tabot*, or altar slab, consecrated to Mary the Mother of Christ. Both artefacts were hidden from the Italians at Wula Gebeba, near the church of Weberi Washa located on a secluded ledge below a rocky outcrop at the edge of the plateau above the monastery.[13]

Another instance of artefacts being hidden occurred at the historic church of Cheleqot Sillassé ('Church of the Trinity') in southern Tigray (Map 9), whose clergy had been entrusted with many precious items in the 19th century. However, in this case the outcome was tragic, for the Italians killed the church treasurer when he refused to reveal where the ecclesiastical treasures had been hidden.[14]

Personal Artefacts

There is also the question of personal artefacts stolen from the clergy and monks when they were killed. For obvious reasons there is very little information available on this subject. Nonetheless, the various reports of items such as silver hand crosses, prayer books and prayer staffs (sometimes silver-topped) being taken from massacre victims are consistent and undoubtedly correct. Tibebe Kassa of Debre Libanos reported not only that the Italians removed hundreds of personal hand crosses, manuscripts, vestments and prayer staffs from the captives before their execution at Laga Weldé, but also that he travelled to Debre Birhan in an Italian military truck in which many of these artefacts were being transported.

It should be noted that such personal items were not included in the Italian inventory of Debre Libanos. Since an estimated 1,300–1,700 of the victims executed at the two sites of Laga Weldé and Borale were monks, priests or deacons, and since a large proportion were adults wearing ecclesiastical vestments, who would have been carrying at least one cross or parchment manuscript (and in some cases one of each), it may be estimated that the total number of such items unaccounted for from the massacres of Debre Libanos alone could be in excess of a thousand. Countrywide, there are thus thousands of personal ecclesiastical artefacts to be accounted for.

What Happened to the Loot?

Ethiopian clergy who survived the massacres of the occupation and who were interviewed by the present author in the 1990s generally believed that the majority of artefacts stolen from the churches by the Italians were taken to Italy. According to the Debre Libanos monastery council, none of the items known to have been removed from the monastery church were returned. It is not known if the lesser items were actually taken to Addis Ababa as planned, according to Maletti's report;[15] they have never been traced. During the research conducted into the matter by the present author together with Richard Pankhurst and Degife Gebre-Tsadiq in 1991–2, the clergy of Debre Libanos said that they believed that some—perhaps all—of the stolen manuscripts found their way into the Vatican library, where, they assumed, they are still held.[16]

The evidence supporting these beliefs is compelling. It is well attested that the Italian military commanders removed substantial amounts of Ethiopia's tangible heritage when they left the country. Pietro Badoglio, the first Italian viceroy, appropriated half of the 1.7

million Maria Theresa thalers in the Bank of Abyssinia, and installed in his Rome villa the astonishing number of 300 crates of booty that had been flown from Ethiopia by the Regia Aeronautica. Graziani returned to Italy in 1938 with no less than 79 crates of artefacts, and Attilio Teruzzi, the minister of Italian Africa, took away four truck-loads after a single, brief visit in 1939.[17]

In the case of Graziani, at least some of the items reappeared in public, for in 1939 several Ethiopian treasures, including a number of royal crowns, coronets, lion's-mane headdresses and other objects, were exhibited in Rome for the official opening of the Museo Coloniale, the museum of the Ministry of Italian Africa. Mussolini, who donated the collection to the Museum, was reported by the Fascist authorities to have been given the collection by Graziani. There can be little doubt about this, since the room housing items from the collection was named the Graziani Room.

The display case in the left foreground in the photograph of part of the Graziani Room published by the Italian government in 1939 (Fig. 51) contained 'the precious crowns of the last four Ethiopian emperors'.[18] This case, which in the photograph contains four elaborate Ethiopian royal crowns together with what appears to be a fine ecclesiastical crown, formed the *pièce de résistance* of the newly created exhibition. All four royal crowns are in the 19th-century style or earlier, and could well have belonged, as the Italian sources indicated, to the most recent Ethiopian emperors.[19]

These five crowns are likely to be those stolen from the church of St Tekle Haymanot at Debre Libanos, although they were—not surprisingly—omitted from the Italian inventory. The question is: what happened to them? We know that they did not remain for long in the Graziani Room at the Museo Coloniale, for the contents of that museum were dispersed not long afterwards. When he was caught and executed by Italian partisans in April 1945 at Dongo, in northern Italy, the *Duce* reportedly had in his possession over 60 kg of gold, several thousand pounds sterling in various currencies, letters from world leaders, and a number of Ethiopian royal crowns. It is apparent that these artefacts were being carried for their resale value, suggesting that the Ethiopian crowns were thought by Mussolini to be made of gold.[20]

After Mussolini's execution, partisan leaders General Raffaele Cadorna and 'Colonel Valerio' (Walter Audisio), who personally shot the dictator, were photographed with these crowns, which are clearly the same crowns displayed in the Museo Coloniale, and even carry the museum display cards (Fig. 52).

So what happened to these crowns, described by the Italians as the 'most valuable part of the Dongo treasure',[21] in the short interlude between the partisans proudly displaying them and their return being requested by the Ethiopian government? According to the peace treaty finally signed in 1947, all of these artefacts should have been restored to Ethiopia:

> The question of loot taken from Ethiopia during the Fascist occupation (as well as the tragic fate of the monks and deacons of Debre Libanos) was raised by the Ethiopian Delegation to the Paris Peace Conference of 1946. The Italian government was forced under Ethiopian pressure to agree in Article 37 of the peace treaty of 1947 that: 'Within eighteen months ... Italy shall restore all works of art, religious objects, archives and objects of historical value belonging to Ethiopia or its nationals and removed from Ethiopia to Italy since October 3, 1935', i.e., the date of the Fascist invasion.[22]

Given the considerable importance and value evidently attributed to these artefacts not only by the Fascists but also by the partisans, it is difficult to imagine that the new Italian government, which included several of the partisan leaders, were unaware of their existence and location at the time of the peace conference. However, more than seven decades later, Ethiopians are still waiting for the Italian government to abide by the terms of the 1947 peace treaty.

Of the thousands of artefacts stolen during the occupation, only two have been returned; a statue of an Ethiopian lion, which had been removed from outside the Addis Ababa railway station, and the great stela of Aksum, the latter having been returned reluctantly and only after repeated refusals by the Italian government led to a fierce international campaign for its reinstatement. The voices of condemnation finally led to Italian capitulation and the return of the stela to Ethiopia in 2005 and its re-erection in Aksum in 2008.

APPENDIX II

So far as the present author is aware, none of the ecclesiastical and state treasures looted from Ethiopian churches and monasteries during the invasion and occupation, nor the numerous personal artefacts that were confiscated, have ever been returned. It is not even clear what steps, if any, the Italian government has taken to trace Ethiopia's cultural patrimony that it is still bound under the 1947 Peace Treaty to return to Ethiopia. As Andrea Riccardi put it in 2017, 'There is a whole patrimony still to be recovered from [Italian] religious bodies.'[23] A striking comparison may, however, be drawn with Italy's current policy concerning the restitution of cultural heritage to their countries of origin. It is ironic that 21st-century Italy has emerged as a European leader in that field, in its successful quest to recover looted artefacts of Italian patrimony acquired by museums in America.

APPENDIX III

MAJOR QUERCIA'S REPORT OF 14 MARCH 1937 (PAGE 1)

COMANDO DEL GRUPPO DEI CARABINIERI REALI DI ADDIS ABEBA

N° 184-12-21 di prot.   Addis Abeba, 14 marzo 1937-XV°-
OGGETTO: Accertamenti ed indagini in Debra Libanos sull'attentato del
         19 febbraio c.a.

AL COMANDO SUPERIORE DEI CC.RR. DEL GOV.GEN.A.O.I.

ADDIS ABEBA

Rispondo al foglio 21/231 Ris.dell'8 corrente.

Dagli accertamenti eseguiti dall'Arma in Debra Libanos e a Ficcé é risultato quanto segue:

I°- il convento di Debra Libanos ove é venerata da tutti i cristiani copti la salma del santo TECLAIMANOT,tigrino,é composto da una chiesa principale dedicata al santo;di altra della S.Croce ad 800 m.circa dalla prima;da un centinaio di tombe di grandi capi abissini sparse tra le due chiese,a guardia delle quali stanno frati e casci;da varie centinaia di tukul ove abitano monaci,frati,diaconi,studenti,suore,sparsi e nascosti alla vista,in zona boscosa di olivastri acacie ed eucalipti dell'ampiezza di chilometri 5 per 3 e mezzo circa.

Presso questo convento giornalmente si recano pellegrini a pregare e a bagnarsi nelle acque che scorrono in una grotta,perché benedetta dal santo Teclaimanot che ivi morì.-

Non é possibile controllare il traffico delle persone.Solo quelle di rango elevato che si recano alla chiesa di Teclaimanot vengono conosciute dal priore,capo del convento,che a mezzo del Negaby (fornitore dei viveri) fa loro distribuire gratuitamente il vitto.-

2°- Nel convento,e precisamente nella casa del frate Abba Hanna (confessore del negus e che lo seguì nella fuga),a circa 300 metri della chiesa principale ed a 500 da quella del priore del convento,si erano ritirate,da oltre IO mesi,dopo l'occupazione di Addis Abeba le tre uoizerò Birchenesc Besciá,le sorelle Sergutè e Lachec Dillinessau.Costoro hanno condotto vita ritirata.

Nella stessa casa,fino al settembre 1936 abitò certo Mogos Asghedon, amico del ricercato Abrahà Deboc.Il predetto vi ritornò il 9 febbraio

o/o

APPENDIX IV

TELEGRAM NO. 35049, PIETRO MALETTI TO RODOLFO GRAZIANI, 22 MAY 1937

TELEGRAMMA DI STATO

SG/ AD/
GOVERNO GENERALE
DELL'AFRICA ORIENTALE ITALIANA

Assegnazione
GABINETTO

GABINETTO - UFFICIO CIFRA
N. 35049

Provenienza Gen. Maletti il
Ricevuto il   22/5/1937   Ore 02.00

Telegramma in arrivo

Per conoscenza

GABINETTO S.E. VICE RE

ADDIS ABEBA

2152/op/./ Confermo che tutti indistintamente personaggi segnalati sono stati definitivamente sistemati/./

Generale Maletti

APPENDIX V

TELEGRAM NO. 9325, RODOLFO GRAZIANI TO PIETRO MALETTI, 24 MAY 1937

TELEGRAMMA DI STATO

Mittente: GABINETTO

N. 9325 di prot.

Addis Abeba lì 24 Maggio 1937.XV°

Indicazioni di urgenza

M.P.A. SU TUTTE LE M.P.A.

Graziani

Telegramma in partenza

GOVERNO GENERALE DELL'AFRICA ORIENTALE ITALIANA
GABINETTO - UFFICIO CIFRA

Copia per conoscenza
S.E.V.Gov.Gen.
Stato Maggiore
Dir.Sup.AA.PP.
Uff.Politico
Uff.Giust.Mil.
Com.Sup.CC.RR.

GENERALE MALETTI

26606 _ GABINETTO /./ Ras Hailù da me interrogato conferma pie_
namente responsabilità convento Debra Libanos /./
Ordino pertanto at V.S. di passare immediatamente per le armi
tutti i diaconi di Debra Libanos meno i ragazzi /./
Assicuri con parola "" LIQUIDAZIONE COMPLETA "" /./

GRAZIANI

APPENDIX VI

TELEGRAM, RODOLFO GRAZIANI TO THE *RESIDENTE* AT FICHÉ, 27 OCTOBER 1937

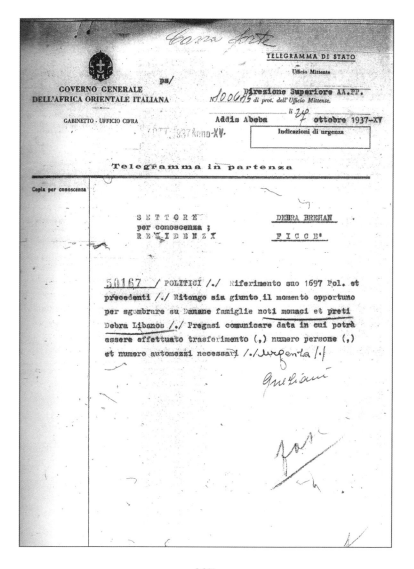

APPENDIX VII

THE ITALIAN INVENTORY OF ITEMS REMOVED FROM DEBRE LIBANOS

Allegato 4 al foglio 2091 del 22/maggio

COMANDO SETTORE NORD-ORIENTALE

La sottonotata commissione, riunitasi oggi 21 maggio 1937 -XV° in Debra Libanos, in seguito a ordine 2058 stessa data del comando settore nord-orientale, per accertare e depositare a verbale i valori e gli oggetti sacri di qualche importanza raccolti nelle chiede di Taclè Haimanot e di Mascal Biet, ha accertato quanto segue:

A) ELENCO DEGLI OGGETTI RINVENUTI NELLA CHIESA SANTUARIO DI TACLE' HAIMANOT IN DEBRA LIBANOS.

1 tappeto persiano usato dimens; approssimativa		m.	2,60 x 1,40
1	idem	idem	1,70 x 100
1	"	"	1,90 x 1,50
1	"	"	2,50 x 1,50
1	"	"	2,80 x 1,40
1	"	"	2,80 x 1,40
1	"	"	2,80 x 1,90
1	"	"	2,60 x 1,40
1	"	"	3,00 x 1,40
1	"	"	2,80 x 1,60
1	"	"	2,80 x 1,50
1	"	"	2,90 x 1,80
1	"	"	1,90 x 1,40
1	"	"	3,00 x 2,00
1	"	"	2,50 x 1,60
1	"	"	2,80 x 1,80
1	"	"	2,80 x 2,00
1	"	"	2,00 x 1,30
1	"	"	2,80 x 1,60
1	"	"	2,80 x 1,80
1	"	"	2,20 x 1,50

2 tappeti usati di tipo vario
2 mascal grandi dorati
4 " medi in argento
5 " piccoli di metallo
45 campanelle in ottone
10 coperte di tipo vario
20 ombrelli
12 piviali
18 paludamenti vari da sacerdote
6 paramenti vari da altare
7 piviali
22 libri sacri
2 tavole scolpite
1 piatto e 1 cucchiaio in argento
1 coppa di ottone
1 vassoio di ottone
2 nafore di ottone
16 campanelle in argento

//..//

HOLY WAR

- 2 -

13 paramenti da chiesa
24 vesti da sacerdote
70 indumenti vari da sacerdote
6 coperte da altare
35 paludamenti vari da sacerdote
4015 talleri M.T.
1584 lire italiane
1 anello di oro
3 mascal grandi dorati
2 mascal medi in argento
2 anfore in argento
2 anfore in metallo
16 campanelle in argento
4 mitre di metallo dorato
  alcuni piccoli oggetti in argento
1 coppa in argento
1 calice in metallo
1 calice in metallo dorato
2 coppe piccole in argento
2 calici in argento dorato
1 calice in ottone
1 anfora in argento dorato
2 sigilli in argento

B) ELENCO DEGLI OGGETTI rinvenuti nella chiesa della Croce Mascal Biet) in Debra Libanos.

1 tappeto persiano usato dimens. approssimativa			m. 1,90 x 1,40
1	idem	idem	3,00 x 2,00
1	idem	idem	3,50 x 1,80
1	idem	idem	1,70 x 1,40
1	idem	idem	1,40 x 1,20
1	idem	idem	1,50 x 1,20

6o libri sacri
1 custodia per croce in argento
1 croce in argento
1 croce in legno scolpito (I)
32 indumenti vari per sacerdote

(I) è la croce che secondo la leggenda sarebbe caduta dal cielo in Debra Libanos, e perciò oggetto di particolare venerazione.-
Tutti gli oggetti sopra elencati sono stati riuniti a parte per il loro trasporto in sede da indicarsi e affidati ad apposita guardia.-

Fatto letto e chiuso in Debra Libanos il 21 maggio millenovecento trentasette - ore 9 - -

MEMBRO
(Cap.CC.RR. L.Romerio)

MEMBRO SEGRETARIO
(Cap. S. Montuori)

IL PRESIDENTE
(Maggiore Massimo Taggi)

F. C. C.
IL TEN. COL. AIUTANTE DI CAMPO
(Carlo Marenco)

ACKNOWLEDGEMENTS

The programme of research that culminated in this book began thirty years ago, in 1991, with *Ato* Degife Gebre-Tsadiq, chief librarian of the Institute of Ethiopian Studies (IES), Addis Ababa University, and with the support of the indefatigable Professor Richard Pankhurst, founder of the IES, to whom this volume is dedicated. The death of both of these co-researchers, which occurred before the project was completed, constituted not only a personal blow to the author but also a great loss to the field of Ethiopian studies.

Over a period of more than twenty-five years Professor Richard and Rita Pankhurst participated in many field visits and rendered invaluable assistance over tea and biscuits in their beautiful and historic Addis Ababa home, by discussing, reviewing and assessing findings as they emerged. Professor Pankhurst also kindly provided photographs from the collection of his mother, Sylvia Pankhurst, with permission to publish.

A special thank-you goes to Professor Emeritus Shiferaw Beqele of Addis Ababa University, who has also been a constant source of information and good advice throughout the many years that it has taken for this book to come to fruition.

I am most grateful to the late David Buxton, a pioneering Ethiopianist responsible for gathering, analysing, compiling and publishing important material on the cultural history of Ethiopia. In 1990 he generously presented me with the negatives of the photographs he took of the monastery of Debre Libanos shortly after

ACKNOWLEDGEMENTS

liberation (which were published in his *Travels in Ethiopia*), together with permission to publish.

The late Dr Birhanu Abebe, scholar, historian and author, formerly Professor of History at Addis Ababa University, and later researcher at the Centre Français des Études Éthiopiennes, who was also a dear friend and mentor, rendered invaluable support and encouragement in many early morning meetings over coffee at the little café opposite the Greek Orthodox church in Addis Ababa's Piazza district.

I commenced the first phase of research jointly with *Ato* Degife in 1991, focusing largely—though not exclusively—on the May 1937 massacre at the monastery of Debre Libanos of Shewa. These investigations were conducted with the generous assistance of His Holiness *Abune* Paulos, patriarch of the Ethiopian Orthodox Church, archbishop of Aksum and *ichegé* of the See of St Tekle Haymanot, who graciously facilitated the research and opened many doors.

The first phase also had the good fortune to benefit from the invaluable support and advice of the late *Fitawrari* Nebiyye-Li'ul Tekle-Tsadiq, son-in-law of *Li'ul-Ras* Kassa Haylu, who joined and guided us in several field trips. It was largely due to the *fitawrari*'s encyclopedic knowledge of Debre Libanos, and his energetic assistance, that it was possible to determine the circumstances of the massacre of the clergy of that monastery, identify reliable eyewitnesses, and locate the first of the two execution sites. Welcome support was also provided by *Ato* Demeqe Birhan of the University of Addis Ababa, and Dr Ing. Birhanu Gizaw Hayle-Maryam of the College of Telecommunications and Information Technology, Addis Ababa.

Another aspect of the research at this stage was the exemplary repression carried out by the Italians in Bulga, for which I was fortunate to be accompanied in December 1993 by *Ato* Gétachew Beqele, a leading authority on the 20th-century history of Bulga, who had personally experienced the Italian onslaught as a young boy.

Dyakon Kifle Assefa and *Ato* Fisseha Taddesse (then of the Holy Trinity Theological College, Addis Ababa) were indispensable assistants throughout the second phase of research in the late 1990s, which concentrated on the second execution site of the monastery of Debre Libanos, and Italian attacks on monasteries in Ethiopia's Rift Valley. That phase also benefited from the generous support of

ACKNOWLEDGEMENTS

my dear friend and colleague *Ato* Welde Aregay, who introduced me to the energetic *Ato* Girma Demissé, attorney and head of the Fiché Association, and *Ato* Laqew Regarssa of the College of Commerce, Addis Ababa University. In particular, I would like to thank *Ato* Laqew for kindly giving me a copy of a publication by the monastery of Debre Libanos that, *inter alia*, lists some of the members of staff executed by the Italians.

I am indebted to Dr Deressé Ayenachew and *Ato* Alebachew of the University of Debre Berhan, and PhD student *Ato* Téwodros Siyum, for their support and companionship in accompanying Professor Shiferaw and me during our last visit to the execution site at Borale—a deeply moving experience—and familiarising us with hitherto unknown Patriot execution sites in and around Debre Birhan.

Assistance was also generously provided by His Highness Prince Asfa-Wossen Asserate, historian, and son of *Li'ul-Ras* Asserate Kassa; Dr Joachim Persoon, scholar and author, formerly of the Ethiopian Orthodox Church Theological College; the tireless Kidane Alemayehu, executive director of the Global Alliance for Justice— The Ethiopian Cause; and *Dejazmach* Zewdé Gebre-Sillassé.

Weyzero Herane Birhane-Mesqel Kassa graciously provided information about the family of her grandfather, *Li'ul-Ras* Kassa Haylu, while the knowledgeable *Weyzero* Alem-Seged Feqade-Sillassé Hiruy, granddaughter of *Ras* Imru Hayle-Sillassé and stepdaughter of *Blattén Géta* Lorenzo Ta'izaz, always had a warm welcome in her cosy verandah in Kazanchis for *Dejazmach* Zewdé, Dr Birhanu and me, where I would be regaled with stories of life in Ethiopia under the emperor and during the Italian period, over Sunday afternoon tea.

The third phase of research, which was concentrated on the historical connections between the Ethiopian and Roman Churches, and the activities of the Italian government, the Holy See, the Vatican and the Italian Catholic clergy during the 1930s, began with a study of the Rev. Dr Mikre-Sillassé Gebre-Ammanuél's detailed thesis on the subject, and benefited from the generosity of Ethiopianist Andrew Hilton, who threw open his beautiful hideaway in Trastevere as my pied-à-terre in Rome.

Cardinal Berhaneyesus Demerew, metropolitan archbishop of Addis Ababa (Ethiopia), Father Petros Berga and Antonello

ACKNOWLEDGEMENTS

Carvigiani of tv2000 facilitated a very rewarding visit to the Vatican, and Antonello provided important archival documents. It was also in the Eternal City that *Avvocato* Luigi Panella kindly gave me access to his archive on the Italo-Ethiopian war—a rare treasure trove in the elegant surroundings of via Frattina. I am also grateful to *Avvocato* Panella for providing his expert opinion of key Italian military documents.

Giancarlo Penza and Cecilia Pani of the Community of Sant'Egidio in Rome were most helpful, providing both information and translation services, and in kindly organising a visit to Münster, which afforded opportunities for meeting kindred spirits. Professor Paolo Borruso and Professor Lucia Ceci have been of great assistance, answering questions, pointing me towards important sources, and providing valuable documentation.

Dyakon Daniél Kibret of Addis Ababa, the well-known broadcaster and authority on the Ethiopian Orthodox Church, greatly facilitated the fourth and final phase of the project, which broadened the scope of the research in Ethiopia. *Dyakon* Daniél graciously provided access to his valuable archive containing primary Amharic sources detailing attacks by the Italians on individual Ethiopian churches, monasteries and clergy. The theologian and prolific author *Qéssis* Kefyalew Mehari was also generous in giving of his time, knowledge and a considerable body of published material, while my long-time friend *Ato* Mengesha Werqineh, together with *Ato* Fireqal Yigrem, assisted with research in Gojjam. Many thanks are also due to Tekalign Gedamu, a friend and colleague of many decades, who came to the rescue just in time to fill a gap with little-known information about the circumstances of the execution of Bishop Mikaél.

Of especial importance during this phase were the contributions of Dr Ahmed Hassen Omer of Addis Ababa University, who patiently answered my many questions about the exemplary repression conducted by the Italians in Northern Shewa in mid-1937. Thanks are also due to Dr Agidew Redie, commissioner of the Ethiopian Orthodox Church Development and Inter-Church Aid Commission (EOC-DICAC), and the Rev. *Memhir* Daniél Seifemikaél for information, advice and assistance.

ACKNOWLEDGEMENTS

Critical to this stage were the contributions of cultural heritage specialist *Ato* Tesfaye Yimer and my dear friend and colleague *Ato* Tamene Tiruneh Matebe, who rendered valuable services in arranging and facilitating interviews.

I can never repay the debt I owe to the following eyewitnesses and informants, who kindly provided critical testimony between 1991 and 2018, many of them on the very sites of the events concerned. They are listed below in alphabetical order:

- *Weyzero* Abebech Ezenah of Misir Duket, between Debre Birhan and Ankober;
- *Maitre-artiste* Afewerq Teklé, celebrated Ethiopian artist, of Addis Ababa;
- *Aleqa* Akaz Geda of the church of Gebre Menfes Qiddus at the monastery of Midr Kebd, near Lake Zway;
- *Weyzero* Alemash Sibahtu, daughter of *Dejazmach* Tsibahtu Yohannis, private secretary and interpreter to Viceroy Rodolfo Graziani;
- *Ato* Alle Felega Selam, well-known artist, raconteur and grandson of *Aleqa* Hiruy of the church of Fiché Giyorgis;
- *Aqqabé* Bi'isé Tiruneh, a monk at the church of Debre Werq in Gojjam;
- *Ato* Demissé Hayle-Maryam, distinguished resistance fighter during the Italian occupation, of Nazareth, Ethiopia;
- *Ato* Derbi Tsegé of Borale, Ingécha, near Debre Birhan;
- *Ato* Feleqe Asress of Misir Duket;
- *Ato* Feqyibelu Yirgu of Borale, Ingécha;
- *Meggabi* Fiqre-Iyesus of the monastery of Debre Libanos;
- *Abba* Gebre-Giyorgis, monk, resident at the monastery of Debre Libanos as an anchorite from 1913 to 1937;
- His Excellency Girma Welde-Giyorgis, president of Ethiopia from 2001 to 2013 and a kind and helpful friend, who was able to answer many questions about the Italian period;
- Ambassador Imru Zelleke, author of *My Journey*, who was imprisoned with his mother and baby sister by the Italians in Danane concentration camp, and is a mine of information on life in Ethiopia before, during and after the occupation;

345

ACKNOWLEDGEMENTS

- His Grace *Abune* Matéwos, archbishop of Jerusalem and *Tsebaté* Hayle-Mesqel of the monastery of Debre Libanos in the 1950s;
- *Immahoy* Hiruta of the church of Be'ata Maryam, Addis Ababa;
- *Blatta* Mehari Kassa, scholar and author, who lived through the massacre of Addis Ababa;
- *Abba* Mika'él of the church of Gebre Menfes Qiddus at the monastery of Midr Kebd, near Lake Zway;
- Rev. Dr Mikre-Sellasie Gebre-Ammanuel, Church historian specialising in the Italian period, of Addis Ababa;
- *Weyzero* Mulatwa Yirgu of Borale, Ingécha;
- *Ato* Negash Yirgu of Borale, Ingécha;
- Dr Syoum Gebregziabher, international public servant, who lived through the massacre of Addis Ababa;
- Taddesse Tiruneh, distinguished Patriot, of Addis Ababa;
- *Abba* Tibebe Beyene of the monastery of Debre Libanos;
- *Abba* Tibebe Kassa of Wusha Gedel, Debre Libanos, who was imprisoned in Danane concentration camp;
- *Nebura'ed* Tefera Menissé of the church of Béta Maryam, Addis Alem, and formerly *aleqa* of the monastery of Debre Assebot;
- *Ato* Tekle-Tsadiq Mekuriya, historian and former minister of culture, who was imprisoned in Danane concentration camp;
- *Memhir* Tibebu Welde-Maryam of the monastery of Debre Libanos;
- *Ato* Welde-Sillassé Habte-Sillassé, former treasurer and *dyakon* at the church of Kundi Giyorgis, north of Ankober;
- *Ato* Wend'afrash Welde-Giyorgis of Misir Duket;
- *Abba* Werqu, a monk at the monastery of Debre Libanos;
- *Debtera* Zelleqe of the church of St Tekle Haymanot at Debre Libanos;
- the son of *Ato* Mengesha Negeda of Misir Duket.

Much of the information gathered for this book has been provided by Ethiopian informants and Amharic-language published sources. However, use has also been made of primary Italian written sources. In this regard I have drawn principally on the microfilmed communications and associated reports in the United States National

ACKNOWLEDGEMENTS

Archives (USNA), Maryland, USA, and the IES. For relevant documents in *Fondo* Graziani in the Archivio Centrale dello Stato, Rome, but not included in the USNA or IES microfilm collections, I have relied principally on the extensive research already carried out on these documents by specialists Professor Angelo Del Boca, Professor Giorgio Rochat, Professor Pankhurst and Professor Alberto Sbacchi. Nonetheless, it was necessary to undertake some additional studies of archival documents in Rome, and I am grateful to Antonello Carvigiani and *Avvocato* Panella for their assistance in that regard.

For information in the Vatican Secret Archives and other Catholic archives in Italy, I have relied on the work of Professor Paolo Borruso, Professor Lucia Ceci, Professor Emma Fattorini, Professor David Kertzer, Professor John Pollard and Professor Nicolas Virtue.

For information on Baron Eric S.A. Leijonhufvud, Ethiopian advocate general during the negotiations between the Ethiopian government and the UN War Crimes Commission, I am grateful to Dr Lars Wikström, chief genealogist of the House of Nobility, Genealogical Department, Stockholm.

For translation services from Amharic to English I am indebted particularly to *Ato* Tamene, *Ato* Lemma Argaw and *Ato* Begashaw Wukaw of Addis Ababa; for translation services from Italian to English, warm thanks are due to Caterina Ruggero and Matteo Marchisio of Washington, DC, and Roberta Di Chiara of Rome, the last-mentioned kindly facilitated by Carlo Di Chiara of Addis Ababa. I am grateful to Dennis Chan of Mississauga for drawing the maps, and to Archivio Luce, Awen Films, the Burton Holmes Archive, Zeno Calantoni, Daniél Kibret, Herane Birhane Mesqel Kassa, Mondadori Portfolio, Luigi Panella, Richard Pankhurst and Gabriele Zorzetto for kindly giving permission for the reproduction of photographs.

Finally, I am greatly indebted to Professor Shiferaw, Professor Emeritus Paul Gifford and *Ato* Tamene for kindly reviewing successive drafts of the text and making many helpful suggestions.

NOTES

PREFACE

1. *Debre Libanos*, by Antonello Carvigiani, was directed and photographed by Andrea Tramontano, and edited by Dolores Gangi.
2. Riccardi, A., 2017A. See also Beltrami, A., 2017.
3. Beltrami, A., 2017.

1. A MOST ANCIENT CHURCH

1. Diamant, J., 2017.
2. Some sources indicate a date of AD 330 for the conversion of Ezana, king of the state of Aksum and a forebear of the emperors of Ethiopia. The Ethiopian Orthodox Church generally holds that before this date St Philip the Evangelist baptised an Ethiopian man in Gaza, thereby marking the beginning of the Ethiopian Church at an even earlier date.
3. Emperor Theodosius I (r. 379–95) declared Christianity the state Church of the Roman Empire through the Edict of Thessalonica in AD 380.
4. The full name of the Ethiopian Orthodox Church (referred to hereafter as the Ethiopian Church) is the Ethiopian Orthodox Tewahido Church, the Amharic term *tewahido* meaning 'united', indicating that Christ is one, united and composite in nature and person. Binns, J., 2017, p. 153.
5. Sergew Hable Sellassie, 1972, p. 181.
6. Sergew Hable Sellassie, 1972, p. 186.
7. Kaplan, S., 2007B, p. 988.
8. For a summary of the history of Debre Libanos of Shewa, see Derat, M.-L., 2005. For a detailed account of the early stages in

the development of the monastery, see TADDESSE TAMRAT, 1972, pp. 169–74.
9. For a discussion of the various movements of the body of St Tekle Haymanot in relation to the geography of the monastery, see CAMPBELL, I.L., 1994A, p. 5.
10. KAPLAN, S., 2014, p. 446.
11. Debre Libanos of Ham is in today's Eritrea. For information on this monastery, see BAUSI, A., 2005.
12. The patriarch of the Ethiopian Orthodox Church still carries the title '*Ichegé* of the See of St Tekle Haymanot'.
13. While most monasteries have only one *meggabi*, Debre Libanos is unusual in having below the principal *meggabi* a number of *meggabis*, each in charge of a specialised function.
14. MEINARDUS, O., 2005.
15. PEDERSON, K.S., 2007, p. 274.
16. DERAT, M.-L., 2010.
17. DERAT, M.-L., 2005B.
18. FIACCADORI, G., 2007, p. 236; FIACCADORI, G., 2010, p. 529.
19. ANTONIOS ALBERTO, 2013, p. 122, citing ADHANOM, S., 1969, p. 15.
20. AYELE TEKLEHAYMANOT, 1999A, pp. 211–12. Antonios Alberto gives a date of 1440; ANTONIOS ALBERTO, 2013, p. 122.
21. DEBRE-KIDDUS ESTEFANOS, [c.1971], p. 3; ANTONIOS ALBERTO, 2013, p. 123, citing ADHANOM, S., 1969, p. 18.
22. BONECHI, M., 2011; SALVADORE, M., 2017, p. 74.
23. SALVADORE, M., 2017, p. 72.
24. NÚÑEZ, J.G., 2018, p. 209.
25. BECKINGHAM, C.F. & HUNTINGFORD, G.W.B. (EDS.), 1961, vol. 1, pp. 262–3.
26. Description by the 19th-century historian Asma Giyorgis, cited in AYELE TEKLEHAYMANOT, 1994, pp. 98ff.
27. ŠIHĀ B AD-DĪ N AHMAD BIN 'ABD AL-QADER BIN SALEM BIN 'UTMAN, 2003, pp. 186–92.
28. BECKINGHAM, C.F. & HUNTINGFORD, G.W.B. (EDS.), 1961, vol. 1, pp. 340–1; DERAT, M.-L., 2007.
29. ŠIHĀ B AD-DĪ N AHMAD BIN 'ABD AL-QADER BIN SALEM BIN 'UTMAN, ALSO KNOWN AS 'ARAB FAQĪ H, 2003, pp. 246–7.
30. TADDESSE TAMRAT, 1972, p. 301.
31. Tesfa Siyon, who signed himself 'Tesfa Zeon Malhizo' in MS Vat Lib Aeth. 16, f. 61v in the Biblioteca Apostolica Vaticana, had been much troubled by the devastating invasions of Ahmed Grañ. BAUSI, A. & FIACCADORI, G., 2014, p. 525.

32. ANTONIOS ALBERTO, 2013, p. 123.
33. BAUSI, A. & FIACCADORI, G., 2014, p. 525. See also SALVADORE, M., 2017, pp. 186–7, 192.
34. AYELE TEKLEHAYMANOT, 1999A, pp. 374–5, 451–6; AYELE TEKLEHAYMANOT, 1999B, pp. 203–18, 299–308.
35. SALVADORE, M., 2017, pp. 75, 160–1.
36. SALVADORE, M., 2013; SALVADORE, M., 2017, pp. 193–4.
37. BAUSI, A. & FIACCADORI, G., 2014, pp. 525–8.
38. www.annasromguide.dk/personer/dicaantoniolomere.html.
39. NICKELSBURG, G.W.E., 2006.
40. CERULLI, E., 1967, pp. 7–8; PANKHURST, R., 2003B; ANTONIOS ALBERTO, 2013, p. 124.
41. ANTONIOS ALBERTO, 2013, p. 125, citing ADHANOM, S., 1969, p. 27.
42. Tesfa Siyon of Debre Libanos died in Tivoli on 28 August 1550 (or possibly 1552), aged 42. BAUSI, A. & FIACCADORI, G., 2014, p. 525. Matteo Salvadore indicates 1552. SALVADORE, M., 2013; SALVADORE, M., 2017, p. 194.
43. On the side wall of the Chapel of the Saviour (also called the Cinque Chapel, having been built by the Cinque family) in the church of Santa Maria degli Angeli e dei Martiri, Rome, the painting, usually referred to as 'The Praying Pope', and sometimes as 'Kneeling Devotees of the Madonna', is generally attributed to Giulio Mazzoni. The upper register of the painting depicts eight female founders of the basilica, a group that includes an unidentified Ethiopian woman. See TOWNLEY, J., 1821, p. 61.
44. SERGEW HABLE SELLASSIE, 1993, p. 33, citing a manuscript in the church of Mahdere Maryam in Begémdir.
45. SALVADORE, M., 2017, p. 184.
46. Matteo Salvadore states that although Mendez bore much responsibility for the eventual failure of the Jesuit mission, the plans for the mission drawn up by Ignatius of Loyola were partly based on questionable assumptions. SALVADORE, M., 2013. Furthermore, Juan Núñez points out that armed riots against Emperor Susinyos's pro-Catholic policies were already under way during the time of Páez. NÚÑEZ, J.G., 2018, pp. 106–7.
47. PANKHURST, R.K., 1982, pp. 110–12. Azezo adjoins today's Gondar airport, where the monastery church, since rebuilt, is still named Azezo Tekle Haymanot. CAMPBELL, I.L., 1994B; CAMPBELL, I.L., 2004B.
48. UHLIG, S., 2005; DERAT, M.-L., 2007.

2. BAD NEIGHBOURS

49. For a traditional account of the determination of the original site of the monastery church at the time of Emperor Yohannis IV, see CAMPBELL, I.L., 1994A, p. 7.

2. BAD NEIGHBOURS

1. GARRETSON, P.P., 1993, p. 41; SALVADORE, M., 2017, pp. 40–1.
2. KNOX, M., 2000, p. 12.
3. ALOISI, P., 1957, p. 382, cited in KNOX, M., 1986, pp. 34–5. Contemporary historians and Alessandro Lessona himself agreed that Mussolini was only interested in the conquest of Ethiopia for political reasons, and to enhance the international power and prestige of Italy and Fascism. SBACCHI, A., 1997, p. 54 n. 79, citing, *inter alia*, LESSONA, A., 1958, pp. 269–70.
4. For Mussolini's draft directive of 30 Dec. 1934 informing Marshal Badoglio of his plans for the invasion of Ethiopia, see ROCHAT, G., 1971, pp. 102–4 and Doc. 29, pp. 376–9; and ROBERTSON, E.M., 1977, pp. 112, 227 n. 65. For an English translation of the directive, see ADAMTHWAITE, A.P., Doc. 14, pp. 133–4.
5. Harar had been absorbed into the Ethiopian empire by Emperor Menelik in 1887.
6. MIKRE-SELLASSIE GEBRE-AMMANUEL, 2014, pp. 45–6.
7. In the north, under the jurisdiction of the Sacred Congregation of the Oriental Churches, was the Vicariate Apostolic of Abyssinia, while the Vicariate Apostolic of Oromo, and the Prefecture Apostolic of Kaffa in the south-west, were the concern of the Sacred Congregation for the Propagation of the Faith.
8. At the time, these envoys were known as ministers.
9. DUGAN, J. & LAFORE, L., 1973, pp. 85–92.
10. DEL BOCA, A., 1969, p. 21.
11. JONAS, R., 2011, p. 307.
12. JENKINS, P., 2015, pp. 65–6.

3. AN UNHOLY ALLIANCE

1. FATTORINI, E., 2011, p. 8.
2. ANTONIOS ALBERTO, 2013, pp. 160–1.
3. HAILE SELLASSIE I, TR. & ANNOT. E. ULLENDORF, 1999, p. 103.
4. 'Pope Congratulated Mussolini: Emperor Gave Site for Catholic Church in Jerusalem', *New Times and Ethiopia News*, 23, 10 Oct. 1936.

5. KENT, P.C., 1981, pp. 62–3; CECI, L., 2010, pp. 32–3; RAINERI, O. & MARTINEZ D'ALÒS-MONER, A., 2010, p. 1054.
6. ANTONIOS ALBERTO, 2013, p. 127.
7. DEBRE-KIDDUS ESTEFANOS, [c. 1971]; ANTONIOS ALBERTO, 2013, pp. 128–9.
8. ANTONIOS ALBERTO, 1998, pp. 321–3.
9. Ethiopia did not have an ambassador accredited to the Holy See who might have been in a position to garner a degree of support from Pius XI to counter the impact of the Italian clerics.
10. MIKRE-SELLASSIE GEBRE-AMMANUEL, 2014, p. 135, citing TEELING, L.W., 1937, pp. 3–4.
11. CECI, L., 2016, p. 182.
12. FATTORINI, E., 2011, p. 38.
13. BINCHY, D.A., 1970, p. 341.
14. DUGGAN, C., 2013, p. 197.
15. LACROIX-RIZ, A., 1994, p. 53.
16. LACROIX-RIZ, A., 1994, p. 52, citing letter of Charles-Roux, 15 Feb. 1935.
17. Secretary of State Eugenio Pacelli, often considered one of Mussolini's most influential supporters in the Vatican City, would succeed Pope Pius XI as Pius XII in March 1939.
18. LACROIX-RIZ, A., 1994, p. 53, citing letter of Truelle, 16 May 1935.
19. SALVEMINI, G., 1969A, p. 192.
20. KERTZER, D.I., 2014, p. 214.
21. JENKINS, P., 2015, p. 66.
22. A figure of 13,154 churches and monasteries was published in 1965–6. NOSNITSIN, D., FRITSCH, E. & DIMETROS WELDU, 2003, p. 740.
23. SBACCHI, A., 1997, p. 36.
24. For a succinct overview of the history of slavery in and through Ethiopia, see TESHALE TIBEBU, 1995, pp. 53–67.
25. See, for example, CURTIN, P.R., 1983.
26. *Antischiavismo*, March 1927, cited in 'Italian Opinions on Slavery in Ethiopia', *New Times and Ethiopia News*, 15, 15 Aug. 1936; STRANG, G.B., 2017, p. 294.
27. SMIDT, W., 2010, p. 681.
28. BUSTORF, D., 2010, p. 679.
29. BUSTORF, D., 2010, p. 678.
30. Yperite is a highly toxic warfare agent that creates large blisters on the skin and in the lungs, and can be fatal. The name refers to its use by the German army at Ypres, Belgium, in the First World War. Arsine, the most toxic form of arsenic, is a colourless and odourless chemical

warfare agent. Phosgene is a very insidious poison, also used in the First World War, Lethal, colourless and odourless, it was generally used more extensively than arsine as it is non-flammable and thus safer to store and deploy.

31. SBACCHI, A., 1997, p. 36, citing, *inter alia*, ACS-PNF/Pol. 25, folder Torino, 20 Sept. 1935.
32. *La Tribu'*, Spring 1936; ACS-Cultura 155/13, *Various Information Collected at Private Gatherings*, Rome, 20 Aug. 1935; ACS-Int/C. 15/27, Istra, Zagreb, 8 June and 6 July (1935); ACS/SPD-R 2/13 Bis-R/1, *Memorandum for Mussolini (State of Mind of Officers and Soldiers on the Eve of the Italo-EthiopianWar)*, Aug. 1935; ACS-Int/C., Ministry of Interior to Border Police Headquarters, 26 Aug. 1935, cited in SBACCHI, A., 1997, pp. 38, 50 nn. 22–6.
33. *The Tablet*, London, 4 July 1935, p. 7, cited in POYNTER, J.W., 1936.
34. *DDI*, series 8, vol. I, no. 450, Talamo to Mussolini, 27 June 1935, cited in KERTZER, D., 2014, p. 455 n. 8 and VIRTUE, N.G., 2012, p. 295 n. 33.
35. *Rapporti con l'Etiopia—Atteggiamento della Santa Sede*, Talamo to Grazzi, 27 July 1935, ASMAE, AISS, *busta* 56, *sf* 1-b, cited in VIRTUE, N.G., 2012, p. 295 n. 34.
36. SALVEMINI, G., 1936, p. 1.
37. MIKRE-SELLASSIE GEBRE-AMMANUEL, 2014, pp. 145–6.
38. GIOVAGNOLI, A., 2008, pp. 243–4, citing *Discorsi di Pio XI*, D. Berletto, Città de Vaticano, Libreria Editrice Vaticana, 1985, vol. III, pp. 361–2.
39. SBACCHI, A, 1997, p. 39.
40. CECI, L., 2010, p. 33; FATTORINI, E., 2011, pp. 7–8; VIRTUE, N.G., 2012, pp. 296–7; KERTZER, D.I., 2014, pp. 214–17; KORNBERG, J., 2015, pp. 214–15.
41. VIRTUE, N.G., 2012, pp. 295–6.
42. MANHATTAN, A., 1949, pp. 121–2; SALVEMINI, G., 1969A, p. 192.
43. Pacelli to Mussolini, 14 Sept. 1935, ASMAE, AISS, *busta* 56, *fasc* 1, *sf* 1c, cited in KERTZER, D.I., 2014, p. 218. Kertzer notes that according to an informant (ACS, DAGR, *busta* 1320, *informatore* n. 52, Roma, 12 Sept. 1935), the pope sent his envoy Tacchi Venturi on a secret mission to England to lobby local Catholics to support the invasion, but that no evidence has yet come to light to suggest that the trip actually took place. KERTZER, D.I., 2014, p. 456 n. 21. The Holy See considered sending a private letter to Mussolini to attempt a peace initiative, but by 22 September the idea had been dropped. VIRTUE, N.G., 2012, p. 298.
44. ARMSTRONG, K., 2001, pp. 473–6.

45. POLLARD, J., 2014, pp. 158–9.
46. The iconography of the Madonna of the Manganello was actually based on a much earlier theme known as La Madonna del Soccorso (The Madonna of Succour), a canonical rendering of the Mother of Christ. This representation portrayed the Holy Virgin protecting children by striking down the Devil, who was often depicted as an African, or 'Moor'. DUGGAN, C., 2007, between pp. 432 and 433; www.yeshua.it/il%Bestiario%20incensato/la_Madonna_con_il_manganello.htm.
47. For an account of how the popes delegated control over crusaders, see RILEY-SMITH, J., 2009, pp. 50–2.
48. FRANZINELLI, M., 2008, p. 261.
49. FRANZINELLI, M., 2008, p. 261; CECI, L., 2010, p. 126, citing FRANZINELLI, M., 1992, p. 577 and GIULIANI R., 1937.
50. CECI, L., 2010, p. 126, citing FRANZINELLI, M., 1992, pp. 574–7.
51. NOVATI, G.C., 2007, p. 241; CECI, L., 2010, p. 126.
52. MANHATTAN, A., 1949, p. 122.
53. CECI, L., 2008B, p. 130; VIRTUE, N.G., 2012, p. 287.

4. MISSIONARIES OF THE CROSS

1. In his determination to show the League of Nations that Ethiopia was not the aggressor, and confident that the League would take action against Italy, Haile Selassie delayed mobilisation of the Ethiopian military for a year before the invasion. He finally gave the order to mobilise on 28 Sept. 1935—only one week before the invasion was launched. DEL BOCA, A., 1969, p. 37.
2. Haile Selassie's American legal advisor John Spencer points out that the Italians actually launched their southern invasion from bases already established inside Ethiopia. SPENCER, J.H., 1987, p. 60.
3. PEARCE, J., 2014, pp. 163, 564 n. 7, citing DE BONO, E., 1937, p. 253.
4. For a summary of the war of invasion, see OFCANSKY, T.P., 2007.
5. DUGGAN, C., 2013, p. 263, citing Fondazione Mondadori, *archivio Bottai*, *busta* 62, f. 2739, letters to wife, 20 October 1935, 24 Feb. 1936.
6. FALASCA-ZAMPONI, S., 1997, p. 175; SANNEH, L.O., 1996, p. 27. See also NOBILI, E., 2008, p. 273.
7. KERTZER, D.I., 2014, p. 224, citing FRANZINELLI, M., 1995, pp. 311–12.
8. SALVEMINI, G., 1969A, p. 196.
9. BINCHY, D.A., 1970, p. 721.
10. KERTZER, D.I., 2014, p. xxv.

11. CECI, L., 2010, p. 178, citing 'Etiopia religiosa', in *La Civiltà Cattolica*, LXXXVI, 1935, vol. 4, pp. 89–105, esp. p. 93.
12. ASMAE, AISS, *busta* 102, cited in KERTZER, D.I., 2014, pp. 215, 462 n. 35.
13. TESHALE TIBEBU, 1995, pp. 7–12; BINNS, J., 2017, pp. 25–6.
14. *Kirchenzeitung*, Salzburg, 24 Oct. 1935, cited in DESCHNER, K., 2013, pp. 45, 247 n. 139; www.catholic-hierarchy.org.
15. MARTIN, W.C., 1936.
16. KERTZER, D.I., 2014, p. 260.
17. KERTZER, D.I., 2014, p. 207.
18. NOBILI, E, 2008, p. 273; CECI, L., 2010, pp. 86–7; KERTZER, D.I., 2014, p. 222.
19. BINCHY, D.A., 1970, p. 679; BAER, G.W., 1976, p. 161; LACROIX-RIZ, A., 1994, p. 53; NOBILI, E., 2008, p. 273; CECI, L., 2010, pp. 86–7; MIKRE-SELLASSIE GEBRE-AMMANUEL, 2014, p. 159; KERTZER, D.I., 2014, p. 222; CECI, L., 2016, p. 182.
20. FRANZINELLI, M., 2008.
21. CECI, L., 2010, pp. 100, 130, 132.
22. PARSONS, G., 2008, p. 68.
23. SALVEMINI, G., 1969A, pp. 191–2.
24. NOBILI, E., 2008, pp. 267–9.
25. GEMELLI, A., 1935A, cited in NOBILI, E., 2008, pp. 267–9.
26. KERTZER, D.I., 2014, p. 222.
27. CECI, L., p. 100, citing GEMELLI, A., 1935.
28. CROCIANI, P. & BATTISTELLI, P., 2010, pp. 8–9, 26.
29. For an interesting analysis of Fascist construction of the morality of the invasion, see FALASCA-ZAMPONI, S., 1997, pp. 171–83.
30. SALVEMINI, G., 1936, p. 1.
31. FRANZINELLI, M., 2008, p. 257.
32. BAER, G.W., 1976, p. 161. See also BINCHY, D.A., 1970, p. 678.
33. SALVEMINI, G., 1969A, p. 193; BINCHY, D.A., p. 168. See also BAER, G.W., 1976, p. 162; MIKRE-SELLASSIE GEBRE-AMMANUEL, 2014, p. 160.
34. KERTZER, D.I., 2014, p. 225, citing DE FELICE, 1974, p. 761; *Il Popolo d'Italia*, 19 Dec. 1935.
35. PARSONS, G., 2008, p. 68.
36. NOBILI, E., 2008, p. 271.
37. CECI, L., 2010, p. 178, citing 'Il cristianesimo degli Abissini', in *La Civiltà Cattolica*, LXXXVI, 1935, vol. 4, pp. 47–87, esp. p. 486.
38. CECI. L., 2010, pp. 98–9; KERTZER, D.I., 2014, p. 229, citing TERHOEVEN, P., 2006, pp. 102, 104, 105 and CECI, L., 2012, p. 92.
39. DUGGAN, C., 2013, p. 259.

40. KERTZER, D.I., 2014, p. 228, citing ASV, AESI, *posiz* 967, vol. 5, f. 201r, 'Istruzioni per Monsignor Roveda da impartire verbalmente ai vescovi d'Italia', 30 Nov. 1935.
41. DUGGAN, C., 2013, p. 275.
42. ZEWDÉ RETA, 2005 EC, p. 312.
43. ZEWDÉ RETA, 2005 EC, p. 307, based on Zewdé's translation of the letter into Amharic.
44. ZEWDÉ RETA, 2005 EC, p. 307, based on Zewdé's translation of the letter into Amharic.
45. CECI, L., 2010, pp. 43–54; CECI, L., 2016, pp. 178–9.
46. KORNBERG, J., 2015, p. 217.
47. BAER, G.W., 1976, pp. 121–46.
48. NYSTROM, H., TR. GEBREYEHU TEFERI & DESSALEGN ALEMU, 2014, pp. 178–9. See also MOCKLER, A., 1984, p. 72.
49. PERSOON, J. & NOSNITSIN, D., 2005; HENZE, P., 2006. In 2001 *Memhir* Gebre Aregawi provided Paul Henze with a foundation date of 1327 EC (1334/5). HENZE, P., 2006, pp. 664–5.
50. DANIÉL KIBRET, 1999 EC, p. 511, giving a date of 11 Tahsus, 1928 EC (22 Dec. 1935) for the bombing. See also HENZE, P., 2006, pp. 663–5.
51. At the time of Ethiopianist Paul Henze's visit to the restored monastery in 2001, the monastery consisted of around 120 monks, nuns, priests and deacons, with between 300 and 400 students attending the monastic school. HENZE, P., 2006, p. 664.
52. USSME, D5, *busta* 123, *fasc* 8, f. 020066 of Badoglio, 25 Dec. 1935, cited in DOMINIONI, M., 2008, p. 46.
53. HAILE SELLASSIE I, TR. & ANNOT. E. ULLENDORF, 1999, p. 259.
54. VAN DONZEL, E., 2010; WUDU TAFETE KASSU, 2010;
55. GENTILLI, R., 1992, p. 139.
56. KERTZER, D.I., 2014, pp. 223, 233, 461 n. 26.
57. KORNBERG, J., 2015, p. 217.
58. KENT, P.C., 1984, p. 141, citing FO J429/180/1, Montgomery to Eden, 3 Jan. 1936; LENTZ, H.M., 2002, p. 105.
59. SALVEMINI, G., 1969A, p. 194.
60. BAER, G.W., 1976, p. 162; LACROIX-RIZ, A., 1994, pp. 53–4.
61. KERTZER, D.I., 2014, pp. 229–30.
62. LACROIX-RIZ, A., 1994, p. 54, citing letter of Charles-Roux, 9 Jan. 1936.
63. CECI, L., 2010, p. 178, citing G. Goletto, 'Il clero eretico dell'Abissinia', in *Missioni Consolata*, XXXVIII, 1936, 1, pp. 6–8.
64. HAILE SELLASSIE I, TR. & ANNOT. E. ULLENDORF, 1999, p. 263.
65. CECI, L., 2010, p. 126, citing FRANZINELLI, M., 1992, p. 577.

66. CECI, L., 2010, p. 127; NOVATI, G.C., 2007, p. 241.
67. The Italians named a street in Addis Ababa after Reginaldo Giuliani.
68. BAER, G.W., 1976, p. 161. Baer refers to Colli incorrectly as archbishop of Parma, an appointment he received later, in 1955.
69. MIKRE-SELLASSIE GEBRE-AMMANUEL, 2014, p. 159, citing *New Times and Ethiopia News*, 3 Oct. 1936 and SALVEMINI, G., 1969A, p. 193.
70. The four cardinals present on 23 February were Vincenzo La Puma, who had been appointed cardinal by Pius XI in December 1935, Carlo Salotti (December 1935), Camillo Laurenti (June 1921) and the very senior Domenico Serafini, prefect of the Congregation for the Propagation of the Faith (May 1914). SALVEMINI, G., 1969A, p. 194; www.catholic-hierarchy.org.
71. SALVEMINI, G., 1936, p. 1.
72. SALVEMINI, G., 1969A, p. 193.
73. CECI, L., 2010, pp. 130–1; caption, Fig. 5 between pp. 146 and 147. The references to *veterani* and *soldati invalidi* in Ceci's text (citing Salvemini) indicate that the Blackshirt company accompanying the icon was the strongly Fascist 6th 'Tevere' Division. This in turn indicates that the destination would have been Mogadishu rather than Massawa.
74. CECI, L., 2010, p. 131.
75. CECI, L., 2010, p. 133, citing VIOLI, R.P., 1996, p. 83.
76. FRANZINELLI, M., 2008, pp. 255–6.
77. CECI, L., 2010, p. 131–2.
78. CECI, L., 2010, p. 131, citing FRANZINELLI, M., 1992, p. 566.
79. CECI, L., 2010, pp. 130–5. No doubt some, if not all, of these icons were consecrated copies of the originals, which can still be seen in their original sanctuaries in Italy.
80. HELDMAN, M.E., 1993, p. 71. The church, has, however, since been reconstructed on at least one occasion.
81. GERSTER, G., 1970, pp. 95–8; MERCIER, J., 2014, pp. 20–30.
82. KERTZER, D.I., 2014, p. 216.
83. NOBILI, E., 2008, p. 278.
84. HAILE SELLASSIE I, TR. E. ULLENDORF, 1999, pp. 235, 273; DEL BOCA, A., 1969, pp. 104, 165; MOCKLER, A., 1984, p. 76.
85. CONSOCIAZIONE TURISTICA ITALIANI, 1938, p. 442.
86. 'The Patriots as Seen at the Time—Report from Harar—September 7', extract from *New Times and Ethiopia News*, 15 Oct. 1936, in *Ethiopia Observer*, III, 10, p. 319. See also PANKHURST, S., 1955, p. 541, and MIKRE-SELLASSIE GEBRE-AMMANUEL, 2014, p. 184.
87. PEARCE, J., 2014, p. 285.

88. BERNOVILLE, G., 1948, pp. 332–3.
89. MIKRE-SELLASSIE GEBRE-AMMANUEL, 2014, pp. 167–8, citing *The Tablet*, 30 May 1936, p. 688.
90. HAILE SELLASSIE I, TR. & ANNOT. E. ULLENDORF, 1999, p. 295.

5. A HAPPY TRIUMPH

1. KERTZER, D.I., 2014, p. 237, citing ACS, CR, *busta* 68, Tacchi Venturi to Mussolini, Rome, 6 May 1936.
2. CECI, L., 2010, p. 116.
3. CECI, L., 2010, pp. 116–17.
4. BINCHY, D.A., 1970, pp. 648–52; CECI, L., 2010, pp. 159–60; POLLARD, J., 2014, p. 258.
5. KENT, P.C., 1984, p. 144.
6. MIKRE-SELLASSIE GEBRE-AMMANUEL, 2014, pp. 154–5. The complete speech is in *Civiltà Cattolica*, 2, 1936, p. 422.
7. BINCHY, D.A., 1970, pp. 648–51.
8. BINCHY, D.A., 1970, p. 650.
9. BAER, G.W., 1976, p. 281; BOTTAI, G., 1949, p. 125.
10. See, for example, LACROIX-RIZ, A., 1994, p. 54.
11. 'The Patriots as Seen at the Time—Report from Harar—September 7', extract from *New Times and Ethiopia News*, 15 Oct. 1936, in *Ethiopia Observer*, III, 10, p. 319. See also PANKHURST, S., 1955, p. 541, and MIKRE-SELLASSIE GEBRE-AMMANUEL, 2014, p. 184.
12. Thursday was actually 7 May. According to Anthony Mockler, the Italians arrived in Harar on Friday, 8 May, killing, in the process, 'two hundred Amhara'. MOCKLER, A., 1984, p. 145.
13. 'The Patriots as Seen at the Time—Report from Harar—September 7', extract from *New Times and Ethiopia News*, 15 Oct. 1936, in *Ethiopia Observer*, III, 10, p. 319. See also PANKHURST, S., 1955, p. 541, and MIKRE-SELLASSIE GEBRE-AMMANUEL, 2014, p. 184.
14. LE HOUÉROU, 1994B, p. 823.
15. DEL BOCA, A., 1969, p. 112.
16. MOCKLER, A., 1984, p. 127.
17. GRAZIANI, R., 2001, pp. 52–3; MOCKLER, A., 1984, pp. 127, 145. George Baer says that Graziani 'broke some bones'. BAER, G.W., 1976, p. 274.
18. 'Directive and Plan of Action to Solve the Abyssinian Question', memorandum, Mussolini to Badoglio, Rome, 30 Dec. 1934; ADAMTHWAITE, A.P., 1977, pp. 133–4.

19. DEL BOCA, A., 1969, p. 214, citing *New Times and Ethiopia News*, 6 June 1936.
20. ANON., 1936.
21. MINISTRY OF JUSTICE, 1950, p. 24, quoting Italian sources. For the use of gas by the Italians in Ethiopia, see DEL BOCA, A., 1996; GENTILLI, R., 2003; BAUDENDISTEL, R., 2006.
22. DUGGAN, C., 2013, pp. 336–7, citing CALAMANDREI, C., 1982, pp. 86–7.
23. Affidavit No. 88, *Basha* Desta Amanuel, MINISTRY OF JUSTICE, 1950, p. 3.
24. Affidavit No. 88, *Basha* Desta Amanuel, MINISTRY OF JUSTICE, 1950, p. 3.
25. GOVERNO GENERALE, STATO MAGGIORE, A.O.I., 1939, pp. 13–15.
26. 'The Patriots as Seen at the Time—Report from Harar—September 7', extract from *New Times and Ethiopia News*, 15 Oct. 1936, in *Ethiopia Observer*, III, 10, p. 319. See also PANKHURST, S., 1955, p. 541 and MIKRE-SELLASSIE GEBRE-AMMANUEL, 2014, p. 184.
27. CONSOCIAZIONE TURISTICA ITALIANI, 1938, p. 561.
28. CONSOCIAZIONE TURISTICA ITALIANI, 1938, p. 561.
29. LÁSZLÓ, S., 2015, pp. 113–14.
30. GOVERNO GENERALE, STATO MAGGIORE, A.O.I., 1939, pp. 22–6.
31. Personal communication, Seifu Kassa, Garland, Texas, to the present author, 10 May 2016. See also the documentary *If Only I Were That Warrior*, Awen Films.
32. SELTENE SEYOUM, 2003B.
33. MERSHA ALEHEGNE, 2010, p. 140.
34. LÁSZLÓ, S., 2015, p. 115.
35. MOCKLER, A., 1984, p. 161.
36. FESSEHA MEKURIA & RUBENSON, S., 2000.
37. LÁSZLÓ, S., 2015, pp. 115–16. The viceroy was not, however, personally present at the tribunal to witness Pétros's address.
38. POGGIALI, C., 1971, p. 76. See also LE HOUÉROU, F., 1994A, p. 74.
39. LE HOUÉROU, F., 1994A, p. 73, citing GIOVANNI GEBRE-IYESUS, 1984, p. 351. Giovanni was the son of Ethiopia's scholarly former ambassador in Rome, Afe-Werq Gebre-Iyesus. ROUAUD, A., 1991, pp. 301–2.
40. PEARCE, J., 2014, pp. 363, 598, citing Konovalov, F., unpublished manuscript as newly translated by J. Calvitt Clarke III, in CLARKE, J. C., 2008.
41. MERSHA ALEHEGNE, 2010, p. 140.
42. LE HOUÉROU, F., 1994A, p. 74, citing GIOVANNI GEBRE-IYESUS, 1984, p. 342.

43. Telegram, Graziani to Lessona, no. 8906, 20 July 1936, MINISTRY OF JUSTICE, 1949, Doc. 23, p. 14.
44. SELTENE SEYOUM, 1999, pp. 236–7, 383, citing interview, Ato Mäket Zäläqä, 20 Jan. 1995, Dangela, Ethiopia.
45. SELTENE SEYOUM, 1999, p. 237.
46. 'The Patriots as Seen at the Time—Report from Harar—September 7', extract from *New Times and Ethiopia News*, 15 Oct. 1936, in *Ethiopia Observer*, III, 10, p. 320.
47. 'The Patriots as Seen at the Time—Report from Harar—September 7', extract from *New Times and Ethiopia News*, 15 Oct. 1936, in *Ethiopia Observer*, III, 10, p. 320.
48. 'The Patriots as Seen at the Time—Report from Harar—September 7', extract from *New Times and Ethiopia News*, 15 Oct. 1936, in *Ethiopia Observer*, III, 10, p. 320.
49. Telegram, Graziani to Lessona, 30 July 1936, MINISTRY OF JUSTICE, 1949, p. 14.
50. MIKRE-SELLASSIE GEBRE-AMMANUEL, 2014, p. 162, citing *Gazzetta del Popolo*, 22 Oct. 1936.
51. KENT, P.C., 1984, p. 147.
52. www.catholic-hierarchy.org.
53. *Foreign Relations of the United States Diplomatic Papers, 1936, Vol. III, the Near East and Africa*, Washington, 1953, 865D.404/7, Minister Resident in Ethiopia to Secretary of State, No. 193, 15 Oct. 1936.
54. KENT, P.C., 1984, p. 147, citing PRO, FO, J8531/3957/1, Roberts to Eden, 27 Oct. 1936, and J8291/4321/1, Mallet to Eden, 28 Oct. 1936. See also SUNDKLER, B. & STEED, C., 2000, p. 614.

6. CIVILISING ACTIONS

1. Born in Campobasso in 1877, Pirzio-Biroli fought in Libya in 1911–14, and was a colonel in the First World War. Commander of the Italian army in Eritrea, he was appointed governor of Amhara on 15 June 1936. DOMINIONI, M., 2002, pp. 4–5.
2. Telegram, Graziani to Lessona, 11 Sept. 1936, DEPARTEMENT DE LA PRESSE ET DE L'INFORMATION DU GOUVERNEMENT IMPERIAL D'ETHIOPIE, c.1945, p. 22.
3. Telegram, Graziani to Pirzio-Biroli, 11 Sept. 1936, MINISTRY OF JUSTICE, 1949, Doc. 44, p. 26.
4. Telegram, Pirzio-Biroli to Graziani, 11 Sept. 1936, quoted in telegram, Graziani to Lessona, 12 Sept. 1936, DEPARTEMENT DE LA

Presse et de l'Information du Gouvernement Imperial d'Ethiopie, n.d., p. 29; Ministry of Justice, 1949, Doc. 45, p. 26.
5. Kertzer, D.I., 2014, p. 465 n. 9, citing Gentile, E., 1993, p. 127.
6. Haile Selassie I, ed. H. Marcus, 1994, pp. 13–15.
7. The church had been rebuilt by Emperor Menelik's minister for war, *Fitawrari* Habte-Giyorgis.
8. Interview, *Abba* Mikaél, with Richard and Rita Pankhurst, Degife Gebre-Tsadiq (of Addis Ababa University), and the present author, at Midr Kebd, May 1997. According to *Abba* Mikaél, some members of the armed gang, who said at the time that they were fighting for the Italians, were reportedly later shot by the Italian officers, which suggests that some bandits had infiltrated the group.
9. Telegram, Graziani to Cabinet, 21 Oct. 1936, Ministry of Justice, 1949, p. 22. See also Chernetsov, S., 2005, p. 423.
10. Gentilli, R., 2003, p. 142; Rochat, G., 2008, p. 41. See also Gentilli, R., 1992, pp. 132–3. The amount of yperite contained in a C-500T bomb varied as the technology evolved. An average of 212 kg is assumed here. Pedriali, F., 1996, p. 95.
11. Mikre-Sellassie Gebre-Ammanuel, 2014, pp. 187–8, citing Adugna Amanu, 1969, p. 24. Mikre-Sellassie adds that the monks who survived the strikes on the monastery were rounded up and taken to the town of Mojo (see Map 6), where they were executed. This event actually relates to a later attack on Ziqwala, in June 1937. See Chapter 15.
12. Baer, G.W., 1976, p. 161: See also *Popolo d'Italia*, 29 Oct. 1935, cited in Mikre-Sellassie Gebre-Ammanuel, 2014, p. 158.
13. Teeling, L.W., 1937, pp. 128–9, cited in Mikre-Sellassie Gebre-Ammanuel, 2014, p. 144.
14. Pollard, J., 2016, p. 182.
15. Mikre-Sellassie Gebre-Ammanuel, 2014, p. 144, citing *Gazzetta del Popolo*, 22 Oct. 1936.
16. Telegram, Graziani to General Bergonzoli, 24 Jan. 1936, Doc. 7, Ministry of Justice, 1949, p. 6.
17. Telegram, Graziani to General Gallina, 27 Oct. 1936 quoted in a telegram of the same date from Graziani to Rome. Ministry of Justice, 1949, Doc. 37, p. 22.
18. Taddesse Mécha, [c.1943 EC], p. 71 in the small-format (21x16 cm) edition; p. 67 in the large-format (24x17 cm) edition. See also Mockler, A., 1972, p. 205; Mockler, A., 1984, pp. 157, 165, 167; Kefyalew Mehari, 2001, p. 110; Borruso, P., 2002, p. 204.

19. ANON., 1986 EC, p. 36. This article (in Amharic) was based on an unpublished manuscript, *Illubabor*, by Zewdé Dubale, and an interview with *Aleqa* (later, *Liqetebebt*) Indale Biresaw in Gore.
20. ANON., 1986 EC.
21. Immediately after the bishop's execution, in front of the assembled townspeople, the Italian officer who had given the order to shoot asked *Aleqa* Biresaw Yimer, head of the church of St Mary in Gore (and father of *Liqetebebt* Indale), if the execution had not been the appropriate punishment for the bishop's defiance of Italian rule. The *Aleqa*, a good friend of the bishop, appeared to reply that the bishop's death was good. The interpreter had translated his words literally, ignoring, or perhaps unaware of, the deliberate ambiguity of the erudite cleric's Amharic, of which the hidden meaning (which of course the Italians failed to grasp) was that the Italians had killed a good man. ANON., 1986 EC, p. 37; BORRUSO, P., 2009, p. 24; TEKALIGN GEDAMU, 2011. p. 19 and n. 6, p. 463; interview, Tekalign Gedamu, by the present author, Addis Ababa, February 2020. Tekalign Gedamu is the grandson of *Aleqa* Biresaw Yimer, and the niece of *Liqetebebt* Indale Biresaw.
22. Telegram, Graziani to Lessona, 11 Dec. 1936, quoting Pirzio Biroli, MINISTRY OF JUSTICE, 1949, p. 9.
23. Letter, Graziani to Aberra Kassa, 11 Dec. 1936, SALOME GEBRE-EGZIABHER, 1966, pp. 303–4, citing MELESELIÑ ANILEY, 1947 EC, p. 38. Salome provides the date of 11 Dec. from the Amharic version of the letter.
24. Letter, General Tracchia to Aberra Kassa, date in the month of Tahsas (Dec.–Jan.) not given, as quoted in the testimony of *Lij* Hayle-Maryam Gazmu, MINISTRY OF JUSTICE, 1950, p. 2. See also SALOME GEBRE-EGZIABHER, 1966, p. 301.
25. According to Salome Gebre-Egziabher, they were also beheaded. SALOME GEBRE-EGZIABHER, 1966, p. 301.
26. Telegram, Graziani to Lessona, 21 Dec. 1936, MINISTRY OF JUSTICE, 1949, Doc. 13, p. 10. See also the testimony of Hayle-Maryam Gazmu, MINISTRY OF JUSTICE, 1950, pp. 2–3.
27. MIKRE-SELLASSIE GEBRE-AMMANUEL, 2014, pp. 162–3, citing *L'Osservatore Romano*, 23 Jan. 1937 and *New Times and Ethiopia News*, 13 Feb. 1937.
28. DUGGAN, C., 2013, p. 288.
29. Castellani was appointed vicar apostolic of Addis Ababa and apostolic delegate to Italian East Africa on 25 March 1937; www.catholic-hierarchy.org.

30. PERRET, M., 1986, p. 65, citing letter, Col. Azolino Hazon to Governo Generale, No. 21/358, 22 March 1937, ACS, *fondo* Graziani, *sc* 48, *fasc* 42, *sf* 12, and report by General Maletti, 30 Aug. 1937, ACS, *fondo* Graziani, *sc* 31, *fasc* 29, *sf* 42.

7. TERROR IN THE CAPITAL

1. For a detailed account of the conspiracy behind *Yekatit 12* as summarised here, see CAMPBELL, I.L., 2010.
2. Paolo Borruso provides a figure of 'around 2,500 poor' present at the ceremony. BORRUSO, P., 2020, p. 88.
3. See CAMPBELL, I.L., 2017 for a detailed analysis of the massacre of Addis Ababa.
4. Dr Shashka blamed a certain Madame Dabbert, whom he referred to as a sinister Russian, for informing Italian military officers about the treasure trove in the cathedral while masquerading as a devoted friend of Ethiopia. SAVA, L., 1941B.
5. SAVA, L., 1941B; LE HOUÉROU, F., 1994A, p. 80.
6. POGGIALI, C., 1971, p. 183; DEL BOCA, A., 1986, p. 85.
7. Affidavit, Captain Toka, MINISTRY OF JUSTICE, 1950, p. 8. According to Alberto Sbacchi, based on Italian sources, twenty mines were placed to blow up the cathedral. SBACCHI, A., 1997, p. 85. However, if this is true, they were either not detonated or were ineffective, for the building survived intact.
8. TEMESGEN GEBRÉ, 2001 EC, p. 93.
9. POGGIALI, C., p. 183; DEL BOCA, A., 1986A, p. 85.
10. Report and Covering Memorandum 147/30/37, 1 March 1937, Great Britain, Public Record Office, File FO/371/20927, p. 4, para. 5.
11. See CAMPBELL, I.L., 2017, p. 193, and phonogram, 21 Feb. 1937, Giovanni Sindico, Fascist Party Office to Chef de Cabinet, p. 397.
12. MINISTRY OF JUSTICE, 1950, p. 7.
13. Telegram, Mussolini to Graziani, No. 93980, 21 Feb. 1937, cited in DOMINIONI, M., 2008A, pp. 179, 330 n. 7.
14. Interview, *Dyakon* Dawit Gebre-Mesqel, Addis Ababa, 24 Feb. 2009.
15. Interview, *Dyakon* Dawit Gebre-Mesqel, Addis Ababa, 24 Feb. 2009.
16. Interview, *Dyakon* Dawit Gebre-Mesqel, Addis Ababa, 24 Feb. 2009.
17. Interview, *Agefari* Gebre-Medhin, who had served the church of St Peter and St Paul since 1909/10, Addis Ababa, 1963, cited in HAILE GABRIEL DAGNE, 1987, pp. 66, 77 n. 7.
18. Haile Gabriel Dagne has the full name of this church as Tserha Ariam Rufael. HAILE GABRIEL DAGNE, 1987, p. 68.

19. Interview, *Liqetebebt* Sawita Selassie, who had lived in the area of the church of St Rufael since childhood, and *Qes Gebez* Welde Kidan, church administrator, Addis Ababa, 1963, cited in HAILE GABRIEL DAGNE, 1987, pp. 68, 77 n. 10.
20. Interview, *Liqetebebt* Sawita Selassie and *Qes Gebez* Welde Kidan, Addis Ababa, 1963, cited in HAILE GABRIEL DAGNE, 1987, pp. 68, 77 n. 10.
21. Interview, *Liqe Mezemeran* Tefere-Werq, head of the church of Lideta Maryam since 1932/3, Addis Ababa, 1963, cited in HAILE GABRIEL DAGNE, 1987, pp. 72–3, 78 n. 77.
22. STRACHAN, B., 2014.
23. Interview, secretary of the church of Yeka Mikaél, *Abba* Kebede Welde Tsadiq, *Aleqa* Gebre Selassie Yeshanew and *Ato* Kibru, Addis Ababa, 1963, cited in HAILE GABRIEL DAGNE, 1987, pp. 65–6, 77 n. 5. See also CHERNETSOV, S., 2005, p. 422 for mention of reprisals against the church of St Michael.
24. Interview, Melake Tsehay Zeleke Habtemariam, the head of the church of Intotto Maryam, and *Memhir* Gebre-Selassie, Addis Ababa, 1963, cited in HAILE GABRIEL DAGNE, 1987, pp. 61, 77 n. 3.
25. KAPLAN, S., 2007.
26. HAILE GABRIEL DAGNE, 1987, pp. 74, 77 n. 20, citing the journal *Menen*, 7, 5, Yekatit 1955 EC.
27. Interview, *Qes* Ermyas (general secretary, Emperor Menelik Memorial Organisation), Addis Ababa, 1963, cited in HAILE GABRIEL DAGNE, 1987, pp. 75, 77 n. 21.
28. SAVA, L., 1941.
29. KENT, P.C., 1984, p. 148, citing PRO, FO, R1427/135/22, 25 Feb. 1937; POLLARD, J., 2014, p. 258.
30. MIKRE-SELLASSIE GEBRE-AMMANUEL, 2014, pp. 163–4, citing *Fides News Service*, 10 July 1937, pp. 162–3, based on an interview of Cardinal Tisserant.
31. GRUBB, N., 1943, p. 119.
32. GRUBB, N., 1943, p. 137. It is not clear which cathedral Grubb is referring to here.
33. The BCMS was unique among the Protestant missions in Ethiopia in adopting this policy of working with the Ethiopian Orthodox Church. LAUNHARDT, J., 2004, p. 65; MIKRE-SELLASSIE GEBRE-AMMANUEL, 2014, pp. 39–40.
34. GRUBB, N., 1943, p. 153.
35. See, for example, LASS-WESTPHAL, I., 1972, p. 99.
36. GRUBB, N., 1943, pp. 156.
37. GRUBB, N., 1943, pp. 153–4.

38. TEKLE-TSADIK MEKURIA, 2008 EC, pp. 62–3; CAMPBELL, I.L., 2017, p. 201.
39. TEMESGEN GEBRÉ, 2001 EC, pp. 99–100.
40. TEMESGEN GEBRÉ, 2001 EC, p. 100.
41. Temesgen uses the Amharic term *menekosat*.
42. TEMESGEN GEBRÉ, 2001 EC, p. 100.
43. The surviving prisoners were released when Ethiopia was liberated in 1941. QUINTON, A.G.H., 1949, pp. 28–9.

8. A BUNGLED MISSION

1. Personal communication to the author by Simi'on's nephew, Bishop (later, Cardinal Archbishop) Birhane-Yesus Suraphael Demirew, Addis Ababa, 1997.
2. While local informants were under the impression that the search party of 22 Feb. was under the command of Colonel Arduino Garelli, a *carabinieri* report by Major Quercia states that it was led by Major Biancoli. Report No. 184-12-21, Mario Quercia, Addis Ababa, 14 March 1937, p. 2.
3. Interview, Tibebe Kassa, Sella Dingay, 2004. Tibebe was not related to *Ras* Kassa Haylu.
4. Interview of Father Aklilu Gebré conducted by Dr Birhanu Abebe during the making of the film *La conquista di un impero*.
5. Interview, Tibebe Kassa, Wusha Gedel, Debre Libanos, 1995.
6. The church of Kateba Maryam was founded in the 15th century by Merha Kristos, the ninth abbot of Debre Libanos, during the reign of Emperor Zer'a Ya'iqob.
7. Interview, Tibebe Kassa, Wusha Gedel, Debre Libanos, 1995.
8. Interview, Tibebe Kassa, Wusha Gedel, Debre Libanos, 1995.
9. 'Bonus Clip: The Massacre of Debre Libanos—If Only I Were That Warrior', Awen Films, https://vimeo.com, 24 March 2017. *Meggabi* Welde-Tinsa'e's knowledge of this little-known episode supports his credibility as an informant on the history of the monastery during the Italian occupation.
10. MINISTRY OF JUSTICE, 1950, p. 10.

9. A BEAUTIFUL CONQUEST

1. Telegram, Graziani to General Nasi, Governor of Harar, 1 Mar. 1937, MINISTRY OF JUSTICE, 1949, Doc. 27, pp. 16–17, 48.

2. Telegram, General Nasi to his subordinate officer, 2 Mar. 1937, quoted in Graziani's telegram to Rome of 3 March 1937, Doc. 11, MINISTRY OF JUSTICE, 1949.
3. DEPARTEMENT DE LA PRESSE ET DE L'INFORMATION DU GOUVERNEMENT IMPERIAL D'ETHIOPIE, n.d., pp. 64–5; DEL BOCA, A., 1969, p. 224. The original Italian refers to 'stregoni e ribelli'.
4. *New Times and Ethiopian News*, 6 Mar. 1937.
5. STEER, G.L., 2009, p. 40.
6. CAMPBELL, I.L., 2017, pp. 274–8.
7. PERSOON, J., 2007.
8. PERSOON, J., 2007. The date of the attack (Megabit 12, 1929 EC, i.e., 24 March 1937) is provided in KEFYALEW MEHARI, 2001, p. 112. One of Father Kefyalew's informants claimed that the final death toll was in excess of 513 monks. KEFYALEW MEHARI, 2001, p. 112. See also CHERNETSOV, S., 2005, p. 423.
9. KEFYALEW MEHARI, 2001, p. 112.
10. DANIÉL KIBRET, 1999 EC, p. 511.
11. MIKRE-SELLASSIE GEBRE-AMMANUEL, 2014, p. 168, citing *Fides News Service*, 10 July 1937, pp, 162–3; *New Times and Ethiopia News*, 17 July 1937, p. 7.
12. Telegram, Graziani to Lessona, 26 Mar. 1937, Doc. 40, MINISTRY OF JUSTICE, 1949, pp. 23–4.
13. SELTENE SEYOUM, 1999.
14. BOSC-TIESSÉ, C., 2007.
15. SELTENE SEYOUM, 1999, pp. 54, 73.
16. KEFYALEW MEHARI, 2001, p. 112.
17. Interview, Reverend Daniél Seifemikaél, 9 Aug. 2018, offices of the Ethiopian Orthodox Tewahido Church Development and Inter-Church Aid Commission, Addis Ababa.
18. WION, A., 2010.
19. Local traditions—not uncommon in Ethiopian church communities—trace its roots as far back as the 4th century, and the establishment of Christianity as Ethiopia's state religion.
20. BOSC-TIESSÉ, C. & FIACCADORI, G., 2005.
21. HABTEMICHAEL KIDANE, 2005.
22. Interview, *Abba* Bi'isé Tiruneh, at the age of 68 years, with scholar Firekal Yigret, Debre Werq, 31 July 2018. Information on the attack is also published by the church of Debre Werq Maryam in a pamphlet, DEBRE WERQ MARYAM, 1991 EC, available at the church. The priests say that the bomb contained chemicals. Although there were instances of Italian artillery ammunition containing gas, these were sometimes

problematic for the Italians, so their use by artillery was less common than the use of gas by the Regia Aeronautica.

23. There are also ancient vestments of Ethiopian sovereigns, a crown of the king of Gojjam, and other sacred artefacts. Bosc-Tiessé, C. & Fiaccadori, G., 2005; Debre Werq Maryam, 1991 EC.
24. Seltene Seyoum, 1999, pp. 54, 73.

10. PREPARING THE KILLING FIELDS

1. Campbell, I.L., 1994A, p. 5.
2. Report, General Pietro Maletti to Graziani, 'Convento di Debra Libanos', 21 April, 1937, ACS, *fondo* Graziani, *busta* 48, *fasc* 42, *sf* 12.
3. Report, Major Mario Quercia to Governo Generale, No. 184-12-21, 14 March 1937, together with cover sheet, Colonel Azolino Hazon (chief commander of the *carabinieri*) to Governo Generale, No. 21/297, 16 March 1937, ACS, *fondo* Graziani, *busta* 48, *fasc* 42, *sf* 12. See also Le Houérou, F., 1994B, p. 82 and Perret, M., 1986, p. 69.
4. In 1995 Tibebe Kassa provided information to the present author about the Debre Libanos *carabinieri* station, which was also mentioned by Aklilu Gebré in his interview in *La conquista di un impero*. In 1994 *Fitawrari* Nebiyye-Li'ul explained that *Ras* Kassa had a house in Wusha Gedel (not to be confused with his house at Chagel), but that it had since been demolished.
5. Telegram, Graziani to Tracchia, No. 720, 11 March 1937, ACS, *fondo* Graziani, *busta* 48, *fasc* 42, *sf* 12.
6. 'Bonus Clip: The Massacre of Debre Libanos—If Only I Were That Warrior', Awen Films, https://vimeo.com, 24 March 2017. Knowledge of this little-known fact on the part of *Meggabi* Welde-Tinsa'e again indicates that he was a well-informed interviewee.
7. Information provided by *Fitawrari* Nebiyye-Li'ul and Tibebe Kassa. See also Debre Libanos Gedam, [c.2010], p. 6, which states that the event was to incorporate the inauguration of the new *ichegé*, and that the order to attend came from General Tracchia.
8. The term *attentato* was regularly used by Graziani in reference to the attack of 12 Yekatit. Although 'strike' may be a more accurate literal translation, the term 'attempt' is adopted here.
9. For more details of the various claims made by the royal military advocate involving the Patriots and the monastery of Debre Libanos in the attack at the Governo Generale, see Campbell, I.L., 2014, pp. 76–9.

10. Memorandum, Franceschino, 21 Apr. 1937, cited in Borruso, P., 2001.
11. Quoted from Franceschino's report (no date mentioned) in Graziani's telegram to Lessona of 21 May 1937, Doc. 31, Ministry of Justice, 1949, pp. 18–19.
12. For a more detailed commentary on the findings considered by Franceschino, see Carvigiani, A., 2019.
13. General Maletti replaced General Tracchia in that capacity. Perret, M., 1986, p. 71 n. 1.
14. Labanca, N., 2007.
15. Telegram, Graziani to Lessona, 19 Mar. 1937, Doc. 28, Ministry of Justice, 1949, p. 17.
16. Interviews, *Debtera* Zelleqe and *Meggabi* Fiqre-Iyesus, Laga Weldé, 1994. The site of Laga Weldé is referred to as Chafé in Debre Libanos Gedam [c.2010], p. 8.
17. Although the Italian documents refer to executions having taken place at Shinkurt, the execution site of Laga Weldé is actually around 4 km from Shinkurt.
18. Following realignment, the present Debre Birhan–Ankober road runs some 2 km south of the execution site. The old road is disused in this section. In 2015 access to the site was facilitated by a new road turning east off the Dessie road.
19. Information about Awsene Amba was provided to the author in April 1998 by local resident Wend'afrash Welde-Giyorgis, based on what he was told by his father, Mengesha Negeda, who witnessed the executions at Ingécha.

11. ENCIRCLEMENT AND CAPTIVITY

1. Maletti, P., 1937, p. 1. See also Del Boca, A., 2005, p. 217, citing ACS, *fondo* Graziani, *2° anno dell'impero, busta* 60, *parte* VI, *cap* 2, p. 14; Borruso, P., 2001, p. 63. The population of Menz in the 1930s is estimated at no more than 100,000, so with an average of around five people to a household, the number of residential *tukuls* in Menz would hardly have exceeded 20,000. Given Graziani's more typical figure of 15,302 *tukuls* burned on 18 May, it is possible that Maletti's figure should have read 15,422.
2. For Maletti's 'police action' in Northern Shewa from mid-April to mid-June 1937, see Dominioni, M., 2008B, pp. 51–6.
3. Telegram, Graziani to Generals Geloso and Giren, 17 May 1937, Doc. 20, Ministry of Justice, 1949, p. 13.

4. Extract from Graziani's telegraphed report to Rome of 19 May 1937, Doc. 41, MINISTRY OF JUSTICE, 1949, p. 24.
5. There are actually two areas south of Debre Libanos known as Guerene. It is not known which of these two areas was referred to by Maletti.
6. MALETTI, P., 1937, p. 1.
7. MALETTI, P., 1937.
8. DEL BOCA, A., 2005, p. 218, citing ACS, *fondo* Graziani, 2° *anno dell'impero*, *busta* 60, *parte* VI, *cap* 2, p. 14.
9. Interview, *Memiré* Beyene Gemmé, *La conquista di un impero*. The monastery authorities report that General Tracchia's troops were responsible for the encircling of the monastery. DEBRE LIBANOS GEDAM, [c.2010], pp. 5–6. They may not have been aware that General Tracchia had by that time been replaced by General Maletti.
10. Telegram, Maletti to commanders in Addis Ababa, Dessie and Debre Sina, 11 pm, 19 May 1937, USNA Captured Enemy Documents, T-821, roll 468, frame 45.
11. MALETTI, P., 1937, p. 2. See also telegram, Maletti to Governo Generale, Addis Ababa, 11 pm, 19 May, USNA Captured Enemy Documents, T-821, roll 468, frame 45.
12. Interviews, *Debtera* Zelleqe and *Meggabi* Fiqre-Iyesus, Laga Weldé, Debre Libanos, 1994.
13. MALETTI, P., 1937, p. 3.
14. MALETTI, P., 1937, p. 2. Since the abbot of Debre Libanos held the *ex officio* position of *ichegé*, in the 20th century that meant moving to Addis Ababa. He would thus delegate his duties at Debre Libanos to his next-in-command, the *tsebaté*. So, for all practical purposes, the *tsebaté* was head of the monastery, and was referred to by the Italians as 'the prior'. The next most important official was Gebre-Maryam, referred to by the Italians as 'the vice prior'.
15. MALETTI, P., 1937, p. 2.
16. MALETTI, P., 1937, p. 3.
17. Interview, Tibebe Kassa, Debre Libanos, 1994.
18. See Appendix I, 'The Loot', below.
19. MALETTI, P., 1937, p. 3. See also telegram, Maletti to Governo Generale, Addis Ababa, No. 34931, 11 pm, 19 May, USNA Captured Enemy Documents, T-821, roll 468, frame 45.
20. Interview, Tibebe Kassa, Wusha Gedel, Debre Libanos, 25 Jan. 1998.
21. DEBRE LIBANOS GEDAM, [c.2010], p. 7. In his report, General Maletti did not describe or name the site to which the captives were moved.
22. Interview, Tibebe Kassa, Wusha Gedel, Debre Libanos, 25 Jan. 1998.

23. DEBRE LIBANOS GEDAM, [c.2010], pp. 7–8.
24. Telegram Graziani to Maletti, No. 8922, 19 May 1937, USNA Captured Enemy Documents, roll 468, frame 46. A carbon copy is reproduced in LE DEPARTEMENT DE LA PRESSE ET DE L'INFORMATION DU GOUVERNEMENT IMPERIAL D'ETHIOPIE, n.d., p. 128. See also a different copy in ACS, *archivio* Graziani, *busta* 48, *fasc* 42, *sf* 12. This telegram is quoted in Maletti's report (MALETTI, P., 1937, p. 3), and is translated into English in MINISTRY OF JUSTICE, 1949, Doc. 31, pp. 18–19, 51–4.
25. SBACCHI, A., 1985, p. 195.

12. DEATH IN THE AFTERNOON

1. Letter, Captain Corvo to *Ato* Guila Guiorguis [sic], 20 May 1937, MINISTRY OF JUSTICE, 1949, Doc. 33, p. 20.
2. The identity of officers accompanying General Maletti was provided by Dr Luigi Panella, Rome, 28 June 2017.
3. MINISTRY OF JUSTICE, 1950, p. 10.
4. MALETTI, P., 1937, p. 3.
5. Interview, Tibebe Kassa, Wusha Gedel, Debre Libanos, 1994.
6. Interview, Tibebe Kassa, Wusha Gedel, Debre Libanos, 25 Jan. 1998.
7. Telegram, Maletti to Graziani No. 34713, 20 May 1937, USNA, Captured Italian Documents, T-821, roll 468, frame 44.
8. DEBRE LIBANOS GEDAM, [c.2010], p. 7.
9. Information provided by Dr Luigi Panella, Rome, 28 June 2017.
10. As explained by Luigi Panella on TG2000 website, 15 March 2017.
11. According to the monastery, the prisoners were taken in four trucks to spend the night at a site near the church of Chagel Medhané Alem, near *Ras* Kassa's house.
12. Telegram, Maletti to Graziani No. 34713, 20 May 1937, USNA, Captured Italian Documents, T-821, roll 468, frame 44.
13. MALETTI, P., 1937, p. 4.
14. Telegram Graziani to Lessona, 21 May 1937, No. 26320, MINISTRY OF JUSTICE, 1949, Doc. 31, pp. 18–19, 51–3. Also ACS, *archivio* Graziani, *busta* 48, *fasc* 42, *sf* 12. Mockler states that Colonel Garelli was in charge of the executions, but Maletti's report of 22 May 1937 (MALETTI, P., 1937) makes no mention of Garelli in this connection. See also MOCKLER, A., 1984, p. 180.
15. Telegram Graziani to Maletti, 21 May 1937, No. 26151, USNA Captured Italian Documents, T 821, roll 468, frame 42.
16. Interview, *Debtera* Zelleqe, Laga Weldé, 1994.

17. Described as 'peasant farmers, traders and weavers'. DEBRE LIBANOS GEDAM, [c.2010], p. 7.
18. Interview, Tibebe Kassa, Wusha Gedel, 1994. The notes on the back of *Tenente* Virgilio Cozzani's photographs confirm this belief on the part of the Italians.
19. Telegram Maletti to Graziani, No. 2072.OP, 21 May 1937, USNA, Captured Enemy Documents, T-821, roll 468, frame 39.
20. The vehicles lined up below the escarpment at Debre Libanos in *Tenente* Cozzani's photograph are all heavy trucks, of which the most numerous was the Fiat 634N, followed by the Lancia Ro-Ro and the Isotta-Fraschini D80NM. As they are all of a similar shape and size, it is difficult to identify those in the photograph. However, they are most likely Fiat 634Ns, which had a load-bed area 12.6 sq metres, and could thus easily accommodate 30–40 prisoners in a standing position.
21. Interview, Tibebe Kassa, 25 Jan. 1998.
22. Information provided by *Aleqa* Mekonnin Solomon and *Debtera* Habte-Gebri'él, as cited in DEBRE LIBANOS GEDAM, [c.2010], p. 7. The present author does not know whether these two clergymen were eyewitnesses as children, or whether they learned about the speeches later.
23. It is not known whether *Tenente* Cozzani was the only commander in charge of the 45th Colonial Battalion assigned to the executions at Laga Weldé.
24. Graziani informed Rome that the executions began at 1 pm. Telegram, Graziani to Lessona, No. 26320, 21 May 1937, MINISTRY OF JUSTICE, 1949, Doc. 31, pp. 18–19, 51–2, 54. Another of Cozzani's photographs shows a *muntaz* giving the *coup de grâce* with a pistol, which is consistent with the eyewitness accounts. According to the monastery, some of the victims were finished off with bayonet stabs. DEBRE LIBANOS GEDAM, [c.2010], pp. 5, 7.
25. Paolo Borruso indicates that Maletti deployed irregulars known as the Mohammed Sultan group for the massacre of Debre Libanos. BORRUSO, P., 2002, p. 202. However, Luigi Panella finds no documentary evidence that they were deployed in Northern Shewa before June 1937. He is of the opinion that though apparently badly dressed and undisciplined, the soldiers responsible were all regulars. Private communication, Luigi Panella to the present author, 27 June 2018.
26. The identity of the officers on site was kindly provided by Luigi Panella, Rome, 28 June 2017. The website albertoparducci.it has the major's name as 'Castellani'.

27. As this book went to press, some of these photographs of the massacre of Debre Libanos were published in ZORZETTO, G., 2020.
28. Tibebe's recollection that a fleet of four or five trucks was used for the prisoner transport convoy is consistent with the statement published by the monastery that a fleet of four trucks was involved in the evacuation to Mesqel Massaya. The published statement that two additional trucks were deployed later is also consistent with *Tenente* Cozzani's photograph showing four trucks lined up ready to transport the captives, with an additional two in the background. DEBRE LIBANOS GEDAM, [c.2010], pp. 7–8.
29. DEBRE LIBANOS GEDAM, [c.2010], p. 7.
30. BIRHANU DENQÉ, 1937 EC, p. 64.
31. DEBRE LIBANOS GEDAM, [c.2010], p. 7.
32. Interview, *Debtera* Zelleqe, Laga Weldé, 1994.
33. Although the figure of 18 truck-loads reported by Tibebe differs from that of 39 reported by Zelleqe, who watched the trucks drive to the execution site, the two accounts are not inconsistent. Tibebe, one of the last prisoners to be removed from the Chagel camp, was taken away at around 3.30 pm, whereas Zelleqe counted the trucks arriving with victims at the execution site until 6 pm. Furthermore, whereas Tibebe was aware only of the prisoners taken from the Chagel camp who had been there with him since the previous day, Zelleqe said that many of the trucks he saw were bringing prisoners directly from the monastery.
34. MINISTRY OF JUSTICE, 1950, p. 10.
35. PANKHURST, A., 1994, p. 27. If so, then the nuns were most likely shot at the monastery, or at Laga Weldé after 3 pm. In addition, nuns could well have been among the visitors executed; some of the victims in *Tenente* Cozzani's photograph wearing white with their heads covered could be women.
36. MALETTI, P., 1937. Also cited in PERRET, M., 1964, p. 72 n. 4.
37. Telegram, Graziani to Lessona, 21 May 1937, MINISTRY OF JUSTICE, 1949, Doc. 31, pp. 18–19, 51–2, 54.
38. PERRET, M., 1986, p. 67.
39. It is sometimes erroneously assumed that the people separated from the first batch of execution victims were released.

13. MASSACRE AT BORALE RIVER

1. MINISTRY OF JUSTICE, 1949, Doc. 31, pp. 19, 52, last paragraph.
2. Interviews, Tibebe Kassa, Wusha Gedel, Debre Libanos, 1994, 1995, and Sella Dingay, 25 Jan. 1998.

3. MALETTI, P., 1937. See also PERRET, M., 1984, p. 67.
4. Telegram, Maletti to Graziani, No. 2152/op/, USNA, Captured Enemy Documents, T-821, roll 468, frame 38. No dispatch time or date is shown, but there is an arrival time of 2 am, 22 May 1937.
5. Telegram, Graziani to Maletti, No. 26609, 24 May 1937, USNA Captured Enemy Documents, roll 468, frame 37. A facsimile of a copy is published in LE DEPARTEMENT DE LA PRESSE ET DE L'INFORMATION DU GOUVERNEMENT IMPERIAL D'ETHIOPIE, n.d., p. 132.
6. Interview, Tibebe Kassa, Wusha Gedel, Debre Libanos, 25 Jan. 1998.
7. Mulatwa told the present author that there were three trenches dug, of which two were used. Interview, Mulatwa Yirga, in her residence overlooking the execution site at Borale River, Ingécha, 1998.
8. According to Feqyibelu, there were around 400 soldiers. Interview, Feqyibelu Yirgu, Borale, Ingécha, 12 April 1998.
9. Interview, Feleqe Asress, at the age of 76 years, Borale, Ingécha, 12 April 1998.
10. Interview, Derbi Tsegé, at the age of 68 years, Debre Birhan–Ankober Road, near Ingécha, Jan. 1998.
11. Neither Letarge nor Gebre Gonete was interviewed by the present author. Letarge died in 1997. Negash Yirgu was interviewed in 2015.
12. Feqyibelu Yirgu recalled seven trucks; Derbi thought there were eight. Mulatwa, Feleqe, and Mengesha Negeda's son and Negash Yirgu thought there were six.
13. In 1998 Feqyibelu's homestead was located where the convoy stopped.
14. The large military trucks such as the Fiat 634N and the Lancia Ro typically carried 30–40 standing adult prisoners on short journeys. At Laga Weldé most observers estimated around 40 prisoners per truck. The figure of 70 per truck reported by Feqyibelu at Borale can be explained only by the fact that they were tied together, and included many youngsters.
15. Interview, Negash Yirgu, Borale, Ingécha, 21 March 2015.
16. After the executions, these clothes created problems for Mulatwa Yirgu, who was accused by the Italians of stealing them. CAMPBELL. I.L., 2014, p. 176.
17. Interview, Feqyibelu Yirgu, Borale, Jan. 1998.
18. The visiting researchers were Professor Shiferaw Beqelé, Addis Ababa University; Dr Deressé Ayenachew and *Ato* Alebachew Belay of Debre Birhan University; and *Ato* Téwodros Siyum, a PhD student. During this visit, on 21 March 2015, GPS coordinates of the execution site were taken.
19. Interview, Negash Yirgu, Borale, Ingécha, 21 March 2015.

20. i.e., Europeans and Eritreans. Interview, Feleqe Asress, Borale, Ingécha, 12 April 1998.
21. Information provided by Dr Lars Wikström, chief genealogist of the House of Nobility, Genealogical Department, Stockholm, Dec. 1995, and Richard Pankhurst, Jan. 1998.
22. Leijonhufvud, E.S.A., 1948, opp. p. 161. The original caption is 'Massakern på munkarna från Debra Libanos'.
23. YeQedamawi Hayle Sillassé Tor Timhirt Bét, 1950 EC, between pp. 108 and 109. The date of publication is recorded as Tir 1, 1950 EC, equivalent to 9 Jan. 1958.
24. In the case of mass executions in urban areas, mass graves were sometimes dug, such as in the town of Debre Birhan, where archaeologists from the University of Debre Berhan have carried out excavations. At one such execution site, in 2015, the present author saw the remains of the hands of victims tied together with wire, as described by witnesses of the executions at the Borale River.
25. Maletti, P., 1937. See also Perret, M., 1984, p. 67.
26. Feqyibelu estimated that there were around 70 victims tied together in each truck. He recalled seven trucks, implying a total close to 500 victims. Feleqe thought that there were 600 victims, but this seems unrealistically high, given the fleet size. The most likely scenario would seem to be eight trucks, as reported by Derbi, each containing an average of around 60 captives tied together. It is also possible that the non-Debre Libanos captives arrived later, in separate trucks.
27. With an average weight of 70 kg/body, equivalent in volume to approximately 70 litres, 1 cubic metre could theoretically accommodate 14 bodies. Thus one trench could accommodate 630 bodies, and two could hold 1,260 bodies. So even allowing for a wide margin of error and the added soil, 500 bodies could be accommodated in the two trenches that Mulatwa Yirgu saw being used.
28. Maletti's initial figure of 155 deacons less Tibebe's figure of 30 boys (including himself), who were later acknowledged by Maletti not to be deacons, gives us 155−30 = 125 deacons. Ministry of Justice, 1950, p. 11.

14. TELLING THE STORY

1. Graziani's report to Rome of 27 May 1937, Ministry of Justice, 1949, Doc. 32, pp. 20, 53.
2. Maletti, P., 1937, pp. 4–5.

3. Telegram, Graziani to Lessona, No. 14440, 21 Mar. 1937, Ministry of Justice, 1949, Document 29, p. 17. See also facsimile in Le Departement de la Presse et de l'Information du Gouvernement Imperial d'Ethiopie, c.1945, p. 66.
4. Despite Graziani's report that the 30 boys were sent home to their families, they were definitely all sent to Danane concentration camp. Details of their journey to Danane, life in the camp, and information on the other prisoners there were provided by one of the boys concerned to the present author in a series of interviews in the 1990s. Campbell, I.L., 2014, pp. 197–202.
5. Telegram, Graziani to Lessona, No. 27136, 27 May 1937, USNA, Captured Italian Docs., T-821, roll 468, frame 20; Ministry of Justice, 1949, Doc. 32, pp. 20, 53.
6. Telahun Paulos et al., 2002, p. 53.
7. Maletti's plan of action contained an estimate that the number of 'clergy, servants, the poor and pilgrims' present would total, in all, 'two to three thousand people'. Report, *Convento di Debra Libanos*, Maletti to Graziani, 21 April 1937, ACS, *archivio* Graziani, *busta* 48, *fasc* 42, *sf* 12.
8. Telegram, Graziani to Lessona, 27 May 1937, Ministry of Justice, 1949, Doc. 32, pp. 20, 53. This report was sent after the execution of the deacons at Borale.
9. The present author is indebted to Luigi Panella for bringing this incident and the supporting documents to his attention in Rome, in June 2019.
10. Telegram, Regia Aeronautica, Addis Ababa, to Graziani, 19 Feb. 1937, Luigi Panella archive, Rome.
11. Telegram, Maletti to Graziani, 11.20 pm, 20 May 1937, Luigi Panella archive, Rome.
12. Luigi Panella suggests that Graziani would have had no scruples in sending instructions to kill civilians, and that the secret message could have been instructing Maletti to seize the monastery's most valuable treasures, such as the imperial crowns, which were looted by Maletti's troops but were missing from the Italian inventory of looted artefacts. The crowns eventually ended up in Mussolini's possession (see Appendix II). Personal communication, Luigi Panella to the present author, 2 Feb. 2021.
13. Interview, Negash Yirgu, Borale, Ingécha, 21 March 2015.
14. Mikre-Sellassie Gebre-Ammanuel, 2014, pp. 166–7, citing an interview with Cardinal Tisserant in *Gazzetta del Popolo*, 22 Oct. 1936.

15. Thiessen, J.C., 1961, p. 300, cited in Mikre-Sellassie Gebre-Ammanuel, 2014, p. 167 n. 104.
16. Pacelli contacted Mundelein, and replied on behalf of the pope, refusing to apologise for the archbishop's speech unless the German government stopped its attacks on the Church. Kertzer, D.I., 2014, pp. 261 and 468 n. 21.
17. Kertzer, D.I., 2014, pp. 261–2.
18. Kertzer, D.I., 2014, pp. 152–3.
19. Ceci, L., 2010, pp. 134–5.

15. PERSECUTION OF THE HOUSE OF TEKLE HAYMANOT

1. Sbacchi, A., 1997, p. 178.
2. Interview, Tibebe Kassa, Wusha Gedel, Debre Libanos, 1998.
3. Maletti, P., 1937, pp. 4–5.
4. Telegram, Graziani to Lessona, 29 May 1937, Doc. 52, Ministry of Justice, 1949, p. 29.
5. Del Boca, A., 1969, p. 224 n. 30.
6. For the history of Zéna Marqos, see Raineri, O., 2014.
7. Maletti, P., 1937.
8. *Debtera Liqetebebt* Abbebe Yirafu gives a date of 29 Ginbot (6 June) for the destruction of Debre Bisrat.
9. Kefyalew Mehari, 2001, p. 111.
10. Affidavit, *Ras* Abebe Aregay, for the UN war crimes trials, in Ministry of Justice, 1950, Doc. 5, p. 4.
11. Ahmed Hassen Omer, 2000, p. 155, based on information from local informants. Calvin Shenk notes that though the Italians themselves had burned the church, in 1938 they blamed it on a certain *ras*. Shenk, C.E., 1972, pp. 131–2. Nonetheless, Graziani informed Minister Lessona that his troops had burned the monastery. Personal communication, Luigi Panella, Rome, 6 June 2019.
12. The monastery is listed as 'Debre Wageg Sillassé' in the records of the Patriarchate of the Ethiopian Orthodox Church. Ethiopian Orthodox Church Development Commission, Doheny, K. & Ryan, M.T., 1975, Statistics section, p. 5.
13. Father Kefyalew Mehari states that the work was undertaken by *Aleqa* Gebre-Medhin. Kefyalew Mehari, 2003, pp. 37–8.
14. Ayelè Teklehaimanot, 1981, p. 57. See also Persoon, J., 2005A.
15. Telegram, Graziani to Nasi, No. 10009 (apparently altered from 999), 2 June 1937, USNA, T-821, roll 472, frame 426.

16. Telegram, Graziani to the Minister for Italian Africa (Lessona), No. 10062, 2 June 1937, USNA, T-821, roll 472, frame 427.
17. KEFYALEW MEHARI, 2001, p. 111.
18. Interview, *Nebura'ed* Tefera Menissé of Béta Maryam, Addis Alem (formerly *aleqa* of the monastery of Debre Assebot), Ambo, 2011.
19. KEFYALEW MEHARI, 2003, pp. 31–2.
20. Telegram, Maletti to Spinelli *via* Governo Generale, No. 48350, 6.30 pm, 18 July 1937, USNA, T-821, roll 468, frame 24.
21. Maletti used the term *oculatezza*. Telegram, Maletti to Spinelli *via* Governo Generale, No. 48350, 6.30 pm, 18 July 1937, USNA, roll 468, frame 24.
22. MINISTRY OF JUSTICE, 1950, Doc. 15, pp. 11–13.
23. See affidavit by *Blatta* Bekele Hapte Michael, judge at the High Court of Ethiopia, Addis Ababa. MINISTRY OF JUSTICE, 1949, p. 69; MINISTRY OF JUSTICE, 1950, Doc. 18, pp. 16–17; SBACCHI, A., 1997, p. 132.
24. WALSTON, J., 1997, p. 181, citing DEL BOCA, A., 1988, p. 178.
25. For further information on Danane, see DEL BOCA, A., 1987.
26. SBACCHI, A., 1997, p. 132.
27. See, for example, Mikaél Tessema's testimony in MINISTRY OF JUSTICE, 1950, p. 13; IMRU ZELLEKE, 2016, pp. 31–2; CAMPBELL, I.L., 2017, pp. 232–3.
28. SBACCHI, A., 1977, p. 216.
29. Museo virtuale della intolleranze e degle stermini, www.zadigweb.it/amis/schede.asp?idsch-115&id=7, accessed May 2019. In 1938 Tekle-Tsadiq Mekuria was one of the inmates at Danane used as slave labour at the Genale plantations. Interview, Tekle-Tsadiq Mekuria, Addis Ababa, 10 Feb. 1998. The Italians also introduced forced labour on their cotton plantations in southern Ethiopia. See, for example, Charles McClellan's research in the 1990s, recording testimony: 'We were not paid ... those who did not show up or did not work hard enough were whipped ... Nearly all of us had been whipped.' McCLELLAN, C., 1998, pp. 188–90.
30. SBACCHI, A., 1977, p. 217.
31. MINISTRY OF JUSTICE, 1950, p. 13.
32. KEFYALEW MEHARI, 2001, p. 111.
33. Interview, Father Michael, Midr Kebd, May 1997.
34. BUSTORF, D., NOSNITSIN, D. & ALIEV-GUTGARTS, Y., 2014, p. 182.
35. KEFYALEW MEHARI, 2001, p. 111.
36. MINISTRY OF JUSTICE, 1950, Doc. 19, p. 17.

16. AN ITALIAN JIHAD

1. Ahmed Hassen Omer, 2000, p. 149.
2. Dechesa Abebe, 2016, p. 26.
3. Ahmed Hassen Omer, 1995, pp. 1–2.
4. Ahmed Hassen Omer, 2000, p. 152.
5. Telegram, Graziani to Minister of Italian Africa, No. 10713, 11 June 1937, IES.
6. 'Addis Ababa: Il giorno dei martiri', *Osservatorio Democratico sulle Nuove Destre Italia*, 19 Feb. 2017, https://www.facebook.com/asservatoriodemocraticosullenuovadestre/posts/.
7. Ahmed Hassen Omer, 1995, pp. 2–3, citing interviews with *Sheikh* Mohammad Salih, *Weyzero* Momina Ali, *Ato* Hassan Omar, and *al-Haj* Mohammad Wale Ahmad.
8. Taddesse ZeWeldé, 1955 EC, p. 372; Ahmed Hassen Omer, 2000, pp. 152–4. See also Ahmed Hassen Omer, 2006, p. 24.
9. Some of the atrocities of the Maletti–Mohammed Sultan *jihad* were so shocking that Italian officers had what Gabriele Zorzetto calls a 'crisis of conscience'. He describes one lieutenant being so appalled that he ordered his Eritrean *askaris* to chase and kill the troops concerned. Zorzetto, G., 2020, p. 125.
10. Dominioni, M., 2008A, pp. 189–92.
11. Ahmed Hassen Omer, 2000, p. 155.
12. Interview, Ahmed Hassen Omer, Addis Ababa, 24 April 2018.
13. One of the victims of the Maletti–Mohammed Sultan *jihad* in the Ankober area was the young Afewerq Teklé (1932–2012), who, though seriously mutilated, survived to become Ethiopia's most celebrated artist. Personal communication, Afewerq Teklé to the present author, Addis Ababa, 1996.
14. Ahmed Hassen Omer, 1995, p. 3; Ahmed Hassen Omer, 2000, pp. 153–4; Interview, Ahmed Hassen Omer, Addis Ababa, 24 April 2018. See also Dechesa Abebe, 2016, pp. 31–5. Ahmed Hassen's informants pointed out that there were also Muslims who fought as Patriots throughout the occupation. Ahmed Hassen Omer, 1995, p. 4.
15. Ahmed Hassen Omer, 1995, p. 3 n. 21.
16. Ahmed Hassen Omer, 2000, p. 156.
17. *Sheikh* Mohammed Sultan was shot dead by a local farmer named Teshebbiru. Ahmed Hassen Omer, 1995, p. 4; Ahmed Hassen Omer, 2000, p. 157.
18. Interview, Ahmed Hassen Omer, Addis Ababa, 24 April 2018; interview, Shiferaw Bekele, Addis Ababa, 20 May 2018.

19. AHMED HASSEN OMER, 2000, p. 159.
20. Interview, Dr Ahmed Hassen Omer, Addis Ababa, 24 April 2018.
21. VIRTUE, N.G., 2016, p. 176.
22. VIRTUE, N.G., 2016, p. 176, citing Graziani, R, *Il secondo anno dell'impero*.
23. VIRTUE, N.G., 2016, pp. 152–3.
24. Pankhurst, S., 1946; HAILE SELASSIE I, ED. H. MARCUS, 1994, pp. 25–7 (in which the list of complaints is abbreviated); BORRUSO, P., 2002, p. 207.
25. BORRUSO, P., 2002, p. 207; CECI, L., 2010, pp. 195–6.

17. THE HOLY WAR TURNS FULL CIRCLE

1. SBACCHI, A., 1985, p. 196; DOMINIONI, M., 2008A, p. 47.
2. Telegram Graziani to Pirzio-Biroli, Addis Ababa, 29 July 1937, cited in DOMINIONI, M., 2003, p. 170 n. 13. See also DEL BOCA, A., 2005, p. 233.
3. KIRSCH, J., 2008, p. 92 n. 81.
4. MOCKLER, A., 1984, p. 185; SBACCHI, A., 1985, p. 197; DOMINIONI, M., 2008A, pp. 263–4.
5. BORRUSO, P., 2002, p. 204.
6. MIKRE-SELLASSIE GEBRE-AMMANUEL, 2014, p. 371.
7. KEFYALEW MEHARI, 2001, p. 112.
8. One British estimate put the number of churches in Gojjam as high as 5,000. *The State of the Church in Abyssinia*, fol. 42, Lambeth Palace Library, Douglas Papers, p. 69, cited in MIKRE-SELLASSIE GEBRE-AMMANUEL, 2014, p. 206.
9. GEREMEW ESKEZIA, 2017, pp. 5, 8.
10. LENTAKIS, M., 2005, p. 61.
11. DOMINIONI, M., 2008A, pp. 264–5.
12. SELTENE SEYOUM, 1999, pp. 135–6.
13. SELTENE SEYOUM, 1999, pp. 237, 239, citing interviews with local Gojjami elders; GEREMEW ESKEZIA, 2017, p. 7.
14. SELTENE SEYOUM, 1999, pp. 238–40.

18. A WIND OF CHANGE

1. For insights into the cause and timing of the growth of resistance in Gojjam, see SELTENE SEYOUM, 1999, and SELTENE SEYOUM, 2003A, pp. 42–5.
2. PANKHURST, R.K., 1997, p. 28.

3. PERRET, M., 1986, p. 72 n. 7.
4. BINCHY, D.A., 1970, p. 360, citing *The Times*, 14 March 1937.
5. KENT, P.C., 1984, pp. 146–7.
6. LESSONA, A., 1958, pp. 306–7, cited in PANKHURST, R.K., 1997, pp. 26–7.
7. Prof. Seltene Seyoum pointed out to the present author that Graziani had agreed to move to Asmara on the understanding that it would provide a better location from which to control the insurgency.
8. Telegram, Petretti to *Residente*, Fiché, No. 90843, 25 Aug. 1937, USNA, T-821, roll 468, frame 17.
9. Telegram, Maletti to Governo Generale to be forwarded by air to the *Residente*, Fiché, No. 57268, 27 Aug. 1937, USNA, T-821, roll 468, frame 16.
10. KENT, P.C., 1984, p. 149, citing PRO, FO, J4228/548/1, Acting Consul General in Addis Ababa, 27 Sept. 1937.
11. *Corriere dell'Impero*, 3 Oct. 1937; SHENK, C.E., 1972, pp. 126–30.
12. Telegram, Graziani to *Residente*, Fiché, No. 100645, 27 Oct. 1937. USNA, T-821, roll 468, frame 15.
13. BINCHY, D.A., 1970, p. 679.
14. Circular, Guglielmo Nasi, 17 March 1940, Doc. 22, MINISTRY OF JUSTICE, 1949, p. 14.
15. Phonogram, Direttore Superiore, Governo Generale, to Comando Superiore CC RR, 2 Nov. 1937, USNA, T-821, roll 468, frame 13.
16. Telegram, Graziani to *Residente*, Fiché, No. 100645, 2 Nov. 1937. USNA, T-821, roll 468, frame 14.
17. Interview, Tibebe Kassa, Wusha Gedel, Debre Libanos, 25 Jan. 1998.
18. Interview, Tibebe Kassa, Wusha Gedel, Debre Libanos, 25 Jan. 1998. According to prisoner Tekle-Tsadiq Mekuria, interviewed in 1997, the prisoners were generally accommodated in huts. However, by the time Tibebe arrived, the population at Danane had swollen to several thousand inmates, and many prisoners were in tents. This was confirmed by another former inmate: 'The women's compound consisted of some large military tents surrounded with barbed wire. Later on, when the number of prisoners increased, they had to build yet more camps with tents and fences.' See http://dir.groups.yahoo.cn/group/ESAi/messages/330.
19. Interview, Tibebe Kassa, 25 Jan. 1998, Wusha Gedel, Debre Libanos, 25 Jan. 1998.
20. MINISTRY OF JUSTICE, 1950, p. 13.

19. MORE CLERGY TO THE SWORD

1. SHENK, C.E., 1972, pp. 126–7.
2. Following the battle in which *Sheikh* Mohammed Sultan was killed, some of the *tabots* and other ecclesiastical valuables stolen during the *jihad* of June 1937 had been recovered by the Patriots, who returned them to the churches concerned. AHMED HASSEN OMER, 1995, p. 4; AHMED HASSEN OMER, 2000, p. 157.
3. This reconstruction of the Italian church-burning campaign along, and to the west of, the Ankober peninsula in late October and early November 1937 is based on discussions and interviews with Father Welde-Sillassé Habte-Sillassé and other elders of the church of Kundi St George, by Professor Richard Pankhurst, Rita Pankhurst, *Dyakon* Kifle Assefa and the present author at the church of Kundi St George, 22 March 1998.
4. This church is referred to as Maryam Ager Yohannis in DANIÉL KIBRET, 1999 EC, pp. 375–87.
5. Diocesan records, DANIÉL KIBRET, 1999 EC, pp. 375–89.
6. Diocesan records, DANIÉL KIBRET, 1999 EC, p. 574.
7. Diocesan records, DANIÉL KIBRET, 1999 EC, p. 371.
8. Diocesan records, DANIÉL KIBRET, 1999 EC, p. 305. A few days later the Air Force was dispatched instead, to carry out a surprise bombing raid on one of the other churches, Ankober St George, where they managed to kill one priest, Father Tekle-Giyorgis. Diocesan records, DANIÉL KIBRET, 1999 EC, p. 306.
9. Diocesan records, DANIÉL KIBRET, 1999 EC, p. 305.
10. Diocesan records, DANIÉL KIBRET, 1999 EC, p. 619.
11. Diocesan records, DANIÉL KIBRET, 1999 EC, p. 365.
12. Diocesan records, DANIÉL KIBRET, 1999 EC, pp. 375–89.
13. Diocesan records, DANIÉL KIBRET, 1999 EC, p. 426.
14. GAITACHEW BEKELE, 1993, p. 31.
15. GAITACHEW BEKELE, 1993, pp. 34–5; GEBRE-IGZIABHER ELYAS, ED. R.K. MOLVAER, 1994, pp. 571–3; MOLVAER, R.K., 2007. Melake-Tsehay functioned as a rallying point for the Patriots of Shewa for a little over a year, and when he died following a week's illness, some suspected foul play.
16. GAITACHEW BEKELE, 1993, p. 35
17. GEBRE-IGZIABHER ELYAS, ED. R.K. MOLVAER, 1994, p. 574.
18. Subsequently some of the Oromo converted to Christianity; others to Islam.
19. GEBRE-IGZIABHER ELYAS, ED. R.K. MOLVAER, 1994, pp. 571, 574.

20. Diocesan records, DANIÉL KIBRET, 1999 EC, p. 342.
21. Diocesan records, DANIÉL KIBRET, 1999 EC, p. 370.
22. Diocesan records, DANIÉL KIBRET, 1999 EC, p. 370.
23. Diocesan records, DANIÉL KIBRET, 1999 EC, pp. 370–87.
24. Diocesan records, DANIÉL KIBRET, 1999 EC, p. 387.
25. WUDU TAFETE, 1997, pp. 101–5.
26. Not to be confused with Ziqwala in the Rift Valley, where the famous monastery of Gebre Menfes Qiddus ('Abo') is located.
27. MOCKLER, A., 1984, pp. 183–4; WUDU TAFETE, 1997, pp. 104–5, citing local informants Asmerom Werqneh and Bayu Tafete.
28. DANIÉL KIBRET, 1999 EC, p. 322, giving a date of 24 Hidar 1930 EC based on diocesan records. According to Ethiopian Church historian Father Kefyalew, the Italians slaughtered 143 priests at Addis Alem. KEFYALEW MEHARI, 2001, p. 111, giving a date of 28 Hidar 1929 EC (7 Dec. 1936).
29. Diocesan records, DANIÉL KIBRET, 1999 EC, p. 316.

20. KISSING THE CROSS

1. *I primi venti mesi dell'impero*, ACS, *fondo* Graziani, *Sc* 31, *fasc* 29, *sf* 40, cited in PERRET, M., 1986, p. 74 n. 16.
2. KENT, P.C., 1984, p. 140.
3. The other surviving Ethiopian bishop, Isaac, protested against the severance from the Coptic patriarchate and was imprisoned by the Italians until he accepted their arrangements. MIKRE-SELLASSIE GEBRE-AMMANUEL, 2014, p. 202.
4. BORRUSO, P., 2001, pp. 73–7.
5. ASDMAE, MAI, *posiz* 181/55, *fasc* 255, telegram no. 07730, Graziani to Lessona, Addis Ababa, 22 Feb. 1938, cited in DOMINIONI, M., 2008A, p. 47, n 36.
6. SHENK, C.E., 1972; MIKRE-SELLASSIE GEBRE-AMMANUEL, 2014, Appendix IV, pp. 394–5. As noted earlier, in some areas the Italians actually started repairing some churches before this time—in fact during the last months of Graziani's tenure. See SHENK, C.E., 1972, n. 32, citing *The New Abyssinia*, London, 1937.
7. MIKRE-SELLASSIE GEBRE-AMMANUEL, 2014, Appendix IV, p. 395.
8. GREENFIELD, R., 1965, p. 241.
9. HAILE SELASSIE I, ED. H. MARCUS, 1994, pp. 40–2.
10. SHENK, C.E., 1972, p. 127.
11. SHENK, C.E., 1972, p. 135.

EPILOGUE

1. KERTZER, D.I., 2014, p. 354.
2. *Corriere della Sera*, 10 June 1938, cited in MANHATTAN, A., 1949, pp. 125–6; KERTZER, D.I., 2014, pp. 271–3.
3. BINCHY, D.A., 1970, p. 683.
4. KERTZER, D.I., 2014, pp. 276–80.
5. Ciano to Holy See, 15 July 1938 and Teruzzi to Ciano, 6 Aug. 1938, ASMAE, *busta* 44, *ss* 6-5 (1939), cited in KENT, P.C., 1984, p. 150; BORRUSO, P., 1989, p. 62, citing ASMAI/Gab, p. 181/59, f. 293, telegram, Cerulli to Minister of Italian Africa, 26 July 1938, communication Terruzi to *Duce*, 17 May 1937, and ASMAI/Gab, p. 181/59, f. 291, *pro memoria*, Teruzzi to *Duce*, 17 May 1938.
6. BORRUSO, P., 1989, p. 63.
7. KENT, P.C., 1984, p. 150, citing ASMAE, *busta* 44, *ss* 6-5 (1939), Ciano to Minister of Italian Africa, 26 July 1938; ibid., *busta* 39, *ss* 5-Germania, Pignatti to Ciano, 26 July 1938; ibid., Pignatti to Ciano, 10 Aug. 1938. See also BORRUSO, P., 1989, pp. 62–4.
8. KERTZER, D.I., 2014, pp. 306–7, citing Archivio Segreto Vaticano, Segreteria di Stato, Affari ecclesiastici straordinari, Italia, *posiz* 1007c, *fasc* 695, ff. 37r–39r, 'Nota da me presentato al Duce la sera di venerdi 12 Agosto', Tacchi Venturi, 12 August 1938.
9. FATTORINI, E., 2011, pp. 187–93; KERTZER, D.I., 2014, p. 373.
10. Affidavit, *Lij* Abebe Shinkurt, Doc. 22, MINISTRY OF JUSTICE, 1950, pp. 18–19.
11. Affidavit, *Blatta* Mane Agegnehu, Doc. 23, MINISTRY OF JUSTICE, 1950, p. 19.
12. PANKHURST, R.K., 2001, p. 244.
13. PANKHURST, R.K., 2001, p. 245, citing H. GIBSON (ED.), 1946, pp. 3, 42.
14. HAILE SELASSIE I, ED. H. MARCUS, 1994, p. 159.
15. Italian forces around Gondar under General Nasi continued to hold out under very difficult conditions and heavy losses until their surrender in Nov. 1941. DEL BOCA, A., 1969, p. 259.
16. HAILE SELASSIE I, ED. H. MARCUS, 1994, p. 165.
17. DEL BOCA, A., 1969, p. 259.
18. MIKRE-SELLASSIE GEBRE-AMMANUEL, 2014, pp. 350–1, citing Public Record Office, London, 35642, J1995, 'Italo-Catholic Subversive Activities', memo by Egyptian Department, Foreign Office.
19. MIKRE-SELLASSIE GEBRE-AMMANUEL, 2014, pp. 350–1, citing Public Record Office, London, 35642, J1995, 'Italo-Catholic Subversive Activities', memo by Egyptian Department, Foreign Office.

20. MIKRE-SELLASSIE GEBRE-AMMANUEL, 2014, pp. 351–2, citing Public Record Office, London, FO 371, 27530, J3578/173/1, M.S. Lush, Deputy Chief Political Officer, Ethiopia, to the Chief Political Officer, Addis Ababa, 11 Oct. 1941.
21. MIKRE-SELLASSIE GEBRE-AMMANUEL, 2014, pp. 358–9.
22. PARIS, E., 1961, pp. 4, 9. Paris provides a figure of 750,000 Serbs (in addition to 60,000 Jews and 26,000 Roma) killed between 1941 and 1945, citing Serbian Orthodox bishop Dr Nikolaj Velimirović, in the ecclesiastical review *Svećenik*, 1954, and Hermann Neubacher in *Sonderauftrag Südost 1940–1945: Bericht eines fliegenden Diplomaten*, Göttingen-Berlin-Frankfurt, 1956, pp. 31–2.
23. DUGGAN, C., 2013, pp. 420–1.
24. PANKHURST, R.K., 1999B, pp. 123–4, citing FO 371/63171, J5671, Leijonhufvud to Ledingham, 17 Nov. 1947.
25. MINISTRY OF JUSTICE, 1949, p. 2.
26. MINISTRY OF JUSTICE, 1949, Docs. 31, 32, pp. 18–20, 51–4.
27. MINISTRY OF JUSTICE, 1950, Docs. 13, 14, pp. 10–11.
28. MINISTRY OF JUSTICE, 1949, pp. 3–4.
29. DEPARTEMENT DE LA PRESSE ET DE L'INFORMATION DU GOUVERNEMENT IMPERIAL D'ETHIOPIE, n.d..
30. PANKHURST, R.K., 1999B, pp. 133–4; CAMPBELL, I.L., 2017, pp. 246–50. For a detailed study of the reasons for the absence of an 'Italian Nuremberg', see FOCARDI, F. & KLINKHAMMER, L., 2004.
31. LE HOUÉROU, F., 1994A, p. 826, and www.comandosupremo.com/Graziani.html.
32. www.catholic-hierarchy.org.
33. The statue was renovated in 1987–8. ANON., 1986 EC, p. 37.
34. Also influential were CARVIGIANI, A., 2019 and BORRUSO, P., 2009.
35. BORRUSO, P., 2020.

REFLECTIONS

1. For a persuasively argued thesis that the fundamental passions of crusading reach down to the present day, see ARMSTRONG, K., 2001.
2. For an account of Vatican reactions to anti-Fascists in the USA, see D'AGOSTINO, P.R., 2003, pp. 258–81.
3. DOINO, W., Jr., 2004, p. 121; FATTORINI, E., 2011, pp. 137–41; KERTZER, D.I., 2014, pp. 276–8.
4. SALVEMINI, G., 1969A, p. 193.
5. JENKINS, P., 2014, pp. 200–5.
6. JENKINS, P., 2014, pp. 213–14.

7. Romanchurches.wikia.com: Santo Stefano degli Abissini.
8. *Appeal by His Majesty Haile Selassie, Emperor of Ethiopia, to the Christian Churches of the World*, July 1937, Lambeth Palace Archives, LPA-EOC, f. 77. See also BORRUSO, P., 2002, p. 207.
9. US GOVERNMENT PRINTING OFFICE, 1953, p. 680, Engert to Secretary of State, No. 47, 11 am, 20 Feb. 1937.
10. POLLARD, J., 2005, pp. 56–7.
11. ZEWDÉ RETA, 2005 EC, pp. 308–14.
12. ZEWDÉ RETA, 2005 EC, pp. 312–13.
13. ZEWDÉ RETA, 2005 EC, p. 313.
14. Personal communication, Lucia Ceci to the present author, 13 Oct. 2017. Prof. Ceci pointed out that she cannot be certain that there are no such documents—only that she was unable to find any.
15. FATTORINI, E., 2011, p. 89.
16. BINCHY, D.A., 1970, p. 652.
17. See, for example, ASANTE, S.K.B., 1974.
18. BINCHY, D.A., 1970, p. 621, citing *L'Osservatore Romano*, 24 August 1938.
19. POLLARD, J., 2014, pp. 164–5.
20. BINCHY, D.A., 1970, p. x.
21. GASCOIGNE, B., 2003, pp. 78–9, citing BRADFORD, E., 1967, p. 184.
22. At this point the relationship between the Catholic Church of Italy and the Fascists was still excellent. Mussolini's ambassador to the Holy See was able to assure him that 'faith in the *Duce* is absolute and beyond discussion in all the episcopal hierarchy and clergy'. Thus Pacelli managed to persuade Mussolini to get the Italian ambassador in Berlin to intercede, although with only partial success. KERTZER, D.I., 2014, pp. 244, 255, 464 n. 13.
23. KORNBERG, J., 2015, esp. pp. 299–301.
24. POLLARD, J., 2014, p. 153. The dollar figure is calculated at 1929 exchange rates.
25. POLLARD, J., 2005, p. 175.
26. POLLARD, J., 2014, pp. 245, 248.
27. BINCHY, D., 1970, p. 303.
28. LO BELLO, N., 1969, p. 72.
29. POSNER, G., 2015, pp. 69–70.
30. POSNER, G., 2015, pp. 69–70.
31. POLLARD, J., 2005, p. 175.
32. Caproni bombers models Ca.101, Ca.111, Ca.133 and Ca.142 accounted for 378 of the total of 679 aircraft used for combat

operations against the Ethiopians. GENTILLI, R., 1992, pp. 205–7. CAN became a subsidiary of Caproni.
33. POLLARD, J., 2005, p. 175.

APPENDIX I: THE FINAL TOLL

1. PANKHURST, S., 1955, p. 548, and KALI-NYAH, I., 2001, p. 112.
2. HAILE SELASSIE I, ED. H. MARCUS, 1994, p. 169; SBACCHI, A., 1997, p. 91.
3. Provisional figures published by Sylvia Pankhurst in 1946—presumably before the Paris Peace Conference—omitted the estimate of civilian casualties. PANKHURST, S., 1946, p. 1.
4. Memorandum, Ethiopian Government to Conference of Commonwealth Prime Ministers, London, September 1945, St Clements Press, 1946, cited in SBACCHI, A., 1997, pp. 91, 101 n. 33.
5. KALI-NYAH, I., 2001, p. 112 n. 5.
6. www.globalallianceforEthiopia.org.
7. OFCANSKY, T.P., 2007, p. 229.
8. DEL BOCA, A., 1969, p. 37.
9. SBACCHI, A., 1997, pp. 91, 101 n. 34, citing Del Boca, A., *Gli italiani in Africa orientale: La conquista dell'impero*, Rome, 1979, p. 720.
10. SBACCHI, A., 1997, p. 91.
11. For a concise overview of the resistance, see SELTENE SEYOUM, 2010.
12. CAMPBELL, I.L., 2017, pp. 308–29.
13. CAMPBELL, I.L., 2017, pp. 379–89.
14. ZERVOS, A., 1936, p. 12.
15. HAILE SELASSIE I, ED. H. MARCUS, 1994, p. 169. In his memoir the emperor gives a slightly different estimated total of 750,000 people killed.
16. See also CAMPBELL, I.L., 2014, p. 171.

APPENDIX II: SPOILS OF WAR

1. *The Convention with Respect to the Laws and Customs of War on Land*, 1899, Section II, Chapter I, Articles 27 and 28; Section III, Articles 47 and 56.
2. Circular, Amadeo di Savoia to staff of A.O.I., 19 Jan. 1940, MINISTRY OF JUSTICE, 1949, Doc. 42, p. 25. See also Doc. 26, p. 16 and SBACCHI, A., 1985, p. 196.
3. CAMPBELL, I.L., 2017, pp. 143, 330–1.
4. See, for example, 'Servisio Decreto G.G. 15 ottobre 1937-XV, N. 738, Confisca beni di sudditi indigeni', in *Giornale Ufficiale del Governo*

Generale dell'Africa Orientale Italiana, Year II, no. 22, 1 Nov. 1937-XVI, p. 468; 'Servisio Decreto G.G. 25 October 1937-XV, N. 751, Confisca beni di sudditi indigeni' and 'Servisio Decreto G.G. 25 October 1937-XV, N. 752, Confisca beni di sudditi indigeni', in *Giornale Ufficiale del Governo Generale dell'Africa Orientale Italiana*, Year II, no. 23, 1 Dec. 1937-XV, pp. 527–8.

5. Maletti, General, *Comando Settore Nord-Orientale: Scioglimento convento Debra Libanos*, 22 May 1937, Enclosure 4, f. 2091 of 22 May, ACS, *fondo* Graziani, *sc* 48, *fasc* 42.
6. The theft of these items by the Italian military was confirmed by *Memhir* Tibebu Welde-Maryam at a meeting of the Council of the monastery with Professor Richard Pankhurst, Dr Alula Pankhurst, Ato Degife Gebre-Tsadiq and the present author, at Béta Marfak, Debre Libanos, 24 Oct. 1992. For a more detailed analysis of information available at that time of the looting at the monastery, see CAMPBELL, I.L., 2014, pp. 217–39.
7. Maletti, General, *Comando Settore Nord-Orientale: Scioglimento convento Debra Libanos*, 22 May 1937, Enclosure 3, f. 2091 of 22 May, ACS, *fondo* Graziani, Rodolfo, *sc* 48, *fasc* 42.
8. CAMPBELL, I.L., 2014, pp. 225–6; Interview, *Memhir* Daniél Seifemikaél, offices of the Ethiopian Orthodox Tewahido Church Development and Inter-Church Aid Commission, Addis Ababa, 9 Aug. 2018.
9. Interview, *Memhir* Daniél, offices of the Ethiopian Orthodox Tewahido Church Development and Inter-Church Aid Commission, Addis Ababa, 9 Aug. 2018.
10. MINISTRY OF JUSTICE, 1950, Doc. 14, p. 11.
11. Interview, *Memhir* Daniél, offices of the Ethiopian Orthodox Tewahido Church Development and Inter-Church Aid Commission, Addis Ababa, 9 Aug. 2018.
12. ZEMEDKUN BEQELE, 1995 EC, p. 182.
13. Interview, *Fitawrari* Nebiyye-Li'ul, Addis Ababa, 1991.
14. Interview, *Memhir* Daniél, offices of the Ethiopian Orthodox Tewahido Church Development and Inter-Church Aid Commission, Addis Ababa, 9 Aug. 2018.
15. According to Michel Perret, the items in the inventory were transferred to Debre Birhan. PERRET, M., 1986, p. 67. However, according to Maletti's report, they were to be taken to Addis Ababa. Maletti, General, *Comando Settore Nord-Orientale: Scioglimento convento Debra Libanos*, 22 May 1937, Enclosure 3, f. 2091 of 22 May, ACS, *fondo* Graziani, *sc* 48, *fasc* 42.

16. Council meeting, Debre Libanos monastery, Béta Marfak, 24 Oct. 1992. CAMPBELL, I.L., 2014, pp. 221–23.
17. PANKHURST, R.K., 2001B, p. 10.
18. The Graziani Room collection was illustrated in Year II, no. 2 of *Gli Annali dell'Africa Italiana* of July 1939, between pp. 702 and 703; see MONDADORI, A., ED., 1939.
19. It should be noted that Ethiopian sovereigns traditionally had a number of similar crowns made, which were kept in the treasury of important churches in various locations.
20. PANKHURST, R.K., 1993; PANKHURST, R.K., 1999A.
21. For an account of Mussolini's capture at Dongo and his demise shortly thereafter, including the description of the crowns as the most valuable part of the Dongo treasure, see LAZZERO, R., p. 48.
22. PANKHURST, R.K., 1993.
23. RICCARDI, A., 2017.

BIBLIOGRAPHY

ABERA JEMBERÉ, 1952 EC, *YeQedamawi Hayle Sillassé: Bego Adiragot Dirijit: Memesret* (Amharic), Addis Ababa, Birhanina Selam Printing Press.

ADAMTHWAITE, A.P., 1977, *The Making of the Second World War*, London, George Allen & Unwin.

ADHANOM, S., 1969, 'Primi pellegrini etiopi a Roma', in 'Pontificio Collegio Etiopico, giubileo d'oro 1919–1969, Città del Vaticano', *Rivista Semestrale degli Alunni del Pontificio Collegio Etiopico*, VIII, 16, 1969.

AHMED HASSEN OMER, 1995, 'Italian Local Politics in Northern Shäwa and Its Consequences 1936–1941', *Journal of Ethiopian Studies*, XXVIII 2, December 1995, pp. 1–13.

———, 2000, 'The Italian Impact on Ethnic Relations: A Case Study of a Regional Policy in Northern Shoa (Ethiopia), 1936–1941', *Annales d'Éthiopie*, XVI, 2000, pp. 147–59.

———, 2006, 'Centres of Traditional Muslim Education in Northern Shäwa (Ethiopia): A Historical Study with Particular Reference to the Twentieth Century', *Journal of Ethiopian* Studies, XXXIX, 102, June–December 2006, pp. 13–54.

ALAZAR TESFA MICHAEL, 1948, 'Eritrean Heroes', *New Times and Ethiopia News*, 26 June 1948, pp. 1–2.

ANON., n.d., *Italian Atrocities in 1911* (English and Arabic), London, St Clements Press.

ANON., 1974 EC, 'And YeJegninet Mi'araf – Abriha Debochna Moges Asgedom' (Amharic), in *Dehnenet*, Hamle, 1974 EC, Addis Ababa, pp. 41–8.

ANON., 1986 EC, 'Ityopiyawiw Sena'it: Abune Mika'él Papas ZeAzéb Ityopiya' (Amharic), in *YeGoré Timhirt Bét:YeWerq Iyobéliyu*, Miazya 1986 EC, Addis Ababa, Yellubabor Meredaja Idir, pp. 36–7.

BIBLIOGRAPHY

ANTONIOS ALBERTO, 1998, *The Apostolic Vicariate of Galla, a Capuchin Mission in Ethiopia (1846–1942): Antecedents, Evolution and Problematics*, Addis Ababa, Capuchin Franciscan Institute of Philosophy and Theology.

———, 2013, *Ethiopian Review of Cultures, 6: A Modern and Contemporary History of the Catholic Church in Ethiopia (16th–20th Centuries)*, Addis Ababa, Capuchin Franciscan Institute of Philosophy and Theology.

ARMSTRONG, K., 2001, *Holy War: The Crusades and Their Impact on Today's World*, New York, Anchor Books, Random House.

ASANTE, S.K.B., 1974, 'The Catholic Missions, British West African Nationalists, and the Italian Invasion of Ethiopia, 1935–36', *African Affairs*, 73, 291, April 1974.

ASFA-WOSSEN ASSERATE, 2007, *Ein Prinz aus dem Hause David und warum er in Deutschland blieb*, Frankfurt, Scherz.

———, 2015, *King of Kings: The Triumph and Tragedy of Emperor Haile Selassie I of Ethiopia*, London, Haus.

AYELÈ TEKLEHAIMANOT, 1981, 'Un faro di luce Cristiana brilla da secoli sull'Ogaden', *Quaderni di Studi Etiopici*, pp. 56–64.

AYELE TEKLEHAYMANOT, 1999A, *Ethiopian Review of Cultures, 2–I: 'Miscellanea Aethiopica'*, Addis Ababa, Capuchin Franciscan Institute of Philosophy and Theology, St Francis' Friary.

———, 1999B, *Ethiopian Review of Cultures, 3 – II: 'Miscellanea Aethiopica'*, Addis Ababa, Capuchin Franciscan Institute of Philosophy and Theology, St. Francis' Friary.

AYMRO WONDMAGEGNEHU & MOTOVU, J., ED., 1970, *The Ethiopian Orthodox Church*, Addis Ababa, Birhanina Selam Printing Press.

BAER, G.W., 1976, *Test Case: Italy, Ethiopia, and the League of Nations*, Stanford, Stanford University.

BAHRU ZEWDE, 1991, *A History of Modern Ethiopia*, Addis Ababa, Addis Ababa University Press.

———, 2003, 'Abriha Däboch', in *Encyclopaedia Aethiopica*, vol. 1, A-C, ed. S. Uhlig, Wiesbaden, Harrassowitz, p. 47.

———, 2008, 'The Ethiopian Intelligentsia and the Italo-Ethiopian War', in *Society, State and History, Selected Essays*, Addis Ababa, Addis Ababa University Press, pp. 215–37 (previously published in *International Journal of African Historical Studies*, 26, 2, pp. 271–95).

BAIRU TAFLA, 2003, 'Abärra Kassa', in *Encyclopaedia Aethiopica*, vol. 1, A-C, ed. S. Uhlig, Wiesbaden, Harrassowitz, p. 7.

———, 2005, 'Darge Śahlä Śəllase', in *Encyclopaedia Aethiopica*, vol. 2, D-Ha, ed. S. Uhlig, Wiesbaden, Harrassowitz, pp. 102–3.

BARKER, A.J., 1968, *The Civilising Mission: A History of the Italo-Ethiopian War of 1935–1936*, New York, The Dial Press.

BIBLIOGRAPHY

―――, 1971, *Rape of Ethiopia 1936*, New York, Ballantine Books.
BAUDENDISTEL, R., 2006, *Between Bombs and Good Intentions: The Red Cross and the Italo-Ethiopian War, 1935–1936*, New York, Berghahn Books.
BAUSI, A., 2005, 'Däbrä Libanos', in *Encyclopaedia Aethiopica*, vol. 2, D-Ha, ed. S. Uhlig, Wiesbaden, Harrassowitz, pp. 28–9.
BAUSI, A. & FIACCADORI, G., 2014, 'Täsfa Ṣəyon', in *Encyclopaedia Aethiopica*, vol. 5, Y-Z, Addenda, Index, ed. A. Bausi, Wiesbaden, Harrassowitz, pp. 525–8.
BECKINGHAM, C.F. & HUNTINGFORD, G.W.B. (EDS.), 1961, *The Prester John of the Indies: A True Relation of the Lands of the Prester John, being the Narrative of the Portuguese Embassy to Ethiopia in 1520, written by Father Francisco Alvarez*, tr. Lord Stanley of Alderley (1881), Cambridge, Hakluyt Society Works, series 2, vols. 114, 115.
BELTRAMI, A., 2017, 'Etiopia: Debre Libanos, gli 80 anni di un eccidio senza scuse', *Avvenire*, 12 May 2017.
BEN-GHIAT, R. & FULLER, M., 2008, 'Introduction', in *Italian Colonialism*, ed. R. Ben-Ghiat and M. Fuller, Basingstoke, Macmillan, pp. 1–12.
BERHANOU ABEBE, 1998, *Histoire de l'Éthiopie d'Axoum à la revolution*, Addis Ababa, Centre Français des Études Éthiopiennes; Paris, Maisonneuve and Larose.
BERNOVILLE, G., 1948, *L'épopée missionnaire d'Éthiopie: Monseigneur Jarosseau et la mission des Gallas*, Paris, Éditions Albin Michel.
BINCHY, D.A., 1970, *Church and State in Fascist Italy*, Oxford, Oxford University Press.
BINNS, J., 2017, *The Orthodox Church of Ethiopia: A History*, London, I.B. Tauris.
BIRHANINA SELAM, 1939 EC, *Calendar for 1939 EC (1946–7)* (Amharic), Addis Ababa, Birhanina Selam Printing Press.
BIRHANU DENQÉ, 1937 EC, *YeAmistu YeMekera Ametat Acher Tarik* (Amharic), Addis Ababa, Birhanina Selam Printing Press.
BONECHI, M, 2011, 'Four Sistine Ethiopians? The 1481 Ethiopian Embassy and the Frescoes of the Sistine Chapel in the Vatican', *Aethiopica: International Journal of Ethiopian and Eritrean Studies*, 14, 2011, ed. A. Bausi, pp. 121–35.
BORRUSO, P., 1989, 'Le missioni cattoliche italiane nella politica imperiale del fascismo (1936–40)', *Africa: Rivista trimestrale di studi e documentazione dell'Istituto italiano per l'Africa e l'Oriente*, 44, 1, March 1989, pp. 50–78.
―――, 2001, 'La crisi politica e religiosa dell'impero etiopico sotto l'occupazione fascista (1936–1940)', *Studi Piacentini*, 29, pp. 57–111.
―――, 2002, *L'ultimo impero cristiano: Politica e religione nell'Etiopia contemporanea (1916–1974)*, Milan, Guerini e Associati.

BIBLIOGRAPHY

———, 2009, *Martiri cristiani in Etiopia tra occupazione italiana e guerra mondiale (1936–41)*, Milan, EDUCatt, Catholic University.

———, 2020, *Debre Libanos 1937: Il più grave crimine di guerra dell'Italia*, Rome, Editori Laterza.

BOSC-TIESSÉ, C., 2007, 'Märṭulä Maryam', in *Encyclopaedia Aethiopica*, vol. 3, He-N, ed. S. Uhlig, Wiesbaden, Harrassowitz, pp. 801–2.

BOSC-TIESSÉ, C. & FIACCADORI, G., 2005, 'Däbrä Wärq', in *Encyclopaedia Aethiopica*, vol. 2, D-Ha, ed. S. Uhlig, Wiesbaden, Harrassowitz, pp. 51–2.

BOTTAI, G., 1949, *Vent'anni e un giorno*, 2nd edn, Rome, Garzanti.

BOTTONI, R. (ED.), 2008, *L'impero fascista: Italia ed Etiopia (1935–1941)*, Bologna, Il Mulino.

BRADFORD, E., 1967, *The Great Betrayal: Constantinople, 1204*, London, Hodder and Stoughton.

BUDGE, E.A.W., 1928, *The Book of the Saints of the Ethiopian Church*, vols. 1-4, Cambridge, Cambridge University Press.

BUONASORTE, N., 1995, 'La politica religiosa italiana in Africa orientale dopo la conquista (1936–1941)', *Studi Piacentini*, 17, pp. 53–114.

BUSTORF, D., 2010, 'Slavery: Domestic and Court Slavery', in *Encyclopaedia Aethiopica*, vol. 4, O-X, ed. S. Uhlig, Wiesbaden, Harrassowitz, pp. 678–80.

BUSTORF, D., NOSNITSIN, D. & ALIEV-GUTGARTS, Y., 2014, 'Zəqwala', in *Encyclopaedia Aethiopica*, vol. 5, Y-Z, Addenda, Index, ed. A. Bausi, Wiesbaden, Harrassowitz, pp. 181–5.

BUXTON, D., 1957, *Travels in Ethiopia*, London, Ernest Benn.

CALAMANDREI, C., 1982, *Diario, vol. 1 (1939–41)*, ed. G. Agnosti, Florence, LaNuova Italia.

CAMPBELL, I.L., 1994A, 'The Church of St Tekle Haymanot at Debre Libanos', *Sociology and Ethnology Bulletin*, I, 3, February 1994, pp. 4–11.

———, 1994B, 'The Royal Fortress at Azazo', in *New Trends in Ethiopian Studies: Ethiopia 94; Papers of the 12th International Conference of Ethiopian Studies, Michigan State University, 5-10 September 1994*, ed. H.G. Marcus, New Jersey, Red Sea Press, pp. 6–15.

———, 1999, 'La repressione fascista in Etiopia: Il massacro segreto di Engecha', *Studi Piacentini*, 24–25, pp. 23–46.

———, 2004A, 'Reconstructing the Fascist Occupation of Ethiopia: The Italian Telegrams as Historical Sources', *International Journal of Ethiopian Studies*, 1, 2, Winter/Spring 2004, pp. 122–8.

———, 2004B, 'Portuguese and Indian Influences on the Architecture of the Lake Tana Region: An Enquiry into the Role of Gänätä Iyäsus', in *The Indigenous and the Foreign in Christian Ethiopian Art: On Portuguese*

BIBLIOGRAPHY

Contacts in the 16th–17th Centuries; Papers from the Fifth International Conference on the History of Ethiopian Art (Arrábida, 26–30 November 1999), ed. M.J. Ramos with I. Boavida, Aldershot, Ashgate, pp. 37–48.

———, 2010, *The Plot to Kill Graziani: The Attempted Assassination of Mussolini's Viceroy*, Addis Ababa, Addis Ababa University Press.

———, 2014, *The Massacre of Debre Libanos: Ethiopia 1937; One of Fascism's Most Shocking Atrocities*, Addis Ababa, Addis Ababa University Press.

———, 2017, *The Addis Ababa Massacre: Italy's National Shame*, London, Hurst.

CAMPBELL, I.L. & DEGIFE GABRE-TSADIK, 1997, 'La repressione fascista in Etiopia: La ricostruzione de massacro di Debra Libanos', *Studi Piacentini*, 21, pp. 79–128.

CARVIGIANI, A., 2019, 'Documenti inediti: Le "fake news" del fascismo su Debre Libanos', *Avvenire*, 28 November 2019.

CATALDI, A., 2018, 'La fede italianizzata', *Nigrizia*, 15 March 2018.

CECI, L., 2008A, 'Il Fascismo manda l'Italia in rovina: Le note inedite di monsignor Domenico Tardini (23 settembre – 13 dicembre 1935)', in *Rivista Storica Italiana*, 1, 2008, Naples, Edizioni Scientifiche Italiane, pp. 294–346.

———, 2008B, 'La guerra di Etiopia fuori dall'Italia: Le posizioni dei vescovi cattolici europei', in R. BOTTONI (ED.), 2008, pp. 117–43.

———, 2010, *Il papa non deve parlare: Chiesa, fascismo e guerra d'Etiopia*, Rome, Gius, Laterza and Figli.

———, 2012, 'The First Steps of "Parallel Diplomacy": The Vatican and the U.S. in the Italo-Ethiopian War (1935–1936)', in *Pius XI and America*, ed. David Kertzer et al., Berlin, LIT Verlag, pp. 87–106.

———, 2016, *The Vatican and Mussolini's Italy*, tr. P. Spring, Leiden, Brill Academic Publishers.

CERULLI, E., 1967, 'Two Ethiopian Tales on the Christians at Cyprus', *Journal of Ethiopian Studies*, V, 1, January 1967, pp. 1–8.

CHADWICK, O., 1988, *Britain and the Vatican during the Second World War*, Cambridge, Cambridge University Press.

CHERNETSOV, S., 2005, 'Ethiopian Orthodox (Täwahǝdo) Church: History from the Second Half of the 19th Century to 1959', in *Encyclopaedia Aethiopica*, vol. 2 D-Ha, ed. S. Uhlig, Wiesbaden, Harrassowitz, pp. 421–4.

CHIARI, G.P., 2009, *Guide to Aksum and Yeha*, Addis Ababa, Arada Books.

CIANO, G., 1952, *Ciano's Diary, 1937–1938*, tr. A. Mayor, London, Methuen.

CLARKE, J.C., 2008, 'Feodor Konovalov and the Italo-Ethiopian War', Part 1, *World War II Quarterly*, 5, 1, 2008, and Part 2 in 5, 2, 2008.

BIBLIOGRAPHY

Consociazione Turistica Italiani, 1938, *Guida dell'Africa Orientale Italiana*, Milan, CTI.

Conti Rossini, C., 1928, 'Tabelle comparative del calendario etiopico col calendario romano', in *Pubblicazioni dell'Istituto per l'Oriente*, Rome, Instituto per l'Oriente, pp. 3–47.

Crociani, P. & Battistelli, P., 2010, *Italian Blackshirt 1935–45*, Oxford, Osprey Publishing.

Curtin, P.R., 1983, 'Laboratory for the Oral History of Slavery: The Island of Lamu on the Kenya Coast', *American Historical Review*, 88, 4, 1 October 1983, pp. 858–82.

D'Agostino, P.R., 2003, *Rome in America: Transnational and Catholic Ideology from the Risorgimento to Fascism*, Chapel Hill: University of North Carolina Press.

Daniél Kibret, 1999 EC, *Ye Bét Kristiyan Merejawoch* (Amharic), vol. 1, Addis Ababa, Be Etiopiya Ortodoks Tewahido Bét Kristiyan.

De Bono, E., 1937, *Anno XIIII: The Conquest of an Empire*, London, Cresset Press.

De Felice, Renzo, 1974, *Mussolini il duce: Gli anni del consenso, 1929–1936*, Turin, Einaudi.

Debre-Keddus Estefanos, [c. 1971], *The Pontifical Ethiopian College in the Vatican City*, Rome, Typografia S. Pio X.

Debre Libanos Gedam, [c. 2010], *Zena Abeyomu Lesema'atat ZeDebre Libanos deqiqu LeTeklehaymanot* (Amharic), Monastery of Debre Libanos.

Del Boca, A., 1969, *The Ethiopian War 1935–1941*, tr. P.D. Cummins, Chicago, University of Chicago Press.

———, 1986, *Gli italiani in Africa orientale, vol. III: La caduta dell' impero*, Milan, Mondadori, Biblioteca Universale Laterza.

———, 1987, 'Un lager del fascismo', *Studi Piacentini*, 1, pp. 59–70.

———, 1988, *Gli italiani in Libia: Dal fascismo a Gheddafi*, Rome: Laterza.

———, 1996, *I gas di Mussolini: Il fascismo e la guerra d'Etiopia*, Rome, Riuniti.

———, 2003, 'The Myths, Suppressions, Denials and Defaults of Italian Colonialism', in *A Place in the Sun: Africa in Italian Colonial Culture from Post-Unification to the Present*, ed. P. Palumbo, Los Angeles: University of California Press, pp. 17–36.

———, 2005, *Italiani, brava gente?*, Vicenza, Neri Pozza Editore.

Departement de la Presse et de l'Information du Gouvernement Imperial d'Ethiopie, n.d., *La civilisation de l'Italie fasciste en Ethiopie*, Addis Ababa, Gouvernement Imperial d'Ethiopie.

———, 1946, *La civilisation de l'Italie fasciste en Ethiopie*, vol. II, Addis Ababa, Gouvernement Imperial d'Ethiopie.

BIBLIOGRAPHY

Derat, M.-L., 2005A, 'Däbrä Libanos', in *Encyclopaedia Aethiopica*, vol. 2 D-Ha, ed. S. Uhlig, Wiesbaden, Harrassowitz, pp. 25–8.

———, 2005B, 'Dawit II', in *Encyclopaedia Aethiopica*, vol. 2, D-Ha, ed. S. Uhlig, Wiesbaden, Harrassowitz, pp. 112–13.

———, 2007, 'Mäkanä Səllase', in *Encyclopaedia Aethiopica*, vol. 3, He-N, ed. S. Uhlig, Wiesbaden, Harrassowitz, p. 672.

———, 2010, 'Wədəm Rä'ad', in *Encyclopaedia Aethiopica*, vol. 4, O-X, ed. S. Uhlig, Wiesbaden, Harrassowitz, p. 1177.

Deschner, K., 2013, *God and the Fascists: The Vatican Alliance with Mussolini, Franco, Hitler and Pavelić*, New York, Prometheus Books.

Diel, L., 1939, *'Behold Our New Empire': Mussolini*, tr. K. Kirkness, London, Hurst and Blackett.

Doino, W., Jr., 2004, 'An Annotated Bibliography of Works on Pius XII, the Second World War, and the Holocaust', in *The Pius War: Response to the Critics of Pius XII*, ed. J. Bottum and D.G. Dalin, Lanham, Lexington Books, pp. 97–280.

Dominioni, M., 2002, 'Il 1937 nel Governatorato dell'Amara: Le cause della grande rivolta', in *Studi e materiali dale tesi di Laurea*, III, Università ca' Foscari Venezia, Milan, Unicopli.

———, 2003, 'La repressione italiana nella regione di Bahar Dar', *Studi Piacentini*, 33, pp. 159–70.

———, 2008A, *Lo sfascio dell'impero: Gli italiani in Etiopia 1936–1941*, Rome, Editori Laterza.

———, 2008B, 'Il sistema di occupazione politico-militare dell'Etiopia', in *Politiche di occupazione dell'Italia fascista*, L'Annale Irsifar, Istituto romano per la storia d'Italia dal fascismo alla Resistenza, Milan, FrancoAngeli, pp. 43–57.

Dugan, J. & Lafore, L., 1973, *Days of Emperor and Clown: The Italo-Ethiopian War 1935–1936*, New York, Doubleday.

Duggan, C., 2007, *The Force of Destiny: A History of Italy since 1796*, Boston, Houghton Mifflin.

———, 2013, *Fascist Voices: An Intimate History of Mussolini's Italy*, New York, Oxford University Press.

Ethiopia Tourist Trading Corporation, n.d., *Ethiopia: Around Ziqualla*, Addis Ababa, ETTC.

———, 1997, *Yeltyopya Bét Kristiyan Tinantnana Zaré: The Church of Ethiopia Past and Present* (Amharic and English), Addis Ababa, Ethiopian Orthodox Church.

Falasca-Zamponi, S., 1997, *Fascist Spectacle*, Berkeley, University of California Press.

BIBLIOGRAPHY

Fattorini, E., 2011, *Hitler, Mussolini and the Vatican: Pope Pius XI and the Speech That Was Never Made*, tr. C. Ipsen, Cambridge, Polity Press.

Fiaccadori, G., 2007, 'Italy, Relations with: Relations during the 12th–19th Cent.', in *Encyclopaedia Aethiopica*, vol. 3, He-N, ed. S. Uhlig, Wiesbaden, Harrassowitz, pp. 236–9.

———, 2010, 'Santo Stefano dei Mori', in *Encyclopaedia Aethiopica*, vol. 4, O-X, ed. S. Uhlig, Wiesbaden, Harrassowitz, pp. 528–32.

Finaldi, G., 2019, 'Fascism, Violence, and Italian Colonialism', *Journal of Holocaust Research*, 33, 1, pp. 22–42.

Focardi, F. & Klinkhammer, L., 2004, 'The Question of Fascist Italy's War Crimes: The Construction of a Self-acquitting Myth (1943–1948)', *Journal of Modern Italian Studies*, 9, 3, 2004, pp. 330–48.

Forgacs, D., 2014, *Italy's Margins: Social Exclusion and Nation Formation since 1861*, Cambridge, Cambridge University Press.

Franzinelli, M., 1992, 'Il clero e le colonie: I cappellani militari in Africa orientale', *Rivista di storia contemporanea*, XXI, 4, 1992, pp. 558–98.

———, 1995, *Stellete, croce e fascio littorio: L'assistenza religiosa a militari, balilla e camicie nere (1919–1939)*, Milan, F. Angeli.

———, 2008, 'Il clero italiano e la "grande mobilitazione"', in R. Bottoni (ed.), 2008, pp. 251–65.

Gaitachew Bekele, 1993, *The Emperor's Clothes: A Personal Viewpoint on Politics and Administration in the Imperial Ethiopian Government 1941–1974*, East Lansing, Michigan State University Press.

Garretson, P.P., 2003, 'A Note on Relations between Ethiopia and the Kingdom of Aragon in the Fifteenth Century', *Rassegna di Studi Etiopici*, 37, 1993, pp. 37–44.

Gascoigne, B., 2003, *A Brief History of Christianity*, London, Robinson.

Gebre-Igziabher Elyas, ed. R.K. Molvaer, 1994, *Prowess, Piety and Politics: The Chronicle of Abeto Iyasu and Empress Zewditu of Ethiopia (1909–1930)*, Cologne, Rüdiger Köppe Verlag.

Gemelli, A., 1935A, 'L'Italia nell'ora presente', *Vita e Pensiero*, XXI, 12, December 1935, pp. 683–5.

———, 1935B, 'Tutti gli Italiani uniti nella lotta per la pace', *Vita e Pensiero*, XXI, 12, December 1935, pp. 733–55.

Gentile, E., 1993, *Il culto del littorio*, Rome, Laterza.

Gentilli, R., 1992, *Guerra aerea sull'Etiopia 1935–1939*, Florence, Edizioni Aeronautiche Italiane.

———, 2003, 'La storiografia aeronautica e il problema dei gas', in Del Boca, A., 2003, pp. 133–47.

Geremew Eskezia, 2017, 'Local Response to Italian Occupation in Yilmana Dénsa District (West Gojjam) and the Battles of Yizora and Yidibi

BIBLIOGRAPHY

(1937)', *Ethiopian Journal of Social Sciences*, 3, 1, 2017, pp. 1–13.

GERSTER, G., 1970, *Churches in Rock: Early Christian Art in Ethiopia*, London, Phaidon.

GIBSON, H. (ED.), 1946, *The Ciano Diaries, 1939–1943*, New York, Doubleday.

GIOVAGNOLI, A., 2008, 'L'Africa nella "geopolitica" di Pio XI', in R. BOTTONI (ED.), 2008, pp. 233–49.

GIOVANNI GEBRE-IYESUS, 1984, *Dall'Etiopia imperiale all'impero rosso*, Turin.

GIULIANI, R., 1937, *Per Cristo e per la Patria*, Florence, Salani.

GOVERNO GENERALE, STATO MAGGIORE, A.O.I., 1939, *Il I° anno dell'impero*, vol. III, Addis Ababa, Superiore Topocartografico.

GRAZIANI, R., 2001, *Una vita per l'Italia: 'Ho difeso la patria'*, Milan, Mursia.

GREENFIELD, R., 1965, *Ethiopia: A New Political History*, London, Pall Mall Press.

GRUBB, N., 1943, *Alfred Buxton of Abyssinia and Congo*, London, Lutterworth Press.

HABTEMICHAEL KIDANE, 2005, 'Dəggwa', in *Encyclopaedia Aethiopica*, vol. 2, D-Ha, ed. S. Uhlig, Wiesbaden, Harrassowitz, pp. 123–4.

HADIS HIWET, 1964 EC, *Nihineni Nanisosu Wuset Hadas Hiywet*, Addis Ababa, Tinsa'é Zegube'é Printing Press.

HAILE GABRIEL DAGNE, 1972, 'The Gebzenna Charter 1894', *Journal of Ethiopian Studies*, X, 1, pp. 67–80.

———, 1987, 'The Establishment of Churches in Addis Ababa', in *Proceedings of the International Symposium on the centenary of Addis Ababa, November 24–25 1986*, ed. Ahmed Zekaria et al., Addis Ababa: Institute of Ethiopian Studies, Addis Ababa University, pp. 57–78.

HAILE LAREBO, 2008, 'Empire Building and Its Limitations: Ethiopia (1935–1941)', in *Italian Colonialism*, ed. R. Ben-Ghiat and M. Fuller, Basingstoke, Macmillan, pp. 83–94.

HAILE SELASSIE I, ED. H. MARCUS, 1994, *My Life and Ethiopia's Progress: Haile Selassie I King of Kings of Ethiopia, volume 2: Addis Ababa, 1966 E.C.*, East Lansing, Michigan State University Press.

HAILE SELLASSIE I, TR. & ANNOT. E. ULLENDORF, 1999, *My Life and Ethiopia's Progress: Volume One 1892–1937: The Autobiography of Emperor Haile Sellassie I* (photographic reprint of 1976 edition), Barbados, Research Associates School Times Publications.

HELDMAN, M.E., 1993, 'Maryam Seyon: Mary of Zion', in M. Heldman with S.C. Munro-Hay, *African Zion: The Sacred Art of Ethiopia*, ed. R. Grierson, New Haven, Yale University Press, pp. 71–100.

HENZE, P., 1999, 'The Monastery of Mertule Maryam in Gojjam: A Major Medieval Ethiopian Architectural Monument', in *Äthiopien gestern und heute. Akten der 1. Tagung der Orbis Æthiopicus Gesellschaft zur Erhaltung und Förderung der äthiopischen Kultur*, ed. P.O. Scholz, Warsaw, Internationales Jahrbuch für koptische, meroitisch-nubische, äthiopische und verwandte Studien, pp. 131–62.

———, 2006, 'The Monastery of Däbrä Abbay: Ǝnda Abunä Samu'el', in *Proceedings of the XVth International Conference of Ethiopian Studies, Hamburg 2003*, ed. S. Uhlig, Wiesbaden, Harrassowitz, pp. 663–9.

IMRU ZELLEKE, 2016, *A Journey: Memoirs*, North Charleston: CreateSpace Independent Publishing Platform.

JENKINS, P., 2014, *The Great and Holy War: How World War I Became a Religious Crusade*, New York, HarperCollins.

JONAS, R., 2011, *The Battle of Adwa: African Victory in the Age of Empire*, Cambridge MA, The Belknap Press, Harvard University Press.

KALI-NYAH, I., 2001, *Italy's War Crimes in Ethiopia (1935–1941): Evidence for the War Crimes Commission*, Chicago, The Ethiopian Holocaust Remembrance Committee.

KAPLAN, S., 2007A, 'Matewos', in *Encyclopaedia Aethiopica*, vol. 3, He-N, ed. S. Uhlig, Wiesbaden, Harrassowitz, pp. 867–8.

———, 2007B, 'Monasteries', in *Encyclopaedia Aethiopica*, vol. 3, He-N, ed. S. Uhlig, Wiesbaden, Harrassowitz, pp. 987–93.

———, 2014, 'Monasticism', in *Encyclopaedia Aethiopica*, vol. 5, Y-Z, ed. A. Bausi, Wiesbaden, Harrassowitz, pp. 443–7.

KEFYALEW MEHARI, 2001, *Saints and Monasteries in Ethiopia*, Addis Ababa, Commercial Printing Enterprise.

———, 2003, *Saints and Monasteries in Ethiopia II*, Addis Ababa, Commercial Printing Enterprise.

KENT, P.C., 1981, *The Pope and the Duce: The International Impact of the Lateran Agreements*, New York, St Martin's Press.

———, 1984, 'The Catholic Church in the Italian Empire, 1936–1938', in *Historical Papers / Communications Historiques*, 19, 1, 1984, pp. 138–50.

KERTZER, D.I., 2014, *The Pope and Mussolini: The Secret History of Pius XI and the Rise of Fascism in Europe*, New York, Random House.

KIRSCH, J., 2008, *The Grand Inquisitor's Manual: A History of Terror in the Name of God*, New York, HarperCollins.

KNOX, M., 1986, *Mussolini Unleashed 1939–1941: Politics and Strategy in Fascist Italy's Last War*, Cambridge, Cambridge University Press.

———, 2000, *Hitler's Italian Allies: Royal Armed Forces, Fascist Regime, and the War of 1940–1943*, Cambridge, Cambridge University Press.

KORNBERG, J., 2015, *The Pope's Dilemma: Pius XII Faces Atrocities and Genocide in the Second World War*, Toronto, University of Toronto Press.

BIBLIOGRAPHY

LABANCA, N., 2008, 'Italian Colonial Internment', in *Italian Colonialism*, ed. R. Ben-Ghiat and M. Fuller, Basingstoke, Macmillan, pp. 27–36.

LACROIX-RIZ, A., 1994, 'Le rôle du Vatican dans la colonisation de l'Afrique (1920–1938): De la romanisation des missions à la conquête de l'Ethiopie', *Revue d'histoire moderne et contemporaine* 41, pp. 327–41.

LASS-WESTPHAL, I., 1972, 'Protestant Missions during and after the Italian–Ethiopian War, 1935–1937', *Journal of Ethiopian Studies*, X, 1, pp. 89–101.

LÁSZLÓ, S., 2015, *Fascist Italian Brutality in Ethiopia, 1935–1937: An Eyewitness Account*, ed. S. Balázs, Trenton, Red Sea Press.

LAUNHARDT, J., 2004, *Evangelicals in Addis Ababa (1919–1991) with Special Reference to the Ethiopian Evangelical Church Mekane Yesus and the Addis Ababa Synod*, Münster, Lit Verlag.

LAZZERO, R., 1968, 'Un passo verso la verità sulla morte di Mussolini: Dongo', *Epoca*, 25 August 1968.

LE HOUÉROU, F., 1994A, *L'épopée des soldats de Mussolini en Abyssinie 1936–1938: Les 'ensablés'*, Paris, L'Harmattan.

———. 1994B, 'Portrait of a Fascist: Marshall Graziani', in *New Trends in Ethiopian Studies Ethiopia 94; Papers of the 12th International Conference of Ethiopian Studies, volume I*, ed. Harold Marcus, Lawrenceville, Red Sea Press, pp. 822–9.

LEFEBVRE, T., 1845–8, *Voyage en Abyssinie éxécuté pendant les années 1839, 1840, 1841, 1842, 1843*, vol. II, Paris, Betrand.

LEIJONHUFVUD, E.S.A., 1948, *Kejsaren och hans hövdingar*, Stockholm, Norstedt & Söner.

LENTAKIS, M., 2005, *Ethiopia: A View from Within*, London, Janus Publishing.

LENTZ, H.M., 2002, *Popes and Cardinals: A Biographical Dictionary*, Jefferson, NC, McFarland Publishing.

LESSONA, A., 1958, *Memorie*, Florence, Sansoni.

LO BELLO, NINO, 1969, *The Vatican Empire: An Authoritative Report That Reveals the Vatican as a Nerve Centre of High Finance – and Penetrates the Secrecy of Papal Wealth*, New York, Trident Press.

MANHATTAN, A., 1949, *The Vatican in World Politics*, New York, Gaer Associates.

MARCUS, H. G., 1995, *Haile Selassie I: The Formative Years 1892–1936*, Lawrenceville, Red Sea Press.

MARTIN, W.C., 1936, 'Rome and Ethiopia', *New Times and Ethiopia News*, 31, 5 December 1936, p. 1.

MCCLELLAN, C., 1998, 'The Tales of Yeseph and Woransa: Gedeo Experiences in the Era of the Italo-Ethiopian War', in *Personality and Political Culture in Modern Africa: Studies Presented to Professor Harold G. Marcus*, Boston, African Studies Center, Boston University, pp. 184–94.

BIBLIOGRAPHY

McCullagh, F., 1912, *Italy's War for a Desert: Some Experiences of a War Correspondent with the Italians in Tripoli*, London, Herbert and Daniel.

Meinardus, O., 2005, 'Ethiopian Monks in Egypt', in *Encyclopaedia Aethiopica*, vol. 2, D-Ha, ed. S. Uhlig, Wiesbaden, Harrassowitz, pp. 243–5.

Meleseliñ Aniley, 1947 EC, *YeArbeññoch Tegel keFashist Gar: keShewa Iska SudanTeref* (Amharic), Addis Ababa, Birhanina Selam Printing Press.

Mercier, J., 2014, *Illustrated Guide to the Monolithic Churches of Lalibela and Churches in ItsVicinity*, Addis Ababa, Shama Books.

Mersha Alehegne, 2010, 'Peṭros', in *Encyclopaedia Aethiopica*, vol. 4, O-X, ed. S. Uhlig, Wiesbaden, Harrassowitz, pp. 140–1.

Mikaël Bethe Selassié, 2009, *La jeune Éthiopie: Un haut-fonctionnaire éthiopien Berhanä-MarqosWäldä-Tsadeq (1892–1943)*, Aresea, L'Harmattan.

Mikre-Sellassie Gebre-Ammanuel, 2014, *Church and Missions in Ethiopia during the Italian Occupation*, Addis Ababa, Rev. Dr Mikre-Sellassie.

Ministry of Justice, 1949, *Documents on Italian War Crimes Submitted to the United Nations War Crimes Commission by the Imperial Ethiopian Government, volume I: Italian Telegrams and Circulars*, Addis Ababa, Ministry of Justice.

———, 1950, *Documents on Italian War Crimes Submitted to the United NationsWar Crimes Commission by the Imperial Ethiopian Government, volume II:Affidavits and Published Documents*, Addis Ababa, Ministry of Justice.

Mockler, A., 1977, *Il mito dell'impero: Storia delle guerre italiane in Abissinia e in Etiopia*, Milan, Rizzoli.

———, 1984, *Haile Selassie's War: The Italian-Ethiopian Campaign, 1935–1941*, NewYork, Random House.

Molvaer, R.K., 2007, 'Mäl'akä Šähay Iyasu', in *Encyclopaedia Aethiopica*, vol. 3, He-N, ed. S. Uhlig, Wiesbaden, Harrassowitz, pp. 688–9.

Mondadori, A., ed., 1939, *Gli annali dell'Africa italiana, anno II° – numero 2 – giugno 1939 – XVII*, Rome, Casa Editrice A. Mondadori.

Nickelsburg, G.W.E., 2006, 'The Book of Enoch in the Theology and Practice of the Ethiopian Church', in *Proceedings of the XVth International Conference of Ethiopian Studies, Hamburg July 20–25 2003*, ed. S. Uhlig, Wiesbaden, Harrassowitz, pp. 611–19.

Nicolle, D., 1997, *The Italian Invasion of Abyssinia 1935–36*, Men-at-Arms series, no. 309, Wellingborough, Osprey.

Nobili, E., 2008, 'Vescovi lombardi e consenso alla guerra: Il cardinale Schuster', in R. Bottoni (ed.), 2008, pp. 267–85.

Nosnitsin, D., Fritsch, E. & DimetrosWeldu, 2003, 'Churches and Church Administration', in *Encyclopaedia Aethiopica*, vol. 1, A-C, ed. S. Uhlig, Wiesbaden, Harrassowitz, pp. 740–4.

BIBLIOGRAPHY

Novak, M., 2004, 'Bigotry's New Law', in *The PiusWar: Response to the Critics of Pius XII*, ed. J. Bottum and D.G. Dalin, Lanham, Lexington Books, pp. 83–8.

Novati, G.C., 2007, 'Italy, Relations with: Relations during the 19th–20th Cent.', in *Encyclopaedia Aethiopica*, vol. 3, He-N, ed. S. Uhlig, Wiesbaden, Harrassowitz, pp. 239–44.

Núñez, J.G., 2018, *Ethiopia: History and Legend*, Addis Ababa, Agencia Española de Cooperación Internacional para el Desarrollo (AECID).

Nystrom, H., tr. Gebreyehu Teferi & Dessalegn Alemu, 2014, *YeTedebeqew Mastawesha* (Amharic), Chibo Light Book.

Ofcansky, T.P., 2007, 'Italian War 1935–36', in *Encyclopaedia Aethiopica*, vol. 3, He-N, ed. S. Uhlig, Wiesbaden, Harrassowitz, pp. 228–34.

Pankhurst, A., 1994, 'Debre Libanos Pilgrimages Past and Present: The Mystery of the Bones and the Legend of St Tekle Haymanot', *Sociology and Ethnology Bulletin*, February 1994.

Pankhurst, R.K., 1969, 'The Ethiopian Patriots and the Collapse of Italian Rule in East Africa, 1940–41', *Ethiopia Observer*, XII, 2, pp. 92–127.

———, 1970, 'The Ethiopian Patriots: The Lone Struggle 1936–1940', *Ethiopia Observer*, XIII, 1, pp. 40–56.

———, 1973, 'Abune Petros: An Ethiopian Patriot Martyr in the Modern Amharic Theatre', *Ethiopia Observer*, XVI, 2, pp. 118–24.

———, 1982, *History of Ethiopian Towns from the Middle Ages to the Early Nineteenth Century*, Wiesbaden, Franz Steiner Verlag.

———, 1993, 'The Mystery of the Debra Libanos Treasure', *Ethiopian Review*, March 1993, p. 40.

———, 1997, 'The Secret History of the Italian Fascist Occupation of Ethiopia, 1935–1941', *African Quarterly*, XVI, IV, April 1997, pp. 1–52.

———, 1999A, 'The Story of Ethiopian Looted Crowns, 3: Mussolini, and the Ethiopian Crowns of Tewedros, Yohannis, Menilek and Haile Selassie', *Addis Tribune*, 1 August 1999.

———, 1999B, 'Italian Fascist War Crimes in Ethiopia: A History of Their Discussion, from the League of Nations to the United Nations (1936–1949)', *Northeast African Studies*, 6, 1-2 (new series), pp. 83–140.

———, 2001A, *The Ethiopians: A History*, Oxford, Blackwell.

———, 2003A, *Sylvia Pankhurst, Counsel for Ethiopia: A Biographical Essay on Ethiopian Anti-Fascist and Anti-Colonialist History, 1934–1960*, Hollywood, Tsehai Publishers and Distributors.

———, 2003B, 'Cyprus, Relations with', in *Encyclopaedia Aethiopica*, vol. 1, A-C, ed. S. Uhlig, Wiesbaden, Harrassowitz, pp. 842–3.

———, 2007, 'Historical Notes on Books, 2: Hakim Workneh, Ethiopia, and the Libyan War', *Capital* (Addis Ababa), 9, 464, 4 November 2007.

PANKHURST, S., 1946, *Italy's War Crimes in Ethiopia*, Woodford Green, Sylvia Pankhurst.

———, 1955, *Ethiopia: A Cultural History*, Woodford Green, Lalibela House.

PARIS, E., 1961, *Genocide in Satellite Croatia 1941–1945: A Record of Racial and Religious Persecutions and Massacres*, Chicago, The American Institute for Balkan Affairs.

PARSONS, G., 2008, *The Cult of Saint Catherine of Siena: A Study in Civil Religion*, Aldershot, Ashgate.

PEARCE, J., 2014, *Prevail: The Inspiring Story of Ethiopia's Victory over Mussolini's Invasion, 1935–1941*, Delaware, Skyhorse Publishing.

PEDERSON, K.S., 2007, 'Jerusalem', in *Encyclopaedia Aethiopica*, vol. 3, He-N, ed. S. Uhlig, Wiesbaden, Harrassowitz, pp. 273–7.

PEDRIALI, F., 1996, 'Le armi chimiche in Africa orientale: Storia, tecnica, obiettivi, efficacia', in DEL BOCA, A., 1996, pp. 89–104..

PERRET, M., 1986, 'Le massacre de Däbrä Libanos', 'La guerre d'Éthiopie et l'opinion mondiale 1934–1941', in *Actes du Colloque de l'INALCO, Paris, 14 décembre 1984*, Paris, Institut National des Langues et Civilisations Orientales.

PERSOON, J., 2005A, 'Däbrä Asäbot', in *Encyclopaedia Aethiopica*, vol. 2, D-Ha, ed. S. Uhlig, Wiesbaden, Harrassowitz, pp. 9–10.

———, 2005B, 'Däbrä Mäwi', in *Encyclopaedia Aethiopica*, vol. 2, D-Ha, ed. S. Uhlig, Wiesbaden, Harrassowitz, pp. 33–4.

———, 2007, 'Mahbärä Səllase', in *Encyclopaedia Aethiopica*, vol. 3, He-N, ed. S. Uhlig, Wiesbaden, Harrassowitz, pp. 653–4.

PERSOON, J. & NOSNITSIN, D., 2005, 'Däbrä Abbay', in *Encyclopaedia Aethiopica*, vol. 2, D-Ha, ed. S. Uhlig, Wiesbaden, Harrassowitz, pp. 7–8.

POGGIALI, C., 1971, *Diario AOI (15 giugno 1936–4 ottobre 1937)*, Milan, Longanesi.

POLLARD, J., 2005, *Money and the Rise of the Modern Papacy: Financing the Vatican, 1850–1950*, Cambridge, Cambridge University Press.

———, 2014, *The Papacy in the Age of Totalitarianism 1914–1958*, New York, Oxford University Press.

POSNER, G., 2015, *God's Bankers: A History of Money and Power at the Vatican*, New York, Simon and Schuster.

POYNTER, J.W., 1936, 'The Italian Church and Mussolini's Aggression', *New Times and Ethiopia News*, 15, 15 August 1936.

QUINTON, A.G.H., 1949, *Ethiopia and the Evangel*, London, Marshall, Morgan and Scott.

RAINERI, O., 2014, 'Zena Marqos', in *Encyclopaedia Aethiopica*, vol. 5, Y-Z,

BIBLIOGRAPHY

ed. A. Bausi, Wiesbaden, Harrassowitz, pp. 178–9.

RAINERI, O. & MARTINEZ D'ALÒS-MONER, A., 2010, 'Vatican and Holy See, Relations with', in *Encyclopaedia Aethiopica*, vol. 4, O-X, ed. S. Uhlig, Wiesbaden, Harrassowitz, pp. 1052–5.

RICCARDI, A., 2017A, 'Ricordare con gesti concreti il massacro dei monaci etiopi', *Corriere della Sera*, 6 March 2017.

RILEY-SMITH, J., 2009, *What Were the Crusades?*, 4th edn, San Francisco, Ignatius Press.

ROBERTSON, E.M., 1977, *Mussolini as Empire Builder: Europe and Africa, 1932–1936*, London, Macmillan Press.

ROCHAT, G., 1971, *Militari e politici nella preparazione della campagna d'Etiopia: Studi e documenti, 1932–1936*, Milan, Franco Angeli.

———, 1988, 'L'attentato a Graziani e la repressione italiana in Etiopia nel 1936–37 (1975)', in *Guerre italiane in Libia e in Etiopia: Studi militari 1921–1939*, ed. G. Rochat, Treviso, Pagus, pp. 174–214 (originally published in *Italia Contemporanea*, 118, Jan.–March 1975, pp. 3–38).

———, 2008, 'The Italian Air Force in the Ethiopian War', in *Italian Colonialism*, ed. R. Ben-Ghiat and M. Fuller, Basingstoke, Macmillan, pp. 37–46.

ROUAUD, A., 1991, *Afä-Wärq: Un intellectuel éthiopien témoin de son temps 1868-1947*, Paris, Éditions du Centre National de la Recherche Scientifique.

SALOME GEBRE-EGZIABHER, 1969A, 'The Ethiopian Patriots, 1936–1941', *Ethiopia Observer* (Addis Ababa), XII, 2, pp. 63–91.

———, 1969B, 'The Patriotic Works of Dejazmach Aberra Kassa and Ras Abebe Aragaye', in *Proceedings of the Third International Conference of Ethiopian Studies, Addis Ababa 1966*, Addis Ababa, Institute of Ethiopian Studies, Haile Selassie I University, pp. 293–314.

SALVADORE, M., 2017, *The African Prester John and the Birth of Ethiopian–European Relations, 1402–1555*, Abingdon, Routledge.

SALVEMINI, G., 1936, 'Professor G. Salvemini on Papal Connivance with Fascism', *New Times and Ethiopia News*, 24, 17 October 1936, pp. 1–2.

———, 1969A, 'The Vatican and the Ethiopian War', in *Neither Liberty nor Bread: The Meaning and Tragedy of Fascism*, Port Washington, Kennikat, pp. 191–200 (from *Christendom*, Winter 1937).

———, 1969B, 'The Ethiopian War', in *Neither Liberty nor Bread: The Meaning and Tragedy of Fascism*, Port Washington, Kennikat, pp. 241-45 (from *Italian Fascism*, 1938, London, Gollancz, pp. 74–84).

SANNEH, L.O., 1996, *Religion and the Variety of Culture: A Study in Origin and Practice*, Atlanta, Trinity Press International.

SARR, F. & SAVOY, B., TR. D.S. BURK, 2018, *The Restitution of African Cultural*

BIBLIOGRAPHY

Heritage: Toward a New Relational Ethics, Paris, Ministère de la Culture.

SAVA, L., 1941, 'Ethiopia under Mussolini's Rule', *New Times and Ethiopia News*, 4 January 1941, p. 1.

SBACCHI, A., 1977, Italy and the Treatment of the Ethiopian Aristocracy, 1937–1940', *International Journal of African Historical Studies*, 10, 2, pp. 209–41.

———, 1985, *Ethiopia under Mussolini: Fascism and the Colonial Experience*, London, Zed Books.

———, 1997, *Legacy of Bitterness: Ethiopia and Fascist Italy, 1935–1941*, Lawrenceville, Red Sea Press.

SELTENE SEYOUM, 2002, 'Emperor Haile Selassie I and the Ethiopian Resistance: 1936–1941', in *Ethiopian Studies at the End of the Second Millennium, Proceedings of the XIVth International Conference of Ethiopian Studies, November 6–11 2000, Addis Ababa*, volume I, ed. Baye Yimam, R.K. Pankhurst, D. Chapple et al., Addis Ababa, Institute of Ethiopian Studies, Addis Ababa University, pp. 477–98.

———, 2003A, 'Review of the Literature on Ethiopian Resistance with Particular Emphasis on Gojjam: 1936–1941', *Journal of Ethiopian Studies*, XXXVI, 2, Dec. 2003.

———, 2003B, 'Asfa Wäsän Haylä Səllase', in *Encyclopaedia Aethiopica*, vol. 1, A-C. ed. S. Uhlig, Wiesbaden, Harrassowitz, pp. 366–7.

———, 2010, 'Resistance', in *Encyclopaedia Aethiopica*, vol. 4, O-X, ed. S. Uhlig, Wiesbaden, Harrassowitz, pp. 379–81.

SERGEW HABLE SELLASSIE, 1972, *Ancient and Medieval Ethiopian History to 1270*, Addis Ababa, Haile Selassie University.

———. 1993, 'Source for the History of Debre Libanos', *Journal of the Archives of Ethiopia*, I, 2.

SHENK, C.E., 1972, 'The Italian Attempt to Reconcile the Ethiopian Orthodox Church: The Use of Religious Celebrations and Assistance to Churches and Monasteries', *Journal of Ethiopian Studies*, X, 1, pp. 125–35.

SHIFERAW BEKELE, 2013, 'Preliminary Notes on Ethiopian Sources on the Italian Invasion of the Country and the Subsequent Occupation', in *L'impero nel cassetto: L'Italia coloniale tra album e archive pubblici*, ed. P.B. Farnetti, A. Mignemi and A. Triulzi, Milan, Mimesis, pp. 31–6.

SIEBERT, F., 1962, *Italiens Weg in den Zweiten Weltkrieg*, Frankfurt am Main, Athenäum.

ŠIHĀB AD-DĪN AHMAD BIN 'ABD AL-QADER BIN SALEM BIN 'UTMAN, *ALSO KNOWN AS* 'ARAB FAQĪH, 2003, *Futūh al-Habaša: The Conquest of Abyssinia* [16th century], tr. P.L. Stonehouse and annot. R. Pankhurst, Hollywood, Tsehai.

BIBLIOGRAPHY

SMIDT, W., 2010, 'Slavery: The Slavery Question in Politics', in *Encyclopaedia Aethiopica*, vol. 4, O-X, ed. S. Uhlig, Wiesbaden, Harrassowitz, pp. 680–1.

SPENCER, D., 2003, *The Woman from Tedbab*, Dorking, Elizabeth Horne Publishing.

SPENCER, J.H., 1987, *Ethiopia at Bay: A Personal Account of the Haile Sellassie Years*, Algonac MI, Reference Publications, Inc.

STEER, G.L., 2009, *Sealed and Delivered: A Book on the Abyssinian Campaign*, London, Faber and Faber.

STRACHAN, B., 2014, 'Yäkka Mika'el', in *Encyclopaedia Aethiopica*, vol. 5, Y-Z, Addenda, Index, ed. A. Bausi, Wiesbaden, Harrassowitz, pp. 16–18.

STRANG, G.B., 2017, *Collision of Empires: Italy's Invasion of Ethiopia and Its International Impact*, New York, Routledge.

SUNDKLER, B. & STEED, C., 2000, *A History of the Church in Africa*, Cambridge, Cambridge University Press.

TADDESSE MÉCHA, [C.1943 EC], *Tiqur Anbessa: BeMi'irab Ityopya* (Amharic), Asmara, Corriere Eritreo, Mahiber Printing Press.

TADDESSE TAMRAT, 1972, *Church and State in Ethiopia 1270–1527*, Oxford, Oxford University Press.

TADDESSE ZEWELDÉ, 1955 EC, *YeAbalashiñ Zemen* (Amharic), Addis Ababa, Birhanina Selam Printing Press.

——, 1960 EC, *Qerin Geremew: YeArbeññoch Tarik* (Amharic), Addis Ababa, Birhanina Selam Printing Press.

TAMASGEN GABRE, 1945, 'Hell on Earth', *Ethiopian Herald*, 24 February 1945.

TEELING, L.W.B., 1937, *The Pope in Politics: The Life and Work of Pope Pius XI*, London, Dickson.

TEKALIGN GEDAMU, 2011, *Republicans on the Throne: A Personal Account of Ethiopia's Modernization and Painful Quest for Democracy*, Los Angeles, Tsehai Publishers.

TEKLE-TSADIQ MEKURIYA, 1983 EC, *Atsé Minilik Ina Yeltyopya Andinet* (Amharic), Addis Ababa, Kuraz.

——, 2008 EC, *YeHiyweté Tariq* (Amharic), Addis Ababa, Eclipse Printing Press.

TELAHUN PAULOS ET AL., 2002, 'Field Trip to Däbrä Libanos: Life in the Monastery', in *Addis Ababa University College Ethnological Society Bulletin vol. I, nos. 1–10 and vol. II, no. 1, 1953–1961*, reprint, Addis Ababa, Addis Ababa University Printing Press, pp. 53–5.

TEMESGEN GEBRÉ, 2001 EC, *Hiyweté (Gile Tariq)* (Amharic), Addis Ababa, Sister Kibre Temesgen.

BIBLIOGRAPHY

Terhoeven, P., 2006, *Oro alla patria: Donne, guerra e propaganda nella giornata della Fede fascista*, Bologna, Il Mulino.

Teshale Tibebu, 1995, *The Making of Modern Ethiopia 1896–1974*, Lawrenceville, Red Sea Press.

Thiessen, J.C., 1961, *A Survey of World Missions*, 2nd edn, Chicago, Moody Press.

Townley, J., 1821, *Illustrations of Biblical Literature Exhibiting the History and Fate of the Sacred Writings, from the Earliest Period to the Present Century*, vol. III, London, Longman.

Tsegay Berhe G. Libanos & Red., 2005, 'Däbrä Damo', in *Encyclopaedia Aethiopica*, vol. 2, D-Ha, ed. S. Uhlig, Wiesbaden, Harrassowitz, pp. 17–20.

Uhlig, S., 2005, 'Gorgoryos', in *Encyclopaedia Aethiopica*, vol. 2, D-Ha, ed. S. Uhlig, Wiesbaden, Harrassowitz, pp. 855–6.

Van Donzel, E., 2010, 'Wag', in *Encyclopaedia Aethiopica*, vol. 4, O-X, ed. S. Uhlig, Wiesbaden, Harrassowitz, pp. 1069–70.

Violi, R.P., 1996, *Religiosità e identità collective: I santuari del Sud tra fascismo, guerra e democrazia*, Rome, Studium.

Virtue, N.G., 2012, 'A Way Out of Isolation: Fascist Italy's Relationship with the Vatican during the Ethiopian Crisis', in *Collision of Empires: Italy's Invasion of Ethiopia and Its International Impact*, ed. G.B. Strang, London, Routledge.

———, 2016, 'Royal Army, Fascist Empire: The Regio Esercito on Occupation Duty, 1936–1943', PhD thesis, University of Western Ontario, http://ir.lib.uwo.ca/etd/4289.

Walston, J., 1997, 'History and Memory of the Italian Concentration Camps', *Historical Journal*, 40, 1, March, 1997, pp. 169–83.

Wilson, A.N., 2005, *After the Victorians: The Decline of Britain in the World*, New York, Farrar, Straus and Giroux.

Wion, A., 2010, 'Tädbabä Maryam', in *Encyclopaedia Aethiopica*, vol. 4, O-X, ed. S. Uhlig, Wiesbaden, Harrassowitz, pp. 807–8.

Wudu Tafete Kassa, 1997, 'Dajjazmac Haylu Kabbada and the Patriotic Resistance Movement in Wag, 1935–41', in *Ethiopia in Broader Perspective, Papers of the XIIIth International Conference of Ethiopia Studies, Kyoto, 12–17 December 1997*, vol. I, ed. K. Fukui et al., Kyoto, Shokado Book Sellers, pp. 97–110.

———, 2010, 'Wag šum', in *Encyclopaedia Aethiopica*, vol. 4, O-X, ed. S. Uhlig, Wiesbaden, Harrassowitz, pp. 1071–2.

YeQedamawi Hayle Sillassé Tor Timhirt Bét, 1950 EC, *YeQedamawi Hayle Sillassé Tor Timhirt Bét Tarik ke 1927 iske 1949 a mi* [The History of Haile

BIBLIOGRAPHY

Selassie I Military Academy from 1927 to 1949 EC] (Amharic), Addis Ababa, Nigd Matemiya.

ZEMEDKUN BEQELE, 1995 EC, *Qidusan Mekanat Beltyopya: Ye54 Pintawiyan Gedmat ina Idbarat Tarik* (Amharic), Addis Ababa, Artistic Printing Enterprise.

ZERVOS, A., 1936, *L'empire d'Éthiopie*, Alexandria, L'École Professionelle des Frères.

ZEWDÉ RETA, 2005 EC, *YeQedamawi Haylesillassé Mengist: Andenya Metsihaf 1923–1948 I.ÉA. 1930–1955* (Amharic), Addis Ababa, Shama Books.

Zorzetto, G., 2020, *XLV Battaglione Coloniale (1936–1938): storia, immagini, uniformi*, Parma, Museo dell'Araba Fenice.

UNPUBLISHED WORKS AND MANUSCRIPTS

ADUGNA AMANU, 1969, 'The Ethiopian Orthodox Church Becomes Autocephalous', Bachelor of Arts thesis, Haile Selassie I University, Addis Ababa.

AMAN WORJI, 1988, 'From Palace to University: A History of Addis Ababa University Main Campus', Bachelor of Arts in History thesis, Addis Ababa University.

DEBRE WERQ MARYAM, 1991 EC, 'Beseme Ab Weweld weMenfis Qiddus Ahadu Amlak Amén: Yedeb Werq Maryam Tarik, 19.09.1991' (Amharic), Debre Werq, Church of Debre Werq Maryam.

DOMINIONI, M., 2002B, 'Italian Repression in the Bahar Dar Area: Continuities between the Fascist Leadership and the Colonial Personnel in Employing Measures of Stringency and Secret Eliminations', collection, Ian Campbell.

ETHIOPIAN ORTHODOX CHURCH DEVELOPMENT COMMISSION, DOHENY, K. & RYAN, M.T., 1975, 'Ethiopian Orthodox Church Report on Monasteries', typed MSS, Patriarchate Library, Addis Ababa.

MALETTI, P., 1937, 'Comando Settore Nord-Orientale: Scioglimento convento Debra Libanos, 22 May, 1937', unpublished, USNA, Captured Italian Documents, Section T-821, roll 468, frames 32–6. (*Note*: The version in the USNA is a retyped version of the original in the ACS (*busta* 48, *fasc* 42, *sf* 12); it bears Graziani's handwritten comments.)

METAFERIA CONSULTING ENGINEERS, PLC, 1999, 'Conservation Strategy of Ethiopia, Phase III: Baseline Study for Ankober Woreda and Preparation of Management Plans for Five Sub-Kebeles', Addis Ababa.

SELTENE SEYOUM, 1999, 'A History of Resistance in Gojjam (Ethiopia):

BIBLIOGRAPHY

1936–1941', PhD thesis, Addis Ababa University, School of Graduate Studies, May 1999.

UNPUBLISHED LETTERS

Seifu Kassa, Garland, Texas, to Ian Campbell, 10 May 2016.

NEWSPAPERS

Capital, Addis Ababa
Corriere della Sera, Milan
Corriere dell'Impero, Addis Ababa
New Times and Ethiopia News, Woodford Green

JOURNALS

African Quarterly
Annales d'Ethiopie, Centre Français des Études Éthiopiennes and Centre for Research and Conservation of Cultural Heritage, Addis Ababa
Dehnenet (Amharic), Addis Ababa
Epoca, Milan
Ethiopia Observer, Addis Ababa
Ethiopian Review, Los Angeles
Historical Journal, Cambridge
International Journal of African Historical Studies, Boston
International Journal of Ethiopian Studies, Hollywood
Journal of Ethiopian Studies, Addis Ababa University
Journal of Holocaust Research, Routledge
Northeast African Studies, East Lansing
Quaderni di Studi Etiopici, Asmara
Sociology and Ethology Bulletin, Dept. of Sociology and Social Administration, Addis Ababa University, Addis Ababa
Studi Piacentini, Istituto storico della Resistenza e dell'età contemporanea di Piacenza, Piacenza
Tablet, The, London

DOCUMENTARY FILMS

La conquista di un impero, Part II: *La guerra (Etiopia)*, directed by Luciano Doddoli and Ivan Palermo, tx Rai, 1987.

BIBLIOGRAPHY

Fascist Legacy, two-part mini-series, directed by Ken Kirby for BBC Timewatch, 1989.
If Only I Were That Warrior, directed by Valerio Ciriaci, cinematography by Isaak Liptzin, Awen Films, 2015.
Debre Libanos: Il più grande massacro di cristiani in Africa, by Antonello Carvigiani, directed and photographed by Andrea Tramontano, and edited by Dolores Gangi, tv2000, 2017.

ITALIAN GOVERNMENT DOCUMENTS

Note: For the purposes of this listing, the following abbreviations have been adopted:

ACS	Archivio Centrale dello Stato, Rome
ASDMAE	Archivio storico diplomatico del Ministero degli Affari Esteri
ASV	Archivio Segreto Vaticano
D/B	Debre Birhan
DeptPresse	DEPARTEMENT DE LA PRESSE ET DE L'INFORMATION DU GOUVERNEMENT IMPERIAL D'ETHIOPIE
Dir. Sup.	*Il direttore superiore*, Addis Ababa
EGLO	Ethiopian Government Liaison Office in Asmara
F	Fiché
f	*foglio* [folio]
fasc	*fascicolo* [file]
Gen.	General
Graz.	Graziani
IES	IES Microfilm collection, Addis Ababa University
MAI	Ministero dell'Africa Italiana
Mesk.	*Meskerem*
MinJ49	MINISTRY OF JUSTICE, 1949
MinJ50	MINISTRY OF JUSTICE, 1950
Mjr	Major
MVDIDS	Museo virtuale della intolleranze e degle stermini, www.zadigweb.it/amis/schede.asp?idsch=115&id=7
Res	*Residente* (actually addressed to *Residenza*)
posiz	*posizione* [position]
sc	*scatola* [box]
sf	*sotto fascicolo* [sub-file]
SGE	SALOME GEBRE EGZIABEHER, 1966

BIBLIOGRAPHY

subcomms	subordinate commands
supcomms	superior commands
USNA	United States National Archives, Captured Italian Documents, 1922–1943, Section T-821
USSME	Ufficio storico dello stato maggiore dell'esercito

OFFICIAL JOURNALS

Giornale Ufficiale del Governo Generale dell'Africa Orientale Italiana, Addis Ababa, Servizio Tipografico del Governo Generale dell'Africa Orientale Italiana

MILITARY TELEGRAMS

	Date	Source
Graz. to Gen. Berganzoli, No. 1004,	24 Jan. 1936	MinJ49, doc. 7, pp. 6; 34-5
Mussolini to Graz., No. 6496	5 June 1936	MinJ49, doc. 10, pp. 8, 36; DeptPresse, pp. 11-12
Graz. to Lessona, No. 8906	30 July 1936	MinJ49, doc. 23, pp. 14, 45
Graz. to Gen. Gallina	27 Oct. 1936	Tel. Graz.–Lessona, 27 Oct. 1936
Graz. to Lessona	11 Sept. 1936	DeptPresse, p. 22
Gen. Pirzio-Biroli to Graziani	11 Sept. 1936	Tel. Graz.–Lessona, 12 Sept. 1936
Graz. to Pirzio-Biroli, No. 15756	11 Sept. 1936	MinJ49, doc 44, pp. 26, 60
Graz. to Lessona, No. 15808	12 Sept. 1936	DeptPresse, p. 29; MinJ49, doc. 45, pp. 26, 61
Graz. to Lessona, No. 22980	27 Oct. 1936	MinJ49 doc. 37, pp. 22, 55
Graz. to Lessona, No. 31306	11 Dec. 1936	MinJ49 doc12, pp. 9, 37
Graz. to Lessona, No. 33444	21 Dec. 1936	MinJ49, doc. 13, pp. 10, 38
Lessona to Graz., No. 36435	22 Dec. 1936	IES
Mussolini to Graz., No. 38446	31 Dec. 1936	IES

BIBLIOGRAPHY

Graz. to Gen. Gelosa	15 Feb. 1937	USNA, 472/75, cited in PANKHURST, R.K., 1997, p. 14
Mussolini to Graz., No. 93980	21 Feb. 1937	Cited in DOMINIONI, M., 2008, p. 330 n. 7
Graz. to Lessona	28 Feb. 1937	MVDIDS
Graz. to Gen. Nasi, No. 10530	1 Mar. 1937	MinJ49, doc. 27, pp. 16-17, 48
Mussolini to Graz.	1 Mar. 1937	MVDIDS
Gen. Nasi to subcomms	2 Mar. 1937	Tel. Graz.–Lessona, 3 Mar. 1937
Graz. to Lessona, No. 11077	3 Mar. 1937	MinJ49, doc. 11, pp. 8-9, 36
Graz. to General Tracchia	7 Mar. 1937	ACS, *fondo* Graziani, R., *Sc* 48, *fasc* 42, *sf* 12, cited in PERRET, M., 1986, n.1
Graz. to Lessona, No. 14154	19 Mar. 1937	MinJ49, doc. 28, pp. 17, 51
Graz. to Lessona, No. 14440	21 Mar 1937	MinJ49, doc. 29, pp. 17, 51, DeptPresse, p. 66
Graz. to Lessona, No. 15287	26 Mar. 1937	MinJ49, doc. 40, pp. 23-4, 57
Graz. to Gen. Geloso, No. 25601	17 May 1937	MinJ49, doc. 20, pp. 13, 42
Graz. to Maletti, No. 25876[1]	19 May 1937	USNA, 468/46; DeptPresse, p. 128; ACS, *fondo* Graziani, R., *sc* 48, *fasc* 42, *sf* 12
Graz. to Lessona, No. 25919	19 May 1937	MinJ49, doc. 41, pp. 24, 60
Maletti to subcomms, No. 2041/op	19 May 1937	USNA 468/45
Maletti to Graz., No. 34713	20 May 1937	USNA 468/44
Maletti to Graz. 2072/op	21 May 1937	USNA 468/39

[1] The facsimile of the carbon copy in DeptPresse (signed by Mazzi) bears the number 25176.

413

BIBLIOGRAPHY

Graz. to Maletti, No. 26151	21 May 1937	USNA 468/42
Graz. to Lessona, No. 26320	21 May 1937	MinJ49, doc. 31, pp. 18-19, 51-2, 54
Maletti to Graz., No. 2152/op[2]	22 May 1937	USNA 468/38; ACS, *fondo* Graziani, R., *sc* 48, *fasc* 42
Graz. to Maletti, No. 26609[3]	24 May 1937	USNA 468/37; DeptPresse, p. 132
Graz. to Lessona, No. 27136[4]	27 May 1937	USNA 468/20; MinJ49, doc. 32, pp. 20, 53
Graz. to Lessona, No. 27400	29 May 1937	DeptPresse, pp. 134-5
Graz. to Lessona, No. 27500	29 May 1937	MinJ49, doc. 52, pp. 29, 65
Graz. to Lessona, No. 27801	31 May 1937	MinJ49, doc. 30, pp. 18, 50
Graz. to Nasi, No. 10009[5]	2 June 1937	USNA 472/426
Graz. to Lessona, No. 10062	2 June 1937	USNA 472/427
Mussolini to Graz.	5 June 1937	DeptPresse, p. 11
Graz. to Lessona, No. 10713	11 June 1937	IES
Graz. to Lessona	22 June 1937	USNA, 468/422-4
Maletti to Mjr Spinelli,[6] No. 48350	18 July 1937	USNA 468/24
Graz. to Pirzio Biroli	29 July 1937	Cited in DOMINIONI, M., 2003, p. 170 n. 15
Petretti to *Res.*, Fiché, No. 90843	25 Aug. 1937	USNA 468/17
Maletti to Gov. Gen., No. 57268	27 Aug. 1937	USNA 468/16
Graz.[7] to *Res.*, Fiché, No. 50167	27 Oct. 1937	USNA 468/15
Dir. Sup. to supcomms[8]	2 Nov. 1937	USNA 468/13

[2] Also numbered 35049.
[3] Also numbered 9325.
[4] Also numbered 9585.
[5] Apparently corrected from No. 999.
[6] Sent via the Governo Generale.

BIBLIOGRAPHY

Graz.[9] to *Res.*, Fiché, No. 50942	2 Nov. 1937	USNA 468/14
Graz. to Lessona, No. 11077	3 Dec. 1937	MinJ49, doc. 11, pp. 8-9, 36
Graz. to Lessona, No. 07730	22 Feb. 1938	ASDMAE, MAI, *posiz* 181/55, *fasc* 255, cited in DOMINIONI, M., 2008, p. 47
Cerulli to Min., Ital. East Africa	26 July 1938	ASMAI/Gab, p. 181/59, *fasc* 293

MILITARY PHONOGRAMS

G. Sindico to Chef de Cabinet	21 Feb. 1937	ACS, *fondo* Graz., *busta* 48, *fasc* 42, *sf* 7
Gov. Gen. to Comm. Sup. CCRR	2 Nov. 1937	USNA 468/13

MILITARY LETTERS AND CIRCULARS

Graz. to Aberra Kassa	11 Dec. 1936	SGE, 1966, pp. 303-4
Gen. Tracchia to Aberra Kassa	n.d.	MinJ50, p. 2
Aberra Kassa to Gen. Tracchia	n.d.	MinJ50, p. 2
Col. Hazon to Gov. Gen., 21/358	22 Mar. 1937	ACS, Carte Graz., *busta* 48, *fasc* 42, *sf* 12, cited in PERRET, M., 1986, p. 65
Capt. Corvo to Guila Guiorguis	20 May 1937	MinJ49, doc. 33, p. 20
Nasi, G., circular	17 Mar. 1949	MinJ49, doc. 22, p. 14

MILITARY REPORTS

Ministry of Interior to Border Police HQ: *Memorandum for Mussolini (State of Mind of Officers and Soldiers on the Eve of the Italo-Ethiopian War)*, August

---

[7] Signed on Graziani's behalf.
[8] Actually a *fonogramma a mano*; not a telegram.
[9] Signed on Graziani's behalf.

BIBLIOGRAPHY

1935, ACS-Int.C, cited in SBACCHI, A., 1997, pp. 38, 50 nn. 22–6.

Badoglio, 25 December 1935, USSME, D5, *busta* 123, *fasc* 8, *f* 020066, cited in DOMINIONI, M., 2008, p. 46.

Graziani, *I primi venti mesi dell'impero*, ACS, *fondo* Graziani (*busta* 56) (Original: tel. No. 31560 to Lessona [ACS, *fondo* Rodolfo Graziani, *sc* 31, *fasc* 29, *sf* 40], cited in PERRET, M., 1986, n. 10).

Quercia, Major, 14 March 1937, cited in PERRET, M., 1986, p. 69 n. 9.

Graziani, *Il primo anno dell'impero*, ACS, *fondo* Rodolfo Graziani.

Graziani, *Il 2° anno dell'impero,* ACS, *fondo* Rodolfo Graziani, *busta* 60.

Franceschino (n.d.), cited in tel. Graziani to Lessona, 21 May 1937.

Franceschino (memorandum), 21 Apr. 1937, cited in BORRUSO, P., 2001.

Maletti to Graziani, *Convento di Debre Libanos*, 21 April 1937, ACS, *fondo* Graziani, *busta* 48, *fasc* 42, *sf* 12.

Maletti, General, *Comando Settore Nord-Orientale: Scioglimento convento Debra Libanos,* 22 May 1937, USNA 468/32-6, and ACS, *fondo* Rodolfo Graziani, *sc* 48, *fasc* 42.

Maletti, General, 30 August 1937, ACS, *fondo* Graziani, Rodolfo, *sc* 31, *fasc* 29, *sf* 42. See also PERRET, M., 1986, pp. 65, 69.

Ministry of Interior to Border Police HQ, August 1935, *Memorandum for Mussolini (State of Mind of Officers and Soldiers on the Eve of the Italo-Ethiopian War)*, ACS-Int/C, cited in SBAACHI, A., 1997, pp. 38, 50 nn. 22–6.

Quercia, Major, No. 184-12-21, 14 March 1937, ACS, *fondo* Rodolfo Graziani, *busta* 48, *fasc* 42, *sf* 12 (with covering memorandum 21/297, 16 March 1937 by Col. Azolino Hazon).

Graziani, *Il 2° anno dell'impero*, ACS, *fondo* Graziani, *busta* 60.

NON-MILITARY CORRESPONDENCE

Teruzzi to *Duce*	17 May 1937	Cited in BORRUSO, P., 1989, p. 62
Ciano to Holy See	15 July 1938	ASMAE *b* 44, *ss* 6-5 (1939) cited in KENT, P.C., 1984, p. 150
Teruzzi to Ciano	6 Aug. 1938	ASMAE *b* 44, *ss* 6-5 (1939) cited in Kent, P.C., 1984, p. 150

NON-MILITARY PRO MEMORIA

BIBLIOGRAPHY

Teruzzi to Duce	17 May 1938	ASMAI/Gab, *posiz* 181/59 *f* 291, cited in BORRUSO, P., 1989, p. 62
Ciano to Min. Ital. East Africa	26 July 1938	ASMAE, *b* 44, *ss* 6-5 (1939), cited in KENT, P.C., 1984, p. 150
Pignatti to Ciano	26 July 1938	ASMAE, *b* 39, *ss* 5-Germania, cited in KENT, P.C., 1984, p. 150
Pignatti to Ciano	10 Aug. 1938	ASMAE, *b* 39, *ss* 5-Germania, cited in KENT, P.C., 1984, p. 150
Note: Tacchi Venturi	12 Aug. 1938	ASV, Seg. di Stato, Affari eccl. straordinari, Italia, *posiz* 1007c, *fasc* 695, *ff* 37r–39r

BRITISH GOVERNMENT DOCUMENTS (PUBLIC RECORD OFFICE)

FO J429/190/1, Montgomery to Eden, 3 Jan. 1936, cited in KENT, P.C., 1984, p. 141

FO R1427/135/22, 25 Feb. 1937, cited in KENT, P.C., 1984, p. 148

FO 371/209127, Report and Memorandum, 1 March 1937

FO 4228/548/1, Acting Consul-General in Addis Ababa, 27 Sept. 1937, cited in KENT, P.C., 1984, p. 149

FO 35642/J1995, Memorandum, Egypt Dept., cited in MIKRE-SELLASSIE GEBRE AMMANUEL, 2014, pp. 350–1

FO 371.27530 J3578/173/1, M.S. Lush to Chief Political Officer, Addis Ababa, 11 Oct. 1941, cited in MIKRE-SELLASSIE GEBRE AMMANUEL, 2014, pp. 351–2

FO 371/63171, J5671, Leijonhufvud to Ledingham, 17 Nov. 1947

AMERICAN GOVERNMENT DOCUMENTS

U.S. GOVERNMENT PRINTING OFFICE, 1953, *Foreign Relations of the United States Diplomatic Papers, 1936, vol. III: The Near East and Africa*, Washington, US Government, 1953 (865D.404/7, Minister Resident in Ethiopia to Secretary of State, No. 193, 15 Oct. 1936; Engert to Secretary of State, 20 Feb. 1937)

INTERNET SOURCES

BIBLIOGRAPHY

DECHESA ABEBE, 2016, 'Peasants and Resistance against Italian Occupation in North Shewa (May 4, 1936–May 5, 1941)', in *Ethiopian Journal of Social Sciences and Language Studies*, 3, 2, pp. 23–43, http://www.ju.edu.et/cssljournal/

DIAMANT, J., 2017, 'Ethiopia is an Outlier in the Orthodox Christian world', Pew Research Center, https://www.pewresearch.org/fact-tank/2017/11/28/ethiopia-is-an-outlier-in-th-orthodox-christian-world; 'Ethiopia Ranked as the Number 1 Religious Country in the World: According to the Global Attitudes 2015 Survey', http://www.addis24.com/news/ethiopia-ranked-as-the-number-1-religious-country-in-the-world

FESSEHA MEKURIA & RUBENSON, S., 2000, *Abune Petros: A Martyr of the Millennium*, http://www.ethiopians.com/abune_petros.htm

LABANCA, N., 2007, 'Pietro Maletti', in *Dizionario Biografico degli Italiani*, vol. 68, www.treccani.it

PANKHURST, R.K., 2001B, *Ethiopia and the Question of the Restoration of Cultural Property: A General Statement*, Afromet, http://afromet.org/generalstatement.html, 30 January 2001

RICCARDI, A., 2017B, *Risposta all'appello di Riccordi sulla strage di Debrà Libanòs: Un gruppo di lavoro al Ministero Difesa*, 22 May 2017, www.riccardiandrea.it

SALVADORE, M., 2013, 'Gaining the Heart of Prester John: Loyola's Blueprint for Ethiopia in Three Key Documents', in *World History Connected: Forum: Jesuits and World History*, www.worldhistoryconnected.press.uillinois.edu/10.3/forum_salvadore.html

www.annasromguide.dk/personer/dicaantoniolomere.html

www.albertoparducci.it

https://www.facebook.com/asservatoriodemocraticosullenuovadestre/posts/

www.catholic-hierarchy.org

www.comandosupremo.com/Graziani.html.

http://dir.groups.yahoo.cn/group/ESAi/messages/330

www.globalallianceforEthiopia.org.

https://romanchurches.wikia.com

www.yeshua.it/il%Bestiario%20incensato/la_Madonna_con_il_manganello.htm

INDEX

Abam Abo (Gebre Menfes Qiddus) church, Ziqwala district, Wag, Ethiopia, burning of, 266
Abeba (protégé of Alfred Buxton), 153
Abebe Aregay (later, *Ras*), 161, 162, 264
Abera Kassa, *Dejazmach*, 116-17, 125, 134-35, 282
Abiyyé monastery, 263
Abmata St. Libanos church, Ziqwala district, Wag, Ethiopia, burning of, 266
Abraham, Bishop, 271-72
Abriha and Atsbiha, early Ethiopian Christian kings, 165
Abriha Deboch, 152, 157, 158, 159, 161, 162, 175, 188
Abriha, *Shum-Bashi*, 197-98
Ada district, 115-16
Adal, state of, 19
Addis Ababa, 11, 30, 38-39, 40, 45, 52, 64, 100, 112, 139, 151, 182, 188, 224, 226-27, 229, 233, 250, 253, 270-71, 278, 282, 312
massacre of ('*Yekatit 12*'), 2, 140-156, 202-03, 235, 239, 240, 243, 282, 293, 299, 300, 301, 314-15, 320, **Fig. 28**
Catholic Cathedral of the Nativity of the Blessed Virgin Mary, 45-46, **Fig. 6**
Parliament building, 110
Teferi Mekonnin School, 110
Marqos (St. Mark) church, Sidist Kilo, 117
Patriot attempt to recapture, 117-19
St. George cathedral, 117, 142, 216, 291
Special Court, 118
Governo Generale, 118
physical building (former Haile Selassie palace), 118, 140, 147, 151, 154, 157, 163
High Command of Italian administration, 140, 152, 188, 227, 249, 252, 271
Sidist Kilo district, 117
Municipality building, 144
conversion to detention centre, 154

419

INDEX

Kidane Mihret church, 146-47
Te'aka Negest Be'ata LeMaryam church, 146-47, **Fig. 31**
Menelik palace, 147
Central Prison, 154-55
University of, 205, 237, 362n8
Haile Selassie Military Academy, 206
Akaki Prison/Concentration Camp, 228, 315-16
Intotto Maryam (St. Mary) church, see St. Mary church, Intotto.
Banca d'Italia, 283
papal legation, 283
railway station, 328
Addis Ababa-Djibouti railway, 115-16
Addis Alem, west of Addis Ababa, 266-67
Addis Alem church of St. Mary, Ethiopia, massacre of, see St. Mary church, Addis Alem.
Adeljan St. Michael church, Ziqwala district, Wag, Ethiopia, burning of, 266
Adi Keyih, 63
Adulis, 34
Adwa, 35
Battle of, 35, 38, 39, 40, 51, 52, 92, 142, 143, 146, 150
Afar region, 238
Depression, 233
Muslim community, 238
Afe-Werq Gebre-Iyesus, 360n39
Afewerq Tekle, *Maitre-Artiste*, 379n14
Affile, Italy, 289
Viri, Ercole, Mayor of, 289
Agat river, 159, 161, 184

Ahmed bin Ibrahim, aka Ahmed Grañ, *Imam*, 20-22, 29, 57, 87, 167, 168, 224, 243
Ahmed Hassen, Professor, 235, 238, 239
Aklilu Gebré, 160
Akrimit St. Michael church, Bulga, Ethiopia, burning and looting of, 267
Aksum, 16-18, 34, 96-97
Obelisk (*stela*) of, 321, 328
Ezana, King of, 349n2 (Chapter 1)
Albigensian crusade, 73
Alebachew Belay of Debre Birhan University, 374n18
Alexandria, Italy, 103
Alexandrian (Coptic) Patriarchate, 18
Alfonso V, King, 33
Aliotta, Captain, 196
Aliyu Amba, 233-34, 236, 237
Alpini, 54
Alvares, Francisco, Father, 20-21
Amba Alagi, 35
Amda Siyon, Emperor, 18
Amde Sillassé, Abba, 165
Amdewerq, 88, 266
Amdewerq Qirqos (St. Quiricus) church, Ziqwala district, Wag, Ethiopia, burning of, 266
America, 39. 53, 60, 89
legation, Addis Ababa, 38-39, 167
Engert, Cornelius Van H., minister in Ethiopia, 121-22
Amhara, 168
Santa Maria Catholic church, Detroit, 296
Amharic language, 23
Ankober

INDEX

town, 178, 233-34, 237, 260
   St. Michael church, looting of, 260
   St. George church, bombing of, 382n8; *see* St. George church, Ankober.
district, 233, 235, 238, 263-65
   Kundi Fort, 258, 260
Aosta, Duke of, 269, 285,
   appointment as Viceroy, 269, 281
   policies of, 270, 312
   repair/reconstitution of Ethiopian churches by, 272, 278, 323
   death of, 289
   cancellation of the principle of war booty by, 320
Apostles, 19
Aragon, 33
Ar'aya, *Aleqa*, 155-56
Archinto, Filippo, Vicar General of Rome, 24, 25, 26, **Fig. 1**
Arditi, 62
Argobba Muslim community, 237-38
Ark of the Covenant, 74
Armenia, 73
Armenian genocide, 140, 300
Ascalesi, Alesio, Cardinal Archbishop, 11, 90-91, 94-95, 107, **Fig. 17**
Aselefech Kassa, 116
Asfawessen Kassa, *Dejazmach*, 100, 116-17, 125, 134-35, 282
askaris, 68, 184
Asma Giyorgis, 350n26
Assab, 34
Atenolfi, Giuseppe Talamo, 55
Audisio, Walter, aka Colonel Valerio, partisan, 328, **Fig. 52**
Avvenire newspaper, 7

Awsene Amba, 178
Ayalew Birru, *Dejazmach*, 86
Ayraka river, Ankober district, 261-62
Ayyele Haylé, Patriot leader, 238
Azezo, 28-29

Bachi St. Mary church, Ziqwala district, Wag, Ethiopia, burning of, 266
Badoglio, Pietro, Marshal, 68, 87-88, 97-98, 109, 288, 312, 352n4
   arrival in Addis Ababa, 101, 103
   appointed Viceroy, 104
   resignation as viceroy, 108
   as War Crimes suspect. 287
   export to Italy of artefacts of Ethiopian cultural heritage by, 326-27
Bahir Dar, Gojjam, 189, 241
Balkans, 36
Barca, Dr., 189-90
Barlassina, Gaudenzio, Monsignor, 52
Bartoli, Antonio, Ambassador, 19
Begémdir, 116, 165, 170, 242-5, 250
Beheret district, Bulga, 263-64
Belay Zelleqe, *Dejazmach*, 280
Benedict XV, Pope, 40-41, 300
Bernadi, Ferdinando, Archbishop, 93, 94
Bernareggi, Adriano, Bishop, 82
Biancoli, Major, 366n2
Bible Churchmen's Missionary Society (BCMS), 152-53
Bichena, Gojjam, 280
   Baranta district, burning and looting of houses in, 280
   Lamchow district, burning of houses in, 280

421

INDEX

Bilbala Giyorgis, 126
Bi'isé Tiruneh, *Aqqabé*, of Debre Werq, 170, 367n22
Binchy, Daniel, 104-05, 276, 302, 304, 309
Biresaw Yimer, 363n21
Birhanu Abebe, Dr., 366n4
Birhanu Denqé, 197
Birhane-Yesus Suraphael Demirew, Cardinal-Archbishop of the Catholic Church of Ethiopia, 366n1
Birru Amedé, *Dejazmach*, 311-12
Biwel Arba'itu Insasa (Four Beasts of the Apocalypse) church, Ziqwala district, Wag, Ethiopia, burning of, 266
Blackshirts, 11, 60-61, 63, 80, 92, 121, 122, 155-56, 160
   'Great Mobilisation' of, 78-80, 90
   2nd Division '28th October' 63
   6th Division 'Tevere', 111, 112, 141, 142, 358n70
   participation of, in massacre of Addis Ababa, 141
   participation of, in attack of St. George's cathedral, 142-44
   11th Battalion, 144-45
   demise of, 278
Blue Nile (Abbay) river, 17, 167, 170, 325
Bohemia, 73
Bologna, 81
Boniface IX, Pope, 20
Book of Enoch, 25
Borale
   river, 178-79, 201, 204, 215
   execution site, 178-79, 191, 201-08, 210, 215, 227, **Fig. 35**

valley, 203, 215
Borruso, Paolo, 242, 292, 364n2
Bottai, Giuseppe, 105
Botticelli, 20
Brancaleon, Nicoló, 170
Brescia, 82
Bruno Bruni, Father, 168-69
Bulga, 263-65
   Berehet district, 264-65
Buxton, Alfred, 152-54
Byzantium (later, Constantinople), 22, 55, 73, 96

Cadorna, Raffaele, General, partisan, 328, **Fig. 52**
Calabria, 6
Calamandrei, Piero, 111
Canaan, 60
Capuchin Mission, Ethiopia, 283-84
   Dire Dawa, 284
   Atsbi Teferi, 284
carabinieri, 174, 182, 201-02,
Carvigiani, Antonello, 6, 349n1 (Preface)
Castagna, Sebastino, 143
Castellani, Giovanni Maria Emilio, Cardinal Archbishop, 121, 136, 137, 167, 283, 299, 363n29, **Fig. 25**
   appointment as Apostolic Visitor, 120-21
   support for Fascism, 121-23
   departure from Ethiopia at end of Apostolic Visitor appointment, 135-36
   appointment as Apostolic Delegate, 166
   meeting with Pope Pius XI, 277
   decision to remain in Ethiopia, 278
   final departure from Ethiopia,

INDEX

284
  appointed Apostolic Nuncio to Guatemala and El Salvador, 290
  death of, 290
Castellano, Major, 196
Catalani, Matteo, 26
Cathars, 73
Cavellero, Ugo, General, 269, 280
Cazzani, Giovanni, Bishop, 71, 78
Ceci, Lucia, 47, 84, 95, 301, 386n14
Cervini, Cardinal (later Pope Marcellus II), 23
Chafé, Debre Libanos, 194
Chagel, Debre Libanos, 158, 184, 187, 191, 201, 212, 221
  Medhane Alem (Saviour of the World) church at, 191, 371n11
Charles V, Holy Roman Emperor, 25, 26
Charles-Roux, François, Ambassador, 48, 49,
Cheleqot Sillassé (Holy Trinity) church, *see* Holy Trinity, church of, Cheleqot.
Chercher, 98
Chir Four Beasts of the Apocalypse (Arba'itu Insasa) church, Ziqwala district, Wag, Ethiopia, burning of, 266
China, 288
Ciano, Galeazzo, Count, 70, 249
Ciarrocchi, Joseph, Monsignor, 296
Civilta Castellana, 82
Civitella, 121
Claudius (Gelawdéwos), Emperor, 24, 26, 169, 323
Cocquio-Trevisago, Lombardy, 292
Cola, Nicola, Bishop, 75-76

Colli, Evasio, Bishop, 93
Community of Sant'Egidio, 7
Como, 78, 82
Concordat, *see* Lateran Treaty
Conference of Commonwealth Prime Ministers, 311
Consolata Mission, 52
  missionaries, 91
  Ethiopia, 283-84
Conte Grande ship, 94-95
Convention with Respect to the Laws and Customs of War on Land, 319-20
Copts (Egyptian Orthodox Christians), 18, 270-71
  Alexandrian Patriarchate, 18, 270-71
  Coptic Church, 117
  Coptic clergy, 56
  Qérillos (Cyril), Archbishop in Ethiopia, 100, 117
Cornwell, John, 289
Cortese, Guido, 122, 143-44, 151, **Fig. 25**
Corvo, Captain, 189, 241, 294
Costa, Giuseppe, Lt.-Colonel, 235
Council of Chalcedon, 73
Council of Florence, 19, 20
Counter-Reformation, 28
Covenant of Mercy Kidane Mihret church, Tiya, Wag, Ethiopia, burning of, 265-66
Covenant of Mercy (Kidane Mihret) church, Zembabit, Ankober district, Ethiopia, massacre of, 265
  Bantiyurgu, Father, killed at, 265
  Mamo Qetsela, Father, killed at, 265
  Mukriya, Father, killed at, 265
  Tedla, Father, killed at, 265

423

INDEX

Tekle-Giyorgis, Father, killed at, 265
Covenant of Mercy (Kidane Mihret) church, Molalé Aradma Agancha, Menz, Ethiopia, massacre of, 237
Cozzani, Virgilio, *Tenente*, 191, 196, 198
Cremona, 71
Croatia, 156, 285
Crown Council of Ethiopia, 100
Curle, A.T., Colonel, 39
Cyprus, Ethiopian community of, 25

da Gama, Christóvão, 22
da Gama, Vasco, 22
Dabat St. Gabriel church, Ethiopia, 86
Dabbert, Madame, 364n4
Dagabour, 120
Dalla Torre, Giuseppe, 49
Daniél Seifemikaél, Reverend, 367n17
Dawit (David) II, Emperor, 19
Dawit Gebre Mesqel, *Dyakon*, 147-48
De Bono, Emilio, General, 39, 67, 68
de Jacobis, Giustino, 57
Debi Tsige of Borale, 204
Debre Abbay monastery, Ethiopia, 86-87, 166
Debre Asbo (later, Debre Libanos of Shewa) monastery, Ethiopia, 17, 18, 173
Debre Assebot monastery, Ethiopia, 224
    massacre of, 224-26, 317
    church of the Holy Trinity, destruction of, 226

    church of Father Samuél, 226
Debre Birhan
    town, 126, 178, 201, 222, 226, 257-58, 388n15
    Italian garrison, 126, 158, 176, 182, 227, 236, 252, 253
    district, 181-82
    Sellassé (Holy Trinity) cathedral of, 201-02
    carabinieri camp, 201-02, 211
    University of, 205, 375n24
    Italian prison at, 221, 226, 228, 316
Debre Bisrat monastery, Ethiopia
    massacre of, 223-24, 317
    church of Zéna Marqos, massacre of, 224, 243
        Welde-Mikaél, Abbot, killed at, 224
        Welde-Ammanuel, Father, killed at, 224
Debre Bizen monastery, Ethiopia (later, Eritrea), 34-35
Debre Damo monastery, Ethiopia, 16, 17, 22,
Debre Genet monastery, Jerusalem, 100
Debre Libanos (of Ham) monastery, Ethiopia (later, Eritrea), 34-35, 350n11
Debre Libanos (of Shewa) monastery, 1, 2, 6-7, 16-18, 26-27, 29, 30-31, 116, 117, 134, 137, 152, 221, 230, 269-70, 281, 282, 299
    Italian massacre and looting of, 1-2, 6-7, 26, 211, 221, 223, 235, 239, 240, 242, 243, 249, 267, 289, 292, 297-98, 299, 301, 312, 317-18, 323, **Fig.**

INDEX

37, **Fig. 44**
intention to carry out, 137, 157-8
attack of February 1937, 159, 162
detailed plan of, 173-75
preparations for, 174-75
rationale for, 175-76
location of first execution site (Laga Weldé) of, 176-77, **Fig. 38, Fig. 39**
location of second execution site (Borale, Ingécha) of, 178-79, **Fig. 35**
encirclement of the monastery of, 181-86
entrapment of first arrivals at, 186-88
looting of, 187, 322-23
massacre at first execution site (Laga Weldé) of, 189-199, 287
massacre at second execution site (Borale, Ingécha) of, 201-208, 214, 258, 287,
Graziani's report to Rome of, 209
death toll of, 211-12
aftermath of, 214-15
arrest of relatives of victims of, 253-54
hiding and preservation of relics of St. Tekle Haymanot, 325
history of, 17-22, 349n8, 352n49
abbot of, 18
tsebate of, 18,
Yohannis Kama, 7th abbot of, 18
16th-century massacre of, 20-21, 23, 24, 161

representation in Rome, 22-24, 26
Yohannis, 14th abbot of, 26
Zatra Wengel, 16th abbot of, 27
Jesuits at, 27-29
Battra Giyorgis, 19th abbot of, 28
House of the Cross (Mesqel Bét), 30, 190, 211-12
looting of, 323
under Emperor Menelik, 30-31
sacristan of, 67-68
Bét Selihom, 185
district, 227-28, 251
reconstitution of, 252-55, 257, 323
library of, 323
Marha Krestos, 9th abbot of, 366n6
Béta Marfak (monastery council hall), 388n6
Debre Libanos tv2000 docu-film, 6-7, 214-15, 292, 349n1 (Preface)
Debre Libanos 1937, book, 292
Debre Marqos, 282
Debre Sina, 235-36, 238
Debre Tabor, 116
Debre Werq monastery, Gojjam, 169-170
shelling of Monastery church of Debre Werq Maryam, 170
Debre Zeyit St. Mary church, Ziqwala district, Wag, Ethiopia, burning of, 266
debtera, order of, 74
Degife Gebre-Tsadiq, 2, 326, 362n8, 388n6
Del Boca, Angelo, 4, 223, 282, 311
Della Costa, Elia, Archbishop, 104
Demissé Abiyyé, *Memhir*, 264
Denneba district, Northern Shewa, 222

INDEX

Derefo St. Mary church, Ankober district, Ethiopia, massacre and looting of, 262; *see* St. Mary church, Derefo.
Deressé Ayenachew, Dr., 374n18
Dessie, 91, 117
  Yekatit 12 massacre of, 315
Desta Damtew, *Ras*, 88, 100, 135, 136, 166
Digwa, liturgical book, 170
Diocletian, Emperor, 25
Dire Dawa, 98-99, 224
Djibouti, 98
Dominioni, Matteo, 241
Duggan, Christopher, 83, 286

Éfrém Tewelde-Medhin, *Blattén Géta*, 139
Egypt, 19, 36
  Desert Fathers of, 16, 31
  Alexandria, 271
  Cairo, 271
Elam, Debre Libanos, 173
Elfinesh Kassa, 116
Enda Sillassé (Holy Trinity) church, Ethiopia, 87-88
Engert, Cornelius Van H., 121-22
Eritrea, 34, 35, 36, 52, 67, 68, 164, 253, 282, 288
  askaris of, 68, 166, 183, 205, 210, 258, 263
  Asmara, 126, 251, 257
  concentration camps in, 142
  2nd Eritrean brigade, 134, 159
  20th Eritrean Battalion, 182
  Nefasit prison, 281
Ermias, *Qes*, 365n27
Ethiopia, Catholic Church vicariates of, 352n7
Ethiopian Ministry of Justice, 287
Ethiopian Orthodox Church icons, 322
Eugene IV, Pope, 20

Farnese family, 25
Fascism, 36
  fasces, 36
  Fascist Grand Council, 105
  Fascism International, 37
  Fascist Party, 36
  and the Catholic Church, 43-44, 47-49, 56-57, 60-63, 127, 110-11, 215-16, 279
  Fascist Salò Republic, 289
Fattorini, Emma, 302
Fasiledes, Emperor, 28, 165
Feleqe Asress of Borale, 204, 205
Feqyibelu Yirgu of Borale, 203, 204-06, 208, **Fig. 41**
Fiamboro, 113
Fiché
  town, 116, 134-35, 198, 282, 291
  Italian garrison, 159, 182, 183, 187, 189-90, 193, 194, 227, 252, 323
  district, 167
Film Luce (later, Istituto Luce), 71
Fincha Wenz, 177, 194-95, 214-15
Fiqre-Iyesus, *Meggabi* of Debre Libanos, 370n12, **Fig. 39**
Firekal Yigret, 367n22
First Battle of Tembien, aka Battle of Uarieu Pass, 92-93
First World War, 36, 40, 62, 76-77, 176
Florence, 104
Four Beasts of the Apocalypse (Arba'itu Insasa) church, Biwel, Ziqwala district, Wag, Ethiopia, burning of, 266
Four Beasts of the Apocalypse

426

INDEX

(Arba'itu Insasa) church, Chir, Ziqwala district, Wag, Ethiopia, burning of, 266
Fourth crusade, 55, 306
Franca, Dr. (Dir., Italian Dept. of Political Affairs, Addis Ababa), 283
France, 36, 64
    legation in Addis Ababa, 38-39
    foreign minister of, 85
    Paris, 56
        Peace Conference, 287, 311, 317, 328
Franceschino, Giuseppe, Major, Royal Military Advocate, 175-76, 198
Francis (Jorge Mario Bergoglio), Pope, 6
Franzinelli, Mimmo, 78
Freemasonry, 151

Gallina, Sebastiano, General, 115-16
Gallina, 'dagger-man', 150
Ganaz St. Mary church, Bichena, Gojjam, Ethiopia, burning of, 280
Gangi, Dolores, 349n1 (Preface)
Garelli, Arduino, Colonel, 183, 235, 324, 366n2
Gebiwoch Saviour of the World church, Ankober disctrict, Ethiopia, massacre, burning and looting of, 260; *see* Saviour of the World church, Gebiwoch.
Gebre-Giyorgis, *Ichegé*, 100
Gebre-Giyorgis Welde Tsadiq, Bishop, 290
    appointed *Ichegé* (known as *Abune* Basilios), 290
Gebre Gonete of Borale, 204

Gebre-Maryam Welde-Giyorgis, *Abba*, Italian appointee as *tsebaté* of Debre Libanos, 162, 175, 185, 211-12
Gebre-Maryam, *Meggabi*, of Debre Abbay, 166
Gebre-Medhin, *Agefari*, of the church of St. Peter and St. Paul, Addis Ababa, 364n17
Gebre-Medhin, *Aleqa* (of the church of The Holy Trinity, monastery of Debre Assebot), 377n13
Gebre-Mikaél, *Meggabi*, of Debre Libanos, 160-61, 162
Gebre-Selassie, *Memhir* (of Intotto Mayram church), 365n24
Gebre-Selassie Yeshanew, *Aleqa*, 365n23
Gemelli, Agostino, Monsignor, 54, 78, 79, 80
Genda Gora hill, 193
Geneva, 273
    Conventions, 69
Genoa, 78, 80
Germany, 36, 62, 285, 288
    embassy in Addis Ababa, 38-39
    Hermannsburg Mission, Ethiopia, 152
    stormtroopers, 62
    Catholic Church in, 276-77, 278-79, 306
    invasion of Austria by, 277, 296
    invasion of Czechoslovakia and Poland by, 279, 297
    invasion of France, 281
    Russian army reaches Berlin, 285
    surrender to Allies of, 285
    invasion of Italy by, 286
    Nuremberg, Charter of the International Military Tribunal in, 287

INDEX

invasion of Yugoslavia, 297
Jesuits in, 306
Gétachew Beqele, 262-63
Gétésémané Maryam, Gojjam, looting of, 325
Gi'iz language, 23, 152
Giovanni Gebre-Iyesus, 118
Giuliani, Reginaldo, Father, 62-63, 70, 77, 80, 92-93, 106, **Fig. 10**
Gobola hill, 177, 193, 194
Gogetti, Ethiopia, massacre of, 298
Gojjam, 167, 168, 189, 241-5, 249-50, 280
   church-burning campaigns in, 318
Golgotha, 100
Gondar, 28, 132, 242
Gore, 132, 292
   St. Mary church, 292
Gorgoryos (Gregory), Father, 29
Gotha, Duke of, 29-30
Graziani, Rodolfo, General (later, Marshal), 86, 117-19, 136, 140, 151, 153, 157, 167, 186, 236-7, 241-242, 249, 252-53, 257-58, 281, 285, 288, 294, 299, **Fig. 21**, **Fig. 25**
   at southern war-front, 86, 88, 97-98, 312
   appointed Marshal of Italy and Viceroy, 104, 108
   reputation in Libya of, 108-09
   defence of Addis Ababa, 112, 117-19, 145
   policy of favouring Muslims, 106, 251
   instructions for gassing of Lasta Patriots, 125-26,
   attitude towards the Ethiopian Orthodox Church, 108, 120, 131-32, 135, 137, 157-58, 188, 264, 269-70, 318
   execution of the Kassa brothers, 133-35,
   and Alessandro Lessona, 137, 202-03, 209, 227, 269-70
   and anti-Protestant campaign, 153, 156
   preparations for the massacre of Debre Libanos by, 173-79
   orders for the massacre of Debre Libanos issued by, 188
   communications with General Maletti during executions at Laga Weldé, 191-94, 198-99, 213-14
   report of massacre of Debre Libanos to Lessona by, 198-99
   communications with General Maletti during executions at Borale, 202-03
   communications with General Maletti after executions at Borale, 207
   persecution of the House of St. Tekle Haymanot, 221-31
   reports of the bombing of Denneba to Lessona by, 222-23
   orders for clandestine census at in Debre Libanos issued by, 227
   sent to Asmara to recuperate, 251
   speech regarding new policy towards the Ethiopian Orthodox Church, 252-53
   exemplary repression in Bulga following the crowning of Melake-Tsehay Iyyasu, 262-65
   termination of Viceroy appointment, 269, 271

INDEX

memoir of, 286
as War Crimes suspect, 287
appointed Chief of Staff of the Italian Armed Forces and Minister for War, 288
receives prison sentence, 288-89
death of, in Rome, 289
burial of, in Affile, 289
telegrams of, 314
maintenance of the principle of war booty by, 319-20
export to Italy of artefacts of Ethiopian cultural heritage by, 327
Great Britain, 36, 288, 297
legation at Addis Ababa, 38-39
foreign minister at Addis Ababa of, 85
arrival of Emperor Haile Selassie in, 101, 153
London, 98
Anglican Bishop of Liverpool, 104
Anglican Bishop of Southwark, 104
Anglican Archbishop, 127
Hinsley, Arthur, Catholic Archbishop, 240
declaration of war against Germany, 281
attack on Italian-occupied Ethiopia by British and Commonwealth forces under the command of, 281-82
British Military Intelligence, 283-84
Foreign Office, 284, 288
Conference of Commonwealth Prime Ministers, 311
Great Schism, 73
Gregory XI, Pope, 20

Grum Kassa, 116
Gubrazel, Debre Libanos, 161, 162
Gultené Mikaél monastery, massacre of, 181
Gur-Amba St. George church, Ziqwala district, Wag, Ethiopia, burning of, 266
Gurenié, Northern Shewa, 182
Gursum, Harar, 112
massacre of, 112, 317
church, damaging and looting of, 112

Habte-Giyorgis, *Fitawrari*, 167
Habtu, *Abba*, of Debre Libanos
Hagere (Ankober district), 265
Hagere St. Mary church, massacre of, 265; *see* St. Mary church, Hagere, massacre of.
Hagere (later, Alghe; now Bule Hora) town, 113
Hagere Maryam (St. Mary) church, massacre of, 113-114, 317
Hague, The, 319
Haile Selassie I, Emperor, 4, 38, 64, 67, 105, 109, 117, 139, 164, 234, 262-63, 284. 291, 311, 323-24, 356n1, **Fig. 11**
education at Harar, 37, 99
contacts with Pius XI, 44-45, 84, 300, 301
Italian propaganda against, 38
coronation of, 39, 45
and the League of Nations, 39-40, 85
and the slave trade, 51-52
hopes for peace, 64
under aerial attack, 91
departure from Ethiopia at time of Italian invasion, 100

429

INDEX

arrival in Jerusalem, 100
arrival in Britain, 101
and the Anglican Archbishop, 127-28
appeal to Pope Pius XI and the international Christian community, 240, 299-300
Christmas 1937 appeal to Americans of, 272-73
restoration of relationship with Coptic Church, 290
negotiated autonomy of Ethiopian Orthodox Church, 290
disappointment with Pius XI, 300
Harar, 20-21, 37, 94, 112, 119, 352n5
St. Anthony's Catholic Mission and Leprosy Centre, 37, 99-100, 300
massacres of, 98-99, 106-08
Hassen Omar, 379n7
Hayle-Gebriél (protégé of Alfred Buxton), 153
Hayle-Gebriél, *Debtera*, of Debre Libanos 372n22
Hayle Maryam (later, Bishop Pétros), 117
Hayle-Maryam Gazmu, *Lij*, 287, 324, 363n26
Hayle Welde-Kidan, *Blatta*, 231
Haylu Kebede, *Dejazmach*, of Wag, 265
arrest and decapitation, 265-66
Hefhef St. Michael church, nr. Ankober, Ethiopia, massacre of, 261; see St. Michael church, Hefhef.
Henze, Paul, 357n51
Hinsley, Arthur, Catholic Archbishop in England, 240

Hiruy Welde-Sillassé, 139, 152
Historia Aethiopica book, 29
Hiruy Welde Sillassé, *Blattén Géta*, 139, 152
History of Haile Sillassé I Military Academy from 1927 to 1949 (Amharic) book, 206
Hitler, Adolf, 1, 38, 40, 62, 151, 216-17, 276-77, 288-89, 306
invasion of Austria by, 277, 296
anti-semitic policies of, 278
invasion of France, 281
suicide of, 285
Hitler's Pope, book, 289
Holetta, 155
Holy See, 7, 40-41, 43-44, 45, 46-47, 48, 49, 55-57, 58, 89, 90, 111, 120, 217-18, 251, 270, 277, 295, 296, 302
Curia, 41, 55, 94
commitment to the invasion, 94
celebrates 'victory' in Ethiopia, 103
failure to respond to atrocities in Ethiopia, 300
separation of Universal Catholic Church and national Catholic Churches, 304
Holy Sepulchre, church of the, Jerusalem, 19, 45
Holy Trinity
church, Mahbere Sillassé monastery, massacre of 165
cathedral, Debre Birhan, 201-02
church, Debre Assebot monastery, massacre of, 224-25
church, Cheleqot, southern Tigray, Ethiopia, killing of treasurer of, 325
Hussites, 73

INDEX

If Only I Were That Warrior film, 366n9, 368n6
Ignatius of Loyola, 24, 351n46, **Fig. 1**
Il Corrieri della Sera newspaper, 7
Il Gèsu church, Rome, 24
Il Popolo d'Italia newspaper, 82
Igwale Jenberu, *YeDigwa Merigéta* of Debre Werq, 170
Iléni, Empress, 168-69
Illubabor, 132
Illubabor unpublished manuscript, 363n19
Imru Hayle Sellassé, *Ras*, 133
Indale Biresaw, *Aleqa* (later, *Liqetebebt*), 363n19, 363n21
India, 22, 29
  masons of, 29
Indode St. Michael church, Berehet district, Bulga, Ethiopia, massacre and looting of, 264; *see* St. Michael church, Indode.
Ingécha, 178, 215
Innitzer, Cardinal Archbishop, 277, 296
Innocent III, Pope, 306
Isaac, Bishop, 100, 383n3
Istifanos monastery, Ethiopia, 17
Italian embassy, Addis Ababa, 38-39
Italian concentration camps, 240, 315
  in Italian Somaliland, 142, 281, 315
  in Dahlak Islands, 281, 315
    Nocra. 315-16
  Danane, 211, 228-30, 252-54, 270, 281, 282, 315
    Genale plantation, 229-30, 254
  types of
    per scopi repressive, 229
    a scopo protettivo, 229
  Akaki, Addis Ababa, 315-16
Italian economy, 308
Italian episcopate, 295
  and Fascism, 48, 275-76
  and Mussolini, 48
  support for the invasion of Ethiopia, 46, 49, 59-60, 70-72, 75-77, 93-94,
  celebration of 'victory', 104
  reaction to atrocities in Ethiopia, 131
  attitude towards the Ethiopian Orthodox Church, 151
  bitterness regarding the new Fascist policy of embracing the Ethiopian Orthodox Church, 270, 278
Italian government, Rome, 271
  invasion of Albania and Greece by, 279, 297
  surrender to the Allies of, 285
  invasion of Yugoslavia, 297
Italian Jews, 276
  anti-semitic laws, 276
  round-up by Germans in Rome and despatch to Auschwitz of, 285
Italian military
  methods of counter-insurgency and exemplary repression, 111-12,
  'Laghi' division, 113-14
  Muslim battalions, 128
  65th infantry division, Grenadiers of Savoy, 144-45
  Fiat Trenta Quattro vehicles, 160
  Colonial units

431

INDEX

45th Colonial Battalion, 182-83, 191, 193-96, 210, 222-23, 234, 237, **Fig. 36**
20th Eritrean Battalion, 182, 222
12th Colonial Brigade, 182
51st Colonial Battalion, 182-83
52nd Colonial Battalion, 182
56th Colonial Battalion, 182, 23rd Colonial Battery, 182
Royal Corps of, 183
death toll of invasion and occupation of Ethiopia, 311-318
Military Intelligence, 311
heavy trucks
Lancia RoRo, 372n20
Isotta Fraschini, 372n20
Fiat 63N, 372n20
Italian prisons
in Mogadishu, Italian Somaliland, 281
in Italy, 281
Italian Somaliland, 52, 67, 68, 70, 108, 316
askaris of, 68, 183, 263
concentration camps in, 142, 281, 315
Mogadishu, 149, 228
Prison(s) of, 226, 281, 316
Iyasus Mo'a, Abbot, 17
Iyyasu, *Lij*, 262-63

Jarosseau, André, Bishop, 37-38, 45, 94, 99-100, 299, 300
Jenkins, Philip, 50, 297
Jerusalem, 45, 50, 116
Ethiopian community of, 19, 25
Jesuits, 24
delegation to Ethiopia, 24,
351n46
expulsion from Ethiopia, 74
in Ethiopia, 27-29, 168-69
La Civiltà Cattolica newspaper, 72, 74-75, 83, 93
Ledóchowski, Wlodzimierz, Superior General, 74-75, 82, 295
Venturi, Pietro Tacchi, emissary between the Holy See and Mussolini, 103
In Germany, 306
Jesus Christ, 11, 59, 60, 127
devotion of Sacred Heart of Jesus, 78
postcards depicting, 60-61, 81, **Fig. 8**, **Fig. 22**
'Covenant of Mercy', *see* Kidane Mihret.
jihad
of *Imam* Ahmed bin Ibrahim, aka Ahmed Grañ, 20-22, 26, 56, 57, 87, 161, 167, 168, 224-25, 234, 243
of Maletti-Muhammad Sultan Group (of irregulars), 258, 278, 289, 316-17
conduct of, 233-39
formation of, 234
death toll of, 239
Jijiga, 98-99, 108, 120
Jimma, *Yekatit 12* massacre of, 315
Johannes Pottam, Father, 23
John XXIII, Pope, 290
Judaism, 151
Julius III, Pope, 25

Kaffa province, 132
Kasem river, 236
Kassa Habte-Maryam, 115-16
Kassa Haylu, *Li'ul Ras*, 67-68, 100,

221, 323, **Fig. 12**
  residence at Debre Libanos of, 175
Kateba Maryam church, Debre Libanos, 160-61
  Massacre of, 162
Kebede Welde-Tsadiq, *Abba*, 365n23
Kefyalew Mehari, Father, 169, 242, 383n28
Kent, Peter, 270
Kenya, 51, 183, 282
  Nairobi, 289
Keren, 166
Kertzer, David, 49-50, 90, 127, 275, 354n43
Kibru, *Ato* (of Yeka Mikaél church, Addis Ababa), 365n23
Kidane Mihret (Covenant of Mercy) celebration, 159
Kidane Mihret (Covenant of Mercy) church, Addis Ababa, 146-47
Kidane Mihret (Covenant of Mercy) church, Molalé Aradma Agancha, Menz, Ethiopia, massacre of, 237
Kifle Assefa, *Dyakon*, 382n3
Konovalov, Fyodor, 118
Kora, Debre Libanos, 161, 192
  St. Tekle Haymanot, church of, 161
Korem, 91
Kornberg, Jacques, 85, 307
Kotichu hill, 193
Kuré Beret, eastern escarpment, Northern Shewa, 238
  Battle of Kuré Wuha, 238

La civilisation de l'Italie fasciste, book, 288
La Civiltà Cattolica newspaper, *see* Jesuits.
La Conquista di un impero film, 366n4, 368n4
La Puma, Vincenzo, Cardinal, 358n70
Lacroix-Riz, Annie, 48
Lady of the Rosary icon, 11,
Laga Weldé, 177-78, 191, 193-94, 195-99, 205, 222, 223, 227, Fig. 38, **Fig. 39**
Lake Hayq, 17
Lake Tana, 27, 28, 241
Lake Zway, 128
Lakes of Rift Valley, 115, 128, 135, 228, 316
Lalibela (city), 17, 97, 116, 125
Lang, Cosmo, Archbishop, 90
Languedoc, 11
Lasta region, 125
L'Armonia newspaper, 103
Lateran Treaty, 40-41, 43, 45, 47, 48, 308
Laurentini, Camillo, Cardinal, 358n70
Lavitrano, Luigi, Cardinal Archbishop, 90
L'Avvenire d'Italia newspaper, 49-50, 55, 56
Le National newspaper, 56
Le Temps newspaper, 56
League of Nations, 1, 38, 39, 59, 67, 81, 85, 100, 164, 273, 286, 295, 304, 356n1
  appeal by Emperor Haile Selassie, 100
  recognition by members of Italian hegemony over Ethiopia, 135, 139
Ledóchowski, Wlodzimierz, *see* Jesuits.

INDEX

Leijinhofvud, Eric, Baron, 206
Lentarkis, Michael, 243
Leo XIII, Pope, 40, 56
Lessona, Alessandro, 108, 119, 135, 142, 146, 299, 352n3
  relationship with Graziani, 137, 251
  as War Crimes suspect, 287
Letarge of Borale, 178, 204
Letyibelu Gebré, *Bejirond*, 139-40
Libne Dingil, Emperor, 20, 22, 23
Libya, 52, 68, 229, 289
  askaris of, 68, 183
  Italian techniques of counter-insurgency in, 105
  resistance leader Omar Mokhtar, 117
  General Maletti in, 176
  Cyrenaica, 229
Lindisfarne, Northumbria, Britain, 298
Lo Duca, Antonio, Father, 24-26,
Lombardy, 78, 80, 82
Lorenzo Ta'izaz, 139
L'Osservatore Romano newspaper, 49
Ludolf, Hiob, 29

Macchi, Alessandro, Bishop, 79, 82
Madonna del Soccorso church, Nicastro, 61
Mahbere Sillassé, monastery, 165
Mahdere Maryam church, Begémdir, massacre and looting of, 170, 325
Malecore, Giuseppe, 61
Maletti, Pietro, General, 158, 226, 249, 252, 267, 287, 292, **Fig. 34**
  preparations for the massacre of Debre Libanos by, 173, 176-79
  encirclement of the monastery by, 181-86
  entrapment of first arrivals by, 186-88
  massacre at first execution site by, 189-99
  massacre at second execution site by, 201-08
  communications with Graziani after the massacre of Debre Libanos, 207, 209-10
  conduct of clandestine census by, 227-28
  as ally of Sheikh Mohammed Sultan, 233-39
  Maletti-Mohammed Sultan campaign, 233-39, 266
  Death toll, 239
  arrest of relatives of victims of the massacre of Debre Libanos, by, 253-56
  church-burning campaigns of, 233-69, 278, 318
  death of, 289
  involvement in emptying/looting of monastery of Debre Libanos, 323
Malta, Giuseppe, Colonel (later, General), 133
Mamitu Kassa, 116
Mangaria, Santina, Bishop, 82
Mantua, 78
Marcellus II (Cardinal Cervini), Pope, 23
'March on Rome', 63, 76, 254
Marchetti-Selveggiani, Monsignor, 45
Marenco, Colonel, 189-90, **Fig. 34**
Martin V, Pope, 20
Massawa, 34, 358n70
Massino, Francesco, Prince, 52
Matéwos, Archbishop, 150

INDEX

Mathias, *Abune*, Patriarch of the Ethiopian Orthodox Church, 292
Mauro, Fra, 128
Maychew, Battle of, 97, 139, 234, 238, 312
Mayflower ship, 60
Mazzoni, Giulio, 351n43
McClellan, Charles, 378n29
McGeough, Joseph, Monsigner, 284
Mecca, 15
Mediterranean Sea, 33-34, 36
Megezez, Mt., 264
Mekane Sillassé church, Ethiopia, 21
Mekonnin Solomon, *Aleqa*, of Debre Libanos, 372n22
Melake-Tsehay Iyyasu, 262-64
Melake-Tsehay Zeleqe Habte-Maryam of the church of Intotto Maryam, 365n24
Mendez, Alfonso, Archbishop, 28, 33
Menelik II, Emperor, 30, 34, 35, 36, 40, 142, 146, 149, 150, 159, 167, 233, 243, 262-63, 323-24
Menen journal, 365n26
Mengesha, *Dejazmach*, 119
Mengesha Negeda, 369n19
Menna, Domenico, Bishop, 78
Menso river, 264
Menz, 162, 181-82, 236
Meqelé, 92
Merhabété, Northern Shewa, 236-37
Mertule Maryam monastery, Gojjam, massacre of, 168-69
Mescha St. John church, Ankober district, massacre of, 258-60; *see* St. John church, Mescha.
Mesqel Massaya, 187, 190-91, 193, 194-96, 373n28
Metemma, 165
Midr Kebd, monastery of, 128, 362n8
massacres of, 128-29, 230, 317
Gebre Menfes Qiddus church, massacre of, 128-29, **Fig. 26**
Mikaél (Michael), Father, of Midr Kebd, 128
Mikaél (Michael), Bishop, 100, **Fig. 27**
early life, 132
arrest and execution, 133, 136, 271, 301
reburial of, 292
statue erected of, 292
canonisation of, 292, **Fig. 50**
Mikre-Sillassie Gebre-Ammanuel, 46, 130-31, 242, 362n11
Milan, 77-78, 295
cathedral, 77, 78
Catholic University of, 54, 71
Minerva, goddess, 61
MIssioni Consolata periodical, 91
Misqa St. Mary church, Ziqwala district, Wag, Ethiopia, burning of, 266
Mockler, Anthony, 4, 108, 242, 359n12
Mogadishu, 149, 358n70
Moges Asgedom, 140, 157, 158, 159, 161, 162, 175
Mohammad Wale Ahmad, *al-Haj*, 379n7
Mohammed Sakih, *Sheikh*, 379n7
Mohammed Sultan, *Sheikh*, 234
as ally of General Pietro Maletti, 233-39
Group (of irregulars), 234-39, 266, **Fig. 48**

435

INDEX

Mohammed V, Sultan, Ottoman empire (Turkey), 300
Mojo, 231, 362n11
  Yekatit 12 massacre of, 315
Momina Ali, *Weyzero*, 379n7
Monteleone (later, Vibo Valentia), 61
Montevergine abbey, 96
Moret district, Northern Shewa, 222-24, 236
Mother Italy (Magner Mater), 60-61
Mount Zion monastery, Jerusalem, 19
Ministry of Defence, Italian, 7
Mulatwa Yirgu of Borale, Ingécha, 203, 204-05, 215, 374n7, 374n16, **Fig. 43**
Műnster, 7
Muhammad, Prophet, 15, 16
Mundelein, George, Archbishop, 216-17
Mussolini, Benito ('*Il Duce*'), 4, 41, 43, 46, 48, 49, 50-51, 57, 58, 59, 62, 63, 64, 101, 145, 164, 229, 279 249-50, 252, 276, 286, 288, 295, 297, 298, 301, 302, 306, 319, 326
  transition from socialism to Fascism, 36
  plans for conquest of Ethiopia, 36-37, 352n4
  justifications for the invasion of Ethiopia, 38-40
  dependence on the Catholic Church, 43
  orders for complete destruction of the Ethiopian army, 69-70, 312
  and Hitler, 76
  'Day of Faith', 80-83, **Fig. 16**
  reaction to League of Nations sanctions, 81
  relationship with Pius XI, 84
  reaction to Pius XI's attempts to end the Ethiopian war, 85
  proclaims new 'Roman Empire', 104
  'War is over' speech, 105-06, 304
  poses as 'Protector of Islam', 111
  change of policy towards the Ethiopian Orthodox Church, 249-51, 269-70
  declaration of war on Great Britain and France, 281
  execution at Dongo of, 285, 327
    while carrying Ehiopian crowns as bullion, 327

Naples, 11, 33, 78, 80, 90-91, 94-95, 96
Nardo, Puglia, 40
Nasi, Guglielmo, General, 112, 163, 224-26, 254, 384n15
Natale, Leopoldo, Colonel, 280
Navarra, Monsignor, 82
Nazis, 70
Nebiyye-Li'ul, *Fitawrari*, 323, 368n4
Negash Yirgu of Borale, 204-05, 215, **Fig. 42**
Negellé, 88
Neubacher, Hermann, 385n22
New Times and Ethiopia News newspaper, 299-300
Nicolas II, Tsar of Russia, 190
Nicholas V, Pope, 20
Nocera Umbra-Gualdo Tadino, 75
Nogara, Bernardino (brother of Archbishop Giuseppe Nogara), 308-09

INDEX

Nogara, Giuseppe, Archbishop, 276, **Fig. 20**
Núñez, Juan, 351n46

Oddo Becho district, 115-16
Ogaden, 67
Omar Mokhtar, 118
Organizzazione per la Vigilanza e la Repressione dell'Antifascismo (OVRA), 53
Oromo communities, 234
Oromo St. Michael church, Ankober district, Ethiopia, massacre and looting of, 261; *see* St. Michael church, Oromo.
Ottoman empire, 20-21, 23, 29, 51, 56
Ottoman Turks, 140, 234

Pacelli, Eugenio, *see* Vatican Secretary of State.
Pachomius, 16
Páez, Pedro, Father, 27-28, 29
Palermo, 90
Panella, Luigi, *Avvocato*, 196, 371n2, 372n25, 372n26, 376n12
Pankhurst, Alula, 388n6
Pankhurst, Richard, 2, 326, 362n8, 382n3, 388n6, **Fig. 35**, **Fig. 41**
Pankhurst, Rita, 362n8, 382n3
Pankhurst, Sylvia, 2, 98-99, 299-300, 387n3 (Appendix I)
Paris Peace Conference, 287, 311, 317, 328
Parma, 93
Patriots (Ethiopian), 111, 112, 176, 235, 281-82, 312, 317-18
Paul III, Pope, 2, **Fig. 1**
Pavelić, Ante, 156, 285, 297
Pawlos, *Abune*, Patriarch of the Ethiopian Orthodox Church, 291, 323
Petretti, Armando, General, 251, 257
and reconstitution of the monastery of Debre Libanos, 253-54
Petronelli, Francesco, Bishop, 81-82
Pétros (Peter), Bishop, 100, 117, **Fig. 24**
early life, 117
arrest and execution, 117-19, 240, 271, 301
statue erected of, 291
square in Addis Ababa named after, 291
canonisation of, 291
Pew Research Centre, 15
phosgene, 53
Pignatti, Bonifacio, Count, 74
Pilate, Pontius, 64
Pilgrim Fathers, 60
Pirzio Biroli, Alessandro, General, 125-26, 133-34, 168, 241-42, 243, 289
appointed Governor of Montenegro, 289
early career, 361n1
Pius XI (Achille Ratti), Pope, 3, 37, 40-41, 43-45, 47, 48, 54-58, 63-64, 71, 74, 78, 83, 89, 101, 127, 140, 278, 286, 290, 294-96, 297, 299, 353n7, **Fig. 7**
decision not to denounce the invasion of Ethiopia, 43-44
Curis ac laboribus apostolic constitution 45, 48
reference to Ethiopian Orthodox Christians as 'heretics', 57-58
consideration of 'just war', 77

437

INDEX

perception by episcopate of, 82
silences of, 84, 96, 127, 151,
    216, 301-02, 304-05, 307-08
attempt to end war, 85
support for pro-war propaganda,
    89
sacralisation of the invasion, 95
removal of Bishop Jarosseau by,
    100
celebration of 'happy triumph'
    by, 104-05
appointment of Castellani as
    Apostolic Visitor by, 120-21
concern about Protestantism,
    151
recognition of King Victor
    Emmanuel as Emperor of
    Ethiopia, 151
appointment of Castellani as
    Apostolic Delegate by, 166
reaction to the massacre of
    Debre Libanos of, 215-16,
    301
illness of, 215-16, 217
displeasure at Fascist
    administration's change of
    policy towards the Ethiopian
    Orthodox Church, 250, 252,
    274, 277-78
and Italian government policy
    towards Islam in Ethiopia,
    251
beginning to regret alliance with
    Fascism, 275
and anti-semitic laws of, 276,
    303
reprimand of Cardinal Innitzer
    by, 277
death of, 279
fear of Fascists' falling from
    power, 301-02

and Spanish Civil War, 302
and racism, 303
influence of his Italian nationality
    on his attitude towards the
    invasion of Ethiopia, 303
and Italian nationality of Vatican
    staff, 304
appointment of Bernardino
    Nogara as Vatican Financial
    Manager by, 308
'allowing evil to happen', 306-10
Pius XII (Eugenio Pacelli), Pope,
    46, 286, 353n17, **Fig. 47**
death of, 289
and anti-semitic laws, 303
and the Holocaust, 307
Playfair, Guy, Reverend, 156
Poggiali, Ciro, 118, 143-44
Poland, 38, 281, 297
Pollard, John, 308
Pompei, 11
    Madonna of, 11, 94-95
    Pontifical Shrine of the Blessed
        Virgin, 11
Portugal, 29, 33
Portuguese, 20, 22, 27-28
    Jesuits 29
Posner, Gerald, 309
Prince of Naples, 140
Puritans, 60

Qérillos (Cyril), Egyptian
    Archbishop, 100, 271, 290
Quercia, Mario, Major, 174, 366n2
Quinico, Lt.-Colonel, 235
Qworata church, Begémdir,
    massacre of, 170

Ragazzoni, Captain, 196
Raguel, archangel, 24
Ramiel, archangel, 24

INDEX

Raphael, archangel, 24
Ravenna, 96
Red Cross, Ethiopian, 99, 104
Red Sea, 33-34, 178, 233
Regia Aeronautica (Royal Air Force), 11, 37, 53, 68, 71, 86, 131, 145, 213-14, 312, 313
  bombing of:
    St. Gabriel church, Dabat, 86
    Monastery of Debre Abbay, 87, 166
    Negellé church, 88
    Sekota and Amdewerq towns, Wag, 88
    Wadara, 88
    Jijiga town, 108
    villages and monastery of Mt. Ziqwala, 130-31, 314, 362n11
    Holy Trinity church, Mahbere Sillassé monastery, 165
    Denneba district, Northern Shewa, 222-23
    Midr Kebd district, 230
    Mt. Ziqwala monastery (second time) 230-31, 314
    churches of Yilmana Dénsa district, Gojjam, 242-43
    monastery of The Saviour of the World, Adét, Yilmana Dénsa district, Gojjam, 242-53
Chemical Warfare
  C-500T yperite bombs, 88, 309
  gassing of:
    Ethiopians at First Battle of Tembien, 92
    Ethiopians at Battle of Maychew, 97
    Lasta Patriots, 125-26
    villages of Mt. Ziqwala, 130-31
  Chemical Warfare Service, 110
  C-100P phosgene bombs, 309
    yperite, 317, 353n30
    arsine, 317, 353-54n30
    phosgene, 317, 353-54n30
  aerial bombardment of Emperor Haile Selassie, 97
  aircraft used in Ethiopia
    Caproni Ca.101 bombers, 309-10. 386-87n32
    Caproni Ca,111, Ca.133, Ca.142 bombers, 386-87n32
    Romeo Ro.37 aircraft, 309
    Savoia-Marchetti bombers, 310
Rerum ecclesiae encyclical of Pius XI, 303
Rhodes, 121
Riccardi, Andrea, 7, 329
Riley-Smith, Jonathan, 3
Robel church, Gishe, Menz, Ethiopia, massacre of, 237
Rome, 19, 45, 50, 60-61, 72, 76, 151, 168, 178-79, 193, 216, 283
  Ethiopian community of, 20, 22, 23
  Ancient, 36
  'March on Rome', 63, 76
  Piazza Venezia, 83, 276
  Castel Gandolfo, 277
  occupied by German army, 285
  Piazza di Porta Capena, 320
  Museo Coloniale, 327, 328
    Graziani Room, 327, **Fig. 51**
Rubattino Shipping Company, 34
Russia, 39,

INDEX

embassy, Addis Ababa 38-39
Russian Orthodox Church, 291, 296-97

Sakala St. Gabriel church, Bichena, Gojjam, Ethiopia, burning of, 280
Saladin, 25
Salome Gebre-Egziabher, 363n23
Salotti, Carlo, Cardinal, 358n70
Salvadore, Matteo, 27-28, 351n46
Salvemini, Gaetano, 71, 78-79, 94, 296
Samuél, Father, of Debre Wegeg, 224
San Vincenzo Mission, Ethiopia, 283-84
Santa Maria degli Angeli e dei Martiri basilica, Rome, 26, 195, 351n43, **Fig. 3**
    Chapel of the Saviour, 26, 351n43
Santa Maria Catholic church, Detroit, USA, 296
Santo Stefano, *see* St. Stephen Promartyr church.
Sariel, archangel, 24
Sartsa Dengel, Emperor, 27
Saviour of the World church, Chagel, Debre Libanos district, Ethiopia, 191, 371n11
Saviour of the World church, Gebiwoch, Ankober district, Ethiopia, massacre, burning and looting of, 260
    Daniél Gizaw, *Debtera*, killed at, 260
    Kelkilé, Father, killed at, 260
    Mogesé, Father, killed at, 260
    Tsenebet, Father, killed at, 260
Saviour of the World monastery, Adét, Yilmana Dénsa district, Gojjam, Ethiopia, massacre of, 242-43
    Kassa Wasé, Father, killed at, 242-43
Saviour of the World monastery, Nicosia, 25
Sawita Selassie, *Liqetebebt*, 365n19
Sayed Raslam, *Sheikh*, 234
Sbacchi, Alberto, 50, 311, 364n7
Scetis, 19
Schuster, Ildefonso, Cardinal Archbishop, 77, 79, 83, 97, 189, 254, 278, 286, 289, 295, **Fig. 14**
    declaration *Dei Sumus adiotores*, 77-78, 86
    denigration of Ethiopian Muslims, 93-94
    reaction to Italian anti-semitic laws, 276-77
Secolo la Sera newspaper, 164
Second World War, 1, 288, 310
Seifu Kassa, 116
Sekota, 88
Selalé, 116, 134-35
Seltene Seyoum, 381n7
Sendefa, 236
Serafini, Domenico, Cardinal, 358n70
Serbelloni, Fabrizio, Cardinal, 26
Serbia
    Serbs, 285
    Serbian Orthodox Church, 297
Seven Archangels, aka the Host of Seven, 24, **Fig. 2**, **Fig. 4**
    Brotherhood of, 25
Shashka, Ladislas, Dr., 113-14, 118, 143, 150
Shenk, Calvin, 273, 377n11
Sheno, 236
Shewa, 17, 116, 167, 176, 242, 250

440

plateau of, 17. 257-58
Northern, 115, 157-58, 167, 178-79, 181-82, 228, 231, 233-39, 253, 257, 289, 316
  Bishop of, 291-92
  Kingdom of, 234
  eastern escarpment of, 238
  Eastern, 280
  church-burning campaigns in, 318
Shewareged Habte-Gebriél, 116
Shiferaw Beqelé of Addis Ababa University, 374n18, **Fig. 42**
Shinkurt, 134, 193
Sicily, 24, 33
Siena, 78
Siga Wedem river, 17, 184, 192, 223
Simión Adefris, 139, 157, 161
slave trade, 51-53, 68
  Ethiopian anti-slavery edict, 51-52
  Antischiavismo journal, 52
  Office for the Abolition of Slavery, 52
Solomon, King, 88
Spanish Civil War, 4, 302
  Franco, General, 105, 302
  departure from Ethiopia of Blackshirts to, 278
Spencer, John, 356n2
Spinelli. Major, 227
St. Anthony, 31, 193
St. Anthony's Leprosy Centre, Harar, 37
St. Bartholomew basilica, Rome, 7
St. Elija monastery, Scetis, 19
St. Frumentius, 165
St. Gabriel, archangel, 24
St. Gabriel church, Tibanzba, Ziqwala district, Wag, Ethiopia, burning of, 266
St. Gabriel church, Qeya, Menz, Ethiopia, massacre of, 237
St. Gabriel church, Sakala, Bichena, Gojjam, Ethiopia, burning of, 280
St. Gebre Menfes Qiddus ('Abo'), 128, 257
  House of, 130
    persecution of, 230-31
  church of, Ziqwala Ethiopia, 130-31
St. Gebre Menfes Qiddus church, Abam, Ziqwala district, Wag, Ethiopia, burning of, 266
St. Gebre Menfes Qiddus church, Midr Kebd, Ethiopia, massacre of, 128-30, **Fig. 26**
St, Gebre Menfes Qiddus church, Yigem, Ankober district, Ethiopia, massacre of, 261-62
  Gebre-Hanna, *Aleqa*, killed at, 262-62
St. George church, Ankober, Ethiopia, bombing of, 382n8
  Father Tekle-Giyorgis, killed at, 382n8
St. George church, Cairo, 19
St. George church, Gore
St. George's cathedral, Addis Ababa, 6, 117, 142-46, 150, 291
  burning of, 142, 151, 216
  looting of, 143, 216
  repair of, 272
St. George church, Gedambo, Menz, Ethiopia, massacre of, 237
St. George church, Gur-Amba, Ziqwala district, Wag, Ethiopia, burning of, 266
St. George church, Werkera, Ankober district, Ethiopia,

INDEX

massacre and burning of, 260-61
Hayle-Mesqel, Father, killed at, 261
Moges, Father, killed at, 261
Subsibé, Father, killed at, 261
Werqineh, *Debtera*, killed at, 261
St. John church, Mescha, Ankober district, Ethiopia, massacre, burning and looting of, 258-60
  Amenshewa, Father, killed at, 260
  Belachew, Father, killed at, 260
  Dirafu Shewa, Father, killed at, 260
  Gebre-Sillassé, *Debtera*, killed at, 260
  Habte-Maryam, Father, killed at, 260
  Tekle-Weld, Father, killed at, 260
  Teshome Belachew, Father, killed at, 260
  Weldeyes, Father, killed at, 260
St. Libanos church, Abmata, Ziqwala district, Wag, Ethiopia, burning of, 266
St. Mark (Marqos) church, Sidist Kilo, Addis Ababa, 117
St. Mary, Blessed Virgin, 17, 59, 60, 96
  'Covenant of Mercy', *see* Kidane Mihret.
  Madonna of the Rosary of Pompei, 11, 94-95
  use by Italian military of icons, paintings and statues of, 19, 21, 86, 91, 95-96
  Madonna of the Manganello, 60-61, 62, 97, **Fig. 9**
    Based on La Madonna de Soccorso, 355n46

Madonna of Divine Love, devotion of, 78
  as 'Queen of Victories', 95, 103
Madonna dell'Oltremare, 96
Madonna di Montevergine, aka 'Black Madonna', 96
as Theotokos ('Mother of God'), 97
Miracles of Mary manuscript, 321
Madonna delle Gracie, **Fig. 20**
St. Mary church, Addis Alem, Ethiopia, 226, 266-67
  massacre of, 267
    execution of seven priests, names unknown, at, 267
    imprisonment of ten priests following, 267
St. Mary church, Bachi, Ziqwala district, Wag, Ethiopia, burning of, 266
St. Mary church, Debre Werq monastery, Gojjam, Ethiopia, shelling of, 170
  Debre Werq Maryam manuscript, 367n22
St. Mary church, Debre Zeyit, Ziqwala district, Wag, Ethiopia, burning of, 266
St. Mary church, Derefo, Ankober district, Ethiopia, massacre and looting of, 262
  Asrat, Father, 262
  Gebre-Maryam, Father, killed at, 262
  Tamré Beyene, Father, 262
  Tesfa Welde-Tsadiq, Father, killed at, 262
  Welde-Tsadiq Mengistu, Father, killed at, 262
St. Mary church, Ganaz, Bichena, Gojjam, Ethiopia, burning of,

442

INDEX

280
St. Mary church, Gétésémané, Gojjam, Ethiopia, looting of, 325
St. Mary church, Gore, Ethiopia, 292, 363n21
St. Mary church, Hagere, Ankober district, Ethiopia, massacre of, 265
   two priests (names not recorded) burned to death at, 265
St. Mary church, Hagere (later, Alghe; now Bule Hora), Ethiopia, massacre of, 113-114
St. Mary church, Intotto, Addis Ababa, 150
   robbery at, 271
St. Mary church, Kateba, Debre Libanos, Ethiopia, massacre of, 162
St. Mary church, Lalibela, Ethiopia 97
St. Mary church, Lideta, Addis Ababa, 149
St. Mary church, Mahdere, Begémdir, Ethiopia, 351n44
   massacre of 170,
   looting of, 325
St. Mary church, Mertula Maryam monastery, Gojjam, Ethiopia, massacre of, 168-69
St. Mary church, Misqa, Ziqwala district, Wag, Ethiopia, burning of, 266
St. Mary church, Tedbabe, Ethiopia, massacre of, 169
St. Mary church, Wadera, Ankober district, Ethiopia, massacre, burning and looting of, 261
   Hayle, Father, killed at, 261
   Kidane, *Debtera*, killed at, 261
   Tsigé Neway, *Debtera*, killed at, 261
   Wenderad Sema'at, Father, killed at, 261
St. Mary church, Weleh, Wag, Ethiopia, burning of, 265-66
St. Mary monastery, Debre Mewi, Gojjam, massacre of, 243
   Boyale Gétahun, *Liqetebebt*. killed at, 243
St. Mary of Zion church, Aksum, Ethiopia, 16, 96-97
St. Michael, archangel, 24, 174, 189
St. Michael church, Adeljan, Ziqwala district, Wag, Ethiopia, burning of, 266
St. Michael church, Akrimit, Bulga, Ethiopia, burning and looting of, 267
St. Michael church, Hefhef, nr. Ankober town, Ethiopia, massacre of, 261
   Abbebe Ayu, Father, killed at, 261
   Asrat, *Debtera*, killed at, 261
   Birhanu, Father, killed at, 261
   Qirqos, Father, killed at, 261
   Welde-Maryam, *Debtera*, killed at, 261
   Yegwala Ishet, Father, killed at, 261
St. Michael church, Indode, Berehet district, Bulga, Ethiopia, massacre and looting of, 264, 267
   Fisseha, Father, killed at, 264
   Hayle-Maryam, Father, killed at, 264
   Mekonnin, Father, killed at, 264
   Zelleqe, Father, killed at, 264
   ZeSillassé, Father, killed at, 264
St. Michael church, Oromo, Ankober district, Ethiopia,

INDEX

massacre and looting of, 261
Aychiluhim Wibé, Father, killed at, 261
Degife Gebre Hiwet, Father, killed at, 261
Desta Gebre-Iyesus, Father, killed at, 261
Hayle Welde-Maryam, Father, killed at, 261
Taddesse Dilnasew, Father, killed at, 261
St. Michael church, Wasda, Bichena, Gojjam, Ethiopia, burning of, 280
St. Michael church, Wegfelé, Bulga, Ethiopia, 263
St. Michael church, Werqa, Berehet district, Bulga, Ethiopia, burning and looting of, 264
St. Michael church, Werqele, Berehet district, Bulga, Ethiopia, burning and looting of, 264
St. Michael church, Yeka, Addis Ababa, 149
  reprisals at, 365n23
St. Michael monastery, Gultené, Northern Shewa, Ethiopia, massacre of, 181
St. Peter and St. Paul church, Addis Ababa, 148, 364n17
  cemetery of, 148
  desecration of, 148-49, **Fig. 30**
St. Peter's basilica, Rome, 6
St. Philip the Evangelist, 349n2 (Chapter 1)
St. Quiricus (Qirqos) church, Amdewerq, Ziqwala district, Wag, Ethiopia, burning of, 266
St. Rufael church, Addis Ababa, 149
St. Stephen Promartyr church (later, St. Stephen of the Abyssinians), Rome, 19, 20, 22, 23, 25, 29, 44, 299
St. Tekle Haymanot, 17, 18, 30, 158-59, 173, 189, 223, 257
  The Contendings of St. Tekle Haymanot hagiography, 27, 186
  House of, 30, 175, 251, 253
  persecution of, 221-31
  cross of, 211
  movement of body of, 350n9
St. Tekle Haymanot church, Addis Ababa, robbery at, 271
St. Tekle Haymanot church, Azezo, Begémdir, Ethiopia, 29, 351n47
St. Tekle Haymanot church, Debre Libanos, Ethiopia, 18, 21, 30, 160, 173, 184, 187, 208, 352n49
  looting of, 323
St. Tekle Haymanot church, Weyn Washa, Tara gedam (monastery), Begémdir, Ethiopia, looting of, 325
Stappachetti, Commandant (of Akaki Prison), 228
Starace, Achille, 70
Steer, George, 164
Stjärne, Per, 152
Sudan, 165, 282
Suez Canal, 33-34
Sultene Seyoum, 119, 169
Susinyos, Emperor, 27, 28, 29, 168-69, 351n46
Synaxarium, 173

Taccabelli, Mario, Archbishop, 78, 82
Taddesech Istifanos (wife of Abriha Deboch), 157, 159, 188
Tama village, 193

INDEX

Tamo, Eastern Shewa, 280
Tara gedam (monastery), Begémdir, Ethiopia, 325
Taranto, 93
Tardini, Domenico, Monsignor, 83, 295
Taytu, Empress, 34, 243
Te Deum hymn, 105-06
Te'aka Negest Be'ata LeMaryam ('Be'ata Maryam') church, Addis Ababa, 146-147
   attacked by Blackshirts, 147-148
   prohibitions set by Graziani, 150
Tebassi, Debre Birhan, 257-58
Tedbabe Maryam church, Ethiopia, massacre of, 169
Teeling, Sir William, 64
Tefere-Werq, *Liqe Mezemeran*, 365n23
Teferi, *Ras*, *see* Haile Selassie, Emperor.
Tegulet, 167
Tekalign Gedamu, 363n21
Tekkezé river, 86-87, 166
Tekle-Giyorgis, *Tsebaté*, 160-61, 162, 176
Tekle-Tsadiq Mekuria, 378n29, 381n18
Temesgen Gebré (protégé of Alfred Buxton), 153
Teramo, 59
Terracina, 82
Teruzzi, Attilio (Minister of Italian Africa), export to Italy of artefacts of Ethiopian cultural heritage by, 327
Tesfa-Maryam, Father, 119
Tesfa, *Abba*, of Debre Libanos
Tesfa Seyon, Father, 22-23, 27, 29, 168, **Fig. 1**
   appointment as Abbot of Santo Stefano, 24
   death of, 25, 351n42
   departure from Debre Libanos, 22
   depiction in painting, 26, **Fig. 1**
   publications, 24
   support for a church of the Seven Archangels in Rome, 25
   aka Tesfa Zeon Malhizo, 350n31
Teshebirru (local farmer who shot *Sheikh* Mohammed Sultan), 379n17
Tewodros Siyum, 374n18
Téwodros (Theodore), Abbot, 18
The Massacre of Debre Libanos: Ethiopia 1937 – The Story of one of Fascism's Most Shocking Atrocities book, 6, 213
The Tablet newspaper, 54
Theodosius, Emperor, 349n3 (Chapter 1)
Thessalonica, Edict of, 349n3 (Chapter 1)
Thomas Welde-Samuél, Brother, 23
Tibanzba St. Gabriel church, Ziqwala district, Wag, Ethiopia, burning of, 266
Tibebe Kassa, 160, 161, 186-87, 194, 197, 201-02, 281, 326, 372n18, 381n18
Tibebu Welde-Maryam, *Memhir*, of Debre Libanos, 388n6
Tigray, 16, 35, 68, 85, 86-87, 88, 91, 92, 164, 165, 167
Tisserant, Eugène, Cardinal, 131-32, 365n30, 376n14
Tiya Kidane Mihret (Covenant of Mercy) church, Wag, Ethiopia, burning of, 265-66
Todi, 121
Tracchia, Ruggero, General, 134,

445

INDEX

158
Tramantano, Andrea, 349n1 (Preface)
Treaty of Versailles, 36, 38
Treaty of Wichalé, 34, 35
Tredici, Giacinto, Bishop, 82
True Cross, 19
Tsebaté hill, 177, 193
Tserha Ariam Rufael (of the church of Rufael, Addis Ababa), 364n18
Tucci, 20
Tullu, 167
Turin, 54
Tuscany, 82
tv2000, 6

Udine, 276
Umbria, 121
Umm Habibah, 16
UNECA, Addis Ababa, 7
U.N. Italian War Crimes Commission, 6, 112, 162, 189, 230, 280, 287, 304
Universal Postal Union, 38
Uriel, archangel, 24
Ustashe, 156

Vatican, 6, 43-44, 46-47, 48, 49, 55-56, 64, 81, 89, 121, 215, 217, 243, 270, 278, 285, 299, 301
   archives of, 19, 49, 275, 301
   Pontifical Ethiopian College, 45, 76, 303
   Palatine guards, 56
   Secretary of State (Eugenio Pacelli), 46, 48-49, 59, 72, 80, 84, 127, 140, 275, 295, 298-99

attitude towards opponents of the invasion, 48
sympathy for Fascism, 49
informing Mussolini that Pius XI would not stand in the way of the invasion, 59
support for the invasion, 90, 94, 307
addressing issue of Archbishop George Mundelein, 216-17
office arrangements of, 217
succeeds Pope Pius XI as Pius Xii, 279, **Fig. 47**
Supreme Congregation of the Roman and Universal Inquisition (later, Supreme Congregation of the Holy Office), 57
policy of neutrality towards national Catholic Churches, 100
Congregation of the Oriental Churches, 131-32, 151, 216, 352n.7
Congregation for the Propagation of the Faith, 151, 270, 358n70
attitude towards the new policy of the Fascist administration towards the Ethiopian Orthodox Church, 277
complaints about policy of Fascist administration towards Muslims in Ethiopia by, 277-78
under siege during German occupation, 285
support for General Franco, 302
attitude to anti-semitic laws, 303

446

INDEX

Italian nationality of staff positions of, 304
compensation received for loss of Papal States by, 308
Bernardino Nogara appointed as Financial Manager, 308
acquisitions and investments made by, 309
library, 326
Vatican Bank 308
interest in arms manufacturers of, 309
Breda, 309
Reggiane (Officine Meccaniche Reggiane), 309
Compagnia Nazionale Aeronautica (CAN), 309
Caproni Ca.101 bombers, 309
Piaggio aircraft engines, 309
Romeo Ro.37 aircraft, 309
Velimirović, Nikolaj, (Serbian Orthodox) Bishop, 385n22
Venice, 26, 33
Venturi, Pietro Tacchi, 103, 278, 354n43
Verona
Institute of, 216
Anti-Blasphemy Committee of, 217
Victor Emmanuel III, King, 38, 40
Vikings, 298
Virtue, Nicolas, 59, 239
Vita e Pensiero magazine, 80
Vittori, Mariano, Canon (later, Bishop), 23

Wadara, 88
Wadera St. Mary church, Ankober district, Ethiopia, massacre, burning and looting of, 261; *see* St. Mary church, Wadera.
Wag, 88, 265-66
Wagshums, 88
Korem, 265
Waldibba monastery, Ethiopia, 86-87
Samuél, Father, of, 87
Wasda St. Michael church, Bichena, Gojjam, Ethiopia, burning of, 280
Weberi Washa, church of, Debre Libanos district, Ethiopia, 325
Wedim Re'ad, Emperor, 19
Wegeda hill, 193
Wegfelé Michael church, Bulga, Ethiopia, 263
Welde-Ammanuel, Father, of church of Zéna Marqos, 224
Welde Kidan, *Qes Gebez*, 365n19, 365n20
Welde-Maryam Ayele, *Blattén Géta*, 84
Welde-Mikaél, abbot of Debre Bisrat monastery, 224
Welde-Mikaél Chaffa, *Meggabi*, of Debre Libanos, 185
Welde Samiyat, Father, shooting of, 148
Welde-Sillassé Habte-Sillassé, Father, of the church of Kundi St. George, 382n3
Welde-Tinsa'e, *Meggabi*, 162, 175, **Fig. 32**
Welde-Tsadiq Zewdé, *Fitawrari*, 263
Weleh St. Mary church, Wag, Ethiopia, burning of, 265-66
Welette-Israél, 243
Wellega, 132

INDEX

Wello, 88, 116, 265-66
Welwel, 39
Wendo, 116
Wend'afrash Welde-Giyorgis, 369n19
Wendwessen Kassa, *Dejazmach*, 100, 116, 125, 133-35
Werqa St. Michael church, Berehet district, Bulga, burning and looting of, 264; see St. Michael church, Werqa.
Werqele St. Michael church, Berehet district, Bulga, burning and looting of, 264; *see* St. Michael church, Werqele.
Wikström, Lars, Dr., 375n21
Werkera St. George church, Ankober district, massacre and burning of, 261; *see* St. George church, Werkera.
Werqineh Isheté, aka Charles Martin, Dr., 98-99, 106, 109, 112-13, 152
Werqu (protégé of Alfred Buxton), 153
Weyn Washa Tekle Haymanot church, Tara gedam (monastery), Begémdir, Ethiopia, looting of, 325
Wula Gebeba, Debre Libanos, 325
Wusha Gedel, Debre Libanos, 158, 160, 175, 184, 187

Yeshaq, Emperor, 18
Yeshitila Kassa, 116
Yigem Gebre Menfes Qiddus church, Ankober district, Ethiopia, massacre of, 261-62; *see* St. Gebre Menfes Qiddus church, Yigem.

Yilmana Dénsa district, Gojjam, 242
Yirga Alem town, 113
Yirgu, Ato (of Borale, Ingécha), 178, 204
Yohannis (John), Bishop, 100
Yohannis (John), Bishop, Fascist appointee, 277
Yohannis IV, Emperor, 30, 34, 323-24
yperite, 53, 126, 130, 353n30
Yugoslavia, 229, 289

Zagwé dynasty, 17
Zelleqe, *Debtera* of Debre Libanos, 193, 194, 198, 370n12, 371n16, **Fig. 38**, **Fig. 39**
Zembabit Kidane Mihret ('The Covenant of Mercy') church, massacre of, 265; *see* The Covenant of Mercy church, Zembabit.
Zéna Marqos, *Abba*, 223, 224 church of, 223
Zer'a Ya'iqob, Emperor, 18, 20, 33, 366n6
Zervos, Adrien, 317
Zewdé Dubale, 363n19
Zewdé Gebru, 214-15
Zewdé Reta, Ethiopian Ambassador to Italy, 300
Zewditu, Empress, 45, 51, 142, 149
Ziqwala monastery, massacre of, 230-31, 267, 314, 362n11
Ziqwala. Mt. 128, 314
Zoretto, Gabriele, 379n9